A Countess IN LIMBO

DIARIES IN WAR & REVOLUTION
Russia 1914–1920 ⌀ *France* 1939–1947

OLGA HENDRIKOFF

ink/light / VANCOUVER

ink/light

Inkflight Publishing
Mailing address
PO BOX 4608
Main Station Terminal
349 West Georgia Street
Vancouver, BC
Canada, V6B 4A1

www.inkflight.com

Russian translation by: Evgeny Zilberov
French translation by: Maureen Ranson
Substantive edit by: Kelsey Attard
Substantive edit by: Suzanne Carscallen
Maps & family trees by: Kathleen Fraser
Designed by: A.R. Roumanis

FIRST EDITION / FIRST PRINTING

LIBRARY AND ARCHIVES CANADA CATALOGUING IN PUBLICATION

Hendrikoff, Olga, 1892–1987
    A countess in limbo : diaries in war & revolution : Russia 1914–1920, France 1939–1947 /
Olga Hendrikoff ; [translations by Maureen Ranson and Evgeny Zilberov].

Includes index.
Translations from the Russian and French.
ISBN 978-1-926606-78-1 (bound). – ISBN 978-1-926606-79-8 (pbk.)

1. Hendrikoff, Olga, 1892–1987 – Diaries.
2. World War, 1914–1918 – Personal narratives, Russian.
3. Soviet Union – History – Revolution, 1917–1921 – Personal narratives.
4. World War, 1939–1945 – Personal narratives, Russian.
5. Paris (France) – History – 1940–1944. 6. Nobility – Russia – Diaries.
I. Ranson, Maureen
II. Zilberov, Evgeny
III. Title.

DK265.7.H45A313 2012   947.08'3092   C2012-906400-9

To our great aunt Lala, whose
words of wisdom resonate with
us today, and to her generation,
who provided the foundation that
enabled us to lead better lives.

To our great uncle Nicholas
Zweguintzoff and the millions
lost in the Russian gulag.

I GO OUT ON THE ROAD ALONE

by Mikhail Yuryevich Lermontov

Alone I set out on the road;
The flinty path is sparkling in the mist;
The night is still. The desert harks to God,
And star with star converses.

The vault is overwhelmed with solemn wonder
The earth in cobalt aura sleeps…
Why do I feel so pained and troubled?
What do I harbour: hope, regrets?

I see no hope in years to come,
Have no regrets for things gone by.
All that I seek is peace and freedom!
To lose myself and sleep!

But not the frozen slumber of the grave…
I'd like eternal sleep to leave
My life force dozing in my breast
Gently with my breath to rise and fall;

By night and day, my hearing would be soothed
By voices sweet, singing to me of love.
And over me, forever green,
A dark oak tree would bend and rustle.

CONTENTS

IMAGES AND MAPS

Countess

OLGA HENDRIKOFF

PART I

Countess Olga Hendrikoff (née Zweguintzoff), better known by the Russian diminutive "Lala," was born June 30, 1892, in Voronezh, Russia, to Nicholas and Olga Zweguintzoff (née Baroness Stael von Holstein). She was second of five children; she had an older brother, Vladimir (Barbos), a younger brother, Nicholas, and two younger sisters, Helen (Ella) Shirkoff and Irina Kobieff. Their father, Nicholas Zweguintzoff, a member of the working aristocracy, was appointed the Russian Governor of Riga in 1905.

Zweguintzoff family costume party, 1905. From left to right: Irina, 7 years old (fled to Yugoslavia in 1920, died in Yugoslavia in 1975); Ella (Helen), 10 years old (fled to Rome in 1920, died in Calgary, Canada, in 1989); Cola (Nicholas), 11 years old (killed in Siberia in 1938); Lala (Olga), 13 years old (fled to France in the 1920s, died in Calgary, Canada, in 1987); Barbos (Vladimir), 14 years old (fled to France in the 1920s, died in Paris in 1972).

The Zweguintzoff line in Russia can be traced back to the 1600s. An area south of Moscow was given to the Zweguintzoff family after they defended this rich farmland from the Turks and other invaders. Later, the family became farm administrators and landed gentry who built schools, hospitals, churches and even a railway station that is still standing today near the small village of Petrovskoye. They were responsible for the welfare of the peasants who lived in the small villages within their large land holdings, which were quite reduced after the revolution of 1905.

Lala's early life was one of great privilege. On their estate the family raised prize horses. Lala became an excellent horsewoman, taking part in riding competitions in St. Petersburg. Summers and school holidays were spent with her extended family on their large estate "Petrovskoye." The family would also holiday in Finland, taking their own railcars loaded with relatives, servants, numerous children, and all their belongings. Later in life, Lala and her sister Ella remembered their happy times in Finland with much joy.

As was customary in Victorian times, tutors and governesses were imported from England and Europe to educate children at home until it was time to attend formal educational institutions. Lala and Ella attended the famous Smolny Institute, an elite, progressive educational institution founded by Catherine the Great. The school stressed deportment, music, art, literature, and languages: Russian, Italian, English, German, and French, the language of the Russian court. Both sisters became fluent in these five languages. Lala graduated with perfect marks in all subjects. The gift of languages later helped both sisters manage as émigrées. After graduation Lala toured Europe with her mother, seldom staying in hotels but in villas and chateaus of friends and relatives where friendships and family ties were renewed.

As a young woman, Lala was appointed lady-in-waiting to both Empresses, the Dowager Empress Marie Feodorovna and Empress Alexandra Feodorovna. For the 300th anniversary of the Romanov dynasty in 1913, Lala was presented with a special token of the appointment, a cipher (broach), and was received on the royal yacht, the *Standart*, by the Empresses. She attended state functions as a lady-in-waiting from 1911 to 1914.

Other members of her family also held positions at the Imperial Russian Court. Her brother Barbos was the personal page of Empress Marie Feodorovna. Her father-in-law, Count V.A. Hendrikoff, was head of the Imperial Chancellery. In 1914, Lala married Count Peter Hendrikoff, Vice-Governor of Kursk and Orel. They divorced after only three years of marriage in 1917, possibly because her husband's counter-revolutionary activities put her at risk.

PARENTS OF COUNTESS OLGA HENDRIKOFF (NÉE ZWEGUNITZOFF)

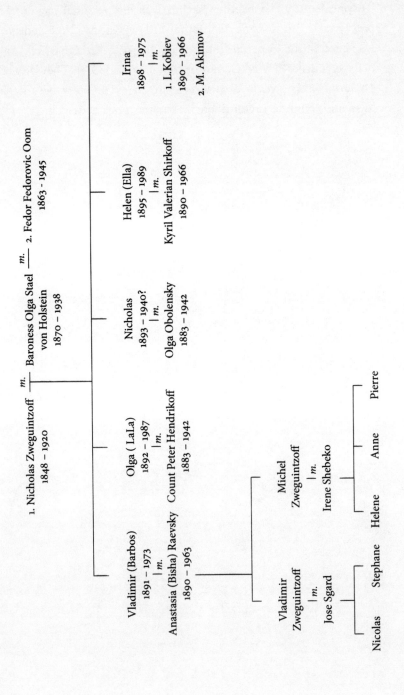

DESCENDANTS OF HELEN SHIRKOFF (NÉE ZWEGUNITZOFF)

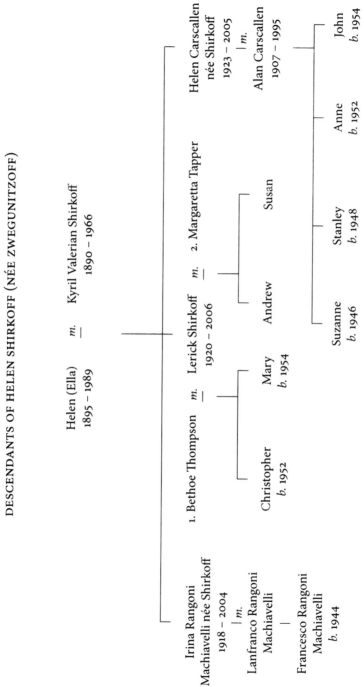

Helen (Ella) *m.* Kyril Valerian Shirkoff
1895 – 1989   1890 – 1966

Irina Rangoni
Machiavelli née Shirkoff
1918 – 2004
m.
Lanfranco Rangoni
Machiavelli

Francesco Rangoni
Machiavelli
b. 1944

1. Bethoe Thompson *m.* Lerick Shirkoff *m.* 2. Margaretta Tapper
1920 – 2006

Christopher   Mary
b. 1952   *b.* 1954

Andrew   Susan

Suzanne   Stanley   Anne
b. 1946   *b.* 1948   *b.* 1952

Helen Carscallen
née Shirkoff
1923 – 2005
m.
Alan Carscallen
1907 – 1995

John
b. 1954

RUSSIA

St. Petersburg
Tsarskoye Selo

RUSSIA

BALTIC SEA

LATVIA
Riga
LITHUANIA

Moscow

BELARUS

Orel
Kursk
Petrovskoye
Voronezh

Kiev

UKRAINE

MOLDOVA

Taganrog

ROMANIA

Odessa
CRIMEAN
PENINSULA
Sebastopol

SEA OF AZOV

THE CAUCASUS

CASPIAN SEA

Kislovodsk

BLACK SEA

BULGARIA

GEORGIA

Constantinople

ARMENIA

TURKEY

THE WAR

"Never before had I kept a diary, but the developments that followed were changing the world around me so quickly that I was afraid that I might forget the sequence of events unless I were to record them."

It was June 15, 1914,[1] just a few days before my wedding to Count Peter Hendrikoff, when I first heard rumours of an imminent war. We had planned to spend a month at his Grafskoye Estate in Volchansk district, Kharkov Governorate, following our June 20 wedding. On my Name's Day,[2] July 11, both my sisters arrived at Grafskoye Estate with their English governess to visit, and in the evening of July 15 we all went to celebrate at the district administrative centre in the city of Volchansk, where a touring troupe was giving a performance. Between acts we were approached by the local land captain who "confidentially" (as he put it) informed us of "unrest at the Russian–Austrian border" and told us that, based on information that he had received, Austria was to immediately declare war on Russia. I was very disturbed by the news – both my brothers were in the military. The younger one had been commissioned from the ranks only a year before, and the elder one was on leave at the Voronezh estate with his wife, who was expecting their first baby within a few days. None of our

1 This date is according to the Julian calendar, which at the time was about 13 days behind the Gregorian calendar used in nearly the entire world today (established in 1582). Russia switched over to the Gregorian calendar in 1918 to keep in step with the rest of the world.
2 In the Orthodox Church, your Name's Day is the birthday of the saint you were named after. For Russian Orthodox at the time, much was made of Name's Day celebrations, including the exchange of gifts.

family members were in St. Petersburg at the time; my father was in Riga – he was the Livonian Governor – and my mother was at a health resort in Austria. I suddenly found that I was no longer paying attention to what was happening on the stage!

The next morning we were awakened by a telephone call around six o'clock in the morning. The telephone office was delivering a telephoned telegram from Kursk Governor Mouratoff, urgently recalling my husband, who at the time was holding the post of Vice-Governor of Kursk. He left immediately, asking me to remain at the Grafskoye Estate for a day or two so that our domestic workers would have enough time to unpack furniture that had been delivered to Kursk following our wedding.

I arranged for the departure of my sisters and the governess to our father's estate, Petrovskoye, but could not send a telegram to my mother in Carlsbad; the post office refused to provide cable services. I left for Kursk on July 18. On my way, I saw evident signs of commotion – the mobilization had already begun. Troop trains were passing by one after another, and soldiers could be heard singing from half-opened doors of boxcars refitted for transporting people.

At the railway stations, crowds of women – commoners – were bidding farewell to husbands and sons, and the air was charged with their heartbreaking wails, which faded as the train moved away from the station and grew louder as it drew near the next stop. In the city of Belgorod, which was my point of transfer, I had to wait a long time. Troop trains were allowed to pass on a first-priority basis. Fortunately the local land captain's wife met me at the railway station, and she took me to a cathedral where the relics of St. Joseph of Belgorod were kept. We also attended a little antique Greek church, so small that one had to bend over double to enter.

The land captain's wife happened to be a very educated guide. She drew my attention to many of the church's architectural elements. Her husband, the land captain, was awaiting our return. He advised me that he had already notified my husband of my delay, and that he was going to contact him as soon as the time of my departure from Belgorod was known. He promised to keep me informed of my train's itinerary. I did not have to wait too long, yet I arrived in Kursk late in the night as a result of frequent stops of the train, picking up mobilized troops running to rejoin their regiments. In the train I met Cleopatra A. Kourcheninoff, who was hurrying off to St. Petersburg with her younger son to bid farewell to her two elder sons, both members of the Horse Guards. Both were killed on the same day soon after, during the early part of the war. In Kursk, where I was met at the station by my husband, no recent news was known, but the mobilization seemed to be of great urgency.

Early in the morning on the following day, July 19, a newspaper was delivered to us with the announcement of war printed in gigantic capitals on the front page. My husband advised me to go to say farewell to my brothers right away because passenger service was to be suspended to give priority to troop trains, and he would initially be busy from morning until night because of the mobilization. At two o'clock in the afternoon, I departed for St. Petersburg by train. The train was packed with military men hurrying to rejoin their army units, as well as wives and mothers of the military trying to extend their time with loved ones. I was lucky to find a seat in a coach with Baroness Wrangel.[3] Poor Olesya was not only experiencing distress because of the separation from her husband, but was also in physical pain, as she had just discontinued breastfeeding her baby as a result of the threat of war.

When I arrived in St. Petersburg, I could instantly feel that we were at war. Military units were continually marching in the streets since the guards that were stationed in St. Petersburg were the very first to go to the front. Although I was not present at the announcement of war by the Monarch, made from the balcony of the Winter Palace, I understood that the Monarch was greeted with a genuine spirit and enthusiasm for the war by those who were in attendance.

---

3 Baroness Olesya Wrangel was the wife of General Peter Wrangel, a courageous and highly regarded leader of the White Russian Army. It is believed that he was poisoned in Brussels in 1928 by the OPGU, a precursor of the KGB, because of his leadership of the ROV, which was composed of thousands of White Russian soldiers in exile.

In St. Petersburg I stayed at the empty apartment of my parents. I was very happy to see my mother, who, to my surprise, returned from Austria toward the evening. The next day we both went to the Alexandrovskaya Station,[4] where the Fifth Battery, which my younger brother belonged to, was entraining. When we reached the point of entrainment, the loading of horses and cannonry into boxcars was in progress. Standing a certain distance from the main body of soldiers, we managed to exchange only a few words with him whenever he had a spare minute. Seeing our worry, yet being equally thrilled himself, he tried to cheer us up with his jokes. Time flew quickly and inexorably until the battery men were called to prayer and the boarding began.

To the strains of martial music, the train, illuminated by the last rays of the setting sun, started pulling away from the platform and soon vanished in the evening darkness. With long-repressed tears flowing without measure, my mother and I stood on the platform for a few more minutes. Eventually collecting ourselves, we returned to St. Petersburg. Early the next morning, I saw off our distant cousin Kyril Shirkoff, a member of the Horse Guards, who was leaving with his squadron. On July 24, I bade farewell to my elder brother, who was catching up with his unit and temporarily travelling with the Hussars squadron. The grey horses of the Hussars squadron, hastily and raggedly painted khaki green, looked dirty and miserable. (This measure failed in its purpose – the paint did not stay on the horses and came off before long!)

Upon my return to Kursk, I had to first pay a number of formal calls, the list of people to be visited being provided to me by an accompanying messenger. At the top of the list were the local eparch and hegumeness of the local monastery, who later became my good friends and helpers.

The battles in August instantly changed the status of Kursk from a city at the deep rear of the war action to an important evacuation point. The wounded began to come in straight from the front and stayed in the city in wait for inland assignment or discharge from

4 Alexandrovskaya Station, built in 1904, was just outside of St. Petersburg.

the forces. Most often the soldiers arrived in lacerated uniforms, sometimes even without overcoats, wearing simply what they wore when the German shell or bullet hit. At first the intendance office did not work according to plan, as Kursk was expected to be a home-front point. Governor Mouratoff was ordered to urgently convert the local boys' and girls' grammar schools to hospitals. In each hospital, "Ladies' Committees" were formed. The committees were responsible for assisting the nursing staff with the registration of the wounded patients, feeding the critically wounded, and so on. In the absence of the intendance office, undergarments, linen, and in some cases even outer garments were given to those who were granted a leave or were discharged from the forces. Initially the Governor had made small appropriations to aid the committees, but from then on they were to seek funding by alternative means: pledges, lotteries, and so on.

I was appointed by Governor Mouratoff to head one of the committees. As the front line drew nearer to Kursk, there were more and more of the wounded in the city, and the quarters situated above our government-owned apartment that used to be occupied by the Governorate Administration were vacated to accommodate the wounded. I was asked by Governor Mouratoff to form a Ladies' Committee in the new hospital as well. Our apartment had a garden, which we placed in the service of the hospital – it offered at least some of the wounded an opportunity to breathe fresh air, weather permitting. Access to the garden from our apartment was rather ingenious – the only way the garden could be entered was through a dining room window. To this end, steps were placed by the dining room window every spring. According to common superstition, cutting an opening for a new outside door in an existing house would result in a "dead body soon carried out through that door." None of the previous tenants in the apartment had the heart to discount the superstition, so we followed suit.

Without difficulty I found good-hearted young ladies as volunteers for both committees, with whom we soon became very friendly. The hegumeness of the local monastery sent several nuns to assist the committees with undergarment and linen mending for the wounded, and generally supported all my initiatives with advice. I shall remember her with deep gratitude.

I spent about two years in Kursk. The city stood on two hills; in winter those who travelled at a fast pace in two-horse open sleighs fell out of the sleighs every so often! Some streets could not be accessed by horse-drawn carriages during winter and could only be traversed on wooden planks that were laid over the pavement. The Streletskaya Sloboda district was flooded by the Tuskar River every spring and for two months remained a canal city, like Venice, that could only be travelled by boat.

The main streets of the city, Moskovskaya and Kharkovskaya, ended at arches and spires, decorated with the Imperial two-headed eagle. One of the arches, put up in commemoration of the passage of Emperor Alexander I through Kursk, still had traces of the inscription that once stated that the arch had been erected "by contributions from the Kursk noblemen." Over the years, however, the inscription lost some letters and, at some point in time, read "Kursk lemon!"

In summer, famous men were often seen in Kursk, including such performers as Smirnoff and Sobinoff.[5] The city of Kursk had a theatre and we often made use of the governor's box that Governor Mouratoff allowed us to occupy; neither he nor his family used it. Before long we had a small circle of friends of various ages with whom we often met. With acquaintances, we had dinners at the Nobility Club. Many of the landed gentry lived permanently around Kursk and many of them used to come to the city to participate in various elections and conventions. Among our frequent guests was V.P. Myatlev, who shared his ingenious impromptus with us. The local public took pleasure in benefit performances, card games, and bingo gambling.

5 Dimitri Smirnoff (1882–1944) was a famous Russian tenor and member of St. Petersburg's Mariinsky Theatre, who sang internationally in Paris, London, and New York's Metropolitan Opera. Leonid Sobinoff (1872–1934) was another famous Russian tenor who began singing at Moscow's Bolshoi Theatre and went on to sing at Milan's La Scala, London's Convent Gardens and others. Recordings of both men are available online.

Back then neither radio nor television existed, so newspapers kept us informed of the latest war news. Distance from the capital, coupled with lack of communication with the masses, kept us in the dark about the pulse of the nation, while locally the positive developments at the front would get everybody's hopes up. It is difficult for those who witnessed World War II to understand the high spirit that the majority of the people felt during the early part of the first war.

The outskirts of Kursk were very picturesque. The Korennaya Hermitage monastery, built in the 16th to 17th centuries, was a short distance from the city. The monastery stood on the riverside in the middle of a vast park with a lake where black and white swans lived. There was a healing spring in the cathedral that bubbled by the root of a tree where, at the end of the 18th century, the *Znamenskaya* icon of the Holy Mother of God had been found. Both the cathedral and its gate were adorned with antique wall paintings. At one time there was a very popular fair near the hermitage that was famous all over Russia – nightingale fanciers from all over the country flocked to the fair, which specialized in nightingales. But in my time, only the ruins of the fair remained. Twice a year the hermitage was visited by groups of pilgrims. In spring the *Znamenskaya* icon of the Holy Mother of God was carried, on the shoulders of the pilgrims, from its winter home at the Kursk Cathedral to Korennaya Hermitage for the summer, only to be moved back to the cathedral in September.[6]

The Kursk Governorate was home to the estates of the Princes Baryatinsky. The Ivanovskoye Estate, belonging to a descendant of the field marshal, was the place where the field marshal's museum was kept. The house where the family of the Princes Baryatinsky lived was appropriately called a palace due to its size and *cour*

6 The *Znamenskaya* icon is a particular style of icon: Mary is portrayed with her arms outstretched to heaven and a medallion of Jesus around her neck. It was a popular style of icon with the last Tsar and his family. The *Znamenskaya* icon from the Korennaya Hermitage Monastery disappeared in 1918 and was found in Serbia in 1919. In 1944 it was in Munich and then travelled to the United States in 1950. It is still housed in a Russian Orthodox Church in New York.

d'honneur architecture. Its chambers abounded with marble statues brought by the owners from Italy over a period of time. A picture gallery contained portraits of Russian monarchs and empresses painted by famous artists. The park in front of the palace bore a resemblance to the Palace of Versailles, with similarly trimmed shrubs and allées leading to a big lake. The park had 100 dessiatines (270 acres) dedicated as a "deer park," where the deer roamed freely.

In close vicinity to Kursk, there was the estate of Count P. Kleinmiehel ("Ryshkovo"). The estate was governed by the count's wife (née Shipova), who lived there permanently with her three children and mother, the daughter of N.N. Goncharova, widow of Pushkin from his second marriage. Even during her middle age, the count's wife's mother, S.P. Shipova (née Lanskaya), resembled the tall, slender, and fine-featured N.N. Goncharova. I once asked the countess whether her mother had ever talked with her about Pushkin. Her answer was, "No, never. When we were little children, we asked her about him on one occasion and she said, 'Do not ask me about Pushkin again. I was very unhappy with him but was very happy with your father.'"[7]

I became very fond of the entire Kleinmiehel family and often went on horseback to visit them on Sundays. I rode a horse from my father's stud farm, which was his gift to me on the occasion of my marriage. Countess Maria Nikolaievna Kleinmiehel[8] once paid a visit to us in Kursk, only to find me in tears as an order demanding dam requisition by the cavalry had just been published. My husband explained to me that I had to comply with this order and part with the horse that my father had given me. The countess immediately reassured me and made an offer to buy my "Déesse," promising to return her as soon as the respective counter-order was published. The countess was apparently allowed to keep a certain

7 Natalya Nikolaevna Pushkina Lanskya (1812–1863), a renowned beauty, married the poet Pushkin at the age of 19. She had four children in the six years they were married. He was killed in a duel with Georges d'Anthes, who apparently was having an affair with Natalya – and was married to Natalya's sister. Natalya's second husband was Peter Lanskoy.

8 Countess Kleinmiehel was a leading society hostess of St. Petersburg known for extravagant parties.

number of dams that was more than she actually had. Subsequent developments denied me any opportunity of seeing my horse again.

In the summer of 1916 my husband was appointed Governor of the Courland Governorate, in Latvia, which at the time was completely occupied by the Germans. Because of its proximity to the front, I could not accompany him there, so I spent the end of the year at his father's estate, Grafskoye. In September of that year, my *belle-mère*, my mother-in-law, passed away, and my husband received an appointment in the city of Orel where, before long, we were caught up in the Revolution.

When we travelled from Kursk to St. Petersburg, we stayed at the Hendrikoffs' house at 3 Mikhailovskaya Square, later renamed Square of Arts. As a matter of fact, the Hendrikoffs no longer owned the house as it had been bought by the State through the personal funds of the Emperor when Count V.A. Hendrikoff died of a stroke in 1912.[9] At the time of his death, my *beau-père* held the post of gentleman-usher to Empress Alexandra Feodorovna. My *belle-mère* was in poor health and was confined to bed from the age of 35 as a result of complications from surgery. Count V.A. Hendrikoff was in charge of all affairs and asset management for the Imperial family. Even though he had no economic expertise and, most probably, no business sense, he undertook various risky ventures that found him running more and more into debt. When, at long last, a major promissory note that he had issued to Prince Kantakouzen-Speransky was not honoured, V.A. Hendrikoff suffered a stroke and passed away without regaining consciousness. The Monarch and the Empress extended considerable sympathy to the bankrupt family. The house at Mikhailovskaya Square was bought by the personal means of the Emperor and my *belle-mère* was allowed to use two floors, at no expense, for the term of her life. Her daughter, Nastenka, was appointed as paid maid-of-honour to the Empress, with the right to live with her mother for the term of her mother's life. The family property was subjected to trust management and a creditors' committee was established to sort out the financial standing of the family. As a re-

9 Count V.A. Hendrikoff (1857–1912), Countess Hendrikoff's father-in-law, was a master of ceremonies at the Russian Imperial Court.

sult, it did not take long for family finances to start changing for the better, yet many ventures, or more properly speaking *ad*ventures of Count V.A. Hendrikoff (such as prospecting in the rich gold-fields in Nevyansk, Siberia), had to be abandoned.

Grafskoye Estate and the house were foreclosed. It later came as a surprise to me that the trust had contracted the former bar-keeper, Andrey, who was a visibly dishonest man, to look after the house and Grafskoye Estate. His daughter wore dresses cut from eastern silk throws that once decorated tables in the Grafs-koye living room. Andrey kept visiting us in Kursk under various pretexts, and his every visit resulted in the disappearance of even more of our belongings. Once he even took my gold watch. He surrendered it later upon my demand, but I made it clear that our house in Kursk was forbidden to him from then on. It must be said that the Revolution put an end to the problem of Andrey, as both debts and proceeds related to the Grafskoye Estate were swallowed by the same abyss. Later I heard that the house at Graf-skoye Estate had been turned into an orphan's shelter. I have no knowledge of Andrey's destiny.

Grafskoye Estate, 1914

I had been at Grafskoye only once, for that very short period of time following my wedding. My attendance there had been at the request of my *belle-mère*, who was kept in the dark about the financial standing of the family. To stay at Grafskoye after her death, we needed to obtain special permission from the trust. The sight of this "Cherry Orchard" left an unfavourable impression on me in spite of the beauty of the surrounding area.[10] The house, furnished with furniture of incompatible styles, was disorderly, while some of the paintings that used to adorn the walls were simply standing in disarray on the floor. In the living room, an oil painting representing a young officer standing near a gigantic horse covered an entire wall. Was it a portrait of Grandfather, or Great Grandfather Hendrikoff, who had a passion for horses? Near the house there was a tremendous empty riding stable and various empty outbuildings of the same style. At the time there were only four horses in the vast deserted stable. They were used in rotation for fatigue duties, and only occasionally were harnessed. The horses were badly schooled and heeded mainly voice, rather than rein. The house itself stood by the side of the Donets River and from its porch one could see the surrounding countryside beyond the river. Traces of former allées in the park could just barely be seen. As I was told by my husband, the family rarely made use of Grafskoye Estate, choosing instead to make trips to Paris or foreign resorts. Having undergone major surgery, my *belle-mère* was no longer travelling abroad and I believe was spending summers in Sestroretsk, Crimea.

Grafskoye was not the ancestral estate of the Hendrikoffs. The original ancestral home had been the nearby Pisarevka, which was either sold or exchanged for Grafskoye. I do not remember the particulars, but when I arrived at Grafskoye the church at Pisarevka was closed and nailed up. Church services were given at the Grafskoye church, which stood nearby. In the Grafskoye church, the old, frail

---

10 "Cherry Orchard" is a reference to the Anton Chekhov play *The Cherry Orchard*. In the play, an aristocratic family must sell their estate because they have run out of money. The family seems powerless to help themselves and consequently (and ironically) the estate is sold to the son of one of their peasant workers. The reference highlights the parallels between the play and the situation that befell Countess Hendrikoff's in-laws.

priest showed us a gold chalice that used to be kept in the Pisarevka church and explained that the chalice was crafted in Rococo style (he pronounced this foreign word as "ro-cho-cho"). At one time it was presented by Empress Elizaveta Petrovna to a Hendrikoff ancestor. In the archives of Pisarevka, a grievance from peasants was still recorded against a Hendrikoff who had trampled their crops while driving game with hounds. The peasants' grievance bore the genuine handwriting of Empress Elizaveta Petrovna, together with her resolution that read, "Hendrikoff, you better keep out of mischief!" I was not so much surprised by the resolution as the fact that such a grievance had reached the Empress herself and was regarded! I was never to see Grafskoye again after war was declared.

The living quarters granted to my *belle-mère* in St. Petersburg for the term of her life, two floors at 3 Mikhailovskaya Square, were notable for their size. Each member of the family had a suite of rooms, not to mention the empty and usually locked public rooms, a ballroom with palm trees standing in every corner, a large dining room and a number of living rooms. Ordinarily the family used a small separate living room and dining room. The main floor was at one time occupied by my *beau-père*. Although at the time he had been dead for a full two years, his suite of rooms was kept exactly as it had been at the time of his demise. His rings and briefcase, together with a wallet, lay on his desk, and his clothes hung in the closets. It looked as if the owner of all these things had left the room for only a few minutes, to return in a moment. Knowing that he was never to come back made me feel uneasy. The majority of the rooms in the house, except for those occupied by Nastenka, were furnished according to late-19th-century fashion, with massive carved furniture, silk curtains and heavy drapes. There were portraits of the family in gilded frames on the walls along with other paintings, including one by Aivazovsky that was considered a rarity, as it depicted a rural landscape with a yoke of oxen moving a haystack: unusual because paintings by Aivazovsky usually depicted seascapes and coastal scenes. Upon the liquidation of the property at Mikhailovskaya Square, the painting with oxen was sold at a ransom price.[11]

11 Aivazovsky's paintings are rarely found outside of Russia, but when one recently sold it fetched over $3 million.

There was a suite of rooms occupied by Nastenka and her former tutoress, Viktorina Vladimirovna Nikolaieva, whom we always called "Vikolka." She was utterly devoted to Nastenka and later followed her to Siberia when the Royal Family was exiled. Nastenka's rooms were very light and covered in *toile de Jouy*. It was in her room that family and friends most often gathered. Near the public rooms was the bedroom of my *belle-mère*, where cold and darkness prevailed: it was kept unheated, even during winter. In this room my *belle-mère* spent year after year in a reclining position in her big bed, all wrapped in wool shawls and wearing knitted wool bonnets on her close-cropped grey head. The bedroom resembled a chapel – it was all cluttered with icons and icing lamps.[12] A folding screen stood by the bed, with icons all over it. When I first met my *belle-mère*, my mind spontaneously went back to the story "A Living Relic" by Turgenev.[13] My *belle-mère*'s pale, almost whey-coloured face was lit up only by sunken, glowing black eyes. The moment she closed them, her face looked as if she was dead! Although physically she was a total invalid, her spirit was remarkably fresh and strong. She was attended day and night by a sister of mercy who went by the nickname of "Sis." None of us would even think of failing to fulfill any of her wishes or demands. Suffice it to say that 24-year-old Nastenka used to dress to her mother's liking in the austere fashion of 25 years ago, and when she finally found it in her heart to get a more modern dress for herself, she never appeared before her mother in it.

During our short stays in St. Petersburg, my husband and I used to allow ourselves some childish fun. We were eager to see our friends and relatives, while my *belle-mère* demanded that we devote all our time to her, especially in the evenings because she had chronic insomnia. Back then we would excuse ourselves, claiming to be tired. We yawned good night, having been blessed with a large iron cross that my unsuspecting *belle-mère* kept under her pillow,

12 An "icing lamp" is a lamp with frosted glass.
13 In Ivan Turgenev's story "A Living Relic," a peasant girl is bedridden and isolated, looking half-dead, like a mummy. She remains in this state a long time, yet manages to have a positive outlook on life.

and then we quickly and quietly escaped by a back door. However, Sis was always on the watch for us and reported all our outings to my *belle-mère*. As a result, my *belle-mère* used to sulk. Before too long, Alec, my husband's brother, who often kept us company in our escapades, put an end to Sis's whispering. One night, having noticed her eavesdropping on us, he gave us a sign to remain talking, crept up on the door and threw it open very quickly. He then pulled the flushed and confused Sis into the room, shoved her into the pantry next door and locked it. He left Sis there for half an hour, ignoring her entreaties and knocking. After finally letting her go, he proclaimed that next time he would keep her in the pantry for the rest of the night. Apparently she believed him – she never again interfered with our adventures.

At the beginning of the war, the eldest daughter of the Hendrikoffs, Alexandra Vasilievna Balashova, whom we addressed as "Inochka," returned to Russia with her four children and husband. She had tuberculosis, so she had been living permanently in the south of France. It was difficult to imagine two sisters who had so little in common, in both appearance and personality, as Inochka and Nastenka. Nastenka took after her father – dark-haired, with a pale complexion. She was petite, although harsh critics noted that she was somewhat unfeminine, with a somewhat awkward gait. All this was redeemed, however, by her straightforward personality, a remarkably high sense of duty and extraordinary devotion to her mother, whom she looked after in her time off from her maid-of-honour duties. Inochka, who looked like her mother, was tall, white-haired, and had big radiant eyes. She was the very picture of charm and femininity, and she fascinated all who ever met her. We all loved her, calling her by different pet names. It was not always apparent to me which sister the family was talking about, and my *belle-mère* used to refer to the German saying *Liebes Kind hat viele Namen* – a good child has many names. Inochka had a lively, rosy disposition until she succumbed to diseases and losses suffered one after another – her two-year-old daughter contracted tuberculosis from her, and then her husband died suddenly of typhus that he caught when serving in the lines.

My *belle-mère* was kept in the dark about the war for a long time and the family made an effort to make up an alternative cause for Inochka's unanticipated return and her husband's departure to the front. Then one day, Alec accidentally let it out and, to our surprise, my *belle-mère* accepted the news calmly. My *belle-mère* died in the autumn of 1916.

Petrovskoye Estate, 1913

I was at Petrovskoye, my father's estate, when the telegram bearing the news reached me. When I arrived at Mikhailovskaya Square, I found Inochka, who had hurriedly come from the Caucasus with her husband. My *belle-mère* was still breathing but was already unconscious. Sadly, over and over, she whispered something we could not understand. Several days and nights passed. The nights were particularly distressing for the family; we were awakened more than once every night and everybody thought that my *belle-mère*'s life was about to end, but she would somehow rally. At long last, she passed away without regaining consciousness. In strict observance of the customs, all women in the family went into full mourning, wearing black crepe dresses with black sleeves and collars. The only finery allowed was a string of black wooden beads around the neck. When going out, we wore small black crepe bonnets with black waist-long veils in front. I had never before worn full mourning dress and felt uncomfortable doing so. Upon the death of my *belle-mère*, the part of the house at

Mikhailovskaya Square occupied by the family was subject to repossession. At the same time, my husband was appointed Governor of Orel and I, without stopping at Petrovskoye, followed him to Orel. Inochka returned to the Caucasus, where she subsequently passed away, while Nastenka took care of disposing of the family possessions at Mikhailovskaya Square. After some time she moved into the palace at Tsarskoye Selo, only to be caught there by the Revolution, which I will write about later.

In the house at Mikhailovskaya Square, in an apartment separate from the Hendrikoffs' quarters, Countess Nadezhda Petrovna Goudovich, a younger sister of my *belle-mère*, lived with her husband and three grown children. She was a very neurotic woman who possessed particular oddities. She was afraid of Fridays and spent them in bed doing nothing and seeing no visitors. By a strange set of circumstances, it was a Friday when she heard about the death of her youngest son. At age of 16 he had gone up the line as a volunteer, despite her wishes, and was killed at the front. For the first time she left her bed that day to quit her Friday seclusions. Her son's death came as a crushing blow. She kept blaming herself for not being able to make him stay at home. She died of galloping consumption within a year. After the Revolution, which scattered all our relatives and friends to the four winds of heaven, I lost touch with the Goudovich family, but I heard that Count Goudovich later married a girl who was unknown to us. The girl had one leg, but I never knew if it was due to an accident or a congenital defect. Apparently it did not prohibit her from giving birth to a son. In the meantime, Alec was appointed adjutant to General Rouzsky.

Upon my arrival at Orel, I was to visit the wives of all the administrative department heads, as well as prominent members of the Orel district council. Orel was a major city with a society far more *bon ton* than that of Kursk. I was told outright that on Sundays I would have to stay at home to receive Orel citizens, of whom I knew very little, and who would be paying formal visits to meet me. In order to ease the formality of those Sunday receptions, to which mothers were bringing their daughters, I asked a few young ladies to take care of the tea table in the adjoining living room and referred all the young children to them, feeling pity for myself for not being able to join them. My husband was very excited over his new status but I, in spite of all the benefits of his appointment in Orel, have warmer memories of the time we spent in Kursk with the friends I had there, and the heartfelt relationships I had with both the mother-hegumeness and eparch of Kursk, whose wise advice during my very first days in my new and challenging capacity was such a great help to me. The eparch of Orel was a stiff-limbed old man of little culture who, possibly just to while away the time, sought to spend most evenings with me. He brought along old Mr. Kulikovsky, the father of the second husband of the Grand Duchess Olga Alexandrovna, sister of the Monarch, whose intellectual endowments were no better than those of the eparch. My husband insisted that I be kind and tolerant to those two old men, but avoided showing up himself!

Early in 1917, on the occasion of the nobility elections in the Governorate, I had to organize a reception for the nobility who had gathered in Orel. Now, when I recall that among the many participants of those celebratory ceremonies, there were only a few people who actually sensed the pulse of the nation, that period of time appears to me as a "feast in time of famine!"

Later, among different letters and notes that survived, I found my description of the first days of the Revolution and they are cited below. Never before had I kept a diary, but the developments that followed were changing the world around me so quickly that I was afraid that I might forget the sequence of events unless I were to record them.

THE REVOLUTION
Notes based on my diary:
Orel, February 26, 1917 (Julian calendar). The first rumours of unrest in the capital were brought to us by an unexpected visitor, D.N. Khvostov. According to his story, mobs were treading the streets of the capital bellowing, "Bread! Bread!" but Khvostov assured us that the manifestations were slight, with no political rationale, and that the people would calm down before long. There was no

mention of unrest in the capital in local newspapers, and operative "agent's telegrams" that my husband used to receive through his position were no longer coming. This, however, did not alarm us, as we believed that it was caused by "temporary" turmoil in the capital. We found out later that it had been in compliance with orders made by the new authorities!

February 27. In the evening my husband and I went to the railway station to see Nastenka, who was to make a stop in Orel. Nastenka had been called by an urgent telegram to attend her sick sister in Kislovodsk. After her mother's death, Nastenka moved into the palace in Tsarskoye Selo to continue her service with the Imperial family. The Tsar's children had caught the measles so they, together with the Empress, were separated from the rest of the court. However, having heard of the telegram received by Nastenka, the Empress insisted on Nastenka's immediate departure to her sister. The atmosphere in the palace was optimistic. According to Khabalov, who I believe served as the governor of the palace, the riots were assumed to have been suppressed. Yet, in spite of his optimism, the gentleman of the Tsar's bedchamber, who always escorted Nastenka in the city, met her in St. Petersburg dressed in plain clothes, rather than in the usual court livery. The court coach, in which she usually travelled in the city, would not be made available to her and she had to walk to the Nikolaevsky Railway Terminal using side streets. She did not hear sounds of firing and the crowd did not seem bloody-minded.

February 28. In the evening we had dinner at Count Kourakin's residence. Count Kourakin was the Governorate Marshal of the Nobility. Among the guests were V.P. Myatlev and Oliv, both of whom stayed in Orel after the nobility elections in the Governorate that had just concluded; Khripunov, a member of the Governorate District Council; and others whom I was to meet later in exile. During the dinner nobody mentioned the developments in St. Petersburg, but towards the end of the dinner Kourakin's valet approached my husband to tell him in a low voice that Gendarmerie Colonel Miller was asking on the telephone for his permission to come over immediately due to a matter of great urgency. Miller came into the room within a few minutes. Count Kourakin and my husband withdrew with Colonel Miller to another room for deliberation. While no one was yet aware of the news Miller had brought, the extended talking in the adjacent room and my husband's voice, occasionally heard when he was calling up unit officers to the Governor's House, contributed to the discomfort of the company that had been perfectly unconcerned up to this point. Having noticed my worry, Countess Kourakina left to clarify the situation and soon returned to tell me that my husband was ready to see me. When I entered the room where the mysterious meeting was taking place, my husband silently extended a telegram to me from Bublikov that was to become renowned before long.[14] It was addressed to "all and everybody" and was sent along the railroad to be intercepted by gendarmes. The telegram informed railroad workers of the fact that on February 28 Bublikov had taken charge of the Transportation Ministry. My husband departed to see Gendarmerie Colonel Dolgov and asked me to not tell a soul of his actions, promising to let me know once he got back to the Governor's House. Upon returning to the dining room, I instantly understood that Count Kourakin had already told some of the guests about the news brought by Miller. Arshounov made no disguise of his jubilance over the news and attempted to persuade me that it was something long expected and that everything was to take a turn for the better from then on.[15]

Then we were unexpectedly joined by Kira Galakhova and Sverbeyev. They had just seen an acquaintance who had come from the capital and shared the latest news with them. They learned that the military had joined the side of the rebels, that the Duma[16] had refused to dissolve, and that a "Temporary Committee" had been established. Everyone started talking at once. While some were in fear of the future, others were very enthusiastic about the developments.

14 Bublikov was head of a group that controlled the railway and telegraph services. He was a powerful man who understood that the success of the Revolution depended on the control of information and troop movements.

15 "Arshounov" is likely Peter Arshinov (1887–c. 1937), an anarchist and later Communist. He is believed to have been a victim of Stalin's purges.

16 The lower house of the Russian Federation.

I returned to the Governor's House in the company of Oliv, who sounded very optimistic, assuring me that he would vouch for the maintenance of peace and order in his district. At the Governor's House the meeting of unit officers was progressing, when all of a sudden agent's telegrams, which we had been missing for the past few days, began arriving and we were able to form a clearer picture of the situation in the capital. Of course we could not go to bed that night! The meeting lasted until four o'clock in the morning.

March 1. At five o'clock in the morning we were visited by the garrison commander, who came to consult with my husband concerning patrol distribution in the city. At six o'clock, his adjutant arrived to report, and around seven o'clock in the morning my husband rode through the city in compliance with his orders. Notwithstanding that the agent's telegrams were then published uncut in newspapers, the city appeared to be calm and the police remained in position.

March 2. On March 2, a long-scheduled open session of the City Duma was to take place. The city mayor, Goumbin, came in the morning to consult with my husband concerning the forthcoming appeal to the public from the City Duma. My husband, for his part, had already addressed the public, calling for patience and peace on the part of the citizens. Having heard of the establishment of the "Committee for Public Safety" in Moscow, members of the City Duma of Orel followed the lead of their colleagues in Moscow. It was reported that the commander-in-chief for the Moscow Military District, Mrozovskiy, had been arrested by insurgents. Furthermore, the central telephone exchange refused to connect my husband with Moscow, referring to their respective orders.

March 3. Early in the morning my husband rode to the railway station in response to a telegram from Prince A.P. Oldenburgsky,[17] who was passing through Orel and wanted to confirm the dreadful rumours that he had heard. The Governor's House was in close vi-

17 Prince Oldenburgsky (1844–1932) was a Major General in the Russian–Turkish War (1877–78), a senator and member of parliament. In World War I he was head of the Russian army's medical service, and established Russia's first medical research institute.

cinity to the barracks and prison. That morning I was sitting in the living room waiting for my husband's return from the railway station when suddenly a continuous buzz and scamper of feet reached my ears. Apprehensively approaching the window and opening it a crack, I saw an excited crowd of soldiers and prisoners, the latter still wearing stripes, running along the street towards the building of the City Duma. Some prisoners even rode on the soldiers' shoulders. Everyone wore red ribbon bows. Attracted by the noise, the household workers ran into the room to pull me back and hastily shut the window. The entry doors of the Governor's House were also hurriedly locked. Fortunately the mob ran past the house without stopping. The only person affected was a police constable who usually stood guard over the Governor's House. He did not have a chance to hide his short fur coat and some fellow from the crowd was quick enough to "confiscate" it as he ran by! In the evening, a revolutionary guard came in and announced to my husband that we were under house arrest from then on and had no right to leave the house. For their part, the revolutionary guards were to occupy the entire main floor of the building and keep watch over the entrance. This period of time lasted until our departure from Orel and became a real test of courage and cordiality for our acquaintances and friends.

Some friends never showed up again. Conversely, Hitrovo, Official for Special Missions, even moved into our house before our departure and went downstairs to calm the drunken guards when they made too much noise at nighttime. Maslov, who I believe was Chairman of the District Administration, visited me every day. The guards did not make it difficult for those who wanted to see us and let them all in! Maslov tried to persuade me to take some air with him, assuring me that it would cause no problems at all, neither for him nor for me. I always refused, however, as I did not want to compromise him in the eyes of the new government. Through Maslov we found out the reason for the mysterious conduct of one of the officials. When delivering his report to my husband, the official suddenly lost his self-control and began crying hysterically for no apparent reason. My husband called for me to give the man some anti-depressant drops. I complied without asking for the reason for the strange behaviour. Afterwards, however, the man came to us to explain. He had been part of a plot aimed at overthrowing the government, but did not feel certain that our family would remain unharmed. My husband's friendly attitude and my young age turned his heart and unsettled him to an extent that he could not bear. He wanted to give us some warning about the conspiracy but was unable to do so.

We received an unanticipated telegram from Nastenka, this time from Kislovodsk. She was hurrying back to St. Petersburg and asked us to meet her at the railway station in Orel. We began deliberating about how to explain our absence at the railway station to her when finally I called the young son of friends, Igor Volodimirov, and asked him to visit us. I do not remember what suitable excuse I thought to give him for the call. He appeared at our house in next to no time and the guards willingly let him in to see us. We asked him to find Nastenka and Vikolka, whom he had never met, at the railway station and explain our absence. We described their dresses and appearances to him and provided him with their photographs. He performed the mission we entrusted to him in an excellent manner. He found them both and delivered our messages to Nastenka. Hardly had Nastenka heard the rumours of the events in Tsarskoye Selo when she became grimly determined to rejoin the Tsar's family and share in their fate.

To the best of my reckoning, we lived this way for another four weeks. My husband received no new orders and it helped him to remain under the illusion that people like him, who had not been in the political spotlight, would keep their posts. He determinately insisted that I not make any arrangements for leaving Orel in advance of any hypothetical departure. He merely ordered me to deposit all our silverware in the National Bank, with the help of our acquaintances. When I dropped a hint of doubt as to its safety at the bank, he lost his temper and said that I did not seem to have any belief in the safety of Russia itself. I could not confess to him that it was exactly what I tended to believe, so I made myself comply with his order. Meanwhile, we began hearing rumours of disturbances, and sometimes even massacres, throughout the governorate towns and lands. We began seeing the first fugitive governors in Orel, which was a bad omen. The possibility of us sharing the same fate in the near future was very disturbing. However, this situation was resolved rather quickly: we received an order for the immediate resignation of my husband, which led to our very prompt eviction from the Governor's House!

I have a rather dim recollection of the days that followed. The guards who occupied the main floor were removed, following some orders that we knew nothing about. Meanwhile my husband pressed me for a hurried departure so I hastily paid off and dismissed the domestic workers. My housemaid asked me to take her along to wherever I was destined, although afterwards she found the situation in post-revolution St. Petersburg so frightening that she chose to return to Orel! The young wife of the Vice-Governor came to me drowning in tears, such was her worry about the fate of her family. The sister of my childhood friend, E.A. Hitrovo, helped me pack, even though she was a fugitive governor's wife, as well.

We took only one trunk with us, and the chief clerk undertook to send the other two to St. Petersburg by regular delivery. We eventually received only one of the trunks, and then all communication with Orel was instantly lost. Since then I have heard nothing about the fate of the civil servants who worked with us in Orel, with the exception of the refugees Maslov and Oliv, who I once met in Constantinople years later, in 1920–21. We left Orel, abandoning there all our furnishings, both our own and those that were the property of the State, including gigantic, floor-to-ceiling portraits of the Hendrikoff family that had been delivered to us with furniture upon Nastenka's departure from the house at Mikhailovskaya Square. We had no chance to sell our property in the short time allowed to us. My husband's optimistic disposition of the first days of the Revolution was gone and he was pressing me for a quick departure from Orel, given that the political situation in the province had turned for the worse. All bank "safes" were soon split open as ordered by the new authorities and the contents of the safes were confiscated under the authority of the new government. We were seen off by a small group of civil servants. At the request of my husband, we travelled in a second-class coach instead of the usual first-class one. In St. Petersburg, our destination, we stayed at first in the empty regimental apartment of my brother, Vladimir (Barbos).

Once in St. Petersburg, we learned that Alec, my husband's brother, had been arrested and admitted to the Nikolaevsky Military Hospital. Of course we immediately went to see him. To our surprise, we found him in the mental ward. We had not been informed that he had been placed there in order to smother his overt action against General Rouzsky, to whom he was attached as an adjutant. According to Alec, he was arrested by soldiers from the St. Petersburg garrison in the first days of the Revolution, moved to the State Duma, which was occupied by the revolutionaries, and then released and sent directly to General Rouzsky at the front, where he was forced to hear, time after time, the general's scornful references to the Tsar's family. Being sincerely devoted to the Imperial family, Alec lost his temper and ran with his weapon at General Rouzsky. Fellow soldiers managed to pull Alec off, arrest him and transport him to St. Petersburg where, under the pretext of a fit of frenzy, he was placed in the same ward with lunatics at the hospital. We found Alec to be in a very nervous state of mind. Quiet mental patients around him suddenly became violent and one of them nearly choked Alec to death. Later we heard that he was transported to the commandant's office where he was kept for five days in a mass cell with those belonging to the lower ranks, and where he had to sleep on the floor. Following this he was suddenly released, and it was explained to him that he had been wrongly arrested. We temporarily fell out of touch with him.

I was puzzled by the high spirits of our friends in St. Petersburg. They all cheered the "Bloodless Revolution" and believed that it would serve as a model for the peaceful change of power in all of Europe. They attended speeches by Kerensky, who hysterically shouted from the stage of an empty theatre, and Lenin, who gave his speech from the balcony of prima ballerina Kshesinska's mansion, confiscated by the new government.[18] Our friends referred to some temporary revolutionary impulse that was to eventually make everything better. They did not give even a single thought to the fate of the Emperor's family.

My father, upon his resignation as the Governor of Riga, happened to be in the area of military operations in the first days of the war. He moved to #35 Znamenskaya Street, our apartment in St. Petersburg, where I went to see him every day.[19] During one of my visits he, without saying a word, held forth a telegram sent by our water mill leaseholder's son. The son offered to buy my riding horse that was temporarily kept at my father's estate. I began to cry and said that I did not want to part with her. My father looked at me sadly and uttered, "Accept it at once. You will never see her again any way!" I realized that he was right and accepted the offer. He telegraphed my consent to the leaseholder's son and instantly paid, with his own funds, the required amount for my "Déesse."

The situation in the country began changing rapidly. We were forced to move out of my elder brother's apartment, as all state-owned and regiment-owned apartments were taken away from previous tenants. I moved into my mother's apartment, where I temporarily shared a room with my sister Elena,[20] who unexpectedly announced that she was going to marry our distant cousin, Kyril Shirkoff. The wedding was prepared hastily; the six-month anniversary of the Revolution was expected in August and everybody was afraid of possible chaos. At the same time, my husband moved into his former club.

My mother returned from Kislovodsk in the Caucasus where many had temporarily moved, to await developments. She left my younger sister in Kislovodsk for a time and, while on her way to St. Petersburg, stopped at the estate of our Grandmother Stahl in Vo-

---

18 Alexander Kerensky (1881–1970) was the Second Prime Minister of the Russian Provisional Government in 1917 before Vladimir Lenin (1870–1924) was elected.

19 #35 Znamenskaya Street was renamed #35 Vosstaniya after the Revolution. Today it is an elegantly restored apartment building in the centre of St. Petersburg.

20 Also known as Ella, or Helen.

ronezh district in order to persuade her to leave for Kislovodsk, but our grandmother adamantly would not leave her small estate, even temporarily. She assured our mother that the peasants knew her very well, and that she knew them too, and that she was safe with them! Sadly it was nothing but an illusion. Our grandmother was subsequently banished from her estate and, as I was to learn later from letters written by our former barkeeper, Ivan Ilyushin, her life ended in the "corner" of a walk-through room in the city of Voronezh. "Corner tenants" were those who could not afford to pay for a bedroom but were allowed to use a corner in a walk-through room, sharing it with other tenants. She first lived with our old housemaid, Anna Alymova, and then by herself after Anna's death. She was fed by our former Tatar cook, Hassan, who found her there after she had become blind. We still do not know when she died or where she was buried; all communication between the Caucasus and the rest of the country was soon discontinued.

My mother persuaded me to leave for Kislovodsk in the Caucasus with her, where Inochka also lived. Prior to my departure, I visited Nastenka to say farewell. Deportation of the Tsar's family to Siberia had already been approved by Kerensky but the Tsar's family was not aware of their destination. If my memory does not fail me, the governor of the palace at Tsarskoye Selo in those days was Kobylinsky, and it was he who notified the families of those who were to go with the Tsar's family to Siberia so that their family members could in turn, and subject to his permission, come to say farewell to their relatives.[21] Due to my planned departure to Kislovodsk, the Hendrikoff family decided that I had to be the first one to say goodbye to Nastenka. My husband took me to Kobylinsky to obtain a permit to enter the palace, and remained outside waiting for me. The governor of the palace was a very courteous man. He issued me the permit and explained that I was allowed to use it to enter the palace through the kitchen entrance. The entrance was watched by two guards who were half-sitting, half-lying, on the edge of chairs. Noticing me approaching, they stood up and

21 The palace referred to here is Alexander Palace, the last residence of the Tsar and his family.

crossed their rifles to prevent me from trying to slip past them into the kitchen yard. I produced my permit, so they sent for another soldier to fetch the officer in charge. A young warrant officer with a red bow in his buttonhole came out to examine my permit. He then ordered the guards to let me in and instructed me to follow him. We first crossed the yard where some young kitchen hands were running back and forth, next we entered a small room with nothing but two chairs. From here the officer sent some soldiers for Nastenka. She, by all appearances, was unaware of the reason she had been called, and looked very frightened. She was still in full mourning over her mother's death, her pale face flushed scarlet, yet turning pale repeatedly. We sat on the chairs provided while the officer stood by the window with his back to us, listening attentively. Hardly had Nastenka asked in a level voice where they were being deported to when he whipped around to terminate my possible answer saying, "I ask you not to answer this question." The Tsar's family had hopes that they would be allowed to live in the Crimea, but other plans were being made for them! The time allowed for our appointment rushed by and, having looked at his watch, the officer announced that it was time for me to say good-bye to Nastenka. Then he called for soldiers who instantly took her away while I was escorted by the officer to the exit, where he waved to the guards to let me out. My husband was waiting for me outside and I asked him to give me some time to collect myself, promising to tell him everything when we got back to St. Petersburg.

Years later, I met Baroness Iza Buxhoeveden (another lady-in-waiting) in both Paris and England, but she never explained to me why she had not shared the same fate as Nastenka, and I never asked.[22] Perhaps the Red authorities of those days could not get to the bottom of her documents. She apparently held a diplomatic passport that she was going to use to see her father, who was working as a diplomat in Scandinavia. When, at the last moment, foreign

22 Baroness Sophie Buxhoeveden (1883–1956), lady-in-waiting to Tsarina Alexandra, followed the Imperial family into exile but somehow managed to escape through Vladivostok. She died in a "grace and favour" apartment in Kensington Palace, London, granted to her by Queen Elizabeth.

nationals were separated from the Tsar's family, the Tsarevitch's English teacher, Mr. Sidney Gibbs; the Swiss national tutor to the children, Monsieur Pierre Gilliard; and Iza were included in the group to be set free. Iza eventually moved to England, where one of Empress Alexandra Feodorovna's sisters assisted in her employment with a very good *maison de retraite*, an old people's home, and where I believe she eventually died during World War II. She managed to have her memoirs written and published but much to my regret, all the books were immediately sold and could not be found anywhere. After WWII I was able to borrow the book from an acquaintance. In her memoirs, Iza tells that the Tsar's family was deported to Tsarkoye Selo in the dead of night of August 13–14, 1917, and learned of their destination (Siberia) only on their way there. As for Iza, she reached Tobolsk later than planned as a result of an appendectomy.

At first the Hendrikoff family received short messages from Nastenka, but then her messages stopped coming. In Kislovodsk, we began hearing rumours that the Tsar's family had been murdered. Many refused to believe it. For me the rumours proved to be true in late 1919 in Taganrog. There, Mrs. Smirnova, a new acquaintance at the time, asked me to visit her place to read me a letter from her husband, who was serving the widow of Prince Ioann Konstantinovich, sister of King Alexander of Yugoslavia. In the letter he described Nastenka's last days, based on information provided by Princess E. Petrovna. The princess had been temporarily arrested by the Soviet authorities and shared a room with Nastenka and Mademoiselle E. Schneider, one of the children's tutors. The princess reported that Nastenka and Mademoiselle Schneider were killed, along with other detainees, in September 1918. Their bodies were found and identified by the Whites who temporarily occupied the area. They were buried in a local graveyard, while their graves were marked with only their last names and date of death.[23] The only one from their group who managed to save his

23 Countess Anastasia (Nastenka) Hendrikoff was later canonized by the Russian Orthodox Church. There is a plaque commemorating her sacrifice in the Russian Orthodox Church on rue Daru in Paris.

life at the last moment was the former palace valet, Volkov, who later published his memoirs in Paris. Having realized where they were being led, he abruptly broke away from the group and got lost in the nearby woods. The guards escorting the condemned attempted to shoot him but presumably decided that he was doomed to die in the unfamiliar woods anyway, and chose not to expend their time chasing him.

Meanwhile the situation in St. Petersburg was changing very rapidly. The part of our family that lived in Tsarskoye Selo could not attend my sister's wedding, which was held on the day of the six-month anniversary of the Revolution. The groom's friend had to give away the bride as well as assume the duties of young icon-bearer and best man! The newly married couple left for Kharkov Governorate to stay with our aunt, while our mother suggested that I go with her to Kislovodsk, where she had left my younger sister and where it was still safe to be. Inochka made arrangements with the landlady of the house where she rented an entire floor, and the landlady agreed to rent out a room to Peter and me, although we were to dine with Inochka. My husband, however, lingered in St. Petersburg, moved into his former club and explained to me that he was part of a plot aimed at overthrowing the Provisional Government.[24] Although all of the conspirers were turned in by the club servants, my husband was able to hurriedly leave for Kislovodsk around Christmas. At the time, travel from St. Petersburg to Kislovodsk was very exhausting; trains were packed with soldiers who were deserting the front lines in order to grab land that had been looted from estates. Not only the coach corridors, but also water closets and roofs were crammed with soldiers who, however, were polite and well behaved. The situation in Kislovodsk was gradually changing for the worse. Many of our acquaintances left, keeping the date and purpose of their departures secret, even from friends. The city attracted men, my husband among them, to compulsory labour, such as ditch digging. After such experiences, Peter soon told me that he, Kutuzov

24 Countess Hendrikoff and Count Peter Hendrikoff divorced in 1917, possibly because his counter-revolutionary activities put her at risk.

and Pashkov[25] had decided to cross the mountains on foot to join Skoropadsky, whose forces were currently stationed in the part of the country that had been freed from the Reds.[26] He asked me to give him the very last precious thing that I had managed to save, a platinum necklace with gem stones from the Urals, leaving me in return with a fur coat that he had pawned at the local consignment shop. The landlady who owned the room where I lived soon demanded the fur coat from me so I had to temporarily move into Inochka's quarters. Before moving I had to first part with my toy dog, as Inochka suffered from a fear of dogs. I placed the dog for a time with some friends, who lived at the opposite end of the city, but my "Snob" returned overnight and within three days Inochka's son found the dog's dead body in a horse stall where he had temporarily placed my pet. I cried all day long and Inochka thought ill of me, saying that one should wail for a child, not a dog!

The situation kept changing, always for the worse. Inochka was forced to change her place of residence time and again. Eventually she caught cold and died, her children were taken by an old grandfather and grandmother, and I fell out of touch with the family for a long time. I moved into the residence of a couple who I had not known before. The husband was a retired general at death's door, while his wife was younger than he and got about on crutches. They had an old live-in female cook who had great sympathy for me and, when her employers went to bed, called me to the kitchen on the quiet and thrust some food into my hands. Kislovodsk was often subjected to the so-called *couvre-feu*, curfew, when everyone had to

25 Both Kutuzov and Pashkov were from distinguished military families. Kutuzov's ancestor Field Marshal Prince Michael Kutuzov was instrumental in the defeat of Napoleon at the Battle of Borodino.

26 Pavlo Skoropadsky (1873–1945) was a Russian army general and commander of a Cossack regiment who saved Kiev from the Bolsheviks. He successfully established an independent Ukraine (short-lived, because foreign allies withdrew their support). As a boy, he was a student the Page Corps cadet school and a member of the Imperial Horse Guards – the same two institutions were attended by Countess Hendrikoff's husband, brother Vladimir (Barbos), and brother-in-law Kyril Shirkoff. Skoropadsky later fled to Germany, where he was killed in a World War II Allied bombing raid.

remain at home! Days after Peter left, the city was occupied by the Reds. I learned that it had been abandoned by the Whites when I finally went down to the city centre. At the last moment before the Whites left, I found Rosen, a horse-guardsman, who had to leave Kislovodsk with a group of officers but had no time to say farewell to his wife – such was the unexpectedness of the occupation by the Reds in the Kislovodsk suburbs. Since I seemed to have no chance of leaving the city in time, Rosen asked me to find his wife and tell her about his departure, which I did promptly.[27]

Early on the changes as a result of the occupation of Kislovodsk by the Reds were not evident to the public. Since Peter's leave, I had been working at the consignment shop where his fur coat had been. I was ordered by the new authorities to appear on a specified day at the official centre for used goods where, according to them, all things rendered for sale to different consignment shops were accumulated. There I discovered that Peter's fur coat was gone for good, along with many other things. The sales staff was managed by a clerk whom I did not know. He called all workers by their first names, and even by pet names, but essentially he was a nice, well-intentioned man. Among my co-workers there was a common humble girl, about 16 or 17 years of age. She was an orphan living with her old grandmother and always invited me to their home, insisting that I stay for dinner.

My landlady, who was renting a room in her apartment to me, requested that I go pay the accrued housing dues on her behalf at the main city settlement office, or the city authorities would threaten her with eviction. She gave me the name of an officer who had an Armenian surname and who I was supposed to see. The landlady knew him personally and said he always helped her in circumstances of this kind. The place bore no resemblance to a real office since the experienced former staff had been replaced with new people. The Armenian man turned out to be a very young and good-looking

---

27 Baron Leon de Rosen, the Russian ambassador to Japan and Sweden, was a relative of Countess Hendrikoff's aunt, Countess Alexandra (Sania) Ruggeri-Laderchi. He was also the father of Léon de Rosen who escaped from Metz prison, France, during World War II.

gentleman. He immediately made all the arrangements for my land-lady and then assailed me with questions, seeking to understand who I was. I gave him answers with great caution and thanked him for his offer to let him know if I experienced any difficulties in the future. After this appointment, he often waited for me when I returned home from work, but behaved with good manners and "knew his distance." I was experiencing difficulties with a permit for housing in Kislovodsk and I once briefly mentioned it in the course of a conversation with my new acquaintance. Two or three days later he quietly, and cautiously, let me know that he had inquired concerning the repeated dismissals of my permit extension by the city authorities. He reproached me for failing to tell him straight off that my name was associated with a noble title! However, he immediately reassured me that he had secured a termless permit for me to stay in Kislovodsk and that from then on I was not to be disturbed by the authorities.

Yet, I was alarmed by recent developments, as the situation in Kislovodsk was changing slowly but relentlessly. We learned about the passage of arms between the Whites and the Reds every time we had an electricity outage. The main electric power station was situated in the town of Mineralnye Vody and the electricity went out once the town was secured by the opposing force. Arrests and executions by firing squads began. From a building that I passed on my way to the city, screeches of the detained were heard. One morning I came across a carriage loaded with uncovered, naked dead bodies. On another day, I went to see my friends in the evening, only to be stopped at the door by their fearful female cook who told me of a raid by a "gang of bandits in Circassian coats" that they had just fallen victim to.[28] The bandits had locked the cook in the kitchen, so she was now afraid to go upstairs to see what had happened to her masters! I had the heart to go upstairs and instantly found myself in a pool of water; the tap in the bathroom remained open with water overflowing onto the floor. I heard my friends calling from behind a locked door. Unlocking the door, I entered the room and my heart

---

28 Circassians are an ethnic group from the north Caucasus region. They fled mainly to Turkey after the Russian–Circassian War of 1862.

was faint! The room was in a mess, with blood stains everywhere, especially on the face of my friend's mother. All the cupboard and wardrobe doors were wide open. It was obvious that they had been ransacked. In another room, my friend's little children cried while the maids were trying to soothe them. Mr. Sh., white as a sheet, was slowly recovering, not saying a word.

Interrupting each other, they all began to describe their experience in detail. While waiting for the lady of the house, who had gone downstairs for a moment to see their neighbours, the family peacefully got ready for dinner. Suddenly they heard feet scampering upon the stairs and, seconds later, a group of men dressed in Circassian coats, which was a popular men's dress in Kislovodsk of those days, burst into the room. They seized Mr. Sh. and held a pistol to his head, demanding money and valuables. The Circassian bandits broke open all the cupboards and wardrobes, throwing each other the things that appeared to them as being of value, most of which were clothes. They were in such a rush that they took away all the left shoes, leaving behind all the right ones! When the elderly mother of my friend begged them to kill her and let the other family members be, one of the bandits shot at her but missed; the bullet only scratched her face and she began bleeding profusely. Hearing the noise in the upper apartment, my friend hurried to her family but was stopped by soldiers who were watching all entrances and exits in the house. The soldiers eventually took compassion and let her go. Next she was seized by one of the robbers. He forced her to her knees and ordered her to pray as he was going to count out loud to "three" before he shot her dead. She closed her eyes and began praying aloud. She could hear the soldier slowly counting but, having come to "three," he stopped and fell silent. At first she was afraid to open her eyes but, having waited a minute in silence, she took a chance, opened her eyes and realized that there was no one else in the room. It was then that I came in and encountered their female cook.

At that time, it was absolutely hopeless appealing for help to the militia but a resident of the house managed to make them arrive. Three elegant militiamen first produced their identification, as required, and then began interviewing all who were present about the raid. The militiamen opened gold cigarette cases and all three began smoking. It appeared that it had not taken them long to understand who was in charge of the raiders, but they told us that the chieftain would not be arrested until the next day because they all had to go celebrate some Revolution-related occasion that evening. In reality, the household maids ran into the raider on the streets a few days later, so before long, the frightened family of Sh. moved to some basement to never leave it until their ultimate departure from Kislovodsk. None of us were informed about where they were hiding.

But there were also examples that allowed us to look at the Russian character another way. Under the order of the authorities, a seaman moved into the house of Natalia Bobrinskaya, a friend of mine whose husband had gone into hiding, leaving her alone with five or six children. The seaman soon proved himself to be a loyal and true-hearted helper to the family. He fed the woman and her children, and protected her from intrusions of his fellow seamen. When Kislovodsk was temporarily reoccupied by the Whites, the seaman could not hide quickly. He was secretly led by Natalia's husband, Murza, who had returned with the Whites, to a safe place where the seaman could easily rejoin his mates, whereupon Murza was able to quickly disappear from Kislovodsk with his family. It was a clever move, because rumours of the seaman saved by Murza spread through Kislovodsk. The tempers of the Whites ran high, just as they had with the Reds shortly before, and I heard from many of the Whites that they were determined to execute Murza by a firing squad if they were ever to capture him.

The position of the Whites in Kislovodsk appeared to be strong, so I began working for a committee of the Volunteer Army, where there was an Armenian supplier who knew many of my acquaintances. In their conversations, they often talked about Murza Bobrinsky and how he would be executed by hanging for having saved that seaman. One evening, when I was walking home, I saw the Armenian man who was waiting to ask me to let him see me home. Having assured himself that there was no one near us, he quickly and nervously explained to me that, for Armenians, being executed by hanging was the most dreadful and degrading way to die. According to his words, his life was under a real threat of such an end because he had also saved a Red, who at one time had saved him from imminent death. Noticing that I was well acquainted with people who had authority, he made the decision that, if he was arrested, I would be allowed to see him before his execution and would have a chance to smuggle poison to him, which he wanted to give to me as we spoke. He could not keep the poison as he would certainly be searched if arrested. Not even waiting for my response, he quickly thrust a small pouch with poison into my hands and disappeared. I was very embarrassed by this request. I knew that I could not grant his wish as it would mean sharing his fate. After that day, however, he kept away from me.

While the area was now under the power of the Whites, the arrests and reprisals continued, the only difference being that it all was done by the Whites now. The dead body of a woman known to the public only as "Madame G." hung for three days in the city centre. Rumour had it that she came from a good family and was the daughter of an army officer, but lived with a Red activist whose last name started with G. She could not go into hiding in good time because she was at the clinic giving birth to G.'s child. She was arrested and sentenced to be hanged. Notwithstanding that her cell was watched day and night, she somehow managed to escape from prison by shinnying down a drainpipe, leaving her newborn child in the cell! She was seized in the neighbouring town of Yessentuki, brought back to Kislovodsk, and executed.

Suddenly, and quite unexpectedly, nothing less than a miracle happened! One day an English general, who was a White front commander at that time, came to the city accompanied by my cousin, D.I. Zvegintzoff, who was serving as the general's interpreter. My cousin instantly found me. He informed me that the future of Kislovodsk was uncertain and that he would promptly try to find me some work with the English corps in the town of Taganrog. He advised me to pack my belongings immediately and be ready to leave the minute I received a telegram from him or from an English representative in Taganrog. Fortunately, the next day, I was able to find the Armenian man to give him back his pouch.

I received the telegram calling me to Taganrog within a few days. The telegram was signed by an English official who was the chief of the translation unit, and I responded to him by telegraph, confirming my immediate departure for Taganrog. My cousin met me at the railway station and took me to the house of a banker where my cousin's friend from his regiment was renting a room. The friend moved out, making the room available to me. For me, those several months that I spent in Taganrog were like an oasis to a footworn traveler. The examination that I had to take as a candidate for the job was not complicated at all. I had mastered the skill of typewriting, with no specific aim and only as a spare-time occupation, when I lived in Kislovodsk. My friends used to make fun of me as they saw it only as an "oddity." Among the staff of the translation unit, I found some women whom I had previously known. During the day we dined in the office, and in the evenings I was fed by the landlady, in return for the bonus food allowance provided by the English that was in addition to my pay. The allowance was delivered to every staff member by a soldier. The landlady's domestic workers could not thank me enough after I presented the landlady with my sewing machine, which, for no explicable reason, I had brought along with me to every place I had stayed in recent years. It was there that I met Ruth Grierson again, who later assumed the surname of Ogareva or Ogareff. I do not remember what the reason had been for her staying at the estate of my friends when the Revolution began, but she somehow had been evacuated from the estate by the English. She had been brought to Taganrog, where she began working in the same unit that I later joined. During the time I spent in Taganrog, I became close friends with Ruth.

Countess
OLGA HENDRIKOFF

PART II

Lala's escape from Russia is documented in her memoir only until she reaches Taganrog, a port on the Sea of Azov. After that, her trail is sketchy at best. She probably went by sea to Yalta and then on to Constantinople. She worked for a British agency in Taganrog and may have had British help in leaving Russia – she worked as a typist and translator at the British High Commission Refugee Registration Centre in Constantinople. She left her employment in Turkey on February 2, 1921.

While working in Constantinople, she heard that someone had seen her sister Ella's husband, Kyril Shirkoff, on a hospital train near Novorossiysk. After several unsuccessful trips to the railway tracks where hospital trains were piling up, Lala heard someone calling her name. She saw standing before her a heavily bearded, haggard-looking stranger in a long cavalry coat, leaning on two canes, who could only whisper, "It's me, Kyril. Don't you recognize me?" An old man at the age of thirty-one, he was left with spotted typhus, yellow fever and lifelong health issues. Much of the family came out of Russia in groups, except for Kyril and Lala, who left alone.

Lala, along with her brother Barbos, his wife Bicha and their two young boys, Vladimir and Michel, her sister Helen (Ella) Shirkoff, Ella's husband Kyril and their daughter Irina, first settled in Rome in 1921. Her much younger sister, Irina Kobieff, had earlier fled to Yugoslavia. Her brother Nicholas stayed in Russia, hoping to help change the political landscape.

Lala, along with Barbos and his family, moved from Rome to Paris in 1924, where Lala's mother had remarried after the death

THIS IS TO CERTIFY that the Countess Hendrikova
has been in the employment of the Anglo-Russian
Refugee Bureau, British High Commission, Constantinople, from 20th April 1920 till 2nd Feb. 1921. Her
services in the capacity of typist and translator
have been invaluable and she has evinced exceptional
interest in her work.

It is greatly regretted that Countess Hendrikova is unable to continue her work at the bureau
as she is leaving Constantinople to join her relatives in Italy.

H. D. Brown

i/c Bureau.

Constantinople,
2nd February, 1921.

British High Commission Reference Letter, 1921

of her father. In Paris they joined the largest Russian aristocratic
émigré population in the world and were reunited with many old
friends and relatives.

Lala had a Nansen passport, given to stateless people, which
made it difficult for her to find work in France. Ever adaptable, she
had many temporary jobs: translating, interpreting, tutoring and
secretarial work. Her journal of her time in France begins with the
looming war and the tumultuous departure of family members.

R. MINISTERO
DEGLI
AFFARI ESTERI
—◆—II—◆—

Ufficio Trattati
e Società delle Nazioni

N. **47872**

Posizione

N. B. — Nella risposta indicare l'Offizio, il numero e la data della presente. In un rapporto trattare di un solo argomento.

Oggetto

Conferenza all'Aja

Roma, 19 AGO 1922

Gentilissima Signora Contessa

Nel ringraziarLa dell'opera da
Lei prestata presso la Delegazione italiana alla
Conferenza dell'Aja in qualità di traduttrice e
dattilografa-segretaria tengo ad assicurarle che
la perfetta conoscenza delle lingue francese ingle-
se tedesca italiana e russa, la Sua intelligente
attività e il suo zelo sono state da me molto ap-
prezzate.

Gradisca , Gentilissima Signora
Contessa, gli atti della mia distintissima consi-
derazione

Contessa OLGA HENDRIKOFF

Villa Bel Respino

presso Contessa Ruggeri-Ladelchi

- SAN REMO -

Italian Reference Letter, 1922

FRANCE

PARIS

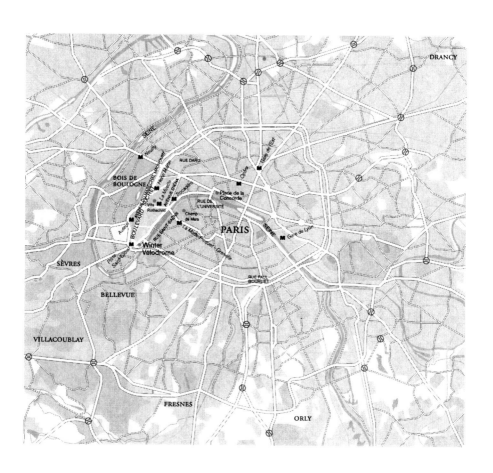

1939

WAR

"All war seems absurd to me anyway. The victors often lose in the exchange, and the vanquished think only of revenge."

21.8.39 I am back in Paris from Le Mouleau, where I spent a few weeks with Diane and Irène de Ganay. The most perfect calm reigned there – nothing could be heard but the song of the cicadas and the sound of the waves breaking against the terrace of the hotel. In contrast, here the city resonates with the sounds of war; no one talks about anything but the impending war with Germany! Tomorrow I am to rejoin the de Ganay's at Royaumont, the property of their grandmother. I took the opportunity to go and see Fyodor Fyodorovich Oom, my stepfather, but he was away. By chance I ran into my sister-in-law Bicha in the street; she just came back from Germany where she had gone with my brother Barbos and their youngest son Michel for her niece's wedding. We sat in a café and talked about the international situation. Bicha says that Germany is armed to the teeth; the Germans loudly shout that they are not looking for another war but will fight if they have to. One feels sorry in advance for the French, for whom the Germans say they harbour no animosity.

22.8.39 Royaumont, in Seine et Oise, is an imposing former Abbey converted into a residence by Countess de Ségur. The *salon* is all Gothic arches and decorative columns. My room used to be a monk's cell, with a crucifix and skulls on the walls, but it has a huge canopy bed. The family spends the day in the cloister, where the silence is broken only by the single note of a small fountain in the

Royaumont Abbey, 1939

courtyard. One wing of the Abbey houses a Cultural Centre open to writers, artists, and so on, who come to spend their vacation for a relatively modest price. The former monks' refectory has been set up as a concert hall where well-known and profitable concerts are held during the Paris season.[29]

Countess de Ségur is full of optimism because she firmly believes in horoscopes, and the astrologer who predicted "the whole truth" for her in 1914 now tells her that there will be a general mobilization but no war. That is also what she keeps telling the footmen and chauffeurs whose units are being recalled and come to say farewell.

23.8.39 In the evening, while we were still at the table, Jean Gradis arrived; he is the son-in-law of Countess de Ségur. He has been recalled and came to say good-bye. I had just seen him at Le Mouleau – gay, carefree, unkempt in fisherman's garb – now here he stands constricted by his military tunic, reserved, somewhat emotional...

29 Royaumont Abbey, founded by St. Louis in 1228, served many diverse functions. First it was a Cistercian Abbey, then a cotton mill, an Oblate Abbey, a nunnery and, during World War I, a war hospital. In 1936, Henry Göuin turned Royaumont into a cultural centre for musicians. Today, Royaumont Abbey continues to be a diverse cultural centre supporting the arts, humanities and sciences. It is open to the public, providing a glimpse of the medieval.

24.8.39 New units are called up every day. The Cultural Centre has closed. Everyone around me is worried and nervous but everyone is trying to act calm and convince others that there will be no war again this time.

The Pope has ordered all good Catholics to pray for peace, and we gather together, master and servant, every day around four o'clock for prayers in the chapel of the Abbey. Countess de Ségur or one of her daughters take turns reading the prayers aloud. One can hear the women crying.

I spent the afternoon with little Be.'s English nurse. She told me about her stay in Spain during the civil war. The family she worked for were Spanish aristocrats. The father was arrested at the beginning of the revolution by the Reds. The mother then took refuge with the nurse and child in a cellar known only to their most intimate friends, who brought them food and clothing. The family's chauffeur, who was very attached to the child – that did not prevent him from being a militant Communist – suggested that the mother send the nurse and child to France. Prior to that, the mother had refused to leave Spain without her husband. After lengthy hesitation, the mother decided to entrust the child and nurse to the chauffeur. He loaded them into the car, placed armed men on the running boards, who kept their revolvers and submachine guns aimed at the nurse all the way, and dropped them safe and sound at the border. The mother ended up reunited with the child in France after her husband's execution.

I asked the nurse if she had been very frightened. She answered me, "Not for a minute. I was sure that man would keep his word."

28.8.39 Any lights visible outside must be turned off starting at nine o'clock in the evening.

We have not had time to paint the windowpanes of the Abbey blue, so in the evening we go up to our rooms with candles in hand, like a procession of pilgrims.

Newspapers, telegrams and telephone conversations are censored. Using public telephone booths and making telephone calls from a restaurant or café are prohibited in Paris. You can still make a telephone call from a post office, but you have to show your identification card, and the employee marks the number you ask for in a special register, along with your name and address.

29.8.39 All the men from the property have been recalled.

30.8.39 Spent the day in Paris. Most of my friends do not believe war is possible.

1.9.39 We are now in Courances, at the property owned by Marquis de Ganay, and are meant to stay here until the end of the summer holidays.[30]

The château reminds me of a smaller version of the château at Fontainebleau – the same main courtyard, horseshoe-shaped staircase, and so on, surrounded by moats where swans are swimming. On the garden side, the château overlooks groomed and manicured French-style parterres, with boxwood shrubbery around the statues and a large ornamental pond. The interior is luxuriously and tastefully furnished. Woodwork covers most of the walls, while some of the rooms are decorated with pastoral paintings of ancient scenes and subjects inspired by the *Fables de La Fontaine*. There is quite a crowd in residence at this time at the château. Seated at the dinner table are twenty-two of us, wearing the obligatory smoking jackets

Château Courances, near Milly, France, 1939

30 Courances is still owned by the de Ganay family. The chateau, and its lovely gardens with many water features, is open to the public.

and long dresses, and that only includes the children and grandchildren of the Marquis and Marquise de Ganay.

The radio announced a general mobilization at midnight tonight. Count B. de Ganay came to say good-bye to his family, and his two brothers also leave today. Despite all that, there are still those who continue to hope that the "Miracle of Munich" will repeat itself.

The German armies have entered Poland.

2.9.39 The Polish government has left Warsaw, and the German armies are advancing at a formidable pace.

In Paris, hospitals are being evacuated and, in the museums, paintings and statues wrapped up.

3.9.39 At twelve-thirty, the radio announced that England has declared war on Germany, and France will follow its example at five o'clock unless Germany gives a satisfactory reply about Poland.

Another war with Germany seems incredible to me when no one has yet forgotten the last one; however, it is clear now that war can no longer be averted. We awaited the five o'clock news in a tense and anxious atmosphere. Marquise de Ganay had us all working, gathering dry leaves from the garden paths, and then playing *mahjong* "to avoid going completely mad," as she put it.

At five o'clock, we gathered around the radio in the *salon* and waited in absolute silence. The announcer said, "No, there has been no miracle this time... France has entered the war..."

Then the Marquise said, "Now that this blunder has been committed, we must see what we can do to make ourselves useful."

4.9.39 The declaration of war on Germany was read by the current mayor of Milly, the Marquis de Ganay, in the little village square, where people came running when they heard the drum roll of the local guard.

Horses and cars have been requisitioned. Windowpanes and light bulbs are painted blue. Newspapers no longer publish more than four pages. In Paris, *Grands Magasins* will only stay open from eleven o'clock in the morning until five o'clock in the afternoon instead of nine to six-thirty. A large proportion of the Parisian population has left the capital. Milly is already full of Parisian refugees in businesses, old people's homes, and so on. The Place du Marché reminds me of

Russian railway stations during the civil war, with women and children looking for a place to stay sitting on their suitcases. In the street, the older ladies in Milly stare curiously, and severely, at Parisian women in shorts with bare legs. The roads are lined with taxis and cars, with mattresses on the roof, fleeing Paris. Trains take only military personnel for the time being. Paris–Milly bus service has stopped.

We have no newspapers or mail and live from one radio broadcast to the next. All the French news is now broadcast at the same time with only one script written by the French radio news centre.

Louis XVI used to be severely criticized for writing in his journal "went hunting" or even "nothing" at decisive times. I too note only minor events, because I feel crushed by the major ones. I have not managed to absorb them.

5.9.39 An order has been issued prohibiting foreigners to travel outside their local *commune*.

Many foreigners have been arrested as a result of denunciations. Many Parisian businesses are dismissing their foreign employees. How difficult our position as émigrés has become! I think back to the war in 1914, how different it was, in spite of the fact that it affected us much more. One was oblivious to the possibility of being considered suspect, at least in the setting where I lived. The spectre of being without work and without bread the next day never presented itself. I look around me. The men are leaving, but the setting remains roughly the same; the routine goes on unbroken.

(Copy)
Mayor's Office
Courances, Seine et Oise
No. 28

Permanent Travel Authorization
Granted to *Madame* Hendrikoff, née Zweguintzoff,
Residing at Courances, Seine et Oise,
for travel to Sèvres, Seine et Oise, via Paris by ground or rail

Courances, September 17, 1939
For the Assistant Mayor
(Signed)
Stamped by the Mayor's Office

ORDERS THAT APPEARED IN THE NEWSPAPERS:

1) **Theatres and cinemas to close at eight-thirty in the evening from now on**
Police department announcement:
"At the request of the military authorities, the police department has ordered that theatres, playhouses, and cinemas will close at 8:30 p.m. starting today."

2) **Special authorization required to employ foreign workers**
"Foreigners may not be employed without prior authorization from the placement office in the department where the workplace is located.
The prohibition does not apply to employers of farm workers.
As a transition measure, employers who currently employ foreign workers will have fifteen days to request authorization.
Foreigners without a 'worker' card who are placed by the offices must obtain a card within an eight-day period."

3) **Radio transmitters and receivers no longer allowed in vehicles**
Police department announcement:
"At the request of the military authorities, the police chief has ordered the prohibition of radio transmitters or receivers in cars, motor vehicles, horse-drawn vehicles, and motorcycles.
Any radio sets and accessories currently installed in vehicles must be removed immediately."

4) **Weather information cancelled**
The National Weather Office announces that, as a result of the state of siege, weather information will not be released until further order.

5) **Equestrian meets cancelled**
The horse breeders' association announces:
"As a result of the recent requisition of the Vincennes racetrack, the impossibility of maintaining order, and the general mobilization, the race meet to be held at the racetrack today, Saturday, September 2, is cancelled."

6) **No bus**
The public transit system, the *Société des transports en commun de la région parisienne*, announces:
"Due to the general mobilization, bus service is cancelled in Paris as of this morning. Buses will continue to operate in suburban areas."

7) **Be wary and discreet or you could be prosecuted**
The Ministry of Information announces:
"Public attention is drawn, in particular, to the danger of lack of discretion in public places.

"In restaurants and cafés and on trains and public transportation, enemy agents may be listening, trying to gather military information revealed involuntarily by relatives of soldiers on leave or employees of official organizations, officers, non-commissioned officers, and soldiers.

"Everyone must constantly bear in mind that careless words risk providing the enemy with valuable information. The German High Command sometimes uses information of that nature to direct enemy submarines and planes.

"Carelessness could cause the death of fellow citizens, even your own children.

"Any flagrant lack of discretion is an offence and may be prosecuted."

6.9.39 We heard an air-raid siren for the first time, at around eleven o'clock in the morning, while we were in Milly. People immediately came out into the streets and listened curiously to the shrieking sirens; there are no shelters in Milly. For the moment, the air-raid warning just means that enemy aircraft have flown over the border.

7.9.39 A census is being taken of foreigners. I went with the Marquise's butler and housemaid, who are Belgian, to register at the Town Hall in Milly. Our fingerprints were taken and added to our identification cards. The butler had to hand over his hunting rifle, most unwillingly, in return for a receipt and a promise that he would get it back as soon as the war ends.

9.9.39 Anyone who goes out in the street without a gas mask is prosecuted; it is sufficient to carry it in your hand. However, foreigners are not entitled to freely distributed masks, and Bicha could not afford the expense for that purchase. Vladimir, my nephew, managed in this way. He dug up an old gas mask, I have no idea where, and put a stick of wood in it; he swings it gravely from his arm whenever he goes out.

13.9.39 The order prohibiting foreigners from travelling outside their *commune* has been postponed to September 20. I took advantage of the delay to go to Paris. A lot of stores are closed, their awnings lowered; often one whole side of a street is just a row of closed storefronts. The windows of the open stores are crisscrossed with strips of paper, often glued on in a careful and artistic design, as a precautionary measure in case of bombing, they say. There is barely any traffic in the streets – one would think it was the annual summer holidays. Place de la Concorde is truly deserted. Many metro entrances are closed and buses cancelled. One has to go kilometres on foot.

On the Paris–Milly road, we saw line-ups of buses loaded with furniture and effects of all kinds, cars with the inevitable mattress on the roof, headlights painted blue, and soldiers on guard duty at bridge crossings.

19.9.39 I often wake up in the morning thinking I have had a bad dream – the war, the departure of friends and relatives... The first few days after war was declared, it was as if I was stunned. I could not bring myself to believe that the country I live in is really at war, and we may see Vimy, Malmaison, and so on happening again. What a painful impression the sight of Berry-au-Bac made on me – the military cemeteries in northern France where the number of graves often exceeds the number of inhabitants living in the neighbouring villages. All that seemed like history at the time, creating a museum atmosphere. To think that it could have been avoided. All war seems absurd to me anyway. The victors often lose in the exchange, and the vanquished think only of revenge.

21.9.39 Princess P.M. came for tea and asked the Marquis for advice about her son, who would like to register for officer training in Orléans. All the women are at somewhat of a loss without men at their sides to take or share responsibility.

The Soviets have occupied part of Polish territory without firing a shot. The process is brutal; however, to be perfectly frank, I am not sorry to see those Russian lands return to Russia. Nevertheless, I hasten to add that I would not like to find myself in territory newly reunited to Russia these days.

25.9.39 Spent the night in Paris at Ruth Ogareff's,[31] because the Paris–Milly bus newly back in operation is still broken down. I was heading toward Place de la Concorde when night suddenly fell. I could no longer find the metro. I could only see the streetlamps, which project a weak blue light and completely disoriented me because they did not light up anything, just made small patches of light in the darkness and made me lose my sense of direction. Taxis brushed me as they passed, like huge, gleaming worms. For a minute, it seemed as if I was going in circles and would never manage to get out of Place de la Concorde.

31 Ruth Grierson, who Countess Hendrikoff spent time with in Taganrog, Russia, in 1917

28.9.39 Surrender of Warsaw. The newspapers announced the potential division of Poland.

29.9.39 Air-raid warning in Paris. When I got off the bus, I did not pay any attention to the siren and was surprised when the siren had barely begun and everyone started running. Cars lined up along the sidewalks and officers wearing helmets stopped passersby and directed them to the nearest shelter, in this case, Hôtel de Ville metro station. Men in semi-military attire posted at the metro entrance were telling people to stay calm.

We had to go down into the tunnel. I sat on my suitcase. Overhead one could hear sinister rumbling, which most of us took for anti-aircraft artillery but was only amplified street noise. Women were crying around me and some even got sick. The alert lasted an hour and a half, then I had to wait an hour for service to start again. The woman beside me pointed out how the pigeons at Hôtel de Ville suddenly took flight a few seconds before the air-raid siren, as if moved by a secret warning; she had often noticed them take flight – before the warning siren every time.

Spent the night at my cousin Kostia Shabelsky's. His mother, Aunt Maroussia, puts her savings in a small cloth bag every evening and hangs it on a nail near her bed; when she hears the air-raid siren, she hangs it around her neck. Russian refugees effortlessly fall back into the rhythm of the years of the Bolshevik revolution in Russia, swiftly adopting again all their trusted old habits of that time.

Security measures: It is prohibited to publish crossword puzzles or personal ads in newspapers, send photographs to another country, correspond by picture postcard, speak other than in French on the telephone, have radios in cars. Foreigners are also not allowed to travel from one *département*[32] to another without a special permit stamped by the gendarmes.

I remember Vladimir Hitrovo telling me, at the time of the Munich Agreement in 1938, "You'll see how easy it will be for everyone if there is war. People who know foreign languages will have guaranteed work." And now employers who have foreigners working for them

---

32 France is divided into 101 *départements*.

have to request authorization to keep them. With Paris half empty, most stores closed, and a large proportion of industrial concerns evacuated, not just foreigners are out of work. The French are, too. There is no war per se but every aspect of life is disrupted. One has the impression that all the sacrifices and petty annoyances and so on are not as necessary as they would be if there were actual fighting.

2.10.39 We often tune in to foreign stations, hoping to find more accurate news than is broadcast on French government stations; England gives more information than France and often announces news that is only broadcast later by the French stations. For now, the two adversaries, Germany and France, are limiting themselves to reconnaissance flights and aircraft duels. Some raids and patrol strikes are reported. The two armies have withdrawn behind the Siegfried and Maginot lines and watch each other without doing any harm. Public opinion is almost in favour of Italy declaring war on the Allies to stop the flow of military supplies being sent to Germany, and also because no one believes the Italian military is worth anything.

All Allied and enemy stations now give information in different languages, and it is often difficult to identify the country of origin of the broadcast at first. The English announcer on German stations is the topic of endless discussion, highly amusing, tongue in cheek, with an Oxford accent and said to be English. The English have nicknamed him "Lord Haw-Haw" and the English newspapers complain that the English listen to him more than they should. The French announcer on German radio, the "Stuttgart Traitor," is less witty than his English counterpart.[33]

6.10.39 I decided to accept the Zweguintzoffs' invitation and go back to join Nancy in Le Mans.[34] It is probably nothing but an interlude but I could not stay indefinitely at Courances, despite all

---

33 The "Stuttgart Traitor" was Paul Perdonnet (1901–1945). It was purported that he broadcast propaganda in French for the purpose of demoralizing the French population. He was executed for treason in 1945. However, a German collaborator, Maurice-Yvan Sicard, believed that Perdonnet wrote the radio scripts but that the actual voice was that of Obrect, a German actor.

34 Nancy is the wife of Countess Hendrikoff's first cousin, Alexander (Sasha) Zweguintzoff. Hannah Nancy Zweguintzoff, née Woolsten, was an American from Philadelphia.

the charming hospitality of the Marquise de Ganay. Madeleine de Ganay has put her daughters in boarding school and is going to work for the Red Cross. I had been waiting for my travel permit for two weeks, and the Marquise sent me to the Ministry of the Interior with her card and a note for a captain in the Second Office and I had my permit in exactly five minutes.

7.10.39 Dined at the C.'s, who are still without news from their oldest son who remained in Poland. Gladys told me, "Sometimes I would prefer knowing he had been killed." Lipsky, the former Polish ambassador to Berlin, was also dining there that evening. He talked about his stay in that city with no animosity, to my surprise. In his time there, he had to give a dinner for Hitler; to absolve himself of all responsibility, he asked to have Hitler's cook and personal valet present for the evening. The cook was to prepare a special menu for his master, and the valet, dressed in Lipsky's livery, was to serve Hitler at the table. When he entered the dining room, Hitler immediately scanned the staff and looked satisfied when he recognized his valet.

10.10.39 Left by car for the château Les Touches in the vicinity of Le Mans. Approaching Le Mans, we encountered convoys of English trucks camouflaged with nets and leaves and coloured strips. The many English motorcyclists, whose helmets were also covered with nets and leaves, made me think of the Spirit of the Forest in Maeterlinck's *The Blue Bird*. The English soldiers look young and tired, offering us friendly little waves as they pass. Children watching for them at intersections greet them with the Roman "thumbs up" sign. At Le Mans, a huge English MP (Military Police) was directing traffic in the large square.

14.10.39 We had barely arrived at Les Touches when, as a foreigner, I had to go to the Town Hall in Brains to declare my stay.

The château Les Touches, a château in name only, is really a large country house and has not been inhabited for years. A few of the rooms in the house still have eighteenth-century woodwork. There is no longer parquet flooring, except in two rooms. In all the others, it has been replaced with red brick floor tiles that incessantly produce a fine dust, which Nancy calls "the good earth" and finds it unnecessary to sweep!

We are camping like refugees, two or three to a room bare of any furniture, except beds, of course. Fortunately the weather is very nice. The park is a dense thicket with very beautiful trees here and there; among them, the neighbouring farmer's cows and sheep graze peacefully. Les Touches reminds me of a Russian property after years of abandon, with the same style of architecture – Empire columns and facade – the same dilapidation, disorder and... freedom. The type of life we lead reminds me of the last years in Russia. All day is spent on domestic tasks, sweeping, washing, chopping wood, heating, and so on. There are no men to help us. There is no central heating, but fireplaces in the *salon* and the dining room and small wood stoves in the bedrooms. The wood is sometimes dry and burns as fast as a matchstick, or too green and does not burn at all but clogs the chimneys. Then we have to take apart all the pipes and unclog them; we end up looking like chimney sweeps after that operation. Irène Nolde and I have become specialists in the task.

A woman from Brains cooks for us. She is misshapen, deaf as a post, and a hunchback, but a real *cordon bleu* cook, although she has never left Brains. Fifteen of us are seated at the table, with a separate menu for the seven children. She is helped by her younger sister, and an old woman, also from Brains, comes to do the bulk of the washing.

15.10.39 Nancy and I went to Le Mans to do the week's shopping. Many English troops are in the streets and camouflaged trucks in the large square. Many stores display the notice, "We speak English."

16.10.39 Nancy and I went to Brains to look for coal for cooking. We dragged the sacks to the car and piled them on the seats – too bad for whoever sits there next.

We picked the last pears and put them away on straw in the attic. I put a few in the linen cupboard, between the sheets, to the great amusement of Baron Nolde, the owner of the château, who asks from time to time if my nightshirts have ripened the pears.

17.10.39 One would think we are thousands of kilometres from Paris. The mail only comes once a day, but we have a radio. The local newspaper, *La Sarthe*, repeats the radio news word for word, that is, something like, "Nothing new on the Western front." What a strange war, so different from all the others! No one is fighting. The German announcers always refer to the English war, started and wanted by England and suffered by France.

The *Royal Oak* was sunk by a German submarine in the Bay of Scapa. The submarine entered the bay at the end of a line of English ships. The English showed sportsmanship by praising the German commander's audacious move.

29.10.39 The Communist party has been dissolved and several party members in military units arrested.

30.10.39 Received a letter from Riga from Lily I. The city is panic-stricken as a result of the Soviet–Latvian agreements. Lily thought she finally had a home base and now she has to start again from nothing and leave, probably for Italy. This summer she was still writing to me about how happy she was in Riga, what satisfaction it had given her to contribute to the rebirth of part of the Pillar property leased to them by the Latvian government, how she hoped I could someday join her and settle there for good...

12.11.39 The radio broadcast a speech by Chamberlain on the subject "Why we are fighting." His voice is the voice of an aging, weak man, with no zest, his arguments utopian and vague: we are fighting to rebuild a new Europe where everyone will be happy, but first, we are going to put everything back in its place, in other words, fuel all the fires of discontent and elements of discord... then we are going to try to make the German people happy; we have no fight with the German people, only with Hitler.

If I was a Tommy "somewhere in France," I would not be too concerned about the reconstruction of a new Europe and the happiness of the German people. The realistic arguments of the French, who fear that Alsace-Lorraine will share the fate of Czechoslovakia, seem easier for me to understand.

Discussion with Madame U., who tried to prove that the German people do not want war and, this very day, would give up all the territory acquired by Hitler. It seems to me that, in the position Germany found itself after the First War – so crushed it could no longer live but not crushed enough to no longer want to live – any German government would have tried to acquire "living space" one way or another and compensate for all the country had lost.

Rationing has been announced, very light rationing. For now, butcher shops are closed Mondays and beef is not sold Tuesdays. There are beginning to be shortages of some products, such as rubber and paper.

4.12.39 It seems to me that world opinion is more affected by the German invasion of Finland than the invasion of Poland. Roosevelt has offered to act as a mediator; collections are being taken up in America. Italy is providing aircraft through Germany. Finland has appealed to the League of Nations, but that stillborn organization has never stopped an armed conflict yet.

Del R., Marina T.'s Italian husband, is here with his wife. He is very pleasant, cultivated, gentle and well brought up. He predicts the end of the capitalist regime in Europe. He thinks the countries that still want to produce and export after this war will have to turn to the Japanese system, where workers are housed and fed, but paid a paltry salary.

Went with Nancy to a "railcar graveyard" where we bought wood for heating, that is, bricks of wood from old railway cars. Again we piled them in the car, something like 300 kg, and brought them back to Les Touches.

8.12.39 Nancy has the flu, so I went to do the week's shopping with the neighbouring farmer. He only has one leg but drives a specially equipped car. On the way, he talked about his forty head of livestock, the bull he wants to sell for 5,000 francs, his daily menu – meat twice a day. The farmers in the neighbourhood are all rich, have superb animals, eat copiously, but do not incur any outside expenses. They dress like their workers. Their houses are bare and sad, furnished only with the strict essentials, with no concern for ornament or embellishment. The family usually spends its time in one large, dark room on the same level as the entry, with a hearth that serves as both stove and fireplace and a dirt floor. The furniture is a long wooden table and benches. The family's abbreviated grooming is done in the yard at the pump, which is frozen in winter!

I was given my travel permit in the blink of an eye, to the astonishment of Baron Nolde, who had to wait a week for his. I did not dare tell him that I won the friendship of the gendarmes by "forgetting" a package or two of cigarettes on their table every time.

10.12.39 Took a walk around Brains. A few of the older women still wear the starched white bonnet typical of La Sarthe,[35] but most go bareheaded or cover their head and shoulders with a large shawl. Men and women dress in dark colours. Not a beautiful breed. As in all small provincial communities, everyone knows what is going on in every neighbour's life.

Traditional dress,
Sarthe region of France, 1940

15.12.39 We just had a visit from an inspector from the *Sûreté*, the criminal investigation department, sent by the military authorities in response to a denunciation. He spent several hours questioning us, asking a wide variety of questions about our occupations,

35 A *département* in the northwest of France

family situations, relations with Russian political groups and the Grand Dukes in exile. He questioned Madame T. in particular at length; her husband works in the office of the Russian daily newspaper published in Paris. That amused us, because Madame T. is indeed the most innocuous person imaginable. I was a little worried for fear of questions about the absence of my brother Barbos and his youngest son Michel but he did not ask me anything; my interrogation only lasted a few minutes.[36]

16.12.39 André Nolde[37] came to spend the Christmas holidays at Les Touches. He is back from China, where he often had occasion to meet members of the Soviet Mission. They seemed ignorant to him, coarse, often incapable of using the military equipment available to them, which appeared excellent to him. However, the Soviet officers boasted about Russian artillery – "the best artillery in the world." André Nolde was surprised by the number of new Russian words, such as *бомбить* – bombing. Most of the words seemed vulgar to him.

18.12.39 Went to Paris by train; we were not asked for our papers en route. If not for the number of soldiers in the street and officers in "pot" helmets, one would think it were peace time. All the stores have reopened. One even sees traffic jams in the streets. The major boulevards are less well lit than usual but are lit at least enough so it does not look like a blackout. The roads leading to the ministries are dark, and one occasionally bumps into passersby.

Spent the evening with my sister-in-law Bicha. We talked about the young Russians who have been mobilized and what help one can give them. Bicha is eventually going to send me the names of the ones who will be stationed at Le Mans, and I promised to go see them. There is frequently some mention in the newspapers about the saltpetre they say is added to the wine and coffee of recruits to prevent them from running after women. We also talked about the final moments of the *Graf Spee*, which has caused a lot of ink to flow, and how the German captain was obliged to go out into open seas where the English fleet was waiting for him like a cat waits for a mouse, how he com-

36 Countess Hendrikoff's journals later suggest that Barbos had been in Germany.
37 André Nolde is the son of Baron Nolde.

mitted suicide after scuttling his ship and was found wrapped in the German flag. According to the newspapers, the sabotage order was given personally by Hitler. If there had been any military operations at the time, the suicide of Captain Langsdorff would probably have gone unnoticed. In the current situation, where nothing is happening, the incident has been discussed at length.

19.12.39 Bicha was called to the police station for questioning about the absence of Barbos and Michel. She answered the questions very frankly and, it seemed to her, the inspector appreciated her candour.

20.12.39 Lunched at the C.'s with Johnny, who looked to me like an escapee from another world. He was at the P.'s when the war broke out. He immediately returned to S., which was already occupied by the Germans, and a swastika was flying over the front door of the château. There, after a brief interrogation, he was ordered to leave the premises immediately. He had time to go up to Gladys' room to get her silver fox stole from an armoire to bring back to her. The neighbouring farmers drove him to the station, and he travelled to Warsaw in a stock car. R. then helped him get the exit papers he needed, camouflaging the date and place of his birth. He is determined to enlist and fight.

25.12.39 I went to Bellevue. Serge Hitrovo read me letters he has received from his many comrades at the front lines. One of them writes, "It's a strange war. We don't shoot at the Germans. The same for them. They don't shoot at us. When aircraft fly overhead, we all come out of our shelters, because we know very well we have nothing to fear from enemy planes. Yesterday, I saw some prisoners guarded by a soldier who wasn't even armed. Unlike their usual habits, lately the Germans started firing guns, so we immediately held up a sign that said 'Please do not shoot at us.' They responded at once, 'Just exercises. You have nothing to fear.'"

I saw André Hallonin, who was in Paris on leave. He spent the night at Cité Martignac. He arrived around eleven o'clock at night, dressed for the country with his backpack and so on. It was the first time he has left the front lines, where he has been since September. He has matured physically and looks like he is in good health. He talked to us about Alsace, where the villages deserted by the people, who have been pushed inland, are being pillaged by the troops. His regiment was among the last to arrive there and they were only able to get their hands on a calf, pig, and goat and only found a single cask of wine. The first to arrive, however, had furnished their trenches and shelters with everything to be found in the neighbouring houses. So he said he felt like laughing when he heard Daladier[38] on the radio saying "Alsatians, you can have confidence that the Army is watching over your homes."

29.12.39 Lunched at the home of the Italian military attaché. He thinks a peaceful settlement of the conflict will be reached, because no one wants to fight. He does not like the Germans, but criticizes the French. He thinks there are not enough young people in the streets yet there are many old people and little dogs that, in his opinion, take the place of children. He also thinks France is regressing in the arts and even in fashion, where it is equalled if not surpassed by America. Italy has an excuse because it is in a period of construction and has never supported development in the arts.

Serge Raevsky, Bicha's nephew, came to see her. He is on leave in Paris. He told us his regiment had no sooner taken a position on the front lines than the Germans were already welcoming them, raising a sign that said, "Salute to the 194th." The newspapers described a similar incident. During President Lebrun's tour of the Army, he was presented with binoculars to review the enemy trenches more effectively and what appeared before his eyes were signs saying, "Welcome to President Lebrun." They even went so far as to say that a squadron of German planes accompanied Daladier's plane as an honour guard when he went to England.

Stores are selling phosphorescent clips to attach to the lapel of one's coat during a blackout. Jock, Bicha's fox terrier, is wearing one on his coat.

30.12.39 It snowed in Paris yesterday. Unemployed workers, who looked like office workers in overcoats and bowler hats, zealously but clumsily worked to clear the roadways and sidewalks of

38 Édouard Daladier was Prime Minister of France at the time.

snow and mud. For the third time, I took the wrong bus in the dark and found myself heading to Neuilly instead of the fifteenth. There are a few theatres open; shows start at six o'clock and end around eleven o'clock. The metro stops running at eleven o'clock, and buses no longer run after eight o'clock in the evening. Brothels stay open until morning and are doing a booming business.

Lighting tests were done in the Champs-Élysées. Officers were given white capes and pedestrian crossings were painted white.

There is no longer any coffee in either Paris or Le Mans.

31.12.39 Back at Les Touches. Snow covers the countryside and it is bitterly cold in the house. The Godin stove in the entrance is not enough to heat this big house. The logs covered with snow we put in the woodbin in the hall on the first floor do not thaw. We live muffled in shawls, sweaters, coats, and boots, and never take them off all day long.

Nancy and Irène left this morning to greet the New Year with their husbands in Paris. I stayed alone with the children and the Nolde's governess. We did not have the courage to stay in the icy *salon* until midnight, so we cheated. We tuned the radio to Rome, which is an hour ahead. At eleven o'clock local time, we heard joyful chimes and a very soft voice sending greetings through space, assuring us that greetings from Rome always bring happiness.

Chamberlain's speech was about the calm before the storm.

1940

WAR AND OCCUPATION

"Occupied Paris is extremely sad, one might say a dead city. Only the hammering of the cast iron soles of German boots and German cars roaring by at crazy speeds resonate in the empty streets."

1.1.40 Up to now, the war has had fewer victims than an earthquake: twelve hundred killed in France and three thousand in England, with only one soldier killed on land. The Allies are making ruinous contracts with Germany's suppliers to take away their markets. England's National Economy Ministry recently stated that those contracts would have made a businessman shudder in normal times.

The *New York Times* notes that Finland's wealth is being exploited by English and Canadian companies and, apart from a natural reaction of sympathy, a certain amount of pragmatism comes into Allied aid to that country. So André Hallonin was right when he wrote, "Let us hope the war ends soon and the social disruption that naturally ensues settles swiftly and wiser men finally understand that there are ways, other than force, to settle conflicts of a purely economic nature – ideology is merely an excuse."

Always the same news release: "Nothing to report." Madame T. told me that a company was carrying out work at the front lines. The Germans opposite them were providing light with searchlights. At some point, the lights went out. The French called out, "Hey, over there, the light." The Germans immediately obliged by turning the searchlights back on.

Irina Shirkoff is currently giving French lessons on Italian radio.[39] To hear her, I started moving the needle along the radio dial and suddenly I heard a familiar voice that reminded me of my sister's and mother's voices. Madame T. came in at that moment and, unable to conceal her surprise, asked me why the plural of words ending in "ou" caused me such emotion.

It is really cold, minus twelve degrees during the day and minus twenty at night. The temperature in the *salon* stays at minus five degrees. Madame T. said uncomplainingly but comically, "I'm not really cold but I feel as though my head is always outside." Washing is truly an act of courage. To top off our misfortune, the pump that supplies water to the house has frozen, despite the spirit lamp that burns beside it night and day and the straw we tenderly place around it at the risk of starting a fire. Now we have to go bring buckets of water from the pump at Alice's, the farmer's wife.

28.1.40 We listened to the "Stuttgart Traitor" on the radio and the French prisoners allowed to send messages to their families on that station.

Irène Nolde came back from Paris reporting defeatist rumours. The government is criticized out loud in cafés, restaurants, and so on, especially by soldiers on leave. In fact, I recopied the instructions Tamara Bertrand's husband, a French airman, showed me, the instructions soldiers are given each time they go on leave:

SOLDIERS ON LEAVE:
Army morale is higher than domestic morale: PROVE IT.
Every soldier has a small share of the responsibility of the General-in-Chief: BE CAREFUL AND DISCREET.
HITLER is spying on your weaknesses: DON'T HAVE ANY.
He is waiting for information: DON'T GIVE ANY.
He is watching for criticism: DON'T CRITICIZE.
Your leave is a step toward Victory.
Try to convince your parents and friends of that fact.
ACT SO THE REAR ENVIES YOUR LUCK AND COME BACK TO WORK AND COMBAT MORE COURAGEOUS.
Remind your friends that the issue in war is: FREEDOM OR BONDAGE.
Don't forget that enemy ears are everywhere: KEEP QUIET.

39 Irina Shirkoff is the niece of Countess Hendrikoff.

Anyone who asks you "What are the goals of the war?" is a conscious or unconscious agent of Hitler.
Answer boldly: VICTORY and don't add anything!

Nancy and I went to Le Mans to visit some young Russian recruits; Bicha had given me a long list of names. We waited quite a long time at the guardhouse at Chanzy barracks, in a tiny room with straw mattresses on the floor; the torn canvas covers let tufts of straw stick out, as dirty as the canvas. The non-commissioned officer did not allow us to choose more than two names on the list. We had brought cigarettes, chocolate, books. The two young soldiers we spoke to did not look too unhappy.

6.2.40 Nancy writes from Paris: "I notice quite a change in Paris in how everybody talks about the war. They say that Germany is very strong (instead of demoralized and starving as they used to say before) and that it will be possible but very difficult to break her. All the military people ask for is that Germany attack but they fear that Hitler is too clever to make that mistake. So you may be relieved to know that the old radio 'English war aims' are not thought of anymore; nor the idealistic United States of Europe; but simply more and more seriously how to win the war."

12.2.40 I had a strange dream. I dreamed I was going up the Champs-Élysées in a car when suddenly aircraft showing the swastika rose above the Arc de Triomphe, pursued immediately by two French planes. I heard the noise of machine guns and saw clouds of smoke around them. Then the German planes descended and headed straight for me, flying under the Arc de Triomphe. They grazed the roof of the car and I crouched low on the seat because I was afraid. Someone shouted, "Run away," and my car sped toward the Bois. In my dream, at times there were bushes and rocks everywhere, and the car had trouble getting through, then the landscape changed and we were going down formal lanes of great beauty. I woke up thinking with relief, "Thank God, it was only a dream seeing German aircraft fly over Paris."

Visited the Melnikoffs, a Russian family who has been established in Le Mans since the Revolution. They have organized a committee to help young Russians who have been mobilized. They send parcels to the ones in the Sarthe and invite young Russian soldiers stationed at Le Mans to their home. The two Melnikoff daughters, who used to look like drooping flowers, have regained their zest for life and take care of their protégés with a great deal of passion. The war has certainly brought a bit of diversion into their dreary provincial life.

29.2.40 Tamara Bertrand's husband was here on leave. Very anti-British, he reproaches the English for their high pay – "an English corporal is better paid than a French colonel" – and the way they spend it, their authoritarian manner – "they act as if they were at home" – and says that the country is becoming a "Dominion."

March 1940 Finland has signed a peace agreement with Russia. We were a bit surprised by such a swift and painful decision for Finland. The newspapers had always assured us that Russia was going from one defeat to the next and published photos of Russian soldiers killed at the front, frozen fields covered with abandoned Russian equipment.

23.3.40 The censors are extremely thorough. All letters between Paris and Le Mans are opened and censored. Recently my letter addressed to Vladimir Hitrovo, in which I asked him for advice on pruning rosebushes, was returned by the military censor marked, "Please write in French." The censor must have taken my innocent sketch of a rosebush for a military map of the area.

26.3.40 In Paris, nearly all the stores are open, and people are buying by the armload in anticipation of upcoming increases. The Melnikoffs told me that they have bought two years' worth of sugar. Rationing is still fairly light but restrictions are increasing day by day. Bread is now being made with a mixture of bean flour; meat is not sold on Monday, Tuesday, and Wednesday; there is no more chocolate; bread is no longer sold by the piece; and the public is encouraged to eliminate anything superfluous from meals.

Charity bridge at the Russian Club to raise funds for young Russians who have been mobilized. Many Russians in French officer uniforms.

8.4.40 Les Touches. In the evening, the radio announced that a fleet of about fifty German ships has left port and is heading north.

Their exact destination was not reported. That is probably German retaliation for setting mines in Norwegian territorial waters.

9.4.40 We missed the news at half past one and were stunned to learn in the evening that Germany has occupied Denmark and Norway.

10.4.40 The Germans landed at several spots in Norway, particularly Narvik. Mr. Chamberlain told Parliament that should surely read "Larvik" in the Bay of Oslo, not "Narvik" in northern Norway. However, there had not been a typing error in the news release and it was indeed Narvik, as unlikely as that may seem. Afterward, it was said that German sailors disguised as fishermen had arrived in Narvik the night before and remained lying down in the bottom of freighters until the time came for landing. The English newspapers also wrote that the landing troops were made up of Germans who had enjoyed Norwegian hospitality in their day. After the First War, many Norwegian families had provided German and Austrian children with hospitality. The Allied press consider the occupation of Norway a serious strategic error by Hitler, and Chamberlain said, "Hitler missed the bus."

20.4.40 A tragic event occurred at Les Touches. The Bertrands' baby was found suffocated in his carriage! We ran to the farmer's, whose name is Gâteau, to get him to drive us to Le Mans, because there is no longer a doctor nearby at Coulans. Nancy and Irène Nolde were in Paris and the only one of us who knew how to drive was Tamara, the baby's mother, but she was crying so hard she was unable to drive. We reached Le Mans in record time, less than half an hour; everyone let us pass when they saw the baby, who was completely blue. He was already blue when he was found in the carriage and could not be resuscitated, despite all the doctor's efforts – artificial respiration, injections, and so on. We left the little corpse at the hospital and then had to attend to a lot of arrangements at the Town Hall, funeral home, and so on.

22.4.40 Tamara's husband arrived late in the night. It is painful to watch him and Tamara. The baby was buried in the cemetery at Brains. Neither Tamara nor her husband wanted to see the child in the coffin, and they asked me to cut a lock of his hair for them. They dropped me off at the hospital; in the viewing area, big black curtains with white crosses surrounded each individual coffin, with the names pinned on each curtain, all watched over by a nun. The nuns had dressed the baby with great care, and he was pink again and looked like he was sleeping. A kind of calm reigned in the room, not the gloomy atmosphere I feared, but an impression of great peace that reconciles one with death.

27.4.40 Russian Easter. The religious service was moved up from midnight to eight o'clock because of the blackout. We listened to the service broadcast on the radio, which was interrupted near the end to go to news.

Vladimir Hitrovo came through Le Mans. We had lunch together. He thinks the war will be long and gradually everyone will be caught up in it. He does not think the English will be able to stay in Norway and thinks all the nonsense we are currently fed by the newspapers – "Brilliant victory for the British forces. We will take what we want on the Norwegian coast" and so on – may someday cause social unrest.

3.5.40 The English announced withdrawal of their troops from Norway on the radio. America appears increasingly interested in the European situation.

4.5.40 We received coal coupons for 50 kg, barely enough for a week. Nancy and I went to see if there was a house for rent in the surrounding area that could be heated more economically. We chanced on a charming property, a two-storey house deep in an old park. Inside was old furniture, paintings, curtains made of *toile de Jouy* – but no running water. The current owners are two fine farmers who had been servants in the household and inherited it from their former employers. However, they could not bring themselves to live there and are living on the farm as they had in the past.

8.5.40 My brother Barbos and his son Michel have just arrived in Paris. I hurriedly went to see them. The train was full of soldiers on leave and German Israelites. Olga Hitrovo met me at the station; I brought her 10 kg of butter from the country, which is no longer to be found in Paris.[40] She told me that the Norwegian campaign was considered over, although that decision has never been officially announced. The English newspapers published interviews with the Alpine Hunters who had just arrived in England; everyone knows they are the very mountain infantry units that made up the expeditionary force for Norway.

There is a shortage of sugar in Paris and rumours that it is going to be rationed.

I still have not seen Michel, because he spent the whole day at the Recruitment Office and in court. He was then sent to the La Tour-Maubourg barracks.

Naturally, Barbos has been assailed with questions on the situation in Germany; however, since he stayed there at a property in a more-than-affluent setting, his field of observation was limited as a result. There are no longer private cars in Germany; only doctors are entitled to a car. However, there are still taxis. Everything is rationed, but all the tickets are honoured. All the stores are open, and dismissing staff is not allowed. People are very against England. In Rome, everyone is saying war is imminent. When the French Consul in Rome learned that Michel was stateless and returning to France to be called up, following orders the Consul was unaware of, he described it a sublime act.

9.5.40 I went to visit Michel at the barracks. He has matured, grown, and still looks like a "young man of good family" despite

---

40 Olga Hitrovo was an old friend of Countess Hendrikoff's. Together they attended the Smolny Institute for Girls of Noble Birth in St. Petersburg. A shrewd businesswoman, Olga became well known as a lingerie designer. As Alexandre Vassiliev explains in his book *Beauty in Exile*, "One Russian designer became sought after just for her lingerie, the plain and stocky Olga Hitrovo, who made it desirable and fashionable to send svelte models down the red carpet wearing nothing but negligees and nighties, and who was lauded by no less than Rita Hayworth for her elegant, fragile and yet sturdily chaste items of *dishabille*." Olga built her business on her inability to find fine lingerie in Paris as she had in pre-revolutionary Russia. At the time, aristocratic women had all of their lingerie handmade out of fine silk by the nuns in the Russian Orthodox convents. Olga remembered this and, copying their designs and methods, ran a successful business which managed to survive World War II. Her husband Vladimir and son Serge are also mentioned throughout Countess Hendrikoff's journals.

the worn and shabby uniform he was wearing. He is somewhat stunned by the conversations of his comrades in the regiment, who have no sympathy for the English; on the contrary, they praise the courage and military exploits of the Germans.

10.5.40   The Germans have invaded Holland, Belgium, and Luxembourg! I was woken up around five o'clock in the morning by the PTT[41] siren a few steps from Cité Martignac, where I was staying this time at the Zweguintzoffs' apartment. The siren was followed almost immediately by the drone of low-flying aircraft and anti-aircraft artillery fire. The racket lasted until seven o'clock in the morning, but I stayed snugly tucked in my bed because, at Barbos' the night before, everyone mocked the people who had rushed down to the shelters at the first wail of the sirens. Calm was finally restored. The morning newspapers had no alarming news and did not even mention the air-raid warning. Around nine o'clock in the morning, when I called Madeleine de Ganay on the telephone, she interrupted me abruptly to say, "Don't you know what happened last night?" The maid who was sweeping the next room heard my exclamations, dropped the broom, and ran to the usual source for any information – the concierge. She came back at once to confirm the unbelievable news: "The Germans have invaded Belgium." Everyone was talking about a German invasion, but no one believed it.

In the morning, I had to go to the Morgan Bank. On my way, the street was completely calm; Parisians seemed unaware of the cause of the air-raid warning. One of the bank managers I spoke to did not want to believe my news and assured me, with reason, that the bank would have been the first to know about the German invasion. Nevertheless, he called a colleague who immediately confirmed that my news was well founded. Leaving the bank at around eleven-thirty, I saw people already grabbing up copies of *Paris-Midi*; a special edition had been published with a headline in large letters announcing the invasion of Belgium! All that could be heard from all sides were comments on the events, anxious ex-

41 Postal, Telephone, and Telegraph siren

clamations. I was having lunch that day with Sasha Zweguintzoff, who advised me to go right back to Les Touches today with Irène Nolde, and I just had time to stop in at the barracks to say good-bye to Michel.

14.5.40 Events are unfolding at lightning speed. Princess Juliana has left Holland for London with her husband and children. The next day, we heard that Queen Wilhelmina had also left Holland.

The Germans have crossed the Albert Canal and pushed as far as Sedan.[42] They are dropping paratroopers behind Allied lines to destroy military objectives and take strategic positions. The paratroopers are equipped with radio sets and folding bicycles. The newspapers even went so far as to say that the paratroopers often dress in civilian clothing or Allied uniforms, and women are often among them. The paratroopers that were captured were summarily executed. The Germans officially protested on the radio, announcing that paratroopers were members of a military corps who wore a special uniform and, if taken, should be treated as prisoners of war. If the Allies did not heed this warning, ten Allied prisoners would be shot for every German paratrooper executed.

The news is now broadcast every hour on the radio; however, one does not learn much. A flood of Belgian refugees have arrived in Paris and the surrounding area and many cars with Belgian licence plates are seen on the road to Le Mans.

15.5.40 Holland has laid down its arms.

Civilians are being armed for the battle against paratroopers. Nancy brought a revolver back from Paris and intends to shoot one or more paratroopers with it. Up to now, she has not been able to distinguish a French uniform from an English uniform, so the inhabitants of Brains had better watch out!

17.5.40 Went to Le Mans to do the week's shopping. The road and the town are full to bursting with refugees, most of them Belgian. We passed trucks and cars with mattresses on the roofs, bicycles tied to the windshields. The traffic in Place de la République is so heavy cars move at a walking pace.

42 The Albert Canal is in Belgium; Sedan is in northwest France.

News from the front is scarce. The Germans have broken through the lines of defence between France and Belgium. However, news releases continue to console the public: "We have succeeded in stopping the German advance," "Brussels is not threatened," "The situation is reassuring," and so on.

18.5.40 The Germans have announced the capture of Brussels and Anvers but the news has not been confirmed by French radio.

19.5.40 Tamara Bertrand has returned from Cambrai; her husband is a member of the Cambrai squadron. She was there when the aerodrome was bombed. Her house was across from the railway station, which was completely destroyed. She took refuge in the basement, which was not a really a shelter and shook as if there was an earthquake. A woman about to give birth clung to her arm and would not let go. Every time there was a moment of calm, Tamara went out to the street hoping to see her husband. Finally, when she had lost all hope of seeing him again, because she knew the aerodrome had been destroyed, the door to the basement opened and she heard her husband call her. They left by car for Beauvais, without waiting for the air-raid warning to end, and it was in the car that Tamara realized what had happened, which broke her nerve, and she admitted she was most afraid.

20.5.40 General Gamelin has been replaced by General Weygand. For the occasion, the newspapers published a photo of Weygand coming out of a bomb shelter looking quite haggard – bad publicity!

Our radio is not working, and we went to listen to the news at farmer Gâteau's house. Italian radio announced that the Germans are marching on Paris and nothing can stop them...

21.5.40 No news releases, which is always a bad sign. The English confirmed that Saint-Quentin has been taken.[43] Irène and I barely have time to mark the advance of the German troops on the map of military operations.

German nationals are going to be put in concentration camps. Nancy's Czechoslovakian nurse, Maddie, has to report to Le Mans tomorrow with a blanket, 30 kg of baggage, and three days of provisions.

43 Saint-Quentin is about 170 km northwest of Paris.

At six-thirty, we listened to Reynaud's speech announcing the capture of Arras, Péronne, and Amiens by the Germans.[44] The reason he gave for the Germans' lightning advance was the poor defence of La Meuse,[45] which was considered impregnable and was guarded by poorly-armed, inexperienced troops, while the best contingents were sent to Belgium. He admits the superiority of the German motorized forces. He ended his speech with a patriotic but desperate cry: "If I were told that a miracle would be needed to save France, I would answer, I believe in miracles because I believe in France."

We listened in despair. He is clearly preparing the public for bad news. Every day lately, official radio broadcasts said nothing or gave hope. Now there is nothing left but to hope for a miracle! We ran to farmer Gâteau's house to listen to the English station because our radio no longer receives foreign stations. The news is no more reassuring; the English announced the collapse of the French front.

Travel is now prohibited without an evacuation order, a measure that is supposed to remedy the bottlenecks on roads where refugees and civilians are mixed with troops advancing to the front or beating a retreat, which creates indescribable chaos. Belgian refugees were sent to the northwest coast at first and then, with the German advance, redirected to Bordeaux. Trainloads of refugees who have not yet received the counter-order continue northward while those who have reached the coast come back by the same route. You really have to see the road with your own eyes to realize the chaos that reigns these days.

22.5.40 I got up and washed and dressed Nancy's two children under the supervision of the nurse, Maddie, who has to leave tomorrow.[46]

23.5.40 Maddie left early in the morning, and Nata kept on repeating "Maddie, Maddie, why aren't you here, Maddie?" in a small, sad voice all day long.

---

44 Paul Reynaud was Prime Minister of France from March 21 to June 16, 1940.

45 A *département* in northwest France

46 Nancy and Sasha Zweguintzoff had two children, Nathalie (Nata) Zvegintzov (b. 1937) and Alexander A. (Sandy) Zvegintzov (b. 1939). Today, Sandy Zvegintzov is a recovering attorney, a part-time ski instructor, park guide and full time painter, who lives in Wilson, Wyoming, with his wife, Mila.

25.5.40 Nancy got back from Paris and announced their decision to leave for America, especially since the American embassy is requiring women and children who are American citizens to leave at once.

Young Maya L., who is only sixteen years old, is a valued help to me with the two children. Her mother sent her to Les Touches, fearing the eventual bombing of Paris. She promised to watch the children while Nancy and I sort things to take and go to Le Mans for the necessary safe-conducts. The road is still in complete chaos; cars are driving in every direction at 20 km an hour. One sees a lot of cars with Parisian licence plates.

Nancy and I went to visit Maddie in her camp with the hope of getting her out. The camp is really a former dance hall decorated with lanterns and coloured paper garlands that clash bizarrely with the group of internees sleeping on straw in a corner. We crossed a courtyard where women's underwear is strung on lines to dry. In the middle of the room sat a board made up of a civilian, a lieutenant, and a soldier acting as interpreter. Nancy and I sat facing them and Maddie was called. Our judges seemed very humane and tried as hard as they could to find a legal reason to free Maddie. According to the spirit of the secret circular they have been given, they told us, she should be freed; however, if they follow it to the letter, she should remain interned. They wanted to send us back to the Second Office but, in the end, decided to mark on Maddie's record "ex-Czechoslovakian" and send her back to Les Touches with orders to report to the Mayor's Office every ten days. Maddie could no longer contain herself and shook the judges' hands and kissed each of the internees one after another; they gathered around and congratulated her, helped her pack up her belongings, carried them to the car for her. Nancy calmed Maddie's delight somewhat by telling her that she and the children are leaving in a few days for America.

When we got back, we found Sasha at Les Touches. He repeated to us the rumour circulating in Paris that Sedan has been taken by surprise. A Chief of Staff arrived and gave the order to fall back and abandon the city. A little later, it was realized that the Chief of Staff was... German. General Giraud, who was coming to take over in Sedan, was taken prisoner when he got out of his car. The War Ministry often receives telephone calls from the German military authorities informing the Ministry that French cities have been captured well before the official announcement of that fact.

Sasha was struck by the sight of the refugees on the road to Le Mans. It made him think of earlier migrations of tribes of people: women and children lying on straw in carts, horses and cows tied behind the vehicles, colts whinnying and gambolling among the crowd on foot following the convoys. Tanks and military vehicles mix with the crowd, threading their way with difficulty through the human flow filling the full width of the road.

26.5.40 The radio announced that from now on, as a precaution, details of military operations or locations occupied by the enemy will no longer be given. The public is asked to have confidence and... be patient.

Irène and I took Nancy and Sasha to the train. On the road, we were stopped several times at military roadblocks to have our papers checked. On the way back, when we were waiting at a railroad crossing, a train went by with guns on the platforms and young soldiers perched on the guns laughing and playing the banjo. They greeted us gaily, waving their helmets – a source of life perched on a source of death!

27.5.40 It seems to me as though we are all gathered around a very sick person who has reached a critical phase in his illness and none of us wants to envision a tragic outcome. It is difficult to believe in a miracle and painful to hope for an armistice.

I went down to the *salon* around eight-thirty in the morning to hear the news. The radio announcer said in a serious voice that Reynaud was going to speak, already creating anticipation of an important event. In a sepulchral voice, Reynaud officially announced the surrender of Belgium. Hostilities on the Belgian front ended at five o'clock in the morning. Reynaud called the surrender a betrayal and declared that France would prevail anyway in spite of everything. At four-thirty in the afternoon, we heard the President of the Belgian Council, Pierlot, announce that his country's government does not accept the King's decision and has declared him divested of power. He enjoins Belgians to resist the King's orders and promises to raise a new army. Tamara Bertrand and Madame Hallonin, Irène's mother, are convinced that the King was "bought" by the Germans, and our cleaning lady reported to us that the villagers are no longer going to welcome Belgian refugees into their homes from now on.

29.5.40 Went to Le Mans. There are fewer refugees in the city but the road is still full of trucks and horse-drawn carts. It is raining. The refugees take shelter as best they can under umbrellas or tarps, a pathetic procession. We have received our first ration cards.

In the evening we listened to Swiss radio. The announcer explained the decision made by the King of Belgium. In the past eighteen days, Belgium has lost more men than during the whole war of 1914. Refugees mingled with troops were hampering military operations. Weygand had discussed the situation with the King and thought he could still hold on for another week, but the swift German advance did not allow any delay.

1.6.40 Nancy has returned from Paris, and her departure is set for Sunday.

Telephone calls to Paris, which is now in the Army zone, are no longer allowed.

3.6.40 We had a surprise visit from an English officer, a visit that caused a particularly funny misunderstanding. André Nolde had written us some time ago to announce a visit to Les Touches by one of his English friends, so when an officer appeared and asked to speak to Captain Nolde, we all in turn thought he was the friend André referred to in his letter. I was the only one in the *salon* when he arrived and naturally also imagined he was André's friend. Then, since he seemed astonished to learn that André Nolde was at the front and assailed me with questions about the *Mladoross*[47] and the political views of the Melnikoffs and Russians in general, I realized

47 Translator's note: movement, party or league of young Russians

that it was a misunderstanding and asked the officer the purpose of his visit. He told me he was from British intelligence and came to investigate as a result of denunciations. At that point, Irène Nolde appeared. Seeing that she also misunderstood the nature of the visit, I hastily made her aware of the situation. Then it was Irène's mother's turn; without waiting to hear our explanations, she immediately urged the officer to have a cup of tea and, from that moment on, he never had time to get a word in, never mind ask a question. Irène's mother took charge of the whole conversation. The officer left rather quickly. When they were finally alone, Irène explained the situation to her mother, who was almost sick with fear. She could no longer remember what she had said in front of the officer, who might, after all, be a "fifth column"[48] agent trying to obtain military information!

The visit caused quite a stir among the inhabitants of the village of Brains! They had barely seen his car enter the grounds of the château before they hurried at once to note its number and went to inform the Mayor. It seems we are being closely watched. That fine gentleman came to the château bright and early the next morning and told us that he was going to report it to the gendarmes; from now on, we are to refuse to answer anyone in his absence. He mainly seemed annoyed that an "English police officer" came to conduct an investigation without being accompanied by a French colleague.

3.6.40 Paris has been bombed.

4.6.40 Italy has declared war on the Allies. Everyone is more appalled than worried.

6.6.40 Nancy came back to Les Touches with Sasha. We are packing the last suitcases.

7.6.40 I went for a walk in the park for the last time with Nata. The weather was glorious and everything was calm around us, as if nature wanted to ignore the battle fought by human beings. Truly nature was indifferent – *равнодушная природа* in the words of the poet...

---

48 A group who falsely sympathize with an enemy for the purpose of overthrowing a nation from within. The term was first used in the Spanish Civil War.

Lala and Nata, Château des Touches, 1939

8.6.40 We left the château by car at seven o'clock in the morning. Sasha and Nancy were in the front seat and I was in the back wedged between suitcases, with the two children on my knees. We travelled without stopping to Bordeaux, weaving our way through thick traffic on the roads, covered with trucks and carts full of refugees travelling in both directions. Near Tours, we passed an English camp with camouflaged tents. Bordeaux is a vast camp of Belgian refugees and also full of Americans who are supposed to leave on the *Washington*. We went from hotel to hotel without finding a single vacant room. We were told that many Americans solved the problem by buying mattresses and sleeping under the stars in the streets and squares of the city. Finally, they dropped me with the two children at a rooming house whose proprietor agreed to let us wait in the hall while Nancy and Sasha went looking for a room.

As the day went on and the noise and coming and going in the hall were making the children agitated, I took them and went to sit outside in a nearby square. A Belgian refugee immediately sat down beside me. She told me she is the wife of a public servant in the Belgian Foreign Affairs department; she has been all over France, bounced like a ball from one city to another, lost all her baggage, and bitterly regrets leaving her home. She told me, "In 1914, I didn't budge and was no worse off." She defended the conduct of King Leopold and begged me not to believe the newspapers. Soon other Belgian refugees joined us and political discussions started; in order to avoid getting mixed up in them, I got up and went to look for another square. I had to carry little Sandy, who is not walking yet and is a good size and heavy to carry, and lead Nata, who was tired and whimpering, by the hand. Finally, around seven o'clock in the evening, Nancy and Sasha appeared; they had found two rooms in a hotel. We put the children to bed; they were exhausted. We entrusted them to the night watchman and went to dinner at the Splendid. The American colony was there in force. The contrast was striking, a noisy pre-war atmosphere, women showily dressed accompanied by pampered dogs, combed and groomed. Everyone seemed to know one another and was conversing between tables.

9.6.40 Sasha left at six o'clock in the morning for Paris. Nancy and I took the eleven o'clock train to Le Verdon, the port of departure; we had sandwiches for lunch on the train and arrived at the harbour station around two o'clock in the afternoon. The *Washington* was there, with the American flag painted on and visible from every angle. There were no porters and all the employees were Belgian refugees who could not provide any information. I saw the most wily passengers getting help from seamen and suggested that Nancy do the same. With their help, we got into the glassed room used for Customs. I went to sit in a corner with the children, surrounded by screaming children soon joined by the screams of Nata and Sandy. It was getting late, and Nancy seemed to still be at the same point. She suddenly had a dizzy spell and a doctor was called who gave her a shot, which allowed her to get through out of turn.

The moment finally came when she was ready to embark. I did not have authorization to board the ship and, at the gangway of the *Washington*, a bellboy took Sandy screaming from my arms while Nancy moved away dragging Nata by the hand, crying and as dirty as a little chimney sweep.

Now I had to get back to Bordeaux, but it was eight o'clock in the evening and the last train left at four-thirty... What was I to do? I set out to look for a charitable soul who could take me by car to Bordeaux. I saw a gentleman who looked like a foreigner to me, that is, someone who was not going to spend the night in Le Verdon. I approached him and, oh, good fortune, he was an American returning to Paris with the military attaché. He remembered seeing me talking to Makinsky, one of his friends, at the Splendid yesterday. There was room for me in the car, and I could go as far as Tours with my saviours. We stopped for dinner in Bordeaux and talked about the military situation; the American military attaché was very optimistic, but that opinion was not shared by the other occupants of the car. En route, I learned that the American I had approached first is the Secretary of the Liberian Legation. Gathering what I remember of geography, I asked him how he came to represent Blacks. He explained that the Liberians are not yet civilized enough to have diplomats of their own colour; the Minister is also white, and Dutch to top it off.

We set off again for Tours. On the road, we were stopped at checkpoints every few minutes by Belgian soldiers who checked our papers. At Poitiers we ran out of gas, but all the passersby and even the officers on duty were Belgian and did not know where gas is sold. We finally came upon a garage and, because again the employee was Belgian and probably did not know the regulations, he gave us gas without asking for coupons.

The military attaché then warned us that he had not slept for thirty-six hours and greatly feared he would fall asleep at the wheel! And almost right away, the car lurched and struck an embankment, which fortunately absorbed the shock. The attaché continued to sleep and we waited in silence for him to recover. He slept like that for about ten minutes then got back on the road. We arrived at Tours around six-thirty in the morning. The train for Le Mans that was supposed to depart at four o'clock in the morning was still there, because the station had just been bombed. It was a military train carrying guns and machine guns and two cars for civilians, which did not reassure the passengers much; however, one had no choice, and I arrived safe and sound in Le Mans after all and even had the good fortune to find that the bus still provides service to Brains.

10.6.40 The news from the front gets worse and worse. The Germans are approaching the capital. Trains to Paris are no longer running. The French army is falling back on all fronts.

Irène Nolde, her mother, and Tamara Bertrand have decided to leave. They are going to take the only car we have. Baron and Baroness Nolde are also making plans to leave and are going to inquire in the village whether it is possible to get the old pickup truck running again. If so, they offered to take me with them, on the condition that I only bring one suitcase with me.

11.6.40 In the evening, German aircraft circled over the château. They sound different than Allied planes. Around four-thirty in the morning, we were woken by a loud detonation and later learned that Le Mans had been bombed. The farmers say that the English headquarters is there now, which is likely, because the last time we went through Le Mans, we noticed a large number of English officers wearing helmets with red bands and a lot of trucks with anti-aircraft guns posted at all the intersections.

Irène, her mother, and Tamara left this morning at five o'clock.

12.6.40 I was working in the vegetable garden when the Belgian refugees who are staying at the Gâteau farm came to ask me the latest news. When we were talking about the bombing of Le Mans, they told me, "Here *they* come again, hot on our heels; we barely find a quiet spot and *they* give the signal to leave again!" Thinking they were talking about the Germans, I tried to reassure them by saying that the Germans were still far away, but to my great surprise, it was the English they meant. Since they left Belgium, the appearance of English troops in an area has always announced the retreat of the soldiers and the flight of civilians!

We listen to Swiss radio. General Herring started by giving the order to evacuate Paris but the order was then revoked and it was even said that "to leave is to lose." I.I.T. thinks that simply means that the French government no longer has the resources to evacuate the population.

In the evening, German aircraft again flew over the château.

13.6.40 Paris has been declared an "open city."

There is no longer any postal service. I went to the village to distribute the clothes left by Nancy. A great many people are making preparations to leave.

14.6.40 Swiss and English radio announced that the Germans have entered Paris...

The first German detachments arrived at the gates of Paris the evening before but camped outside the city, only entering the city the next morning, through Porte Saint-Denis. Police and an unarmed civilian guard maintained order. All men from seventeen to sixty years old left the capital the night before. The bridges have not been destroyed.

I am recording the news I just heard on Swiss radio but have trouble believing it. I remember, on June 11, the newspapers bore the headlines "The French resistance has the Germans in retreat" and "Our tactics are inflicting crushing losses on the enemy" and so on, and here they are announcing that the Germans have entered Paris, apparently without encountering any resistance! Obviously, I know one could hardly have any illusions about the turn the war is taking, but the idea of the occupation of Paris by foreign troops seems unbelievable to me, improbable in this day and age!

15.6.40 This morning I was woken at six o'clock by the farmer's wife, Alice, who came to tell me that two young women were in the yard asking to see Irène. They had naïvely sent a telegram and were astonished that we had not received it. One of them had her little boy with her and was in an advanced state of pregnancy. They had travelled by car all night and had not eaten for twenty-four hours, only had a drink of water they had to pay five francs a glass for on the road. They had a German shepherd they had to abandon en route because the dog was nearly driven mad by the racket all around them during the trip. They thought they had reached an oasis of peace yet could now distinctly hear heavy artillery. They are both Jewish, which makes them especially fearful of the Germans. The Baroness did not want to refuse them hospitality but for practical reasons – we are very short of provisions – she was not overly keen to shelter the refugees for long.

In Brains, where I went around four o'clock for bread, there was a lot of talk of German atrocities. Most of the farmers hesitate to part with their livestock. Moreover, official radio gave the order to stay put and explained that the population exodus was hindering the progress of the troops.

Alice told us that the English left Le Mans during the night. That news did not reassure our two refugees and they decided to go to Le Mans by car to buy gas, which can no longer be found in Brains. Maddie, Nancy's nurse, went with them because, for some reason or another, she had decided to ask the authorities to put her back in a camp.

The *route nationale* is still clogged with refugees who make use of any means of locomotion: men on bicycles, women on foot pushing baby carriages, babies in wheelbarrows pulled like trailers by bicycles, mule- or horse-drawn carriages, strollers... in a word, anything on wheels, anything that rolls, has been mobilized for the exodus. Clearly, although the refugees are fleeing the German advance, they will quickly be overtaken by enemy troops. Cars go by with soldiers lying on the fenders, as was done at the time of the Russian Revolution – officers with their families in the car. Our mayor is surprised and saddened; he considers all those soldiers deserters.

On the way back, I stopped for a minute at the D.'s, who asked me if I had good news from Paris and fell from the clouds when I told them Paris is occupied by the Germans. French radio never announced it to the public.

15.6.40 In the evening, our two refugees came back from Le Mans in a superb Studebaker; enthroned at the wheel was a soldier – completely drunk. Pale and horrified, they told us that Le Mans is deserted; there is no longer a prefect or mayor, nothing but troops scattering in headlong flight on foot or by bicycle. The railway station is closed; the post office employees have emptied all the contents of the mailbags in the street and left as well. The soldier who picked them up sold them military gas and promised to tow them. They hastily gathered their baggage – two toothbrushes and a very heavy statue of Buddha that had our imaginations working overtime. The Baroness was sure it had opium inside. They finally headed in the direction of Laval.

16.6.40 The radio announced that the German flag is flying over the palace of Versailles.

Rumours are circulating that France is going to ask for an armistice; however, the radio denies that. I remember Olga Hitrovo saying, in cases like that, "then it has already been done." Baron Nolde is sure that France can no longer continue to fight.

The Baroness dismissed the two housekeepers and kept only the cook; she divided all the provisions into equal parts and distributed to us everything that will not be used for common meals.

We went to Coulans in the hope of getting supplies; however, the butcher and baker have disappeared, and the gendarmes followed their example.

17.6.40 The cook just got back from Epineux and told us the roads are full of soldiers in retreat, returning home or simply going straight ahead without knowing precisely where they are heading. They have lost any trace of their regiment. It is very easy to get gas now; you just ask any soldier, who sells it to you at a special rate for friends.

The radio announced Reynaud's resignation.

The Soviets have occupied Lithuania and the Baltic States.

At one o'clock, we listened to English news and learned that Marshal Pétain has sent his adversary a request for an armistice.[49] Hostilities have ceased on the French front; however, England is determined to continue to fight. At one-thirty, we listened to the French station broadcasting the speech made by the Marshal, who explained that the Army can no longer continue a fight that is now

49 Marshal Phillippe Pétain would go on to become Chief of the French State, whose government is remembered for collaborating with the Axis forces.

useless against an enemy superior in numbers and arms. He has given himself for his country and asked his adversary to find an honourable solution "between soldiers."

At six o'clock, English radio said that France has already begun talks with Germany. Hitler and Mussolini are going to meet to discuss the conditions of the armistice.

Madame T. came back from Brains and said the ditches are full of drunken soldiers shouting with joy at the announcement of the armistice. How can one continue to fight with troops whose morale has reached that point? Naturally, good Frenchmen do not react that way; however, their proportion is too low not to be alarmed.

18.6.40 French radio announced that the French army has been cut into four with no contact between the four parts anymore. The English proposed a French–English union with France, with only one military command, one government, but two Parliaments, and dual citizenship for nationals of both countries. I strongly doubt that could be achieved. Anyway, the demoralization of the people is already a sign of defeat.

We were surprised to see Maddie, Nancy's nurse, return; she walked all the way from Le Mans to Les Touches pushing her suitcases on a small doll carriage, which she had been happy to find for the price of one hundred fifty francs. When she arrived in Le Mans, there was still an internment camp with thirty-seven German Jews. Then all the detainees were sent to the Basses-Pyrénées.[50] There were no cars to take them to the railway station and they were to carry their baggage themselves, so those who could not do so had permission to stay where they were – in other words, they were set free, because the guards were leaving the camp at once. For three days and three nights, Maddie walked the city, sleeping wherever, in empty hotels or in the street. The large squares in Le Mans have become camps where refugees sleep, eat, and wash in the open air. Maddie, who has some education, compared the sight to scenes from the Russian retreat in 1812.

50 A *département* in the southwest of France

The parish priest in Brains came to the château. According to his information, German detachments are already in Laval and Le Mans; however, "they are not saying anything to anyone and the people are not saying anything to them either." The priest hopes this trial will result in better morale in the country and the return of the peasant to the land.

For the moment, it seems the Germans are behaving like friends rather than conquerors; the farmers in the surrounding area reassure us that they do no more than disarm the soldiers they encounter on the road and send them home, they feed refugees... in short, truly a honeymoon.

Evening B., who gathers farm produce in the countryside, went to sell his merchandise in Le Mans as usual but was stopped by Germans posted where the first houses in the city start and ordered to go back, which means Le Mans is indeed occupied by the Germans.

19.6.40 Alice, the farmer's wife, came to call me around seven o'clock in the morning to see the Germans going by on the main road. Through a hole in the hedge that borders her meadow, we could see a compact line of German trucks, guns, cars, and motorcycles heading in the direction of Laval. Then a neighbour came to tell us that the Germans had stopped and bought cigarettes in Brains; they paid in German marks, their behaviour was very proper, and they did not take French soldiers prisoner, just disarmed them.

Around three o'clock in the afternoon, I went to get bread in Brains as usual. That is when I truly realized the disaster that has befallen the country. Endless lines of trucks and cars with German licence plates were going down the road at high speed. The cars looked more modest and less modern than English cars; often they were only platforms with four raised seats. The officers and soldiers I saw go by seemed amazingly young. The tanned soldiers, most of them blond, freshly shaved, held themselves straight as a rod on their seats, with a military air. In the church square, I saw German soldiers climbing cement poles like monkeys attaching telephone wires at their apex. I saw others in friendly conversation with the locals. One of the Germans was having a friendly conversation with a group of refugees standing around the café; he told them in pidgin French, "Now, over," and his listeners hurriedly answered, "Yes, indeed, over! It's better like that, now we can go back to Paris."

While German troops head toward Laval, the line of refugees is now going the other direction. The tobacco shop clerk in Brains confirmed to me that the Germans bought cigarettes from him and were "very proper." He also assured me that now the Germans are going to re-establish order in the country!

It surprises and saddens me to see people fraternizing with the Germans. The refugees just see the whole thing as the end of the exodus and the opportunity to go back home; the peasants do not seem to realize that things cannot stop there. France has suffered a serious defeat. It may very well be that the majority of the people in the nation never understood why they were fighting. The Germans are steeped in a new mystique they defend with missionary zeal; the French are only defending the status quo and basically completely indifferent to the fate of Czechoslovakia, Poland, or Austria – they have no wish to die for them. The famous cry "Die for Danzig" sowed doubts in many minds.

One sees many French soldiers on the road, wandering disoriented like *Zwei Grenadiere* – two infantrymen. Baron Nolde thinks France will not succeed in reaching a separate peace and it would have been better for the government to go to Africa and continue the battle with the help of England.

Maddie triumphantly brought us a German newspaper published in Paris that she picked up on the road.

20.6.40 One often sees two or three German soldiers in a car or on motorcycles venturing down little country roads, even isolated paths. They seem unafraid of the populace.

The electricity has been cut off, the radio does not work, and reports from farmers are our only source of information.

When evening came, I saw two young French soldiers in uniform without insignia come into Alice's yard. They looked hesitant, like hunted animals. Four of them were sleeping in a barn near the château and they had lost all trace of their regiment. They had walked 200 km and had not eaten for several days. The wife of farmer

Gâteau had shown them to the barn but offered them nothing to eat. With loud shouts, Alice told them to go get their comrades immediately and come and have supper with the family. Just like in the Bible, the poor share their last food with those poorer than they are, while the rich rest easy. They were soon back with their two other comrades and did not have to be asked twice to accept Alice's invitation. During the meal, they kept repeating the same refrain; the officers left first without giving any orders. The soldiers themselves fled blindly in all directions.

The four were from the Eure[51] and had decided not to separate. They were now going to try to reach home; however, despite all the reassuring rumours circulating, they did not have much confidence in the Germans and wanted to find civilian clothing. Alice told them she was going to bury their weapons as well as their uniforms once something was found for them to wear, and I am going to search among the things left by Nancy for items to disguise them.

The routed army made an extremely sad impression on me, making me think of a building intact on the outside but mined by termites from within, crumbling to dust at the first push. The enemy only met resistance in the Vosges and near Tours. The Germans came here as tourists and found a frightened and passive population.

21.6.40 Electrical power was restored yesterday around eight o'clock in the evening, and we rushed to the radio at once to hear the Swiss and English news. We thus heard that French Parliamentarians have left by air for Compiègne. Naturally that is where talks will be held, probably in the famous railcar from the 1918 armistice.

I gave the soldiers some clothing left behind by Nancy: golf jackets, ski pants, pyjamas, and so on. They came around one o'clock in the afternoon to say goodbye to me. They had a real "carnival" look, especially the one in Nancy's cotton pyjamas. The important thing is that they aren't captured and get home to their families. They are going to mingle with the refugee groups returning to Paris. One of them gave me his parents' address and

51 A *département* in the north of France

asked me to let them know that he was safe and sound as of that date. The Germans are now said to be gathering soldiers in uniform on the roads.

Farmer Gâteau came to tell us that Germans slept at his father's; they ordered him to slaughter a calf but paid him with a coupon he is to present to the German authorities, then shared the meat with him. They refused to sleep in the house, because they have orders not to disturb the population. He also told us that German soldiers picked gooseberries in an abandoned vegetable garden and shared them with the village children. He concluded his news by saying, "Maybe all those stories of German atrocities were nothing but a bunch of nonsense after all."

Baron Nolde picked up a German newspaper on the road with a photo of a German artillery unit going up the Champs-Elysées. Who would have thought that possible two months ago!

We heard on the radio that the armistice has been signed.

We worked in the vegetable garden as usual. The traffic circle in front of the château has been transformed into a potato patch. For the past few years, the area has been infested by potato beetles and no one has been able to get rid of them. The peasants even gave up planting potatoes in the Sarthe region. Now that this food product has become so precious, it is being replanted again, and one has to battle the beetles by a totally primitive method. Every day, the Baroness and I carefully pick over the young plants, which are covered with pink larvae that grow bigger before our eyes.

22.6.40 The radio announced that the French plenipotentiaries have met with Hitler and Generals Keitel and Brauchitsch, Admiral Raeder, and von Ribbentrop. The meeting took place in the historic railcar at Compiègne, as it was easy to predict. Hitler sat in Foch's armchair.

23.6.40 Marshal Pétain announced on the radio that the conditions of the armistice were harsh but not incompatible with honour. From his point of view, Churchill said he learned with amazement that an armistice was signed in dishonour.

24.6.40 English radio announced the creation of a National French Committee in England headed by General de Gaulle. The Ambassador from England has left France.

25.6.40 Today is a day of mourning for France; flags will be at half-mast, theatres and stores closed, no music on the radio. A ceremony will be held, in honour of the dead from the first and second war, at eleven o'clock in all the cities, *communes*, and so on, and a minute of silence will be observed by the population.

Around eleven o'clock in the evening, as instructed, we went for the ceremony in front of the War Memorial in Brains, but there must have been a misunderstanding or the inhabitants of Brains set their watches by the sun, because we were the only ones there.

It is truly sad to hear the French and the English accuse each other on the radio of not doing their duty.

26.6.40 Telephones and mail are still not working. Signposts on the highway are covered with German signs.

Madame T. came back from Brains with a lot of information. The *Kommandatur* has been set up in Le Mans. German soldiers are buying everything they can by the armload, especially jewellery, watches, silk stockings, chocolate. They pay in German marks at twenty francs per mark. The grocer told her that one soldier bought two hundred francs worth of chocolate from him. All stores have been ordered to reopen. The hairdresser in Coulans sold all the contents of her shop, right to the last toothbrush. Everyone agrees that the Germans are behaving impeccably; they are friendly and helpful. They tow cars that have broken down and pick up refugees on the road in their trucks. As long as it lasts! It seems to me too good to be true! The time is now officially German summer time, two hours ahead of the sun. Alice often asks me, "What time is it in Berlin?"

From now on, gas and alcohol supplies have to be declared and only five litres of each may be kept.

29.6.40 The Soviets have "peacefully" occupied Bessarabia and Bukovina...

England has recognized General de Gaulle as the leader of all the free French. The government is going to be moved to Vichy.

Radio transmitters are prohibited in homes. Newspapers published in the free zone will not be allowed into the occupied zone. The newspaper *La Sarthe* now publishes small advertisements offering the services of people who speak German.

On the roads, lines of refugees are now heading toward Le Mans. The radio said that eight million French and a million Belgians have left their homes. Reims beat the record; when the Germans entered Reims, they found the city empty and the shops full of merchandise. They immediately distributed the contents of the shops to the refugees, at least, according to the radio – I have trouble believing it!

Madame T., who is the most curious of us all, goes out every day to the highway and then comes to tell us her observations. Today she saw a tractor that was part of a convoy of refugees, a kind of "locomobile," like the ones used to repair tarred roads that move at a snail's pace. Attached to it was a trailer full of refugees, pulling behind it a car likewise filled with refugees. If their intention was to flee the German advance, they certainly must not have gotten very far.

The mail finally came today! Although it only brought letters dated June 6 and 7, we still felt we were once again connected to the outside world. We also received two issues of the local paper, *La Sarthe*. All the news is from German sources; French news releases have been censored. The newsreels on screen at the movies show a parade of German troops along the Champs-Élysées. All private car traffic is prohibited from now on by order of the German authorities.

The Mayor showed Baron Nolde the circulars he receives signed by the Prefect and countersigned by the *Kommandatur*. The people have been ordered to turn in all the weapons in their possession.

English radio announced the arrival of French pilots in England, who came to join General de Gaulle.

30.6.40 Swiss radio describes the critical situation of communications in France; railway employees and equipment have been evacuated to Bordeaux. Many employees have returned home or taken refuge with relatives in the country and it is difficult to make them come back or even find them. In Paris, factories are closed and workers have also dispersed.

2.7.40 It is very warm. Convoys of troops and armoured units roll unceasingly toward the coast. Traffic stops at ten o'clock in the evening. It is prohibited to go out between nine in the evening and six in the morning.

4.7.40 English radio announced the seizure of French ships in Africa by the English. The French fleet offered resistance and the *Dunkerque*, the *Provence*, and the *Bretagne* were sunk. The First Lord of the Admiralty deplored those measures but recalled that Reynaud had promised to hand the French fleet over to England before the armistice was signed. Instead, France released German aviators who were French prisoners.

According to the official list, there are one million nine hundred thousand French prisoners in German hands.

5.7.40 French radio broadcasts in unoccupied territory are allowed starting today.

Baroness Nolde went to Le Mans for the first time by bicycle. She left the house at seven o'clock in the morning and got back at seven o'clock in the evening. She brought us news from the outside world, like the dove to the Ark.

There are many more Germans in Le Mans than there ever were English. The shops have been cleaned out by German soldiers who buy everything they see. The salesgirl at the *Prix Unique* told her they barely have enough merchandise in stock for a week. A large number of shops and the depots at the train station in Le Mans were pillaged by refugees when the local authorities fled. The Baroness had hoped to find her baggage and the baggage sent by the T.'s from Paris a few days before the entry of the Germans. However, she could not find it or get any information about it.

Everyone praises the politeness and helpfulness of the German authorities and soldiers. The Baroness and her companion were brought back to Les Touches by a German truck, which stopped specially to pick them up. She was disagreeably surprised by the number of young people in friendly conversation with German soldiers.

The Gruber café in Le Mans was full of German military personnel, and soldiers were sitting there the same as officers. When the English were there, the café was exclusively reserved for officers and posted a sign: "For officers only."

6.7.40 Today I heard the French news from the unoccupied zone for the first time.

Germaine, the cook, came to bring me St. Odile's prediction, which is circulating throughout the Sarthe region. Everyone is re-copying it and passing it to the neighbours. No one has ever heard of the prophecy but everyone is now applying it to current events and sees in it the certain collapse of Germany.

Irène Nolde had read the predictions of Nostradamus before the war and told me one day that he predicted the invasion of France by the Germans in approximately our era, that they would stop at Poitiers, which the demarcation line did not go beyond, but would finally be conquered and invaded in turn, and France would become a kingdom again in the end.

8.7.40 I received a card from Paris from Vladimir Hitrovo. They have been without news of their son for a month. I went at once to mail a card to my family. The postmaster, who was a defeatist, has become a pro-Gaullist and boasts aloud of listening to London radio every evening.

English radio announced that from now on the motto "Liberty, Fraternity, Equality" has been replaced by "Work, Family and Country."

French prisoners will be on loan by the German authorities to farmers who request them.

We have been given our bread cards, but the baker continues to sell us bread without coupons.

The rules in prison camps have become stricter. Only families who have received a special card sent by the prisoners are entitled to visit them in the camp. Visits are once a month, in alphabetical order.

14.7.40 This morning two German soldiers came to the château and warned us of the arrival of a detachment under the command of an officer. In the evening they came back with a billet order. One of them was a non-commissioned officer, who assured us that *sie werden sich anständig benehmen* – the men would behave properly.

15.7.40 We did not lock the door and, around five o'clock in the morning, we were awoken by the noise of boots in the house. So the Baroness and I went down to show the soldiers the rooms reserved for them. They greeted us very politely. One of them was from Riga and, when he heard us speak Russian, immediately

German soldiers drill,
Château des Touches, 1940

spoke to us in that language. They were all in a good mood and announced to us that they are now going to conquer England. Despite the German–Russian Alliance, they are all of anti-Communist sentiments and assured us that Communism would be obliterated, one way or another.

By eleven o'clock our yard had become a real military camp; all you could see were trucks, mobile kitchens, horses, and so on. The soldiers then announced the arrival of their leader, a very distinguished gentleman – *sehr vonehmer Herr* – by the name of von der Dammerau, if I am not mistaken. They had prepared his room for him with the greatest care. Von der Dammerau introduced himself to us as soon as he arrived, a likable Prussian type, well-bred, but stiff as all Prussians are.

Later we met him again in the vestibule and he immediately started to indoctrinate us: "Hitler has built a great nation, attuned the so greatly opposed interests of workers and management, raised the standard of living of the peasants – the State has eliminated the interest on bank debts owed by peasants. The French mock the heel clicking 'Attention!' and goose-stepping of German soldiers, but that external discipline is matched by an inner discipline. German troops passed through French territory and did not pillage. On the other hand, Vitry-le-François, where the inhabitants shot at the Germans with dum-dum bullets, was completely razed to the ground. German soldiers set animals free in meadows that farmers had left tied up in stables." He even cited a case where "a horse had been bricked in alive. Wherever they went, German soldiers shared their meals with French women and children, by order of the Führer." Von der Dammerau even cited the case of a soldier who threw himself under a truck that was still moving to save a child. Seeing that, the farmwife where he was billeted started to cry and said she could see that the Germans were not the barbarians described to her. He even added that his soldiers would rather incur a punishment than exterminate the stray dogs that came around to German canteens to sit up and beg for a scrap of bread. When I asked him how men who refused to kill animals could kill human beings, he answered that was very different; dogs could not defend themselves. But war could be compared to hunting and all hunting is exciting and should be considered an honourable sport.

He even added that the German press never published articles as disrespectful about the King of England or Lebrun as the articles that were published daily about the Führer in French newspapers. The occupation troops will not make French officers get off the sidewalk or auction off their furniture as happened in Germany under the French occupation in 1918. The time has come for England to be demoted to the second rank of nations; since the Battle of Hastings, no one has ever bothered it and it ended up believing it was invincible. As to Hitler's personality, his worst enemies succumb to his charm after speaking to him.

Listening to von der Dammerau, one might think he was a missionary preaching the Gospel – the same faith and the same fire!

All afternoon a perfect idyll reigned between occupants and occupied. In the yard, soldiers offered Alice some of their soup; others were playing with her grand-nieces. In the kitchen, a soldier ground coffee for the cook, who had previously threatened to quit if she were ever forced to cook for the Germans. And here she was making them omelettes with ten eggs per person and offering them soup "to show the ignorant what good French cuisine is."

I am sure that the English and the Americans do not imagine scenes like that could take place so soon after the country's defeat. Yet I saw what I am describing with my own eyes.

The soldiers paid Alice in French currency for everything they took, except fodder. She was so satisfied with that she renounced going to Le Mans to claim compensation for the fodder.

16.7.40   The German soldiers left this morning around four o'clock. The evening before, von der Dammerau, another officer, and the doctor of the detachment came to take leave of us. The doctor is an educated man, who spoke of architecture and art; the Noldes preferred him to the Wagnerian warrior personified by von der Dammerau.

After their departure, we went to check the bedrooms and rooms that had been occupied by the troops. They had built wooden bunk beds and filled canvas sacks with straw they brought with them, which they used for mattresses. We found everything in perfect order – not a trace of their passage, not a blade of straw on the floor. Everything was as clean and neat as the night before they came.

The inhabitants of Brains are not complaining about their enemies' stay. "They paid for everything" – that seems to be sufficient reason for declaring themselves satisfied. Alas! France has been sorely tried, but has she recovered? I thought the debacle would perhaps be the source of a rebirth of morale. I do not see it around me. Farmers are not interested in the peace terms; they imagine that everything has been said now and they are going to be able to go back to their usual way of life. What bothers them is not the fact that the presence of the Germans is living testimony of defeat but all the little annoyances as a result of the occupation. Madame D. told me: "Parisians are poorly provisioned, and eating is what is most important, isn't it?" I compare those words with von der Dammerau's response when the Baroness complained about not having any coffee: "We have not had coffee since the war started. We live very well without coffee and, in general, all that should not be given too much importance."

17.7.40   To my great surprise, I received an issue of the *New York Times* dated June 30.

Madame T. and I had to go to Le Mans to do the week's shopping. The bus that serves Le Mans was full to bursting and did not stop. We nevertheless decided to start out on foot in the hope that someone would take pity on us and pick us up en route. In fact, we had not gone a hundred steps when a German car with an officer and soldier-driver stopped and the officer asked us if we wanted a ride. On the way, he asked us in German if we were French. Finding out that we were Russian, he hastened to tell us that the German–Russian alliance was purely military and the Germans had no contact, so to speak, with the Soviets. When Madame T. told him that the alliance had really astonished her, he swiftly responded "We were even more astonished than you were!"

I had not been to Le Mans since June 11, and it made a sad impression on me; it really looks "occupied." Echelons of German soldiers march through the streets singing. The shops have almost no merchandise anymore, especially the perfume shops. All soap has disappeared. A lot of signs in German can be seen. At Gruber café, hot drinks and meals are no longer served from two-thirty to six-thirty in the afternoon. We had a sandwich and fruit juice for lunch. The German soldiers who came in and went out saluted the officers by clicking their heels.

We were still able to find tea in a grocery store but could only get a quarter pound of coffee per person with a coupon from the sugar card, and only because the grocery store knows us and we are its best customers, or were in the past.

Then we went to the Melnikoffs'; those good Samaritans are already taking care of Russian prisoners, visiting them at the camp in Auvers and bringing them packages. There are thirty thousand prisoners in the camp. Visits are limited to ten minutes and all packages are opened by the German authorities. The Melnikoffs got the names of Russian prisoners, Russian émigrés, from a certain K., who was acting as an interpreter because he knew German well. On learning that K. was a Russian émigré, the commandant of the camp took advantage of the fact that official prisoners' lists had not yet been drawn up and had him given civilian clothes and let him leave the camp. K. told the Melnikoffs that, when his detachment was taken prisoner, they had not eaten for five days, because the canteens had disappeared first. Inhabitants of the villages they passed through on foot threw them bread and they fought among themselves for a piece.

The first team of French prisoners authorized to work on farms has arrived in Brains. There are twenty or so under the orders of a higher-ranking officer. Each has to answer for the others; the Mayor and farmers who employ them are also answerable to the German authorities.

20.7.40 Received a letter from Paris from the Hitrovos, describing the final days in Paris before the arrival of the Germans. A thick cloud of smoke had descended on the city and surrounding area. The grass and the leaves on the trees in their garden, where they live in the outskirts, are still black with smoke. Explosions could be heard from all sides – gas tanks and factories being blown up. Bellevue was truly deserted; only animals abandoned by their owners wandered the streets. The Hitrovos temporarily adopted a parrot that came and perched on a tree in their garden. All the empty houses have been occupied by the Germans.

21.7.40 All private safe deposit boxes in banks are going to be opened by the German authorities.

The Baltic States have been officially incorporated in Russia, which was done with all the desirable legal formality...

Groups of German soldiers take turns visiting the capital, by order of the Führer. They are driven around Paris in trucks with stops at historic sites; the tour ends with a music hall show.

24.7.40 The château of Les Touches is going to be "occupied" again; soldiers came to present an order to billet fifty-four men, a non-commissioned officer, and an officer. We are entitled to keep three bedrooms and the ground-floor dining room. There will also be one hundred and eighty soldiers billeted in Brains and four hundred in Coulans. The Mayor hurriedly ordered an exceptional distribution of coal, 300 kg per family instead of the regular 75 kg, to avoid potential requisitions. Farmers are also picking all their vegetables and fruit.

Big guns go by every day toward the coast.

28.7.40 We listened to a speech by the English Minister of Supply. He was speaking to English housewives. He recommended that they set aside old metal cans and pieces of scrap metal and repeat every day the litany: "May the Nazis and the order they want to establish be swept from the earth." He closed with this injunction: "Up, housewives, and at them."

The BBC announcer now leaves out the "*Herr*" when he talks about Hitler and the "*Signor*" when he talks about Mussolini.

31.7.40 Went to Le Mans "on the backs of the Germans" as Baron Nolde says in Russian; a German car picked us up en route. Many French soldiers are on the road with backpacks, alone or in groups, not looking military at all anymore but fairly sloppy. Le Mans is even more deserted than the last time. I went to the railway station to distribute things left by Nancy at a refugee centre that was pointed out to me. The employees directed me to the French Red Cross barracks and recommended, in particular, that I not stop at the German barracks I would find on the way. The German barracks had a large notice in German and French, "Refugee Supply Centre," and below that, in large letters, "National Socialist Assistance." The French Red Cross barracks was in a second courtyard and, to be totally impartial, I have to say that the first was much cleaner, better kept, and more welcoming than the second. The German nurses were wearing snow-white caps and aprons, and there were flowers on all the tables. The French nurse told me that the Germans hindered their project, deliberately offering unfair competition. Certainly, there is an element of propaganda in the German assistance.

All mail between the two zones has been suspended until further orders.

Many not-very-fierce-looking young people were accompanied by Germany soldiers.

A German truck picked us up on the road on our return. The soldiers told us that they arrived in France from Holland and Belgium without ever firing a shot. The bridges had been destroyed in their path but they rebuilt them all and went over them a few hours later without any problem. As usual, they added that the day is not far off when German soldiers will stand on English soil.

Received a *New York Times* with a caricature of Marshal Pétain and a poem about Frenchwomen's knitting needles clicking and covering the sound of machinery secretly producing guns and machine guns to fight Germany. That is not exactly what I saw in Le Mans.

3.8.40 The Baron and Baroness went to Le Mans by bicycle to try to find their trunks. They found their clock and a pair of the Baron's shoes in the office of the station chief and had a fair bit of trouble getting them back. In a neighbouring barracks, employees were in the process of selling piles of clothing and various items to the highest bidder – probably the contents of the other trunks.

4.8.40 Madame Poupard, the former farmwife at Les Touches, came to the château this afternoon. She is a big, strong woman about sixty years old and very talkative. She does not understand how, in this day and age, people can kill one another and adds, "If that is progress, then we are too far advanced."

5.8.40 Soap and pasta have been put on the list of rationed products – 125 g of Marseille soap, 250 g of pasta, 100 g of rice per month per person.

Baroness Nolde and I went by bicycle to Loué to find tubs of butter, which already cannot be found in Brains. We rode 30 km and came back loaded with small and large tubs tied to the handlebars of our bicycles and carriers. With her usual energy, the Baroness even tied one on her back.

The July 1 *Times* gave the reasons for the debacle in France: the revolutionary spirit of the people obliged Marshal Pétain to ask for an armistice; disorganization in the army; offices and factories where the leaders were the first to leave. The article ended with the words, "Nobody wins in an earthquake and, in economic value, nobody wins a war."

11.8.40 The newspapers remind people that it is strictly forbidden to listen to English radio.

L. asked for permission to publish a newspaper in Russian. He was told that the newspaper would have to follow an anti-Jewish policy and would be monitored and subsidized by the Germans. L. did not accept the conditions.

14.8.40 Two German *Quartiermeister* came to check the accommodations reserved for the troops arriving Thursday. The two soldiers are living in an empty house in Brains; they have drawn a heart with chalk on the door. Our cook told us that one of them has a girlfriend in Coulans and regularly sleeps at her place, and that many young girls in Loué "have been with" Germans.

15.8.40 The soldiers in the first detachment intended for the château arrived yesterday. They had barely got rid of their packs before they put on shorts and went to wash at Alice's pump. They stayed dressed like that until evening except, of course, for the sentinel who went around in uniform, his helmet on his head and rifle in hand.

German soldiers waiting for their clothes to dry,
Château des Touches, 1940

16.8.40 The soldiers spent the whole day washing and doing laundry; they even washed their uniforms, which they stretched out on planks and scrubbed with brushes and soap. They have already drawn all the water from Alice's pump and are now coming to get water from ours. They go for meals to the canteen set up in the girls' school in Brains and brush their teeth vigorously at our pump after every meal. Some of the soldiers sleep on straw in the *salon*, the others on wooden bunk beds on the ground floor in what are called the refugees' rooms. Their leader is a very young lieutenant who arrived near evening and immediately introduced himself to Baron Nolde.

Alice the farm wife,
her children and a German soldier,
Château des Touches, 1940

German sentry,
Château des Touches, 1940

In the evening, the soldiers played football in the park. They changed clothes again, putting on black shorts, bright blue and white gym jerseys, and slippers.

In Brains, I was going by a house occupied by the Germans when it was time for the change of guard. The two sentinels stand at attention facing one another then goose-step away; they look like wooden soldiers, one might say, in a production by Balieff.[52]

We went to the town hall for another census of foreigners. Regimes change, but for us it is always the same thing – they are never finished counting us.

17.8.40 The soldiers did laundry all day then carried tables and chairs from the house onto the terrace and began to write letters. In the evening, they played ball. Their sportswear was different again. Their habits of cleanliness amaze and annoy the inhabitants of Brains, who keep saying over and over, "When will they be finished washing themselves?"

52 Translator's note: A Russian–Armenian director in the 1920s and '30s

German soldiers doing laundry,
Château des Touches, 1940

19.8.40 Took a refugee train to Paris and was graciously offered sandwiches and milk at the stations by French Red Cross workers. The train was half empty. There were no porters at the station, but demobilized French soldiers offered to carry your luggage home for you.

22.8.40 Occupied Paris is extremely sad, a dead city, one might say. Only the hammering of the cast-iron soles of German boots and German cars roaring by at crazy speeds resonate in the empty streets. Most of the houses have their shutters closed. All the administration offices, ministries, and so on and the big hotels have been occupied by the Germans, as have the private mansions belonging to Jewish families.

German soldiers buy everything they can still find in the shops and markets. Besides the two marks they are each given a day, they are given an additional five hundred francs when they come to Paris, which they must spend and account for to the officer in charge.

Silk stocking shops are completely empty. There is no longer a single pair of silk stockings throughout the city, except a few pairs of black stockings at fifty francs a pair. Apparently they are not in style in Germany. There is no longer any coffee, soap, or cleaning products, and there are line-ups in front of all the food stores. Apparently 60% of leather has been requisitioned.

German posters are stuck on walls. One shows a young German soldier smiling, holding a French child in his arms. He is surrounded by three or four other small children. Below is the legend, "Abandoned people trust the German soldier." Another shows women and children fleeing cities in ruins; the legend says, "All the fault of English soldiers." Often, however, an anonymous hand has erased the last words and replaced them with "Hitler."

People in contact with the Germans tell me they always ask the same questions: "Why do people flee at our approach?" and "Why do Frenchwomen wear so much lipstick?" Barbos thinks the Germans will end up occupying the whole territory and our generation will live to see them still in Paris. Rumours are circulating that Brittany is going to proclaim its independence – this reminds me of the German policy in the Ukraine at the end of the last war – and connect northern France with Belgium and Holland.

24.8.40 There have been a few attacks on Germans. The sentinel on guard in front of the plaza was injured by a bullet fired from a car that fled. Since then, Avenue Montaigne has been blocked at both ends, and French officers guard the entrance to the barricades. Three German soldiers were also killed in the Bois de Boulogne, which has been closed to the public for two weeks.

Had tea at the Noldes' with Mademoiselle R. and Sofka Polotzoff, who recounted how they were walking one evening on the beach in Biarritz and, by chance, came upon a bench where a German soldier was sitting in the semi-darkness. He immediately stood up and timidly and very politely asked them, "Madame, go to bed?" However, he did not insist.

Mademoiselle R. told me that Russian émigrés are having a great deal of difficulty finding work. The few French companies that have not yet been requisitioned by the Germans naturally prefer to employ French people. That only leaves installations that are German or have been requisitioned by the Germans where a foreigner can hope to find work. That could have unpleasant consequences for the foreigner when hostilities end, even though, in fact, everyone is working directly or indirectly for the occupying forces.

27.8.40 Maddie, the Zweguintzoffs' former maid, has moved into the apartment that is currently occupied by Serge and his family.[53] They think she is working for the Germans because she often brings them products that can no longer be found. Bicha is also working for the occupying forces as a chambermaid – *Zimmermädchen* – in a private mansion; the Jewish owner has fled. The building is currently occupied by *Hitlerjugend*, youth about seventeen years old under the command of an officer. The youth are sleeping in Madame's pink muslin sheets.

28.8.40 I did not find work in Paris and returned to Les Touches: not a solution, just an interlude. The Noldes go back to Paris when it gets cold, and the T.'s will leave with them. If I have to end up working in a German installation, which seems to me to be the only possible solution, I still would not want to do political work. On the other hand, I would not like to be a *Zimmermädchen* either...

29.8.40 Fall is swiftly approaching; in the morning, the park is enveloped in thick fog that only dissipates at around nine-thirty, which is seven-thirty in the morning. I would have liked to stop the march of time...

In a letter, Mia G., whom I sent the children's dresses Nancy left, writes that her husband is working as a driver for the Germans, who treat him with great kindness.

30.8.40 The dentist at Le Mans talked to me at length about the strength of the English who will soon come and chase the Germans out of France. Naturally, a Frenchman wants to see his country liberated, but why always count on help from others? I never hear anyone say, "We'll regroup in Africa or somewhere else and chase the occupying forces out of France for good."

In the evening, the non-commissioned officer described to me his comfortable life in Germany, and his surprise at seeing the lack of comfort on farms in France – dirt floors, brick floor tiles, lack of running water, and lack of water in general. "Our wives would never want any part of these interiors," he said.

53 Likely Serge Zweguintzoff

31.8.40 Our occupiers leave the house around five-thirty in the morning and only come back in the evening; they are often gone all night. They tell me they would like to leave here sooner; the local inhabitants avoid them. In Paris, it was different; Parisians immediately started to do business with them. German sentinels are now stationed at intersections, because there have been several attacks. The honeymoon between occupied and occupier seems to be drawing to a close.

I.I.T. thinks that if Germany has not attacked England yet, as it boasted it would do, that means it has given up doing so, and that decision foreshadows the defeat of Germany.

French prisoner camps are going to be closed and the prisoners sent to Germany.

3.9.40 The anniversary of the declaration of war. There was no demonstration by either side.

4.9.40 The radio broadcast a speech by Hitler about *Winterhilfe* – winter relief. The soldiers came to the dining room window, which is on the ground floor, and asked us to let them listen to the speech. They all listened with passionate attention to the Führer's harsh voice, accompanying him with shouts of approval, outbursts of laughter, and so on.

5.9.40 Farmer C. came with loud shouts to reclaim his wheelbarrow, which the soldiers had taken. The sergeant – *Feldwebel* – calmed him down with friendly little pats on the back, calling him *Mein guter Mann*, "my good man," and had the wheelbarrow given back to him.

6.9.40 Charles of Romania has abdicated in favour of his son.

The young lieutenant who commands the detachment came back from leave in Germany and asked to speak to Baron Nolde. He told him that he got engaged while he was in Germany. Today is his birthday, a very important event for Germans. His family and his fiancée were very sad to think he would spend the day all alone in his room. He came to ask the Baron a favour – to invite him to his table that evening. The Baron was a little taken aback; the idea did not appeal to him at all, yet he did not really know how to refuse. I must say, the lieutenant looks more like a big baby than a grown man – blond, pink, with down on his cheeks. The soldiers appear to like him. One of his men is a gardener in civilian life; he does not look the least bit military. His helmet comes down over his ears, and he holds his rifle the way he would hold a shovel. He came to ask our permission to pick a few flowers in the garden to give to the lieutenant, which apparently is the custom. While he was arranging them, he kept on saying, "How beautiful flowers are. How I would like to do nothing but this." In the end, the lieutenant dined at our table, and the Baron sent the Baroness to explain to the cook that he could not refuse the occupier's request, and so on. At the table, the lieutenant indoctrinated us on Hitler, Nazism, and so on. "The Führer is never hasty; he will strike when he thinks the time is right."

The Baron then said, "That is no longer discipline but mysticism!"

There is no longer any water in the pumps; the soldiers have completely drained them. Now they have to take pitchers and fetch water from the pond at the bottom of the hill. Tomorrow they have to pass inspection and went to Brains today for a full rehearsal. Alice admits, "As far as cleanliness goes, they are clean and much better dressed than our men."

11.9.40 The troop of occupiers left at four o'clock this morning. The lieutenant came to take leave of us the night before. The soldiers also came one after another to say farewell. The Baroness complimented them on their exemplary behaviour during their stay at Les Touches and one of them said, "Everywhere we have been, we have always been told we behaved well. That is because we are Saxons. If we are replaced by Saxons, you will see; they will behave themselves just as we have."

The checkers game we lent to them was returned to us with this message written on the back: "*Fremdes Eigentum, sauber halten*" – Foreign property, please keep it clean.

All that seems most idyllic and proves nothing, except that all war is a crime. Certainly, this German detachment was neither barbarian nor belligerent; however, tomorrow in battle, the same soldiers will kill human beings, as peaceful as they are.

12.9.40 The peasants in Brains seem to miss their occupiers. I heard two women talking, saying to one another, "They have left?" "Yes, we would have kept them, they were so nice."

Friendly relations were mainly dictated by commercial interest; the Germans paid for everything they took and gave big tips. I saw two soldiers slip a bank note into the hand of a peasant woman and say, "From Monsieur, our leader."

I read with care the German newspapers left by the soldiers. Among other things, they published the addresses of National Socialist centres, one in every village, where housewives can get referrals and advice on how to make clothing last longer. Women should watch how they sit so as not to wrinkle their dresses. Men should avoid wearing suit jackets during the summer so that, in the fall, with a new pair of pants, they practically have a new suit. All good mental discipline as well! And on how to make shelters *gemütlich* – more homelike. And the addresses of laundries specially reserved for soldiers, where they can not only have their clothes washed but also mended.

16.9.40 Today I sent suitcases and crates of my things to Paris by messenger service, including provisions such as salt, sugar, soap, matches, and so on – products worth their weight in gold these days.

Alice's brother works in an aircraft plant in Saint-Nazaire. He says that the English are bombing the city day and night without destroying any military targets up to now. That information contradicts London radio, so he adds, "I see the English tell the same tall tales our heads have been stuffed with." The remark illustrates people's state of mind pretty well; they no longer believe anything because they remember the pompous speeches and optimistic articles from the recent days of the war.

Mr. Melnikoff, a Russian who now lives in Le Mans, came to see me. He told me that "go-getters" are getting empty trucks from the Germans and taking eggs, butter, and so on as far as Paris and bringing products, such as hosiery, back to the Germans from the capital. Butter and a number of other commodities have disappeared from the market in Le Mans. However, one does not hear many complaints yet, because the inhabitants have stocked up – a neighbour admitted having 200 kg of sugar in reserve. Mr. Melnikoff told me that everyone in Le Mans listens to London radio and hopes the English will come soon to liberate them. Mr. Melnikoff is religious, a real believer, and is convinced that the Germans will perish because of their pagan mentality, "because God has always punished nations that turn away from him and worship idols." The unlimited confidence Germans place in Hitler eventually has to make individuals irresponsible. The current German regime is based exclusively on Hitler's personality and cannot exist under other conditions.

I went with Mr. Melnikoff back to the little train that has just started serving Le Mans and Brains again. I thought it was like looking at a nineteenth-century engraving of "the first train between Paris and Saint-Germain." The engine surely dated from that era. It was like a toy train that stopped in the middle of the fields to pick up farmers and farmwives with their baskets of provisions on their arms – chickens and rabbits. A young man waiting for the train explained to me that he gathers poultry and dairy products in the country and sends them to his wife in Paris. It is exactly like the peddlers with packs – мешочники – in the early days of the Russian revolution. The man obligingly gave me his address in Paris and offered to supply me with all the scarce commodities I need.

26.9.40 We went with the Baron back to the bus that serves Le Mans. The local teacher, L., was waiting with us and shared his observations. He listens to London radio despite the "small waterfall" that attempts to jam reception, but not enough that you cannot listen to the news. There is still one free station anyway, the one the Germans listen to; you just have to find it on the radio dial. The teacher told us that the farmers are upset by the numerous orders and simply refuse to sell their products to avoid doing business with the authorities. How can anyone ever control butter on farms? At the last market in Loué, the Germans requisitioned 800 kg of butter. Cleaning out markets and shops is done so quietly that most French people only notice too late and then are surprised there is nothing left to buy.

The behaviour of the troops stationed at Loué was very "correct" – you hear that said ten times a day. He cites the case of old lady Chaplain who had to put two soldiers up in her home. They always went looking for her glasses when they wanted to show her a word in their French–German dictionary. The night before their departure, they brought her a pound of coffee and gave her a huge bouquet of flowers. When she asked them where they were going, they answered, "Tommies," and added a few onomatopoeic utterances, like "boom" and "pow," showed her their wedding rings, and made her understand that their wives were going to weep for them. "You would have thought it was the song about Marlborough, *Malbrouck s'en va-t-en guerre*," the teacher said in closing.

New food rations: 350 g of bread per day, 90 g of meat per day that the butcher shops are open – they are open four days a week, 50 g of cheese per week, a minimal amount as yet undetermined of fat, 125 g of soap per month.

27.9.40 We listened to the radio broadcast when the Tripartite Pact was signed by Germany, Italy, and Japan. It was the first time I had heard Japanese spoken and had not imagined it was so musical and sounded so Latin.

The current conflict is primarily a political conflict; a right-wing Frenchman sees it differently than his left-wing compatriot.

28.9.40 I am back in Paris for good. Getting off the train, I really had a fright. I was carrying stoneware pots of melted butter in my suitcases, each one weighing 6 kg to 18 kg. Since butter is rationed, it is prohibited to transport it from one *département* to another. If you are caught, it is confiscated and you have to pay a large fine. I decided to run the risk anyway and adopted my most innocent look to get past the city employee. Unfortunately he grabbed one of my suitcases as I went by; finding it too heavy, he asked me to follow him and open all my suitcases. I was so upset; I could not find the key to the suitcases on my key ring. Finally, I opened one and, seeing the books that were right on top, the employee believed, or chose to believe, they were the reason for the weight of the suitcase, told me to close it, and added, "That's okay,

I trust you!" His trust troubled my conscience for a few seconds, but I would have been even more troubled if I had lost the fruit of so much labour, not to mention the expense! After that, a human taxi carried the suitcases to Cité Martignac.

29.9.40 Had tea at the Let.'s. Two right-wing French officers were there. Their party fears a crushing victory by England because it would restart the pre-war situation and return to power all those who thrust France into its current chaos. That does not mean they want to see Germany victorious, dictating terms to France. They would like to see a peaceful agreement with Germany and new leaders at the head of the French government, who would not repeat the errors of the past. Unfortunately, a program tempered by times of crisis has never been a solution.

Restaurants still serve sugar with your coffee, dessert without coupons, as well as pasta, poultry, and cheese.

20.11.40 I am back to my notebooks after a long silence... for good reason. I finally found a non-political job in a German establishment working for a German dentist, despite my total lack of experience in the subject. The dentist is located in three rooms in the Rothschild mansion in La Muette, the *Palais* Rothschild as the Germans call it! The building has been emptied of furniture; I have no idea where it went. One of the dentist's offices still has traces of its original use as a bedroom for two children. The building is occupied for the time being by a German naval reserve detachment. An armed sentinel guards the entrance and only lets people enter with a pass, an *Ausweis*, issued by the personnel office of the establishment where they work. Instruments and equipment of all kinds have been purchased from French firms, including Paz and Sylva, where the dentist saw pocket flashlights with a Maginot Line insignia bearing the proud motto, "They shall not pass." He commented to the sellers that it was about time to put all that away in the attic.[54]

54 The Maginot Line, named after the French minister of war André Maginot, was a line of fortifications between Germany and France that was built after World War I to prevent Germany from invading. The Maginot was neutralized in 1940 when 1500 German tanks raced around the line in the Ardennes.

Rothschild Hotel, Paris, 1940

There are three dentists and two German nurses, who wear striped cotton dresses, aprons, and a white cap with the Red Cross insignia. Up to now, no one has worked because the dentists' office, the *Zahnstation*, is not yet in operation. A Dr. Schier, the head doctor at the German hospital set up in the *Lycée Molitor*, came by lately to talk politics with one of the dentists. He said that in three years we would see an alliance between England and Germany because there are many more common traits and interests between those two countries than between England and France; it is also not in Germany's interest to destroy as large a white racial group as there is in England.

The Germans are now publishing an illustrated magazine, which they call in French *Le Signal*. The colour photos are very beautiful; however, the French text is perfectly ridiculous, translated word-for-word from German, for example, using "big brutes" to mean guns, and so on. The propaganda in the articles is direct and primitive. However, the dentist, Dr. Schark, assures me that the French are not so different from the Germans, and the slogans served up to them daily on posters, radio, and so on will end up influencing them, thus achieving their goal.

Met B., a friend of my brother's, in rue du Val; he accompanied me part of the way home and gave me lots of advice: "Be careful what you say, even outside work and especially in anti-German settings." Working for the Germans is tiring; they demand a big effort from employees but treat them humanely.

25.11.40 I have been staying, temporarily alas, in Nancy and Sasha Zweguintzoff's apartment, which they offered me when they left because their rent is paid until January 15, 1941. It is bitterly cold, a humid cold, in the apartment. The building has not been heated for two years now. The sole source of heat is a small gas radiator in the huge *salon* and, at night, I turn on a little electric sun heater in my bedroom. In the morning, I have to thaw my bath towels in front of the heater and, at night, if I move my head to another spot, I wake up immediately because the pillow is icy. I only take off my fur jacket when I go to bed.

The issue of food supplies is also becoming increasingly difficult. Employees working at the Rothschild building have organized a canteen at ten francs a day per person. Today we had a very thin soup, potato purée in water, and an apple for fruit – not very nourishing, especially for men who do heavy work.

1.12.40 Went to the opera. The performance begins at six o'clock now because of the curfew. All the front rows were occupied by German soldiers. The production was *Fidelio* with Germaine Lubin; the Germans liked it very much.[55] Very few stage and opera stars have stayed in the occupied zone.

3.12.40 I do not know if it is a result of the cold, scarce food supplies, or fatigue, but I constantly have to go back to the *Zahnstation* because I remember I have forgotten something there. The employee who does the cleaning says to me each time, to console me, "Fortunately you have something more important and interesting than the *Zahnstation* to occupy your thoughts." It is true that I have to be there at eight o'clock in the morning, German time, which is six o'clock. I leave home by moonlight, a lovely but fairly unaccustomed sight.

---

55 *Fidelio* is a German opera by Beethoven.

Work is slowly getting organized at the *Zahnstation*. There is now a secretary, a German woman of Polish origin, a fine young woman who is the head doctor's scapegoat, perhaps just because she is Polish. Clients are soldiers or officers of the German Navy, office employees, and so on. When they come in, the sailors come to attention, click their heels, and say *"Heil* Hitler," which is now the official greeting in Germany, and the doctors and employees of the *Zahnstation* respond the same way. Personally, I always say *"Guten Morgen"* and *"Aufwiedersehen."* Anyway, the dentist told me I should use the greeting I am used to, but I have observed that many non-German employees try to be more royalist than the king and greet the Germans with *"Heil* Hitler" and a raised arm.

Yesterday I saw a Gaullist notice posted on the wall of a house on rue Saint-Augustin, a small square of paper with a typewritten invitation to people to stay home on New Year's Day, "thus leaving the occupier free to parade through deserted streets." The notice was only taken down the next day.

10.12.40 Butcher shops now close at eleven o'clock in the morning, because of the scarcity of meat. Serge Hitrovo, who "stands in line," repeats the housewives' conversations to me: "We beat them in 1914 and didn't rule them, why do they want to rule us now?" Everyone was grumbling, reproaching the Germans for taking everything. Then a man standing in line shouted, "Oh! That's it! Were we beaten or not?"

12.12.40 German troops stationed in France are subject to strict discipline; circulars have been distributed to them with instructions on French–German relations. They are not allowed to be seen in public places with Frenchwomen. In spite of that, on Sunday evenings, the streets are full of French–German couples. Quite a number of people openly criticize the conduct of those women and look forward to when they will be called to account.

15.12.40 A model post card has just been introduced for correspondence between the two zones in France. The text is printed, and you just draw a line through sentences that do not apply. For example, you choose between "I'm fine" and "I'm not well."

You are not allowed to add anything whatsoever to the text, as I found out from experience by adding, in all innocence, the word "very" to "affectionate thoughts," which is all the text allows. The card was sent back to me marked, "writing between the lines is not allowed."

It is only two degrees in my bedroom. My stepfather, Fyodor Oom, is freezing on the ground floor, too, but does not want to leave the small apartment where he lived with our mother. He plans to purchase a sawdust stove, a Russian engineer's invention – a stove that burns continuously, only has to be reloaded once a day, and does not produce ashes. The disadvantage is that one must have a basement to be able to keep a stock of sawdust.

21.12.40 All English nationals have been arrested and sent to a camp – in retaliation, they say, for the internment of Germans in England. I ran to Ruth Ogareff's and found out from the concierge that they had come to take her at nine o'clock in the morning. Her neighbours telephoned her husband, who was at work, and he just had time to join her at the police station to say goodbye. He still does not know where she has been taken. I met him leaving the concierge's and he looked like he had aged ten years.

22.12.40 The return of the ashes of the Eaglet has left people in Paris completely indifferent, especially since what was supposed to be an official ceremony and pledge of friendship by the Germany government coincided with the Laval incident, which was hushed by the press and no one really understood.

23.12.40 Ration cards for shoes are going to be introduced starting January 1, so there are endless line-ups in front of stores that sell them.

At Frank's on rue de Passy, the salesgirls all wear velvet gloves supplied, I think, by management; their hands are covered with chilblains because stores are not heated.

Admiral Dönitz came to the *Zahnstation* recently, accompanied by his German shepherd dog, which he at least left in the waiting room. The man is rather short in stature, although well proportioned, and holds himself very erect in an impeccable uniform. It looks as though he is very popular because the soldiers all gathered around when he went by and greeted him joyously.[56]

Another client, Admiral Ciliax, looks very masculine and military. All the officers are very polite, however, and always ask to be introduced, never failing to say a few friendly words.

I recently had the opportunity for a conversation with a Captain Müller, who was in Russia for several years as an engineer. He directed the work at Donbass. Apparently, the Soviets had invited a number of German engineers to come and work for them at that time. Müller lived in the boondocks, as they say, far from any city, and learned to speak Russian without a trace of accent, which amazed me. He told me that people in some parts of the country remain highly uneducated; however, the Soviet government has made enormous effort and progress in the industrial area and, if Russia ever goes to war, it will be a force to reckon with for any enemy. One of the dentists, Dr. Lutowski, whom I suspect is part of an unofficial political force (spy organization), has a completely different opinion, of course; he is sure that Russia is so disorganized it is unable to win a war. Müller answered with great calm and certainty, "God grant that there is never any war between our country and Russia. What I am telling you is based on my personal experience, not propaganda literature."

He also told us how, while he was living in Japan, far from any civilized centre, he was afflicted with a terrible toothache. He was taken to a small Japanese man who had absolutely primitive tools – a foot-operated traction device, and so on. There, in that Japanese backwater, the native dentist treated his tooth perfectly, putting in a filling admired by all the German dentists he has seen since.

A captain whose name I no longer remember also explained National Socialist theory to me at length as it applies to the work unit, which is to replace the monetary unit in the near future. He told me, "The gold standard is no longer of any importance.

56 Admiral Karl Dönitz was the Commander-in-Chief of the German U-boat fleet. After Hitler's death in 1945, Dönitz was, for 20 days, the last German head of state. Dönitz was sentenced at Nuremberg and spent over a decade in Berlin's Spandau prison.

Before the war, Germany had no gold reserves, and its mark has dropped less than the franc and the pound."

I admit that all these conversations and contacts with an unknown element interest me, even though I do not share their political, religious, and other opinions. Interactions with the Germans I have met up to now are straightforward, natural, and require no effort on my part, perhaps because of my familiarity with the Baltic element in Russia.

25.12.40 A Christmas not like Christmas...

31.12.40 Or rather January 1, 1941, because I am writing these lines after bringing in the New Year. We agreed to celebrate before midnight because of the curfew. I was with my brother Barbos and his wife Bicha. We drank to the health of those absent, Michel, our sisters...

1941

OCCUPATION

"Personally, I do not believe for a minute that any nation wants to sacrifice soldiers and money if it does not think it is going to make an attractive profit for itself."

15.1.41 I have left the Zweguintzoffs' former apartment and rented a room from friends, and have my evening meal with them. It is no warmer here than in the Zweguintzoffs' former apartment. The apartment is half heated, which means there is a small Godin wood stove in the bathroom heated with logs that a devoted friend manages to find in Neuilly and drag from there on foot in a shopping bag. By leaving all the doors in the apartment open, a bit of warmth filters into the other rooms; however, we have to keep all the furniture away from the walls because they drip. We only take off our coats to go to bed; there is no question of taking off our fur vests, even indoors.

Laval is now in the occupied zone.[57] We, the general public that is, never knew what happened between him and Marshal Pétain; however, everyone was very surprised to see him sitting between Langeron and Brinon at a symphony concert by the Berlin orchestra.

20.1.41 Yesterday Dr. Vogel, one of the three dentists, showed me the railway travel card he was filling out and under the heading "religion" he put *"gottgläubig"* – meaning he admits the existence of God. I asked him the reason for that wording. He

57 Pierre Laval was a French politician who twice served as the head of government after the armistice with Germany in 1940.

answered that, although he believes in God, he no longer belongs to the Church. He was married in a civil ceremony and his children have not been baptized. I then asked him if that decision was dictated by conviction or political reasons. He answered frankly, "Both."

The German officer who brought Bicha a letter from her sister, Irène Mecklemburg, said to her in conversation, "And, first of all, what is Christianity? It is such a young doctrine when you think of centuries past – barely two thousand years old. Who knows how many times it will still change in centuries to come?" Those are the pagan theories Mr. Melnikoff was talking about.

Our meals consist mainly of rutabaga, with all kinds of sauces or often with no sauce. No one ever heard of the vegetable before the war; it seems to me it was intended exclusively for cattle. Bread rations have been cut for class "A" – that is, adults. You have to register for certain products with a supplier and can no longer buy them in the first store you come across. People who have relatives in the country still manage to receive packages; the sender cunningly includes a pound or two of butter carefully concealed among a few innocent vegetables.

A ration card has been introduced for footwear. To get a pair of shoes, you have to file an application at the Mayor's office, indicating the number of shoes you already own, then wait two or three months for the Mayor's office to issue you a voucher. Shoes are divided into several categories: everyday, street, and dress shoes. For now, wooden-soled shoes are still sold without a voucher. If you know a shoemaker and pay part in cigarettes, he will re-sole them in leather for you at the black-market price.

9.2.41 Langeron, the Prefect of the Seine *département*, was arrested on charges of giving asylum to English nationals and getting them into the free zone.

Léon de Rosen escaped from a prison camp near Metz and got here with false papers. He telephoned me to come and see him. He wants to get to the free zone and then to Africa or England. However, he told me the condition he will set is that he never be sent to the Italian front. He is deeply distressed by all he saw in Paris.[58]

The Hitler youth – *Hitlerjugend* – who occupied the Hotel Reichenbach, where Barbos worked, have been replaced by civil engineers and members of the Armistice Commission, who are more demanding and less friendly than the Hitler youth.

4.3.41   Admiral Arnaud de la Perrière – let me clarify that he is a German admiral! – who was just named Commander of the Southwest Forces, has died, the victim of an airplane accident. The airplane was unable to ascend soon enough on take-off and hit a hangar. There was a National Socialist ceremony, "Wodenesque" as Admiral Kinzel called it, in front of the church of the Madeleine with speeches, Hitler salutes, and so on. Admiral Kinzel is currently head of the German navy yards in Brest. He is decidedly anti-Nazi, but prudent in his speech, although not prudent enough to avoid letting ironic little remarks slip here and there. I met him at the *Zahnstation* and had tea at his place, in mixed company! He showed me the dagger with an Imperial crown he wears on unofficial occasions; on official occasions, he wears a dagger with a swastika. He said of his work, "I am happy that, in these times of destruction, I have a reconstruction and repair job." He lost his son, a seaman like him, early in the war.

Bulgaria has been occupied by the Germans "to prevent the English from taking it." The Soviets wore long faces because the Balkans are their hunting grounds.

5.3.41   The family has committed one gaffe after another. First it was my nephew, Vladimir. At a boy scout meeting, he heard talk that the organization's leader, Colonel Bogdanovitch, was a mem-

---

58 Léon de Rosen is the son of Baron Léon de Rosen, who Countess Hendrikoff mentions earlier having to leave Kislovodsk, Russia, in such a hurry he has no time to say goodbye to his family. Baron de Rosen and his Italian wife Elena Ruggeri-Laderchi fled to France during the Russian Revolution. A lack of resources meant that the younger Rosen quit school and went to work at the Simca car factory as a labourer. He rose through the company to become Deputy CEO. Later he was CEO of Massey-Ferguson France and became the first French representative to the United Nations. He was awarded the Prix Jacques Foucher for his book *A Singular Captivity: In Metz, Under the German Occupation* (L'Harmattan, 2000).

ber of British Military Intelligence in his day and is now in the Gestapo, and obligingly went to warn him. The next day, a Gestapo officer, accompanied by Goshtovt, whose role remained a mystery, came to question Vladimir and demanded the names of those who repeated the rumours. Vladimir said he did not remember, so they asked him to call and give them the names over the telephone. Bicha called me in distress. Of course, Vladimir would never denounce his friend but did not know how to get out of the situation, which fortunately ended abruptly. Vladimir did not call and the Gestapo did not bother him. It should have been a lesson to us all. But no! It was my turn then.

I went to visit Countess K., who was ill. Dr. Schark was there, the dentist who is my boss; he lives in the next apartment and had come to see how she was doing. We were talking about how difficult it is to cross the demarcation line between the two zones. I was not paying too much attention, forgetting that Dr. Schark was sitting there quietly in a corner, and jokingly let slip, "Oh, you know, it's not so difficult if you have friends. In some cafés, they say you can cross for five hundred francs." The next day at work, Dr. Schark suddenly asked me, "Give me the address of the friends you know who help cross the demarcation line between the two zones, the cafés you were talking about yesterday." I had completely forgotten my ill-timed joking remark, naturally, attaching little significance to it, but Dr. Schark had repeated the conversation in high places, giving it a great deal of importance, wanting to distinguish himself in the hope of getting a decoration. For that purpose, he had even called a Lieutenant Lange to come in to the *Zahnstation*; I did not know his position at the time but later learned that he was from the Russian section of the Second Bureau, German military intelligence, *Abwehr III*. In fact, Lange soon appeared. As a man of the world, however, much more astute than Schark, he smilingly told me he would never permit himself to ask me for information about my countrymen or about a French citizen, but passes were issued by the German authorities and it would be of great interest to them to find the guilty Germans. If I could give him details, I merely had to call him at the Plaza. I did not call and Lange did not bother me. I was frightened, however, especially because I really knew people who had crossed with help from the cafés, at locations I knew, and I was mainly afraid that, if I was questioned, I would let slip too much and cause someone harm. Once I saw that the incident would have no consequences, I talked to Dr. Vogel about it; he was very critical of Dr. Schark's actions and said, to console me, "Why didn't you speak to Dr. Lutowski? If you ever have problems, confide in him. He will help you." That only half reassured me because I thought Lutowski might really have a secret political role. I also talked to Admiral Kinzel about it, who told me I was lucky to have gotten out of it that easily and I should pay attention to what I say in future; he added, "Their ideas are often good, but their men are terrible."

10.3.41 There was a rumour going around that powder, lipstick, and other cosmetics were going to be rationed. You could no longer get into a perfume store, where women were pushing one another and pouncing on products they were buying by the armload. One would think, in times like these, makeup would be the least of our worries. But Paris will always be Paris, under any regime!

11.3.41 Had tea at the Gl.'s; he is Serb and she is French. Yugoslavia is on the brink of taking a position in the world conflict. Gl. told me that the country is officially opposed to the passage of German troops. He said, "I know that, in the event of a conflict, the fate of my country is sealed in advance but there are some things we cannot accept." He even talked about the possibility of ending up in a concentration camp, which seems such a contrast with the tasteful and luxurious atmosphere that surrounds them.

The Germans opened a *Deutsches Institut* on rue Talleyrand, where language and literature are taught. There are several subjects in the program, classes for beginners and advanced students; I suppose they also preach the National Socialist faith there. I heard there were already six thousand students registered. Dr. Schark cannot believe that Germans would take French courses in similar circumstances.

13.3.41 The Sold.'s telephoned and invited me for the weekend at the Mortefontaine golf course. A bus rented by the club picks up players Sunday morning at the various gates of Paris and brings

them back there around six o'clock in the evening, the same people as in previous years – that is, many "non-Aryans" and "half-
bloods." Since one now sees very few Jews on Paris streets, it is
surprising. The golf course warrants the nickname "Anyway." The
greens are still green and the food plentiful; the numerous pre-war
staff has been cut down to one couple, chef and housemaid, who
perform all the work to perfection. The Sold.'s have lost all their belongings, pillaged in their absence from Mortefontaine, which they
had to abandon twice. The first time they left by order of the Mayor
in a cart pulled by a workhorse and the second time by order of the
French military authorities, in the Duke de Gramont's car. When
they came back in the fall, they did not find any beds, bedding,
clothing, or personal belongings; even the two bassets they were so
fond of had disappeared. The two Gramont châteaus are now occupied by the Germans.

We were told at the *Zahnstation* that groups of soldiers with
cards bearing the letter "T" were to be sent there and should be
seen before the others. They are combat troops. It seems profoundly illogical to repair part of a soldier who is perhaps going to be
completely demolished. Treating those soldiers makes me think of
grooming a condemned man for the last time.

Staff for buildings occupied by the Germans is recruited by two
offices. One is run by an Austrian of Czech origin named Pospichil,
who does not speak Russian but understands it perfectly. He has
all the failings and qualities of an Austrian; he is friendly, not very
trustworthy, courtly, influenced by the last person he talked to,
mild-mannered, and full of charm. He never speaks to you without calling you dearest madam – "*Liebe, gnädige Frau.*" The Germans do not like him. I think they do not like Austrians, anyway;
they find them too "flexible." The Russian element predominates
at Pospichil's office. The other office comes under garrison headquarters – the *Standortverwaltung*, which recruits staff exclusively
among the French and Alsatians.

April 1941 All the German offices and installations organize
one or more staff outings – *Betriebsausflug* – for their staff each
year. It may be a picnic or an excursion that lasts a day or more or,

if the weather is poor, a dinner in a restaurant. All the costs of the meals, travel, and so on are covered by the German government. All staff take part, and the rank or position of the participants does not matter; an Admiral may have a simple sailor at his side and a plant manager may have a cleaning woman seated beside him at the table. That type of activity is not only intended for employees' entertainment but also to introduce a democratic element into the relationship between leaders and subordinates. It does not appeal to "old-school" types. Professor Fecht, a small German from the south, who attaches great importance to that characteristic, a professor of history in civilian life, almost openly anti-Nazi, has often repeated to me how much he abhors pastimes of that kind. He sees neither their usefulness nor benefit, because he thinks soldiers and cleaning women would have much more fun among themselves. The *Zahnstation* too had its *Betriebsausflug*, which I took part in as the others did. We went out, the three doctors, the secretary, the two nurses, and the technician, in two convertibles driven by two sailors. We stopped to visit the Petit Trianon,[59] then Rambouillet. The park and the château at Rambouillet are occupied by the *Luftwaffe* – air force – and a sign is hung in one of the windows of the château saying that the room is a historical monument and should not be occupied. I did not fully realize the historical importance of the room. We had lunch in a little restaurant in Rambouillet. The two drivers sat at our table. A large mound of butter sat enthroned in the centre of the table. I could not believe my eyes! The doctors themselves were very surprised, because they had not asked for it.

We arrived at Chartres toward evening and dined with the local German Red Cross director, who lives in three requisitioned rooms in the apartment of a French family. The family's maid served the dinner. The director was a highly educated man who took us on a tour of the cathedral, which he knew thoroughly and profoundly admired. We spent the night in a hotel, had breakfast in a very clean, well-organized German Red Cross centre, and then left for

59 On the grounds of the Palace of Versailles

Orléans. The city was bombed by the Italians practically on the eve of the armistice. The city centre was completely destroyed; only the signs set up among the ruins show the location of the former stores and their new addresses. Puddles sparkled among piles of rubble and collapsed walls. It was a very sad sight.

On the way back, I was sitting next to the driver. I had heard him speak quite correct French and asked him where he learned it. He confided to me that he had a French girlfriend who wanted to marry him. For the time being, there is no question of it, because marriages between Germans and French are prohibited for the duration of the war. Then he would never dare bring home a woman with "red lips" – *rote Lippen* seem to make a powerful impression on German soldiers – because his father would drop dead on the spot.

May 1941 English aircraft are dropping tracts on Paris. It is prohibited to pick them up; however, everyone picks them up, and I myself gathered a handful in the garden of an abandoned villa. In metro corridors and on platforms, one often sees the shape of Lorraine crosses, the emblem of General de Gaulle, made of metro tickets laid out on the ground by unknown hands.

The secretary at the *Zahnstation* has been replaced by a tiny German, Fräulein Scheer, who is very knowledgeable and quick; she made us laugh by seriously asking the address and business hours of the "Black Market" she had heard so much about in Germany.

I asked Mademoiselle Kminskowska, the former secretary, to find information for me on the fate of my stepfather Fyodor Oom's daughter Marie, who has been in a care home in Germany for years. The care facility had sent an official letter to him informing him that, because of the current conditions, the patients were going to be transferred to another location, and he would be sent the new address later. However, he has heard nothing further. I did not want to repeat to him the rumours going around about the fate of mental patients in Germany. I heard that Hitler had given orders to exterminate them without telling the families in advance. But so many things have been said about him over time that have proved untrue; perhaps this too is a falsehood.

Admiral Schulze, the *kommandierende Admiral für Frankreich*, came to have dental work done recently at the *Zahnstation*. He looks like a true Prussian – very erect, even rigid, and spoke little. However, while Dr. Schark was gone down to the first floor and he was alone with me for a few seconds, he suddenly asked me what I thought as a Russian about the possibility of war with the Soviets. I answered him that, first and foremost, Russia is the country where I was born and spent my youth and I could not wish for Russia the suffering and privation that usually accompany war. Then he asked me if I would not rejoice to see Communism destroyed. I told him, "Yes, naturally, but I would like Communism to die on its own, not as the result of foreign military intervention." To that he pointed out to me, with some reason, that the regime has been in power for twenty-five years in Russia, and there is no hope of a change. The conversation confirmed for me the current rumours of upcoming war between Germany and Russia, which worry Russian émigrés.

The conversation with Schulze worried Bicha a great deal when I reported it to her. She told me that I was completely insane to talk that way to a German, a high-ranked German to top it off. However, I do not think my individual opinion is of any importance to Schulze. Probably he wanted to find out the prevailing attitude among former émigrés. A lot of Russians naïvely imagine that, if Germany declared war on Russia, it would be to undertake a crusade against Communism, with no self-interest, and already talk about enlisting in the German army. Personally, I do not believe for a minute that any nation wants to sacrifice soldiers and money if it does not think it is going to make an attractive profit for itself and, naturally, there can be no question of common interest.

30.5.41 Dr. Schark has been recalled and Dr. Lutowski is the head dentist now. I am now assisting Dr. Grau, who was the last to arrive and so treats sailors only. The number of sailors is often up to thirty or forty a day; I literally do not have time to sit down for five minutes. Apart from that, I must say that everyone, starting with simple sailors and ending with officers, including medical staff, is very polite, friendly, and humane.

Mademoiselle Kminskowska wrote me that she enquired in all the high places without getting any answer about Fyodor Oom's daughter.

29.8.41 So many events have taken place since my last notes in this notebook!

Yugoslavia has been occupied by the Germans. The King has fled the country and all communication with France has been cut. I remained without news of Irina Kobieff and her husband for an eternity.[60] I finally heard from my sister in Rome, Ella Shirkoff, that they were safe and sound.

Then it was Greece's turn, with spectacular parachuting of German troops, news releases citing the glorious names that used to be sprinkled through our history books: Thermopylae, Olympus, and so on. German uniforms against the background of those classical landscapes seem anachronistic...

Finally Russia was invaded! Hitler chose June 22 to start hostilities, the day Napoleon started the war on Russia, which was noted and criticized by his opponents. Why did I not write anything during that time? I think I was experiencing, and still am, a painful confusion of feelings. I would have never wanted foreign intervention to free Russia, my country. We have always had endless discussions on the subject with Uncle Ruggeri, who saw that as the only solution and would have applauded it, even at the cost of some land concessions. I do not believe in national disinterest. The Crusades, too, may have been inspired by more earthly goals than we were taught in school. What will Germany demand as the price in exchange for the "liberation" of Russia, in the event it is victorious? Russian émigrés are divided into two camps: anti-Communists and patriots. The first are rejoicing, thinking that the immediate result of the war will be to throw out the Communist regime in Russia. The others feel more Russian than "White" and are sad or disturbed. Metropolitan Seraphin, who is from the extreme right, even celebrated a *Te Deum*[61] at rue Daru for the occasion and prayed

60 Irina Kobieff, née Zweguintzoff, was Countess Hendrikoff's younger sister. She escaped to Yugoslavia during the Russian Revolution.
61 An early Christian hymn of praise sung on special occasions in the Russian Orthodox Church

for the victory of the German army.[62] Some former Russian officers went to the German authorities to offer their services. In one of the buildings occupied by the Germans where the staff is entirely Russian, a speech was even sent to the German Führer to thank him for taking the first step toward the liberation of Russia. The employees were invited to sign it on penalty of being considered suspect or losing their job. Since it was the only building where a demonstration of that kind took place, I wonder whether the Russian director of staff was responsible or was "advised" to do it. Moreover, I heard that a number of employees refused to sign.

I read in the German news releases that the Russian people cheer the Germans as they pass, and I sometimes wonder if I was not mistaken, if the war really would not bring Russia a change of regime. Would it suddenly be possible to go back to your own country and see Russian forests again, the rivers you knew as a child, the landscapes you still hold in your heart? Could it really be possible that Hitler only wants to eliminate Communism? Perhaps I was wrong and he will recognize an independent, intact Russia? Barbos always tells me that a Slav does not let himself be assimilated easily, that if the Germans tried to colonize Russia, they are the ones who would be absorbed in the Slavic masses. All those ideas, so contradictory to one another, are at work in me, and I cannot manage to see clearly within.

What is odd is that, in the occupied zone, Russian émigrés have not been bothered, while in the free zone, all the men were arrested and put in a concentration camp.

1.9.41 I changed jobs, with some regret; I feared it was beyond my physical strength. The two young nurses come to see me often and invite me to their homes. The three dentists live in one of the buildings I am going to take care of. Everything is changing from one moment to the next now. For the moment I am supposed to supervise the work of the female staff, of various nationalities, in one of the occupied buildings on Boulevard Suchet. The building is part of a block of requisitioned buildings located on the edge of the

62   A metropolitan is similar to a bishop in the Russian Orthodox Church. The cathedral on rue Daru was the most important Russian cathedral outside of Russia.

Bois de Boulogne. The luxurious buildings with rooftop gardens had been almost completely vacated by their owners and renters when the Germans requisitioned them, because they were occupied in most cases by "non-Aryans" who fled at the last minute, were away from Paris, or stayed in the free zone when the Germans entered the capital. I heard some employees say that, at the time they were requisitioned, the apartments were full of precious objects, masterpieces, clothes, and even jewellery hidden in safes in the bathroom walls. None of all that now remains. The buildings are sparsely furnished in "Levitan" style with furniture requisitioned in Paris from *Grands Magasins* by the *Standortverwaltung*, which limited itself to what is strictly necessary. I was also told that some labourers carried a fortune in jewellery away in their caps, and the Alsatian manager of one of the buildings cut out all the valuable paintings to be found there and left only the frames, on which the names of famous painters can still be seen. "Finders keepers, losers weepers," as the saying goes!

So for the time being, I supervise the work of fifteen or so cleaning women. The male staff and building supervision are the responsibility of the manager, who is currently W.A. Rautsmann, a Russian. French chefs work in the kitchen, which is managed by a German non-commissioned officer who receives supplies directly from the German Supply Corps and distributes them to the cooks. The menu is set by a German unit with headquarters at the Plaza and is the same for all German installations. Twice a week, lunch is an *Eintopf*, a thick soup, usually of pureed peas or barley with added vegetables, macaroni, and small pieces of lard, just one course, followed only by dessert and a cup of coffee. It was introduced in Germany before the war as a savings measure. The restaurant, with its garçons and so on, is also an independent service managed, for now, by a German, while the staff is exclusively French. In each building, there is a *Hausoffizier*, a type of German supervisor, selected from among them, who settles internal matters, is responsible for the conduct of his compatriots, and informs them of the various circulars and regulations, and so on. His duties are fairly undefined and depend a great deal on the personality of the particular *Hausoffizier*. Staff members are paid by Paris Prefecture units.

The Germans who occupy the two twin buildings at 6 and 10 Boulevard Suchet are minor officials, engineers, accountants, and employees of the military supply corps.

September 1941 We have been given interim textile cards, two points for a pair of stockings, and so on. For fabric, one has to request a "purchase voucher."

All kinds of fruit of very fine quality can be found in the shops. The merchants explain that before the war that quality of fruit was exclusively destined for export to England.

15.9.41 There have been a number of attacks on Germans in the metro. Hostages have been shot but that has not put an end to the attacks. Hostility against occupation troops is growing from day to day. Recently again, a German official was struck by a bullet from a revolver when he was getting on a car in the metro. I now avoid standing behind a German in the crowd. Laval and Déat were injured during a farewell ceremony at the *Légion des volontaires français* (LVF), one of the international organizations formed by the Germans, a unit of French volunteers to fight Bolshevism. Many French want victory for the Soviets, because they do not fear Communism becoming established in France and have confidence in the military strength of the Soviets.

Serge R., the Guil.'s nephew, came back from the "no-no" zone, as Parisians call the unoccupied zone. He had been sent to a camp for "workers." The camps were organized in the free zone immediately after the armistice to hold demobilized soldiers who for one reason or another could not return home. In theory, the "workers" were supposed to do farm work and rebuilding. The internal organization of the camps is purely military; colonels head the camps, and so on. Serge revealed to us that the commandants of the camps were quietly gathering horses, trucks, and even weapons for when the time comes for revenge. Food supplies were so miserable that the head of Serge's section had to post an order prohibiting the capture of dogs and cats belonging to private owners because the soldiers were using them "to supplement food supplies."

18.9.41 At the Sv.'s, I met their Dutch brother-in-law who talked about German–Dutch relations and said that attacks are much more numerous in Holland. There is no fraternization between occupier and occupied. As soon as a German enters a café or restaurant, all the Dutch people there ask for the bill and leave without a word.

20.9.41 Last night I missed the last metro and had to go home on foot from the Étoile in total darkness. By a strange chance, I bumped into young Mika in the dark; she was walking home to Clichy, and we were both delighted to go part of the way together.

October 1941 A curfew has been set for nine o'clock in the evening because of the many attacks against the Germans. Big rewards of money, or the release of prisoners, are offered for anyone reporting the killers.

22.10.41 The Germans are 60 km from Moscow and have circled Leningrad. V.B., a friend of my oldest brother, has left for the Russian front as an interpreter. His wife Sophy read us some of his letters. He went through Krasnoe and saw the villas again where he and his comrades stayed in the summer during manoeuvres. From a distance, with binoculars, he also saw St. Isaac's cathedral, tramways, but barely any passersby in the streets of St. Petersburg. He described the misery around him, the children running up to German soldiers and begging for bread. He organized a kind of sponsorship for abandoned children and asked Sophy to take up a collection among her friends and send him clothing and food for the children. There are people who criticize V. and reproach him for going with the German army but I believe in his sincerity.

23.10.41 I am suffering a great deal from the cold in the G.'s apartment. It is odd that, at Cité Martignac, which was not heated at all, I was not as cold. There everything was so solidly frozen that there was no humidity; here it is a humid cold.

Peter Raevsky, Bicha's brother, arrived from the free zone after signing on with the LVF.[63] Yet here he was told that Russian émigrés are not accepted in the LVF. He and DeW. had to be content with jobs as a timekeeper and night caretaker in a German installation.

---

63 LVF refers to the Loyalist Volunteer Force.

26.10.41 There has been a resurgence of attacks. The commandant in Nantes was killed by a bullet in the back. Fifty hostages were immediately shot in reprisal and fifty more will be shot at noon if the killer is not denounced. The German authorities offered a reward of fifteen million francs to whoever finds him.

27.10.41 The Germans announced that they have received information that enables them to find the guilty party and the new hostages will not be shot. The public does not believe that someone really let himself be tempted by the reward. It is generally thought that there was simply a counter-order.

Kharkov, Belgorod, and Kiev have been occupied by the Germans. In Kiev, time bombs exploded in the city centre after the entry of the Germans. Apparently, the bombs were attached to the telephone network and went off as soon as the Germans tried to restore telephone service.

2.11.41 Rautsmann, the building manager at Boulevard Suchet, invited Grand Duke Gabriel,[64] his wife and sister-in-law to lunch in the basement of the building. Despite the fact that I did not approve of the presence of a member of the Imperial family in a building occupied by the Germans – after all, Rautsmann was not in his own home – I agreed to take part to avoid creating an incident that would give the affair too much publicity. The lunch began with a *Te Deum* and the staff choir sang Многие лета – Many Years – for the Grand Duke and the royal family – Августейшая Семья – as well as for Rautsmann and his mistress, with whom he lives in a marital relationship at Boulevard Suchet, which made quite a tangle. During lunch, Grand Duke Gabriel cited Göring's nephew, whom he had just met, recounting how the Soviets are not taking prisoners; however, the Germans had exterminated forty thousand Jews near Kiev. Listening to that reminded me of the words of farmwife Poupard: "If that is progress, then we are too far advanced."

Read a letter from V.B. The population in the area around Leningrad is poor, dirty, and uneducated. The individuals he spoke to

64 Prince Gabriel Constantinovich (1887–1955) was a great-grandson of Tsar Nicolas I and a member of the Imperial family. His book *In the Marble Palace* is a valuable reference for those interested in the Romanov dynasty.

looked like automatons to him and repeated in an indifferent voice, "Perhaps we will live better under German occupation after all." Churches are full and women have their children baptized en masse.

1.12.41   The current tenants at Boulevard Suchet are German Navy officials. The Navy is now the best-represented force in Paris; on first glance, you would think the city was a seaport. The Marine Ministry in Place de la Concorde is occupied by the offices of the German Navy; *Galéries Barbès* has been transformed into a German supply depot; a whole series of buildings on Boulevard Suchet and Avenue Maunoury have been occupied by the Germans; and, in this corner of La Muette, all you hear in the streets is German.

An apartment at No. 6 Boulevard Suchet has been reserved for Minister Schleier, who is the head of the Franco-German committee and, in my opinion, actively working for rapprochement between the two countries. He often has soirées attended by Brinon, Laval, and Spanish and French guests. German guards are posted at the entrances and inside the building on those occasions. I would love to be invisible and attend his receptions. Who are the people who attend and for what purpose? Is there really sincere collaboration between some French and German groups? I have heard that Schleier is a member of the NS party[65] and is the important figure, while Abetz[66] is just there for window dressing. Schleier and his wife keep their distance from everyone and never speak to anyone whatsoever.

4.12.41   New attacks in the eighteenth and tenth arrondissements. The neighbourhoods are in confinement; no one is allowed to leave after six-thirty in the evening.

Birthdays – *Geburtstag* – are important to Germans. Every unit has a list of the birthdays of all employees that are supposed to be celebrated that day by their superiors and co-workers.

December 1941   Grand Duke Vladimir Kirillovich, the pretender to the Russian throne, came to lunch at Boulevard Suchet, accompanied by Grand Duke Gabriel and his family. Vladimir Kirillovitch

---

65   NS refers to the Nationalist Socialist Party, otherwise known as NSDAP. The NSDAP had a 25-point program that set forth the Nazi doctrine.
66   Dr. Heinrich Otto Abetz was the German ambassador to France at the time.

has the same build as his grandfather, Emperor Alexander III. He lacks a princely education or any education at all. He did not say a word to anyone other than his neighbours at the table and made no effort to be friendly with the staff, which was made up mainly of former officers and their wives, who eyed him hungrily. In contrast, Grand Duke Gabriel, who may not be very intelligent, had a friendly word for everyone and, with the hereditary memory of reigning families, spoke to each one about his family or regiment or events he and his listener had attended in their day.

Spent the evening at the Ogareffs'. Ruth has been released; she had to sign an undertaking not to use the telephone, listen to the radio, travel by car, or leave the Seine *département*. She still trembles every time the doorbell rings.

Yesterday I was in a room in the basement at Boulevard Suchet when Admiral Kinzel's driver opened the door and shouted "*Ich habe Sie doch gefunden*" – "Luckily, I found you." He had just covered the six floors of the building at a gallop, a building he is unfamiliar with, whereas the Russian men on staff never find me when necessary. I observe my countrymen and am struck by the sluggishness and laziness of the men; the women, on the contrary, are energetic. It is not resistance on their part; however, they are happy to do nothing and leave all the work to the women, who naturally come and complain. However, I have no authority over the men, who sprawl all day long on the mattresses they dragged into the service rooms. The only place where there is feverish activity is the carpenters' workshop; however, the work they do has nothing to do with German orders. I also see that the furniture in the Levine apartment, which was still furnished when I arrived, is gradually, very discreetly, disappearing. One day, S. had too much to drink and asked me if I was not aware of where Rautsmann's fur overcoat and his mistress' fur coats came from, assuring me they are from the Levine apartment. I cannot prevent the misappropriations; however, by closing my eyes I appear to approve of them...

I was unpleasantly surprised by the sight of the maids' rooms in these luxury buildings. They all overlook a deep, narrow, dark courtyard surrounded by staircases and balconies made of iron; the two service lifts make an infernal racket as they go up and down. The rooms are tiny cells, with no windows and just enough room for a bed and small table and chair. The top of the door is made of glass, which replaces a window.

10.12.41 New attacks have occurred. A curfew has been ordered for six o'clock in the evening. Windows and shutters have to be closed starting at that time. Special passes will be issued to those who have to return home after curfew time for service reasons.

America and England have declared war on Japan. Soviet troops are retaking city after city, and I am again divided between two feelings, the satisfaction of seeing Russia recover its possessions and the fear of reprisals against the people who remain in the cities. The L.'s received news from their relatives who live in the Baltic provinces and are currently in Germany. After describing the atrocities committed by the Soviets when they reoccupied the provinces, the relatives added, "Papa was spared, however, thank God; he died when they came to arrest him."

13.12.41 The curfew will be maintained until Saturday. I obtained a pass and was able to go see our stepfather at the Piccini clinic.[67] The city was completely deserted. It was still light, but the only sound to be heard was the tap of my wooden soles on the asphalt. Despite the official order about closing shutters, I saw many open and even many lighted windows. Yesterday I took the last metro leaving the station around five o'clock in the afternoon. People crushed each other in, laughing and joking. The crowd on the street also looked gay, and I wondered if the carefree attitude showed courage or carelessness...

17.12.41 Restrictions on electricity consumption. All the stores, with the exception of food stores, will close at five o'clock in the evening from now on. Grocery stores, dairy stores, and so on are empty. In their window displays, one sees only turnips, watercress, a few salad greens. However, the black market is organizing and developing. One can find turkeys on the black market for eight hundred fifty and bars of soap for one hundred francs. Dina N.,

---

67 Likely a clinic for those requiring supervised care. Countess Hendrikoff's stepfather's health continued to deteriorate during the war.

who works as a chambermaid at Boulevard Suchet for a monthly wage of twelve hundred francs, spoke to me enthusiastically about a business deal she hopes to make, the sale of an astronomical number of tons of sugar to a German customer she is going to introduce to the manager of the building where she lives and who himself is only an intermediary. If the deal is made, Dina is going to make ten thousand francs.

The newspapers acclaim the exploits of Japanese kamikaze pilots who crash their aircraft full of explosives into enemy ships, setting them on fire, and dying with them.

Hitler spoke on the radio and explained the reason for entering the war against America. This morning, the head of the German Navy unit in the back building at Boulevard Suchet, Lieutenant Prange, likewise gathered the soldiers and spoke to them about the new military situation.

Prange is a man about fifty years old who rose through the ranks and has the appearance and build of a corporal. He is a member of the Party – military ss, which is not exactly the same as civilian ss, although I do not know exactly what the difference is. He is abrupt, unintelligent, and suspicious. He showed me photos of his daughter's wedding – an ss marriage. The couple is standing in front of a kind of altar draped with fabric with swastikas, surrounded by flags with the same insignia. Beside them stand soldiers wearing armbands with swastikas. I naïvely asked, "Where is the pastor?" to which Prange answered self-importantly, "There wasn't one. We no longer belong to the Church. It was an ss who married them." For a man like Prange, National Socialism is surely not a religion or a belief but a way of getting somewhere in life.

I went to see Vladimir Hitrovo in his sanatorium on the outskirts of Paris in Vallée de Chevreuse; he had tried to work as a guide for German soldiers staying in Paris and, of course, had a relapse. It is quite a trip to get there. His condition is serious but he is well cared for; there are two patients in a large, bright, airy room. I had to go part of the way back on foot because there was no room left in the only bus going back to Paris. I walked about 10 km across the fields to the closest railway station. My companions in misfortune were an older gentleman and a young woman who could barely follow us because she was perched on thin high heels. We had to remain standing again in the train, and the young woman fainted in our arms getting off the train.

Vladimir Hitrovo's wife Olga lives in Bellevue; her house is not heated and is appallingly humid. Olga and her son Serge sleep on the ground floor, which is at least warmed by a small wood stove in which they burn trees from their garden. The day I went to see them, the *salon* was in fog and the kitchen walls were dripping. Olga manages as best she can by trying to sell items as foreign to her as railway ties. When she goes to see her husband at the sanatorium outside Paris, she exchanges shoes or products like that for farm produce, vegetables, and so on, which she finds in the area around the sanatorium. The farmers do not accept money. Last summer she transformed their little lawn into a vegetable garden and has thus been able to grow tomatoes, carrots, cabbage, and beans. The Hitrovos' two bassets are so hungry that, when they see me coming bringing them dry crusts of bread I beg for them in the kitchen at Boulevard Suchet, they greet me with howls of joy, jumping play-fully, throwing themselves on the meagre feast and devouring it in the blink of an eye. Lately I saw them devour leftover marinated onions as if they were a delicacy.

The news from the African front is not very bright for the Germans, nothing but "defensive positions" and "counter-attacks."

25.12.41 Christmas is the biggest feast day of the year for Germans. Pospichil's office sent three Christmas trees and decorations that came from Germany; we set them up in the dining room and bar. Candles of any kind are impossible to find here as well as in Germany, so they were replaced by night lights in the shape of a ball, set on coloured paper. Pospichil came in person on the morning of the twenty-fourth and gave Rautsmann and me each a book, *National Socialist Art*, as an official gift and, from himself, gave me a leather book cover and Rautsmann a picture frame, also leather.

Admiral Schulze came around six-thirty in the evening for a short visit to make a little speech; the employees had been ordered to stay out of sight at that time. After dinner was served, the Germans went up to the bar on the sixth floor and sang Christmas carols together, "Heilige Nacht," "O Tannenbaum," and so on. The four young sailors on guard duty looked very sad in the guard room, so I took pity on them and sent them a little coffee and a few slices of brioche that I had made with black-market products. They then took turns coming to thank me politely, without servility. These young Germans appeal to me; they look clean, morally and physically, and full of enthusiasm, as long as that enthusiasm is properly directed in future. What a pity that all young people everywhere in the world do not grow up in an atmosphere of peace!

OCCUPATION

"I envy people who only see one side of things; it simplifies life so much."

4.1.42 The year 1941 is now in the past!

Welcomed the New Year at my brother's. Barbos and Bicha did marvels with the little at their disposal. Drank to the health of those not present. If only we could live all together after the war. In moments of crisis like this, I am more aware than ever that "blood is thicker than water."

Bicha had me read two letters from her nephew Serge Raevsky from August and September. He enlisted in a German unit, although he hates the Germans. He told Bicha when he left, however, that he intends to desert as soon as he sets foot on Russian soil. Bicha thinks that is madness on his part because the Soviet troops will never believe that he is not a German spy. In his letters, he describes the misery of the Russian people, dressed in rags, canvas like a tarp or burlap – *рогожа* – often going barefoot or wearing boots made of canvas. Medical staff is scarce; the wounded are cared for by the women in the villages. He writes that he has succeeded in saving dozens of innocents from the firing squad. The people look like automatons, dazed, indifferent to everything, trembling before the commissars. As soon as they find out that Serge is Russian, White Russian, the inhabitants welcome him, invite him in, share what little they have with him. The harvest is intact near Smolensk; however, the Soviet troops usually destroy everything as they withdraw. Misery reigns in large population centres. Serge goes everywhere freely, unarmed, and is sure he has nothing to fear from the people. The children all know how to read and write, but the intellectual level is low. Serge writes, "Tell my comrades to stop deliberating and drinking, learn a trade, any trade, all of them will be useful here. Even the 'generals' and 'governors' in Meudon will be able to find a job. As for engineers and doctors, they will be worth their weight in gold." He adds that if the war had not taken place, the regime would have lasted another hundred years. No one would have had the power to fight it, even though everyone is unhappy. The people seem as if they are under the influence of a drug. It is truly astonishing and moving that this boy, who left his country as a young child, feels so much affinity and attachment for his country, which he never really knew. He also writes, "You cannot imagine what it means to be in *your* country, to see *your* rivers, *your* forests." In his letter, he put a blueberry and a small branch of the grey absinth so common in our area that gives the milk a bitter taste when the cows eat it.

29.1.42 A very odd dinner at Olga Galitzine's. She telephoned and asked me to come for dinner and help her in her efforts to free Boris Tretiakoff, who was arrested by the Germans for no apparent reason. The Germans appear to have confused him with a Russian by the same name, who, they say, was mixed up in the kidnapping of the Russian General Miller and has fled. I thought I would be the only guest and was rather surprised to find there, first of all, Madame G., the wife of the Russian Admiral with whom Olga is sometimes friends, sometimes sworn enemies, and three Germans unknown to me, two of them in civilian clothes and the third in a uniform I did not recognize that I found out later in the conversation was the uniform of the military ss. Their names, mumbled by Olga, meant nothing to me at first but, as the conversation continued, I began to realize that I had important people before me. All three were highly intelligent and looked like they were watching their hostess carefully and knew more than they were saying. One of them made a reference to Vichy and I understood he had an important position. The military ss, whose name sounded to me like Gellenschmidt – or Hellenschmidt? – told me he "handles Russians" and, near the end of the evening, even spoke pretty fair

Russian to me. One of the civilians was named Knochen. I was completely unaware of his position in Paris and stayed as far away from politics as possible. He was the one who remained the most reserved. The other civilian seemed to me the most astute, or rather the most cunning. I think his name was something like Danneker or Danker, but I did not hear his name clearly.

During dinner, which was elegant and accompanied by wine and liqueur, Olga never stopped talking about her admiration and devotion to Hitler, bragging that she had an autographed photo of him. However, I had the impression that her guests were watching her with a slightly ironic expression and I could not get rid of a feeling of uneasiness due to a hint of something false and artificial in the air. After dinner, Olga took me aside and told me she had invited the Germans because she was trying to get Boris Tretiakoff released and begged me to help her do that; any testimony would help her plead his case. I willingly agreed. In fact, Olga started talking about Tretiakoff, insisting that he had been the victim of an error, and Madame D. and I confirmed her words. Up to then, Olga's conduct seemed altruistic to me, although somewhat imprudent from a political point of view. However, the whole conversation then took a very familiar tone, to say the least, particularly given the amount of liquor served during the evening.

I excused myself and was getting ready to leave, pleading the curfew. At once, the civilian whose name started with D offered to drive me home in his car; I gave him the Boulevard Suchet address. We had barely left Olga's apartment when my companion immediately changed his tone, becoming again the well brought up gentleman he had appeared to me to be at the beginning of dinner, even looking apologetic about the somewhat free tone of the conversation. On the way, he asked me, among other things, how I was related to Olga, who always introduces me as her "cousin." Why does Olga entertain these young people, and why do they come to the home of a woman twice their age? She told me she sees them often. Is it just to eat and drink or to watch her? Madame R., whose husband works for the infamous Gerebkoff, the *Gauleiter* of Russian émigrés appointed by the Germans, assures me that Olga is a dangerous woman and one should be wary of her. I never understood anything about her political activities; first, she was enthralled by Mussolini and took part in all the Fascist demonstrations, had a private audience with Il Duce, and was also given an autographed photograph of him. Then it was Franco's turn, now Hitler. She cannot really share their ideas, yet she openly receives Germans in her home and goes out with them. The day after the dinner party, she telephoned me to tell me how unhappy she is because someone she trusts completely reported to her that she is not well thought of among the Germans, they are very aware of her past, and her husband is not highly regarded either. She had hoped that, by marrying him, she could create the political *salon* she is really made for, she feels.

3.2.42 I asked Dr. Vogel, one of the dentists, who Olga's guests were and felt my knees give out from fear! Knochen is the head of the Gestapo in Paris; Gellenschmidt is in charge of the Russian surveillance unit. He could not tell me about the third one because I could not tell him his correct name. He also told me that he was extremely surprised that I had met them in a private, non-German home and to stay away from Olga because those gentlemen were probably watching her for one reason or another. Otherwise he does not think they would have taken the trouble to go to her home.

7.2.42 The Gerebkoff committee is making a list of Russian émigrés and is going to select instructors from among them for Russian prisoner camps. Gerebkoff lived in Paris for a period of time, where he was a dance instructor in a night club. Then he lived in Germany. Of course, he does not have any authority in Russian émigré circles. It has even been said that the French authorities are no longer going to issue identification cards to émigrés who do not have a census card from the Gerebkoff committee. In fact, the Prefecture ignores the existence of the committee because, when some Russian émigrés showed their census cards to a Prefecture employee, they were told, "That is not of interest to us at all, at all, at all."

10.2.42 German installations are now watched by French officers as soon as night falls; the public is no longer allowed to walk past them. You have to get off the sidewalk and cross the street as soon as you get near.

Highly edifying conversation with Inspector Siewert, one of the German "youth." He told me confidentially that he has already been assigned a position in Russia after the war ends. That does not suit him too well because he is married with two children. He fears the lack of comfort he will find there. According to his information, all the cities the front has passed through are completely destroyed. Smolensk has few houses left intact. The centre of Kiev no longer exists. He is absolutely sure that Germany will never give back the territory it has occupied in Russia, and fear of the "yellow peril" that threatens all countries will make Germany take measures the likes of which will make the Westwall, as the Germans call the Siegfried line, seem like a toy. The territory currently occupied by the Germans will be colonized by German nationals and the Russian population pushed beyond the Ostwall in the Urals. Germany will never allow any other power to play a dominant role in Europe, not even Russia, despite years of peace between the two countries. Germany's takeover of the European continent will guarantee peace for Europe. The Russian people will not be able to oppose that program, because they are now an amorphous mass who have lost all initiative, a moving mass searching for nonexistent shelter and dying on the road.

I listened without saying a word, wondering whether Siewert really believes in that plan and its implementation, but he looked like he believes it and considers it feasible and natural... I listened with unhealthy curiosity, because that is how one can find out the underlying truth. All those plans are never discussed in the newspapers. The word of the day is the crusade against Communism or, as Admiral Schulze suggested to me, the liberation of Russia. I wonder if the "old school" types, like the Admiral, share those ideas and believe in the possibility of colonizing Russia. It seems to me they do not, but can one ever really be sure?

13.2.42 Singapore has been taken by the Japanese, a hard blow for the British, especially coming from the "Yellow Empire."

Collection of warm clothing for the German troops in the East. The guard came to call me. Olga Galitzine asked me to accompany her to see Minister Schleier, who occupies a floor at Boulevard

Suchet. She had rushed to Boulevard Suchet with a large batch of fur coats and was determined to hand them over to Schleier in person, but he did not receive her. I excused myself, saying I was very busy. Since she is the least "giving" person one can imagine, all this seems very strange to me.

16.2.42 Admiral Ciliax broke through the British blockade with three ships, the *Prinz Eugen*, the *Gneisenau*, and the *Scharnhorst*, which had been at Brest for long months. The Germans were exultant at the announcement of the news.

22.2.42 Olga Hitrovo received a letter from relatives in Yugoslavia. They commented on the difficult situation of Russian émigrés, who naïvely formed military units to go fight in Russia beside the Germans. The Germans never sent them to the front but used them in the fight against Yugoslavian partisans. Having enlisted in military units, they cannot now quit, and the population considers them ingrates and traitors, for nowhere have Russian émigrés been welcomed as warmly and generously as in Yugoslavia.

Had news from Olga Zweguintzoff, née Obolensky, my brother Nicholas' wife. She has not heard from him for five years now. She is currently in occupied Russian territory. It was as if I had received a letter from beyond the grave. I have never had news directly from her or my brother since 1926, nothing but news indirectly from Richard Henricksen or the Meyendorfs.[68]

27.2.42 Went to the Neuilly market to buy thread without tickets. Officially, you are only entitled to six francs worth of thread or twelve francs worth of silk in return for the letter "C" on the textile card. At Neuilly, however, you can buy any rationed products freely: thread, cotton, socks, towels, and so on. The famous "flea market" has also become a legal black market centre tolerated by the French and German authorities. The only problem is the choice.

---

68 Richard "Dick" Henricksen, born in 1924 in St. Petersburg, Russia, was a World War II Norwegian resistance fighter. His father, mostly likely a Norwegian diplomat to Russia, either was in direct contact with Countess Hendrikoff or information from him was funneled through Richard. The Henricksens and the Meyendorfs were old Baltic aristocratic families.

3.3.42 I received a reply from Mademoiselle Langheld, a young German who is Admiral Kinzel's secretary. I had asked if she could get news for me about my stepfather Fyodor Oom's daughter and showed her the letter he had received from the institution where she was before. She answered frankly, "I don't need to inquire, I'll give you the answer right now. Your stepfather's daughter is no longer alive. The letter you received is a circular that was sent to all the parents of incurable patients. Doctors were given orders to help them pass on to the next world. Your stepfather will never hear of his daughter again. I find it so horrible that I don't want to talk about it further." Naturally, I did not want to repeat that conversation to Fyodor. It is true that, in a manner of speaking, his daughter no longer exists for him; he has not seen her since the Revolution and she was raving mad. However, our Christian thinking refuses to accept such draconian measures; I'm sure the news would have been painful for him. It is very possible, even likely, that the woman would never have been cured; she had been in an insane asylum for decades and existed, the way plants exist, but did not live. Despite all those excuses, the idea that the State could dispose of an individual because she can no longer be of service to the country and has become a useless mouth to feed seems inhuman, primitive, and unacceptable to me. I remember my discussions at school with our ancient history teacher, whose sympathies clearly lay with Sparta – he was even German – to the point of approving of the extermination of deformed children practised by the Spartans. Now the world seems to be going back to pagan principles.

4.3.42 Spring has made an appearance. Suddenly, without warning, the snow has melted, the sun is out, blackbirds have started their melodious whistling and with spring have come English aircraft flying over Paris. The city was bombed for the first time since the Armistice. Until now, Parisians wholeheartedly believed that the English would never dare touch the city for fear of damaging art treasures, as if such considerations could ever be taken seriously during a war. The raid lasted two and a half hours and took everybody by surprise, starting with the Germans, who have no anti-aircraft artillery in Paris at this time. I was having dinner at Sofka

Polotzoff's on rue Louis David when the first explosion was heard; we did not hear the noise of the aircraft, which were flying at a very high altitude. Since attacks against the Germans had been frequent lately, we often hear the sound of small explosions in the street and do not pay attention. Soon, however, the detonations were following one another in quick succession, and you could clearly hear the roar of aircraft flying at low altitude. Sofka rushed to turn out the lights. We went to the window that looks out on a small garden. The sight was magical! The grass in the garden and the sky were fiery red. The silhouettes of trees with bare branches were etched a sinister black against the sky. Fireballs, rocket flares I was seeing for the first time, came down from the sky so slowly that they seemed to hang in space. The glass in the apartment windows shook with each explosion. We had the impression bombs were falling close to us, which was not very reassuring since the building has no shelter. In fact, the Renault factory was bombed and it is still a good distance from rue Louis David. Around eleven o'clock in the evening, calm had returned, and I decided to spend the night at Boulevard Suchet, which was closer to the Polotzoff's than my actual residence on rue de l'Université. The streets were full of people who apparently had not gone down into the shelters. Groups were gathered on the threshold of buildings in gay discussion, talking loudly. Seeing me walking fairly quickly, a woman shouted at me, "Don't rush, Madame, they're not shooting at us!" Meanwhile, however, rockets continued coming down in clusters of fire, and the sky was streaked with shooting stars, fire from very low-flying aircraft now. I had barely taken a few steps when the bombing started again even more intensely. Detonations were followed immediately by the rat-a-tat-tat of machine guns. I frankly admit I was frightened, because I could not tell how far away the bombs were falling. I found Boulevard Suchet plunged in total darkness; the hall was barely lighted with camouflaged lanterns set on the ground. The building's inhabitants who had gone down to the shelter when the raid began came back up to the ground floor as fast as they could because the roof of the shelter was made of glass. I realized from bits of overheard conversation that German anti-aircraft artillery had been sent to the coast in anticipation of an English landing... One of the Germans also told me that he had climbed up on the roof and clearly seen four fires burning in the direction of the Renault factories.

In fact, English radio, which I listen to morning and night with precautions, announced the next day that it was indeed the Renault factory, where the manager is a notorious collaborator, that had been bombed and the raid was going to be followed by many more.

The next day I went with Olga Novikoff to Boulogne to see the damage. There was not a single window left intact between Place Marcel Sembat and the Sèvres Bridge. Most of the trees were decimated, iron curtains torn off and bent, many houses razed to the ground, their ruins still smoking. Tablecloths, stockings, and various clothing hung from the trees along the avenue. The outside walls of buildings were nearly all destroyed, but we were surprised to see perfectly intact mirrors hanging on the inside wall, ceilings torn open and, in the same room, tidily arranged on their shelves, glass or porcelain containers and crocks that had not suffered any damage. The two Renault buildings to the right and left of the Sèvres Bridge had indeed been hit. Through stretches of wall still standing could be seen a pile of scrap metal that looked like it had been twisted by a giant hand. No access was allowed to the Sèvres Bridge because an unexploded bomb was still half buried in the pavement near the bridge. We teased Olga a lot afterward because when she saw the remains of the bomb, she asked what it was and cried, "And here I thought a bomb was round."

We saw lines of victims pushing handcarts in front of them, as in the time of the exodus, carrying provisions and items they were able to pick up here and there. What is sad is that factories are usually located in working class neighbourhoods and the poorest are left without shelter.

The count to date is seven hundred dead and one thousand five hundred injured. The wife of a Rothschild employee was killed in Boulogne. Her husband and daughter had each gone to a concert. The air-raid warning was not given, so the performances went on in theatres and cinemas throughout the raid. The father and daughter found each other in the darkness in front of the rubble of their home. They worked all night trying to find the mother among the ruins and debris, going so far as to offer five hundred francs to passersby to help them clear the rubble faster, only to find the woman's body in the morning.

Olga Hitrovo telephoned me the next day to tell me that all the windows in their house in Bellevue were broken, and finding panes of glass now is quite a task. Parisians in other districts in the city, on the other hand, were rejoicing about the visit from Allied planes and kept on saying, "You can't make an omelette without breaking eggs."

8.3.42 Most Germans buy butter, eggs, and so on, on the black market, generally through employees in the requisitioned buildings. The Alsatians are incontrovertibly the kings of the black market. Madame C., an Alsatian who is the *Hausdame* in one of the neighbouring buildings, provides her customers with a steady flow of rounds of butter, which I have seen with my own eyes.

10.3.42 Inspector Langheld told me that one of his friends just came back from the Russian front. He had been taken prisoner by the Soviet army then liberated by a German unit. As soon as he was taken prisoner, he was invited to a copious dinner, a plate of meat garnished with potatoes. He could not get over the hospitality. He was then taken to a hangar where cut-up bodies were hung and told that they were the bodies of German prisoners. He was told that he had just dined on the flesh of his comrades, and he and the other prisoners were in turn going to be served as food for future prisoners.

Another time, a group of German sappers were given orders to blow up a bridge. They did not come back from their mission, so their comrades tried to give a hand to free them. They arrived near the bridge only to find the bodies of the soldiers hanging by their throats from slaughterhouse hooks.

April 1942 Daily raids. I sleep poorly. The apartment on rue de l'Université is a few steps from the Eiffel Tower, where there is an air defence post and, when it goes into action, all the windows and doors of the building shake in a way that is hardly reassuring. Then we hear the footsteps of the tenants from the upper floors hurrying to the basement. We get up and get dressed every time as a precaution and each of us keeps a small suitcase handy in our bedroom with our most precious belongings. However, neither the landlady, Mademoiselle Théobald, nor her tenants go down to the basement, which is not a real shelter and does not inspire much confidence in us. When I happen to be kept late at Boulevard Suchet and have to spend the night there, I do not sleep any better there because, as soon as there is a warning, the German guard rings a special signal and goes up to every floor shouting *"Fliegeralarme"* – air-raid warning – and opens all the bedroom doors; everyone is ordered to go down to the shelter. The raids sometimes last two or three hours.

8.4.42 An attempted English landing took place at Saint-Nazaire yesterday. Twelve hundred English soldiers approached the coast on fast patrol boats, pulling an old boat loaded with explosives behind them. The Germans quickly blew them up before they got near the locks. The English soldiers were wearing rubber running shoes. They succeeded in landing and, they say, distributed weapons to the people in Saint-Nazaire, but were finally pushed back. They were probably welcomed enthusiastically because bread rations in the city have been reduced to 50 g a day per person and there have been executions. Everyone understands that the landing was only a trial balloon but it gave people heart again and rekindled hope.

The German Naval Staff has left Lorient and arrived in Paris. Sentinels armed with machine guns are now posted in front of German installations.

20.4.42 At Pospichil's weekly meeting, he explained what measures to take in the event of a raid and bombing. Several employees, *Hausdamen*, asked him the difference between incendiary bombs and liquid-air bombs. Pospichil answered, "If you see or hear bombs falling, forget everything I have just told you and run away as fast as you can."

Laval has been named Head of the Government, *Gauleiter* as London radio ironically calls him.

22.4.42 New attacks. A German was killed at a metro exit. A train carrying soldiers on leave back to Germany was also blown up. Curfew at eleven o'clock. Theatres, cinemas, and so on are closed until Friday, April 24.

An air defence post is going to be installed on the rooftops at Boulevard Suchet. Sandbags have been placed on the landings of all the floors, along with barrels full of water, extinguishers, and so on.

Professor Fecht came to see me at Boulevard Suchet. He went up to the map of military operations in Russia I had updated from German news releases and told me with a slightly ironic look, "You are certainly optimistic!" He then asked if I listen to British radio – he is, of course, sure I do – and what the English are saying about General Seidlitz, who has gone over to the side of the Russian army.

12.5.42 Many officials have been called up to the front and have been replaced by semi-invalids, asthmatics, cripples, and so on. The German guard at the entries to occupied buildings on Boulevard Suchet, nicknamed the *"Kinderwache,"* is made up of young boys seventeen years old.

An unknown hand has written "Danger of Death" on all the Boulevard Suchet buildings where Germans live.

The management of the building at No. 10 has been combined with No. 6 as a result of theft by the *Hausdame*, an Alsatian. I now have to take charge of the male and female staff at No. 10, including the waitresses in the restaurant.

18.5.42 My nephew Michel came home on leave. He has put on weight and matured morally and physically. He is bored in his company, which keeps watch in the unoccupied zone. He had to come to Paris to see an air raid. Their company has not yet seen an airplane. They are fairly well fed, thanks to the economic transactions of their lieutenant, who deals successfully on the black market.

Saw W. Bezobrazoff yesterday, who is in Paris on leave from the Russian front. He is currently an interpreter for a raiding party – *"Stosstruppe"* – with the rank of *Oberleutnant* and wears a uniform at the front that is a compromise: half civilian clothing and half German military uniform. He shares the life of the soldiers; that is, he has often had to sleep in the trenches or outside in fields in all kinds of weather and admits that, at fifty-five years old, fighting a war is no sinecure and he is no longer a young man. I do not think he is going to return to the front. Naturally he has been assailed with questions. He said the morale of the German troops is good; they lack for nothing. However, from what he has seen, the country is in ruins, devastated; there can be no question of Russia contributing to the food supply in Germany or Europe for at least five years. The people welcomed the Germans at first but now are very hostile to them.

25.5.42   One of our inspectors asked me to have two bicycles picked up that he had purchased at the factory with a coupon. The sale of bicycles is prohibited. To buy one, you have to make a special request to City Hall and submit metal coupons and so on, which are only issued very rarely; you have to prove that it is absolutely necessary to own a bicycle. Then you have to wait at least a year for delivery of the bicycle. Bicycles bought on the black market go for astronomical prices. I have never taken advantage of my job to obtain illegal benefits, but this time the temptation was too great, because it is increasingly difficult to get around Paris. Buses have been out of service for a long time; the metro no longer stops at some stations. I have to walk twenty minutes to get to the closest metro to where I live, yet that line does not go all directions. Whole lines have been closed, such as the Boulevards Extérieurs line, and when there is an air raid, metro service only starts again an hour after the signal of the end of the air raid. The German inspector I asked to help me buy a bicycle at a reasonable price lives at Boulevard Suchet; he advised me to speak to Kremer, a civilian. I do not know exactly who Kremer and his friend Hofer are. I think they are accountants in the German navy. They are very generous with staff and always maintain a distance from all their coworkers; Kremer especially gives the impression that he enjoys the good things in life and is always dressed impeccably. Their cleaning women suspect that they are Jews; in any case, they are anti-Nazi. I hardly dare believe his promise but, in short, Kremer immediately promised to take care of getting me a bicycle, on condition that I not reveal the source, allowing me to hope that I will be able to get it at a normal price.

27.5.42   At the time of the declaration of war on Russia, the Gerebkoff committee had circulated query sheets among Russian refugees. Those who signed them committed to accept any position they were offered in the fight against Communism. Many of my compatriots signed those sheets, carried away by the desire to fight the Soviet regime. Since then, the Rosenberg policy in occupied countries, the conduct of the ss in Russia, and the mistreatment suffered by Russian prisoners have all cast a chill on the enthusiasm of the early days. The Gerebkoff committee is currently asking signatories to honour their signatures and enlist in foreign volunteer units leaving for Russia. I am told only twenty-five people have answered the summons. One of them, Rot., who left with the first group, later told me that it was very hard at first. He had to leave his family in France without knowing whether they would be entitled to an allowance; he did not know what clothing to take, and so on. After the first phase, he only thought about the opportunity to finally see his country again and be of use there. Only time will tell whether those men did the right thing to leave under such conditions. Personally, I could never have followed their example; the joy I would feel at seeing my country again could not make me forget the circumstances of seeing it again. I envy people who only see one side of things; it simplifies life so much.

1.6.42 The streets of occupied Paris look entirely different now. First of all, the air is clear because of the absence of motor vehicles. The deserted avenues seem wider, and the whole city seems more majestic, the way a beautiful woman stripped of any ornament or bauble only looks more beautiful. The creative Parisian mind tries its best to remedy limitations and difficulties of any kind. A bicycle, called a "little queen" by the French, has now become the unqualified "queen" and is ridden by all sexes and ages. Common sights nowadays are a cyclist pedalling full speed with a fragile young woman perched on the handlebars, young women on bicycles with peasant skirts gathered at the waist billowing in the wind like a parachute unfurling and little black or tan puppies sitting at attention in baskets attached to the bicycle racks, and couples on tandems towing a small child strapped into a tiny trailer that often swerves dangerously on corners.

Bicycle taxis have appeared on the scene – bicycles or tandems towing inventive vehicles where the passenger sits while the Parisian riksha driver rides the bicycle. They can be rented at intersections such as Place de la Muette. Lately I saw a wedding party leaving the church in a train of bicycle taxis decorated with white ribbons and small bouquets of white flowers.

Women wear the most fanciful shoes, fairly high, reminiscent of Greek buskins, with cloth straps nailed onto wood or cork soles made all in one piece. When women first wore shoes like that, the streets resonated with each step. Stores selling those soles even adopted the advertising slogan "Tap your way down the boulevard." Now strips of rubber cut from old tires are nailed on the bottom of the sole, silencing their steps. Shoes made of raffia or string, even cloth, are also appearing, with the ever-present wooden soles in shapes that vary from store to store.

Leather handbags have also completely disappeared, replaced by cloth bags, enormous in size, worn with a shoulder strap; however, they do not withstand the crush in the metro. Curiously, despite the shortage of any material, women's dress in general has reached outlandish proportions. Their hats are like immense wheels or pancakes, their skirts are very short but very wide, and their hair is parted and massed in a pyramid on the front of their head with the rest floating free down their backs.

14.6.42 Small landings on the coast. Air-raid warnings and heavy bombing in the direction of Boulogne. I was sleeping at Suchet that night and was awoken by the explosions around two o'clock in the morning. The warning only came ten minutes later. I hastily got dressed and went down to the basement, which is not as cold and damp as the shelter, but still glacial, and I had to go back up to my room to get a blanket. The explosions were so loud that it was absolutely impossible to sleep, especially since an air defence unit stationed a few steps from Boulevard Suchet kept up a steady barrage of fire. The aircraft flew so low that one could clearly hear their drone and the rattle of machine guns. Every time a bomb fell, the glass shattered in the windows in the Suchet building. The signal for the end of the air raid was given at around four o'clock in the morning. I wondered how working people in bombed cities manage to go to work in the morning.

16.6.42 The guard told me that, the night of the bombing, bombs had fallen on the Bois de Boulogne and on some of the buildings on Boulevard Suchet.

An air raid in Cologne caused a great deal of damage. The newspapers never mention the bombings in Germany, but we hear about them on British radio because, in those cases, public servants who come from the bombed area immediately go on special leave. British radio played taped recordings of reports from pilots who took part in the raid and described "the glorious sight" of the city in flames. How oddly confusing are the feelings caused by the war! I am convinced that none of those pilots would have the courage to shoot a woman or child in cold blood, yet in a raid humanity disappears, leaving nothing but a hunter mentality.

Molotoff[69] signed a twenty-year mutual assistance pact in London and Washington. I wonder how long those twenty years will last...

Jewish people must now wear a yellow star with the word "Jew" in black letters. Even Jewish children are required to follow the regulation. I find that unnecessary and cruel. In schools, many teachers have recommended that their pupils not make fun of their little Jewish classmates. Madame Citroen, however, has been declared an "honorary Aryan" – what services she rendered and to whom, I do not know.

The fortunes amassed by some people in the black market often reach astronomical figures. A year ago, R. was looking for a job of any kind and now he has offered to buy the Hitrovos' house and land.

An English airplane flew over rue de Rivoli in broad daylight at noon, dropped a tricolour flag, and opened machine-gun fire on the Hôtel du Louvre. Anti-aircraft artillery did not even return fire, so great was the surprise. Apparently the Germans could not believe their eyes and assumed the plane was one of theirs.

23.6.42 The weather is beautiful and warm. Women go out without stockings in Paris and paint their legs with a special product – *41 fin* – that imitates the colour of stockings. On that subject, Olga Novikoff told me, "Now I'm forced to wash my legs every second day."

25.6.42 Lunched at Armenonville with the G.'s then went to Auteuil. There was a crowd at both places. The women were wearing enormous hats draped with tulle, the way they did in 1900. Horse-

69 Vyachesla Moloff was the Russian Minister of Foreign Affairs.

drawn carriages were parked at the entrance side by side with innumerable bicycles. One would have thought we were back in the time of Edward VII. However, the men were bareheaded and in jackets. They say pari-mutuel betting made fourteen million. There were only two yellow stars in the audience, one worn by a bookmaker, and almost no Germans, or else they were in civilian clothes. The black market was all anyone talked about in the grandstands; no one paid any attention to the horses.

7.7.42   Buildings occupied by the Germans along Boulevard Suchet are being camouflaged, painted in wide grey, black and green arabesques, like tanks. I suppose the reason for the camouflage is the proximity to the BSW – the *Befehlshaber der Sicherung West* – behind No. 6, which houses the headquarters of the security zone commander for the West, the German Admiral in command of coastal defence, and the proximity to No. 9 Avenue Maunoury, where submarine crews are billeted and Admiral Dönitz often stays. Admiral Kinzel said that the measures, camouflage and so on, are completely useless, because the Seine cannot be camouflaged and serves as a precise roadmap for the English on nights with a full moon. The building manager, on the other hand, told me that he was distraught about the measure, because the stone of the buildings is porous; it will be nearly impossible to remove the paint once peace has been restored.

Camouflaged German Naval Headquarters,
Boulevard Suchet, Paris 1942–43

The departure of Russian volunteers has been suspended for the time being. The Germans consider them unreliable – *unzuverlässig*.

The industrialist Tretiakoff, the right one this time, has been arrested by the Germans. He is accused of being a Soviet agent, having listening devices in his apartment above the premises occupied by the Russian military veterans' union and hiding Skoblin there after he allegedly delivered General Miller to Soviet agents.[70]

16.7.42 An expectant atmosphere reigned in Paris all day long on July 14. The English had announced on the radio that they were going to liberate Paris that day and had dropped leaflets with the same message inviting Parisians to wave tricoloured flags in the streets. The German guard was hit with a hand grenade – *Handgranaten* – that day, and notices were posted in public places and published in the newspapers warning the public that, in the event of an attack, men in the guilty party's family would be shot, including cousins, women sent to a concentration camp, and children sent to education centres. But the English did not come, and the day went by in calm.

A new order has been issued that Jews are not allowed to visit museums, go to movies, theatres, or restaurants, or be seen on major boulevards. They must travel in the last car on the metro and shop only at certain times in stores, by order of the lofty Höhere ss Führer.

Any request made to officials, even at a local police station, has to be accompanied by a signed form stating that you are not Jewish.

A German press release announced that Povorino has been taken, a large market town with a railway junction about 8 km from our property near Petrovskoye. I often went there on horseback. I try but cannot succeed in imagining battles against the peaceful backdrop of fields and forests. The sun is fiercely hot in that area in this season; injured soldiers left in the field must not survive their injuries long...

70 General Evgeny Miller was a Russian general and a leader of the White Army who was captured and taken back to Moscow, where he was tortured for two years before he was executed in 1939.

V. Bb. came back from the Russian front. He had us taste a shapeless green pancake, as hard as wood, a mixture of potato and sand, which people around St. Petersburg eat! He showed us many photos: partially destroyed palaces, twelve-year-olds breaking stones and paving roads...

22.7.42 Waiting in line, people fervently repeat, "They're coming soon now, they said so; the carrots are already cooking."[71]

I unofficially found out that the Germans have been given secret instructions in the event of Allied parachute landings. From now on, they are to send their valuables and clothing not in use to safety in Germany. Occupied buildings will not be defended, except the Rothschild, say the workers who are employed there. The Germans themselves will have to make their way to certain designated or to-be-designated centres. As for the employees, I suppose they will tuck their heads between their knees.

Lately there have been major roundups of Jews, gathered from everywhere and herded into the Winter Velodrome. The public is not allowed to approach them. There are rumours that they are going to be sent to Poland or Germany, but no one knows exactly what will happen to them after that. A continuous, frightening, low howl can be heard from the Velodrome that sends chills up your back.

A humiliating and insulting article appeared in the newspaper *Das Reich*, Goebbels' mouthpiece, on the "so-called Russian soul."

29.7.42 Lieutenant Pospichil has been arrested. He is accused of espionage! A letter addressed to him was intercepted, referring to a Swiss bank account they say he opened with payments for information he supplied to a third party. Despite the naïveté of the charge – it is highly improbable that a letter of that kind would be addressed to a spy, even admitting that he is one – they did not hesitate to arrest him, which proves that no one is really safe. He was released after a week in Lutétia and spoke to us freely about the incident.

71 Translator's note: The reference in French to carrots cooking would be understood at the time to refer to one of the coded personal messages – *"Les carottes sont cuites,"* which literally means the carrots are cooked – broadcast by the BBC Radio French service from London during World War II to Resistance fighters, in preparation for the Normandy landing.

1.8.42 Military parade on the Champs-Élysées. Marshal Rund-staedt and the head of the military ss, Dietrich, reviewed the ss troops returning from the Russian front. The parade lasted several hours. All the streets with access to the troops' passage were blocked and guarded by German sentinels. The troops looked like they were in perfect condition, all spit and polish, in full dress uniform; one would never have thought they were back from the front.

People are nervous because there have been rumours of a landing on the coast. It was even claimed that paratroopers had occupied the Montparnasse and Gare du Nord railway stations. While I was watching the parade through a window at Boulevard Suchet, Inspector Langheld came up to me and said with satisfaction, "Those troops take no prisoners...

Dined at Admiral Kinzel's. He seems to sincerely believe in the possibility of collaboration. He is meeting with industry representatives and the French authorities at evening events and assured me that they show great understanding and good will. He is convinced that the meetings could have a great influence on Franco-German relations. He also told me that I am cynical and blasé because I said I do not believe in the sincerity of those representatives nor the importance of the meetings!

19.8.42 Another small landing at Dieppe. The English stayed there for nine hours straight.

The regulations for buildings occupied by the Germans have become stricter. Even German women are no longer allowed to enter, and the employees of one building are not allowed to enter the other buildings. When the sailors from the back building at No. 2 Boulevard Suchet leave on exercises or there is a change of guard, armed guards are stationed at intersections facing the public. The entrance doors to occupied buildings are closed at a certain time in the evening, and the soldier on guard aims his revolver and flashlight at anyone who rings, only opens the door halfway, and asks for your name or the password – which, by the way, is usually clearly visible, written on a slip of paper lying on the guards' table!

Manoeuvres have taken place around Suchet that have hardly been reassuring. German infantry occupied the block of houses near the Bois de Boulogne and defended it with rifle, machine gun, and cannon fire – shooting blanks, naturally – against an opposing force advancing by crawling from the Bois. One of the guards told me that the exercises were in anticipation of civil war! In that event, the sailors will leave the buildings they currently occupy and the infantry will replace them. They are digging shelters in advance in the Bois, opposite the BSW, for infantry offices.

2.9.42 Here are the latest jokes going around Paris:

St. Peter rushes to the Lord and announces that Hitler in person is at the gates of Paradise. "Let's hurry," says the Lord, "or he'll start The New Paradise right here, as we speak." They rush off but, unfortunately, get there too late. The angels and archangels are already on parade, goose-stepping, the Milky Way has been skimmed, and the word "Jew" is written in big letters on all the stars.

And this one:

Two tramps are rummaging through garbage cans and find a tract with the title The New Europe.
"Do you know what that is?" asks one of the tramps.
"I have no idea," answers the other.
They see a German officer on the terrace of a café. "Officer," one of the tramps asks, "explain to us what The New Europe is."
"Glad to," answers the officer, "but I have to use examples. A car with one person at the wheel – that is a plutocracy. Several cars, each with one person at the wheel – that is an aristocracy. But when everyone has a car – that will be The New Europe."
The tramp thanks him and goes back to his comrade and says, "I'll explain it all to you. One tramp foraging in the garbage is a plutocracy. Several tramps doing the same thing – that is an aristocracy. But when the whole world is reduced to digging through the garbage, that will be The New Europe."

Professor Fecht liked those jokes very much.

13.9.42 Most of the Russian émigrés who had left for the Russian front have been sent back here "on official assignment." Rumour has it that the German command thought they were fraternizing with the people too much.

Saw the Gl.'s again. I had not seen them since the declaration of war on Yugoslavia. They were arrested and interned in Bodensee then Belgrade, but the Germans treated them properly. We talked about the Russian troops enlisted by the Germans, and Gl. said he admits that the Germans erred by enlisting émigrés, but the Russian émigrés will still have to leave Yugoslavia after the war. Yugoslavians will never forgive them for wearing the German uniform and policing them, especially after the widespread hospitality Russian émigrés enjoyed in Yugoslavia. He also talked about General Mikhailovitch, one of his friends, and said that he and his partisans are not bandits, as the English seem to be saying, but patriots worthy of respect. Gl. added that the Germans behaved differently in Yugoslavia; in France, they have orders to behave "properly" and follow them to the letter. However, in Belgrade, for example, the Germans executed an entire class of young schoolchildren because they were singing patriotic songs. Among them was the son of one of his friends, who told him, "I will wait ten years, twenty years if necessary, but I will avenge my child."

5.10.42 Rationing is going from bad to worse. The September coupons were not accepted. Butter has disappeared, even from the black market.

There was a curfew Sunday at three o'clock in the afternoon. I was at Bellevue when the warning was broadcast and had to stay there for the night.

Occupied buildings will no longer be heated starting November 1.

My nephew Michel is back in Paris. He was demobilized and went to apply for naturalization, which displeased Barbos and Bicha, who think that all hope of returning to Russia is not yet lost. We fear he will be sent to Germany; if he found a job in a German plant, it would at least be some guarantee of being allowed to stay in France. I think of Nancy and how we used to joke at Les Touches when she would say, "I don't want my husband to work like a slave in Germany." She was the one who was right, and we were wrong.

10.10.42 The buildings on Boulevard Suchet look more like a fortress with every passing day. A kind of wall made of wooden planks has been built along rue François Hébert. Whenever there is a reception at No. 6 Boulevard Suchet, where Minister Schleier stays, sentinels armed with machine guns are stationed at the entrance to all the surrounding intersections.

There is talk of an Allied threat at Dakar and in Africa in general.

26.10.42   All the employees of the requisitioned buildings at Boulevard Suchet were called in to try on gas masks. There were quite a few comical incidents, such as when the blond wig of one of the employees slid off her head and there she stood, embarrassed and blushing, with a head of white hair.

11.11.42   We have learned that the Americans have landed in Africa. French troops did not offer any resistance. After that, events unfolded like a movie being filmed. Marshal Pétain assumed command of the Land, Sea and Air Forces. After first appearing in all the newsreels and exhorting the French troops to defend the territory against the Allies, Darlan went to the Anglo-American camp.[72] On the radio, Churchill said that, after promising "toil, sweat and tears," he could now announce the greatest victory the world has ever seen. Rommel has fled. The Germans used to say *"Rommel – das ist der Mann"* – "Rommel is our man." The whole German machine is near collapse. I do not see how Germany will extricate itself from this situation, surrounded as it is by occupied countries that want only its defeat.

Today Parisians were buying, by the armful, cakes with no sugar or fat and sparkling wine to celebrate the liberation of the city, which should not be long now. Everyone thinks the Allies will be in Paris in three months, and collaborators are in trouble. Inspector Langenberg said to me yesterday, *"Jetzt müssen sich die Franzosen entscheiden"* – "Now the French have to make up their minds." As if the French had not *entschieden* long ago! He added that, if the French side with the Allies, they are going to be walking on bodies...

13.11.42   Darlan ended hostilities in Africa in the name of the Marshal, whom Hitler proposed move to Versailles, but the Marshal refused.

72   François Darlan was a French naval officer who played a role in the French government during World War II.

The Germans have occupied the free zone, but restrictions on travel from one zone to another have not been lifted. However, one can write more freely, on special postcards without any printed text.

Dinner at Admiral Kinzel's. He had a southern German there, a Captain Nostitz.[73] I find southern Germans much more like Austrians than Germans usually are, especially Prussians. A cultured atmosphere – we talked literature. Nostitz recited entire passages of Goethe's *Faust*. After he left, Kinzel told me that the latest news leaves no doubt that the situation is very grave. Italy's attitude is highly equivocal; that nation has never ended a war on the side it started anyway. Citing the opinion of the generals, who protested Hitler's decisions during the French campaign, the Admiral added that "despite everything" Hitler has shown military genius and must again be trusted. I told him that, instead of paying unwelcome court to France, who could care less, Hitler might have gained more by courting Russia, whereas his policy in occupied Russia has not only been anti-national but inhuman. To that, the Admiral responded, "Hitler paid court to many nations without success. We have conquered but we have not won."

Admiral Kinzel actually speaks fairly correct French; however, he made me laugh at dinner. When he was being served a dessert with egg whites, which I suppose he is not allowed to eat, he asked the waiter serving him, "Is it albumen?" and the waiter kept a straight face and answered, "Chemically speaking, yes, Monsieur Admiral."

15.11.42 Today all the bells were ringing in England to celebrate the Allied victory in Africa. The Germans evacuated Tobruk. How far we have come from the bells ringing in Germany to celebrate the armistice in 1940.

Despite the military situation so clearly unfavourable to the Axis, a collaboration meeting was recently held at the Winter Velodrome. I went out of curiosity. It was really an odd sight. Young boys and girls in semi-military uniform maintained order; there were a lot of people in the audience. You were frisked at the entrance. On the podium was the writer Châteaubriant, pale, emaciated; his voice was weak and lacking in resonance and did not carry. Beside him were

73 Most likely Count Friedrich von Nostitz-Rieneck (1891–1973)

Déat and a few dignitaries I did not know. The speeches could be summed up in these words: "Germany the Great will save us. Let us not delay in rallying to her. *Vive* Hitler! *Vive* the Franco-German Alliance!" Uniformed youth units stood on both sides of the podium, with a backdrop draped with tricolour flags and swastikas. All of that is beyond me, I must admit. I cannot understand applause like that for the leader of a nation that conquered you. A venue like the Winter Velodrome does not fill up with just the curious.

Yesterday one of the young inspectors was expounding economic theories to me at length. He predicts economic standardization, a few but well-developed models. "We will follow America's example, and the quality will show." While he was talking, the radio signalled a special announcement – *Sondermeldung* – usually an announcement of a German victory, which has not been heard for a long time. The inspector I was talking to immediately commented ironically, "A *Sondermeldung*? What can we announce now? Surely not the capture of Tobruk?" There is quite a group of Germans at Suchet who criticize everything done at this time, almost openly.

18.11.42 Marshal Pétain announced the removal of his heir apparent, the *Dauphin* as the French ironically call Darlan, who has just been appointed Commander in Chief of the Land, Sea and Air Forces by the Command in Africa. The Parisian public has been warned that food supplies would suffer because of the occupation in Africa – no more tea, chocolate, or coffee, and a cut in bread, tobacco, and fat rations.

There are rumours that relations between General Giraud and General de Gaulle are not the most friendly. At the K.'s, Mademoiselle Romanoff told us about Giraud fleeing. He had been arrested by the Germans but later escaped. He calmly took the train and sat in French uniform in a first-class car in the company of German officers. He introduced himself and told them he had just been appointed to conduct talks between the Marshal and Hitler and was on his way to an interview with Hitler. Informed by the German officers of the General's mission, the conductor did not ask for his ticket and did not bother him. It is interesting to see what can be done with a little daring.

A year has passed since the last letter from Serge Raevsky, a sad letter in which he complained of bugs, lice, and so on, asked for insecticides, and said he was suffering from the cold. He added that his sentiments had not changed but he sometimes envied the fate of a comrade who was killed. Then nothing more. It is hard to think he is still alive. If he fell into the hands of the Soviet troops or authorities, he would certainly have been treated as a spy or traitor. From their viewpoint, they may be right. It is sad, however, to think that Serge's idealism has been so poorly rewarded.

28.11.42 Friday evening, Inspector Lehmann approached me and said in a low voice, "Have you heard the latest news? Toulon has been occupied by our troops. The French fleet scuttled itself. The Armistice Army is going to be demobilized." I just had time to run to my room and turn on Swiss radio, which confirmed the news. A secret order from the Commandant in Toulon fell into Hitler's hands, saying that the French fleet was not to offer any resistance to the Allies in the event of a landing.

We are probably on the eve of major events; meanwhile, I keep on handling staff, rooms, restaurants, and so on. It reminds me of Ségur's memoirs of the Russian campaign where he talks about the streetsweeper. In response to his surprise at seeing her calmly continue her work in a city on fire, invaded by the French army, she says, "Oh, my good Sir! I have seen cities captured and recaptured in my lifetime. In spite of all that, the streets still have to be swept!"

29.11.42 German Advent will be celebrated Sunday and the following three Sundays. The Germans are already preparing wreathes of pine branches to be hung from the ceiling, laced with red ribbons and decorated with candles. They light one candle the first Sunday, two the second, and so on, a custom I did not know. There are no candles for sale now in Paris, so the Germans bought wax candles in churches and had them dyed red.

3.12.42 Olga Obolensky, the wife of my youngest brother Nicholas, arrived in Paris for a few days from Berlin. Her son from her first marriage went to meet her at the station and they recognized each other, even though they have not seen each other for twenty-five years. She came to see me and this is a summary of what she had time to tell me.

She was working as a nurse in a hospital at Kalinin (formerly Tver) when the Germans approached the city. Seeing the Soviet officials pack up to leave, she asked whether she should abandon the sick and injured patients and follow the Army in retreat or stay put. She was told, "Do as you think best; we will talk about it again when we return." So she decided to stay. The Germans did not bother her, but they did not remain long that time in Tver, which was bombed day and night during their stay. One morning, when she was out in the city, without a hat or money, she realized that the Germans were preparing to leave the city. She was afraid of reprisals and decided to take the opportunity to follow the troops of refugees leaving the city in the direction of Smolensk, then in German hands. She went part of the way in a sled, but soon had to give up her place to the injured and completed the trip on foot in the cold, at a temperature of 30°F. When she arrived in Smolensk, she found the city full of German troops in retreat and refugees from other regions. The municipality assigned her a corner in a room already occupied by ten other refugees, where she had to sleep on the floor under a table. There was not enough water to wash; she had not had time to bring a brush or comb and was covered with abscesses. The refugees were fed lunch at a "soup kitchen" and the daughter of a priest who lived in the same building gave her potatoes from time to time. Finally, she was fortunate to find a relative who gave her the address of a cousin in Berlin who got her the necessary permits to enter that city. Olga now works at the *Pressabteilung*, press department, in Berlin. When our compatriots complain about the effort demanded by the Germans at work, she answers that she feels like laughing and it is nothing but child's play compared to the effort required of a worker in Russia. One of the merits of the Soviets, she says, is that they have eliminated the proverbial laziness of Russian men. There are no more lazy people in Russia now. She criticizes those who do not want to join forces with the Germans. As long as the Soviet machine remains intact, and it will never disappear on its own, there can be no Russian nation. The flag of "Holy Russia" currently waved by the Soviets is only a temporary weapon they need to reach their goals. As soon as they are certain of victory, they will relegate the flag to the bottom of a drawer.

She told me about my brother Nicholas. He was the one who brought her food and clothing when she was arrested and put in prison in 1924. She and my brother were married in Novgorod, where she was deported when she got out of prison. For a long time, the authorities refused to issue her documents in my brother's name. I did not really understand her explanations. According to her, the Soviets do not automatically recognize the marriages of deportees. Perhaps they were not married in a civil ceremony, only in church, after all. That I am sure of because my brother sent me a few snapshots of a church in Novgorod at the time; he had written on the back of them in pencil, "In this church Madame and I went around the altar three times."

In any case, she uses her maiden name, Obolensky, here; to add to the confusion, it is also the name of her first husband because, in her first marriage, she had married an Obolensky cousin. She explained that was dictated by a desire to avoid harming my brother, in case he is still alive. She does not really believe in that possibility any longer, however. Without noticing, she already uses the past tense when she talks about him: "He *was* very strong physically; he *was* very nervous," and so on.

When she lived in Novgorod, my brother came to see her twice a month. At that time, he was working for Richard Henricksen, a Norwegian who was my only link with my brother for a long time. He wrote to give me news of Nicholas when he went back to Norway on holidays. I was also able to send him packages for my brother at the address of the Norwegian Legation in Finland. In that relatively peaceful period of his life, Nicholas was arrested several times. One of the times, he was released thanks to an involuntary service my father had done in the past for a man named Ouritzky. When he learned during interrogation that Nicholas was the son of the former Governor of Riga, Ouritzky told him that the Governor had done him a great service in his day and now Ouritzky wanted to pay his son the debt of gratitude he owed the father and he would have my brother released. He even added that, if my brother were ever arrested again, he should send word to him immediately. Alas, however, Ouritzky was soon assassinated and my brother lost his

protector. Olga thinks she recalls that my father, who for some reason was entitled to travel certain railway lines at that time between
Riga and St. Petersburg in his parlour car, got off at one of the
little stations along the route and was asked by a station manager
to help a poor student get to the capital. The poor student was the
young Ouritzky; he did not have the money he needed to continue
his journey. Completely unaware of whom he was dealing with, my
father had him board his rail car. The police were after him at the
time; however, naturally, they never thought of looking for him in
the rail car of the Governor of Riga.

In 1926, there was a resurgence of arrests following the murder of
Voïkoff. My brother was arrested again and sentenced to deportation
to the Solovetskiy Islands. Due to bad weather, however, he was held
at Kem on the mainland and spent three years there in a concentration camp forced to work on logging jobs. Food supplies were very
inadequate there, and Olga sent him packages of food. When the
three years were over, my brother had to choose to remain in the
camp as a free worker or live outside but still under surveillance and
look for work, which was impossible to find. Despite Olga's insis-
tence, my brother chose the first option and was soon transferred
with other groups of deportees to the *Bielostroi*, the canal that joins
the White and Baltic Seas, which was dug by deportees and political
prisoners. Olga got permission to join him there and, despite all kinds
of problems and the hard labour my brother had to do, she considers
those years the happiest of their life.

Although Nicholas was officially considered a "free worker," he
was ruled not by an iron hand but a pointed gun. He was constantly
threatened with being arrested again, punished, shot. His intelligence, energy, and abilities immediately distinguished him from the
mass of deportees, and he was assigned duties that involved some
responsibility, which was a great danger for anyone.

He was then transferred to the canal that now joins Moscow and
the Volga. The proximity to the Kremlin was not at all reassuring
for a deportee. This coincided with a period of purges. My brother
was arrested again on an improbable charge. He was accused of
openly taking sides with "Trotskyites" and saying out loud that he

would be happy to hear of Stalin's death. Olga tried everything, in vain, to prove that it was impossible my brother would have spoken those words, which amounted to a death sentence, but nothing worked; his name appeared among the names of Trotskyites at their trial. He barely avoided the death penalty and was sentenced to deportation. Olga went to see him in prison to tell him the changed verdict, but he was an emotional and physical wreck. He was walking with two canes and started to cry when he saw her. She told me, "It was truly horrible to see what that giant of a man had been reduced to." Nicholas told her that he had been examined by a doctor, who led him to believe that he could become paralyzed. He had, in fact, been complaining of pain in his back for a long time. As soon as his work was done, he would lie down and groan. "How my back hurts!" he would say.

When she came back the next day, she did not find him in the prison. He had been taken away. He wrote to her once more to tell her that he had a hernia operation and the incision had not closed. He asked her for food and clothing. She then received a note scribbled hastily in pencil saying that he was being deported to Tchebeya, the harshest camp, beyond the Arctic Circle, considered an "extermination" camp, and had not been allowed to take his belongings with him, always a bad sign. And since then, nothing further. That was in 1937. Olga added that, with my brother's energy and experience in camps, he would surely have found a way to get word to her if he was still alive. Hearing her story, I realized that I would not really want my brother to still be alive. Furthermore, anyone who knows the Soviet attitude toward "another useless mouth to feed" can have no doubt of his fate.

Olga told me about my mother's apartment in St. Petersburg. All the rooms had been divided by partitions based on the number of windows. Each "cell" was divided again by a horizontal partition to create a section to be used as a kitchen by the cell's occupant. The former kitchen was no longer adequate for the thirty or more tenants currently living in the apartment, who were mostly workers and peasants who had been evicted from their apartments or expelled from their villages. On that subject, Olga told me that one often sees a lot of abandoned houses in the villages and, when one asks the neighbours where the owners are, they answer, "deported." Along the roads, one sees endless lines of villagers, with packs on their backs, walking day and night, heading for other regions. Uprooting people opposed to the Party that way is one of the principles of Soviet policy; they are then sent to new territories. Olga considers the "Soviet machine" the most powerful that has ever existed, completely foreign to Russian character, inhuman, amoral. Such an organization dedicated to other goals could have achieved wonderful things. The mass of the population is now stupefied, trembling with fear, completely submissive to its leaders. The regime will never fall on its own. She is convinced that only war can shake it. Olga hopes her next stop will be America; a relative promised her to take care of it.

6.12.42 Barbos, Bicha, and I went to Olga's; she had gone to stay with her son Alek. Getting off the metro, we found ourselves in complete darkness. We did have a flashlight, but the battery was nearly used up. An obliging passerby lit the way and accompanied us to the door. I think that hard times like the times we are going through bring people together. Parisians are much more accommodating than in normal times.

Olga talked about the plan that had germinated in our minds at one time to exchange Nicholas for Soviet prisoners in other countries. She told us that the plan could have had some chance of success, because the Soviets sometimes attached importance to efforts made by a foreign dignitary. However, Nicholas was so discouraged and beaten that he did not want to hear anything about it when we succeeded in getting word to Olga about the plan we had in mind. She told us again that we must not forget that Nicholas had truly been a martyr, and that is how we should speak of him to the children and grandchildren in our family who never knew him.

10.12.42 Had lunch with the G.'s in a little restaurant on Place Saint-Cloud, the Paradou, with modern white and pink decor and filtered pink lighting. The menu was scribbled in pencil on an utterly innocuous piece of grey cardboard. Naturally there was no question of coupons, although the pike meuniere was swimming in black-market butter, the steak came with deep-fried potatoes, and real coffee was served with all the sugar you wanted. The whole meal with a half-bottle of white wine cost eighteen hundred francs, which is more than an average month's salary for eight hours of work a day – I was a guest. I should also add that the restaurant was full.

It is interesting to note that the individuals who now make a fortune in the black market were never in business, in most cases, in normal times. The black-market business done under the cover of German organizations is simply incredible. It is extremely easy to get "black market" products into these buildings on the pretext that they are for Germans. Traffickers generally carry a pass duly issued by some civilian employee in German offices through a friend or other relationship. Once they get the merchandise inside a requisitioned building, they are sure they will not be bothered by the French police anymore, as they are not allowed entry to the buildings. Z., an Armenian who is supposed to handle the staff in an occupied building on rue Henri Martin, is busy all day long delivering black-market merchandise. One day, he proudly showed me his headquarters in the basement; it reminded me of Ali Baba's cave, except instead of jars of gold pieces, there you see mounds of butter, whole wheels of cheese, quarters of meat, and so on. Of course the German authorities are aware of the traffic but tolerate it because they often go to Z. to supplement their meagre rations. I actually almost fell over, however, when Rautsmann, the Russian manager at No. 6 Boulevard Suchet, came to find me to show me the contents of a large room in the basement of No. 6 that is always locked; he always keeps the key on his person. What appeared before my amazed eyes was an actual slaughterhouse. Whole beef carcasses were stacked on tables up to the ceiling. Rautsmann was very agitated and told me, "You can imagine the work I have ahead of me. I have to liquidate this stock by tomorrow morning because we have no ice and the animals were killed a few days ago." I have never seen or heard how the butchered meat was brought in or out.

11.12.42 I was intending to go to the movies when the anti-aircraft artillery started firing. You could clearly see rocket flares bursting in the sky. Professor Fecht was with me at the time. He had just returned from Genoa and brought me news from Italy. He talked about the catastrophe in the tunnel in Genoa. A shelter had been set up in a tunnel that could hold a few hundred people. It was divided in half by a partition that was supposed to be kept open during raids. However, someone forgot to open it and people rushed into the tunnel and perished, crushed and suffocated. The number of victims who perished there was said to be more than three hundred and fifty, while only fifty people were killed in the city.

Building "M" behind No. 6 is empty right now. It was occupied all this time by *Kriegsmarine*. We rarely saw them, because they were always busy going on exercises. Only on Saturday did we see endless lines of them report to the non-commissioned officer on duty for inspection before they were allowed to "go ashore." The young sailors had to take their hankies out of their pockets and show that they were clean; their shoes had to be properly polished; their papers in order. That is one reason why the German soldiers one sees on Paris streets always look like they just came out of the box. I was sitting in the Bois de Boulogne one afternoon when some German sailors went by. The lower-middle class French couple beside me watched them, not very sympathetically, but ended up saying between clenched teeth, "They are well-groomed anyway, better than ours, that's for sure."

The non-commissioned officers on duty at No. 6 and No. 10 Boulevard Suchet told me they were going to be leaving for the front and would be replaced by reservists who are in their sixties or have disabilities. The reservists are nicknamed "*die Schwarze Husaren*" – the Black Hussars – because the uniforms they were given are French sailors' jackets dyed black. They are already on guard in several buildings and look as non-military as it is possible to look. There was even one hunchback among them. Parisians look at them quizzically. Certainly they are separated by an abyss from the young, blond, pink-cheeked athletes who paraded the streets in 1940. It is frightening to think of the human resources this war has swallowed in Germany and Russia. Everywhere the best, the strongest, the most inspired are the ones to disappear.

The guard leaving was made up of men in their forties. They were polite, conscientious, clean, and orderly. Despite the fact that four men in heavy boots and uniforms spent their days and nights in the small concierge's quarters, it was always clean and orderly. The blankets on the bunk beds were pulled tight and smooth, a vase with a few stems of greenery on the table, no discernible smell! I am ashamed to admit that the Russian employees who sleep at Suchet brought lice into their rooms!

The soldiers are leaving with low morale, however; they no longer believe in victory. One of them told me, "If Germany loses the war, not one of us will see his home or family again. Just think of the hordes of prisoners, the Greeks, French, Serbs, and so on, who will suddenly be released, storm our houses, and rape our women. If I have to see that, I would rather put a bullet in my head."

13.12.42   Spent the evening at Barbos'. We discussed the new regulations that apply to hiring employees. It is now prohibited to hire staff for German installations without prior authorization from the German Labour Office, which only gives authorization to those who have already worked in a German installation or in Germany. Pospichil is still waiting for authorization for the newly requisitioned building on rue de Courcelles, which was a brothel, among other things. They made the ladies leave but do not know how to get rid of the many mirrors that cover the walls and ceilings.

As usual, we talked about rising prices, which are no longer keeping step with salaries, and Bicha said out loud what I have always quietly thought. "We ask so little of life," she said. "Not wealth or entertainment, nothing more than to live without trembling that we will no longer have enough to pay for lunch in a few days, no longer have to depend on the whims of others."

14.12.42   At Bellevue, the Hitrovos read me a letter from their brother, an interpreter with the Hungarian army in Russia, who had just visited Kiev and Kharkov. In one of the stores in Kiev, he found a photograph album that belonged to his family, with photos of his parents, friends, and so on. The city has suffered a great deal. The people live mainly by barter, exchanging clothing for bread, and so on. Money no longer has any value. He also writes that his leaders are very polite and kind to him. The letter raised violent discussion. L. de W., who was there, does not want a Communist victory nor a German victory on the Russian front. He thinks a war, which would end disappointingly on that front, would weaken the Communist regime in Russia and reunite that country with the western group of nations from which it has been separated for so long. However, he wants a decisive victory for the Allies in Germany because, in his opinion, it would result in the introduction of the Communist regime in Germany, which would destroy the country. It is difficult to believe that the Allies would accept a Communist Germany, and Vladimir Hitrovo reminded him that, during the civil war in Russia, some of the people used to say, "Neither Lenin nor Koltchak." That political platform did not prove viable because, in periods of such bitter struggle, you have to take one side or the other. The moderate figure some wanted and waited for in 1917 never came. Now, Vladimir continued, we have to take sides with Germany or Russia and consider all the consequences of the victory of one or the other.

22.12.42 Weekly conference with Pospichil, who kept us after to offer sandwiches and a glass of port and wish us a Merry Christmas. He is always attentive and his voice and manners gentle. His Viennese accent softens even the harsh German language and always moves employees, even those who are fully aware that one cannot always count on his word.

26.12.42 This is the third Christmas we have spent under the Occupation.

The gardeners came to decorate the occupied buildings with pine boughs and laurel. Laurel is a plant only seen at funeral ceremonies in Germany, but the French did not know. Many of the Germans protested when they saw it hanging in garlands on the walls of the rooms. But it was already too late to change the building decorations. Engineer Wiedemann said to his cleaning woman, "Do you want to bury us already? This laurel is a bad omen."

The bar at No. 6 was set up to accommodate residents of No. 6 and No. 10, who have permission to invite the German secretaries and typists and dance this evening; Germans had been prohibited from dancing during the war.

I spent Christmas night at Boulevard Suchet to be sure everything was in order and was in my office, which has a couch so it can be used as a bedroom. Engineer Koch came and knocked on my door and asked me to come up to the bar for a few minutes because his comrades wanted to wish me a Merry Christmas. I was truly touched by the attention and followed Koch. The room was lit only by the candles on the Christmas tree. The Germans were sitting at tables in small groups and started singing "O Tannenbaum" then "Stille Nacht" and so on together, crossing arms and holding hands with their neighbour to the left and right. One of them, Engineer Zerbe, sat at the piano and improvised. Inspector Köttgen and a young secretary played duets on the accordion. There was a minor incident because, from among the dance music records, someone inadvertently put on a waltz by the Jewish composer Kalman, who had been blacklisted. One of the hard-liners got up at once and rudely insisted that the record be taken off immediately, which was done, but to a murmur of protest. The spoilsport, a particularly ugly man, a real Punchinello, has the ominous name "Aron." Rumour has it that he deleted an "a" from his name and is of Jewish origin, which would explain his excessive zeal.

Engineer Weidemann was sitting beside me. He had just returned from Marseille, which has recently been occupied by the Germans. He was in the mood for confidences and told me that relations between the Italians and the Germans are fairly tense and even permitted himself to say *"Der nächste Krieg kommt noch"* – "There will still be another war." However, relations between the French and the Germans are much friendlier in the former "no-no" zone than in our zone. Naturally, they are still on their honeymoon! Weidemann does not speak French and had to conduct all the talks with French Navy representatives in English. Then he told me about his early days in the Party, which he joined as soon as it was formed, and the problems he had finding work at that time. He had to be satisfied with a job as a streetcar collector and locksmith. He seemed sincere to me, motivated by patriotism.

The staff of the two buildings had time off starting at noon on the two holidays. On that occasion, one of the cleaning women at

No. 10, a Frenchwoman, even exclaimed, "We are so well off here; I wish it would last forever!" O.W. and I could not get over it.

I accompanied one of the cleaning women from No. 10 to the BSW infirmary. German medical staff are not required to treat civilian staff; however, they rarely refuse. I constantly ask the dentists at the *Zahnstation* not only for myself but also for employees and have never been refused.

The radio announced the assassination of Admiral Darlan, killed with three shots from a revolver by a young man whose name and nationality have not yet been disclosed.

Spent the evening with the Noldes. The Baron commented to me that the French are good colonists, show great tolerance toward the native people, and usually make them fond of their colonizers. Quite the contrary for the English, who succeeded in spite of that, by different methods, in building the greatest Empire in the world.

The Noldes heard Lieutenant Zweguintzoff, our young cousin, on English radio, explaining how England supplies arms to the Soviets via Persia, exactly the opposite of what happened in 1920, when England supplied arms to the Whites fighting against the Reds.

1943

OCCUPATION

"These Frenchwomen had forgotten for the moment that the children were German and just sympathized with a father's pain. How easy it would be to understand one another with a little good will and have pity on each other, but no, the law of nature is inexorable. All living things devour one another, on every level."

1.1.43 1943 will be a decisive year, according to the English.

The military situation does not look very favourable for the Germans: standstill at Stalingrad, English and Allied advance in Africa, Soviet offensive in the Caucasus and toward Veliki Louki.

Had tea at Sofka Polotzoff's. Black-market company. Everyone refused Sofka's cakes, rare as cake is these days, claiming to have eaten too much turkey and goose at Christmas!

12.1.43 The Soviet army has retaken Kislovodsk and Piatigorsk. My thoughts went back to 1918–19: street fighting, hostages being led away, executions... all against a festive natural background of brilliant sunlight, blue and pink mountain ranges. Kislovodsk had to see all that again.

Rotoff came to see me the evening before he left for the Russian front; he was here on leave. He was wearing a German uniform with slightly different epaulettes. He told me that he has been promoted to the rank of captain – by whom? – and is in command of turncoat Soviet prisoners, members of the Russian Liberation Army (the ROA)[74]

74 The Russian Liberation Army or *Russkaya Osvoboditel'naya Armiya* – the ROA or Vlasov army – was founded by Andrey Vlasov with the aim of overthrowing Stalin and the Communist regime. Formerly, Vlasov was General of the Red Army and captured by the Germans in July 1942. He became pro-Nazi likely out of self-preservation. After the war, the Allies sent him back to Russia and he was hanged for treason in 1946.

and German soldiers. He told me that there has never been a desertion in their ranks. His mission was to "clean out" occupied territory, which meant searching for partisans hiding in the woods. He mainly administered territories called municipalities, distributed land among the peasants, and so on. He confirmed that relations between Russian émigrés and Soviet Russians are excellent. I asked him if his current work in that sensitive situation in Russia gave him satisfaction. He answered in the affirmative and added that he is impatiently awaiting the time to return to the front. He is convinced that his activities are useful to the country. "But for most émigrés," he added, "it is still too soon to go back to Russia. They will not be able to find the right balance; they will be too soft or too cruel, also too unaware of local living conditions. Only men from there will be able to manage all the complicated work of rebuilding." Rotoff then told me that the Soviets put a price on his head because he treated the prisoners well and they joined his unit willingly. I never heard from Rotoff again and strongly doubt that he is still alive.[75]

22.1.43 Inspector Roll came through Paris and asked me to go to the theatre with him and one of his friends to thank me for taking care of him during his serious asthma attacks. After the theatre, we went to a nightclub, Le Doge, which is very popular right now, so popular that we had a lot of trouble finding a free table. I was curious to see what an establishment of that kind was like during the Occupation. The room was full to bursting, and people continued to arrive well after midnight – the legal curfew time. Roll told me that everyone there was a black-market dealer and had a safe conduct obtained through friends. Almost no German uniforms. We had barely sat down when an individual approached us, sat down at our table, and started offering coffee, cognac, and so on, in unlimited quantities. The people at nearby tables followed his example and assailed my companions with similar offers. Relatively few couples were dancing; most of the people were involved in animated conversations around tables or in the corners of the

75 This last sentence about Rotoff's fate was likely added to the journals by the Countess later.

room. Many were young people, "swing" and "zazou" types, slov-enly dressed, permanent waves in their hair, which hangs long at the back of the neck.

22.1.43 Rautsmann's daughter got a notice from the German Labour Office at 102 rue de l'Université, informing her that she is to report to the German Recruitment Office in the Seine *département*. She works in a toy workshop, but that type of work is not enough to avoid "worker mobilization."

Until now, worker requisition orders applied only to men. The Ger-man authorities systematically tried to increase the number of unem-ployed workers by replacing male employees with women as much as possible, ordering a reduction in sewing employees, and so on. Unem-ployed workers are reported to the German Office and almost always sent to work in Germany. One of the young cooks at Boulevard Suchet was sent to Germany and assigned to a pharmaceutical products plant there, contrary to all the promises made to him in Paris. He came back on leave and confided to me that he was joining the Resistance.

23.1.43 A German civilian official in his sixties who lived at No. 10 for a while and always professed National Socialist theories, Wr., came by and told us that he "plays soldiers" every Saturday afternoon; they are taught to handle various weapons, including machine guns.

28.1.43 The German army of two hundred thousand men has been surrounded near Stalingrad and partially annihilated, accord-ing to London radio. Only an island of twelve thousand men re-mains, who have no hope of escape. The Soviets offered surrender with military honours, but the Germans refused. Inspector Lehm-ann told me that a new German army is going to be raised to re-place the army in Stalingrad; all officials under thirty-five years old are going to be sent to the front. They expect that it will be possible to mobilize three million men.

There are rumours among Russian émigrés that Hitler is going to make a speech announcing the creation of a national government in Russia, maybe even a monarchy, with Grand Duke Vladimir Kirillov-ich at its head. To be honest, I highly doubt it; one has only to reread *Mein Kampf* to realize that a decision of that kind would never occur to Hitler. As far as the Grand Duke is concerned, I do not think he could ever become a leader; he has always been surrounded by poor advisors. I also doubt that First World War émigrés can have a voice on the subject despite their love for their homeland. They have lived outside its borders too long.

Dined at Admiral Kinzel's. There were six of us at the table: a *Kapitän zur See* (sea captain), Friedrich, along with the wife of a German bank manager, a colleague of Admiral Kinzel's, and Admiral Kinzel's secretary. Friedrich was wearing the Narvik shield on his chest, apparently a very rare decoration. His conversation was perfectly "international" and slightly ironic in tone. He must surely be anti-Nazi. He told me about his stay in Rome before the war; he attended an audience at the Vatican with the wife and son of one of his friends. A group of German soldiers led by an officer was also among the crowd of the faithful waiting to be blessed by the Pope. At the Pope's approach, everyone knelt down except the soldiers and their officer. A cardinal who knew Friedrich was German, even though he was in civilian clothes that day, approached him and asked him to explain to the officer commanding the soldiers that it would be desirable for his group to kneel down too, because that was the custom. Friedrich went to parley with the officer; however, the officer categorically refused to follow the crowd's example. When the Pope went by the soldiers, the group greeted him by clicking their heels and gave the Nazi raised-arm salute. The Pope had stopped in front of each of the faithful to bless them and say a few words but passed by the line of soldiers without stopping, without even looking at them.

The incident took the conversation on a detour to Ribbentrop's famous Nazi salute at an audience with the King of England. *Punch* immediately published a cartoon of an audience at Court with natives saluting head down, feet in the air, and Chinese rubbing noses with the Monarch. I notice that "*Heil* Hitler" and the raised-arm salute seem ridiculous, aggressive, and uncivilized to a whole class of Germans who think any deviation from European etiquette puts them in a position of inferiority. Admiral Kinzel has often admitted to me that he mutters "*Heil* Hitler" unintelligibly and salutes with his wrist only. Later we talked about the agrarian situation in pre-war Russia. In that cultured setting, no one had ever heard of communes – *община* – the community regime where the land belongs to the community not to an individual, or farms belonging to an individual in his own right – *хутора* – or Stolypine's reform. Everyone was convinced that all the land belonged outright to members of the Russian aristocracy.

The German offices in Lorient are going to be transferred to No. 6 Boulevard Suchet. The city of Lorient has almost been completely destroyed in bombings and most of the people have been evacuated.

1.2.43 General von Paulus, commander of the group surrounded at Stalingrad, has just been appointed Field Marshal *in extremis*. He is sure his troops have no hope of getting through the enemy lines that surround them.

Hitler did not make a speech on the anniversary of his taking power. Göring spoke in his place.

Saturday afternoon and Sunday morning, all the officials leave in special buses to go for military exercises. Engineer Koch told me that the site where they have exercises is usually reserved for executions. Recently he noticed that he had blood on the palms of his hands after a crawling exercise and did not understand why. It was explained to him that seventeen people were executed there that morning. He was very nervous and shocked recounting the incident to me, then composed himself and said, "What do you want? This is war."

Yesterday I went into a store that sold girdles made of rubber, a rationed product that cannot be found, after I saw some in the window display. The saleswoman asked me if I had any farm products to offer in exchange, butter and so on. She was not selling her merchandise for money.

2.2.43 Engineers and "inspectors," a vague term that covers any job, have arrived from Lorient and settled in Block "M." They are very demanding. When I think that all the comfort and *Gemütlichkeit* – cosiness – they are looking for are at the mercy of an Allied bomb, the effort seems rather futile. However, perhaps it is a sign of strength to "stoop and build again with worn out tools."[76]

76 Translator's note: a reference to lines from *If* by Rudyard Kipling: "If you can... watch the things you gave your life to, broken, and stoop and build them up with worn-out tools."

10.2.43 The Germans are retreating on the Russian front, while the Soviet armies are advancing with the same speed as the Germans in 1940. The Russian campaign is not turning out the way the Germans expected. It is difficult to find out exactly what is happening and the "why" and "because" of the retreat. German censorship is very strict. British radio broadcasts news unpublished in the newspapers; however, one never knows whether to believe everything it says because the information has often been inaccurate. In any case, von Paulus has been taken prisoner with the rest of his army, Stalingrad has been occupied by Soviet troops again, and German installations in Paris have been given the order to fly their flags at half-mast for a day.

11.2.43 The Germans are evacuating all offices from the coast.

Barbos and I ran every which way to find a clinic or hospital that would agree to care for our stepfather. All those establishments refuse the chronically ill, whom they are trying to send out to the provinces. Fyodor Oom, my stepfather, fell in the street a few months ago and fractured his pelvis; the surgeons refuse to operate on him because of his age and the shortage of anaesthetic. So he is condemned to stay in bed until the end of his days. The fall must also have affected his mind, because he often hallucinates, imagining that a Soviet agent is watching him, sitting beside him or hidden in a cupboard. We have changed hospitals three times, and the hospital where he is currently staying telephoned us to say that if we do not take him immediately, they are going to send him to an insane asylum. The kind of hallucinations he has only trouble him from time to time. Sometimes he discusses things completely reasonably and is perfectly well aware of his condition. He begs me not to abandon him.

Dined at Admiral Kinzel's; he spoke more freely than he usually does. All the offices and installations on the coast that can be dispensed with have been evacuated to the interior out of fear of an Allied landing. The siege of Stalingrad was ordered by Hitler, despite the opposition of his staff. Hitler ignored the advice of his generals, because they had also opposed the plan for the French campaign, which nevertheless ended in success.

20.2.43   The Soviet advance continues at the pace of the *Blitz-krieg*. Kharkov, Kursk, Ekaterinodar have been occupied again in succession by the Soviet armies. British radio considers the Russian campaign over and lost by Germany; however, the Germans still talk about a "supreme effort."

All men twenty to forty-five years old, whether they work for the Germans or not, have to be enumerated and will be sent to work in Germany, except in exceptional cases. Yesterday, I was with Xana Khv., who is responsible for the staff of a requisitioned building, when several of the cleaning women came crying to tell her that their husbands had just telephoned to say they passed the medical and were leaving that very evening for Germany...

Several of the German "inspectors" have told me that one no longer hears German spoken in the streets of Berlin, nothing but foreign languages.

26.2.43   I went to see our stepfather to tell him that I finally found a clinic that would take care of him, a Jewish clinic that hid Jews during the Occupation. I hardly dare believe that I will now be certain he will not be sent to an insane asylum in the country. We are going to have him moved to the new clinic, where he will be more comfortable. When I was leaving the clinic, I was hailed by an officer who told me that the whole district was blocked off as a result of an attack against Germans. It was prohibited to leave until a cyclist came through the streets and gave the order to unblock it. It was already nearly dark, and the stores and cafés were closed. I had no desire to walk the streets, perhaps for several hours, especially since I was two blocks away from the next district, where you could circulate freely. Parisian police officers only enforce all those orders halfheartedly, I must say, so after the officer checked to be sure there was no one except us two on the street, he quickly said to me, "Go, go on, I never saw you." I did not need to be told twice!

28.2.43   All businesses have to send a list of their employees to the German Recruitment Office.

1.3.43   N. Rehb. has been arrested for black-market dealings. His wife, Marina, is running all over Paris trying to get him released. Rehb. was delivering black-market butter to a soap factory that uses it to make bars of soap. The factory gave Rehb. a certain quantity, which he resold, mainly to German offices or barracks. His last delivery was refused for some reason that I do not know. He contacted an intermediary who gave him an address, in this case, a *Luftwaffe* (air force) garage. He had barely arrived there with his truck full of bars of soap when he was arrested by a Gestapo officer. That happened Thursday and it was only the following Tuesday that Marina learned that he was at Compiègne. Marina knows that I am acquainted with Olga Galitzine and had heard that she plays an important role with the Germans (!), so she came to ask me to go with her to Olga's. She thinks Olga can intercede for her husband.

4.3.43 George Bibikoff was given orders to leave to work in Germany. His father, V., is in Paris right now; he just came back from the Russian front with a completely different ideology. He brought photos of the palace at Tsarskoye Selo – broken furniture, pillaged interior – and photos of kids twelve or thirteen years old breaking stones on roads, guarded by German soldiers. He does not say much now and weighs his words. He opened a home for abandoned children at Tsarskoye Selo, and his wife Sophy is going to try to collect clothing to send there. She has also organized a women's committee here in Paris to take care of Russian children deported by the Germans. The children are currently in a camp at Cherbourg, where they work on big construction projects. One of our Russian priests has been given permission to go visit them once a month and takes packages prepared by the committee. Bicha and I joined the committee. I received a naïve and touching letter written in Russian from my "godson" that begins with the words "*Дорогая тётенька, бо не знаю как Вас инше звати,*" meaning, "Dear Auntie, I don't know what else to call you," and ends with a drawing showing two hands holding one another. Below them, the Russian child had scribbled his name, *Сашко* – Sashko, and the word *Тётя* – Auntie.

If we could at least hope this war would soften the regime in Russia! But the War of 1812 did not abolish serfdom!

General Vlasov, the Soviet General taken prisoner by the Germans, is now going to form an anti-Communist Russian army and has published a call for volunteers in all the newspapers.

Das Reich, Goebbels' official newspaper, published a very different article from previous articles we have become used to, which I quote from memory:

> It is impossible to hide from the people the extent of the misfortune that has befallen Germany. It must serve as a lesson and encourage people to grit their teeth and make every effort to reach a final victory. In every war, a time always comes when the last battalions are called up, and they decide the outcome of the battle.

And so it goes on, taking me back to 1940 when the usual slogans were suddenly abandoned and all the French Ministers went to pray at Notre-Dame-des-Victoires. The Germans no longer talk about the "sacrifice for Europe."

From now on, horseback riding is prohibited in the Bois de Boulogne and the Bois de Vincennes. Stores have also been ordered not to display luxury items in their windows anymore. They immediately took the order to ridiculous lengths; most painted their whole window white, leaving only a small transparent circle the size of a five-franc coin, which made all the passersby laugh.

Yesterday I met Bobrikoff in the street, and we walked part of the way together. He was going to the weekly session of the group of former Russian officers he belongs to, which is tolerated by the Germans. No member of that group has ever been able to explain the purpose of the secret organization to me, which is supposed to be the creation of a Russian nation. Vladimir Hitrovo sometimes takes part in the meetings and thinks it would be naïve to believe that any organization could meet once a week, issue membership cards to those who belong, and pursue secret goals, all unknown to the Germans.

23.3.43 Had lunch at the Eristoffs'. Countess Sollohub was there, who is Georgian by birth. She recounted with a great deal of humour how she cannot take two steps in the street without being stopped by gentlemen in civilian clothes, the anti-Jewish brigade, asking to see her papers, taking her for a Jewess. She assured us that she wants to go to the Prefecture and ask for a yellow star, the stigmata inflicted on Jews, so that she no longer has to repeat the same refrain, "No, I'm not Jewish, I'm Georgian."

Lately the owner of the nightclub called Shéhérazade, Nag., has been complaining that business is not doing as well. He only earns five thousand francs a day; the salary of the cleaning women at Suchet is approximately two thousand francs *per month*. There are often raids in his establishment; however, they are only aimed at German customers. The German police recently went to all the tables and checked the papers of diners – only the Germans, however, who were ordered to leave the premises.

2.4.43 Yesterday evening, as I was about to go down to the metro, the anti-aircraft guns started to roar noisily. The moon had not come up yet, and you could clearly see the rocket flares falling like fireworks in cascades of light. There is nothing more treacherous than flying anti-aircraft artillery shell splinters. The next morning I picked up a bunch of good-sized shell splinters around rue de l'Université.

The French press never mentions the Marshal's name anymore.

Erdely went to renew his worker card and was refused by the Prefecture; he was told that all foreigners who have worked for the Germans would no longer have a work permit after the war.

One sees a lot of flower gardens transformed into vegetable gardens. Mima Gag. has planted tomatoes in boxes she set on her windowsills.

I made an arrangement with Josephine, one of the cleaning women who lives at Suchet, and bought a couple of rabbits, which she promised to take care of; we are going to share their progeny. I did it for my stepfather, Fyodor Oom, who has an unfortunate craving for rabbit and refuses to understand that rabbit is no longer sold in the markets. At first, Josephine kept the rabbits in a little locked hut at the back of the yard, but several little rabbits have already mysteriously disappeared. Now she has taken them into an empty maid's room at No. 6 Boulevard Suchet, far from the eyes of the staff and German authorities, and watches them like the most precious treasure. I hope we will not be discovered!

7.4.43 Last Sunday, the Renault factory was bombed again. Sunday afternoon was so peaceful and the sun so radiant that no one could believe there was an air raid at first, especially since there was no air-raid warning. People out walking stopped in surprise; the curious stood at their windows... Then ambulances and fire trucks started speeding down Boulevard Suchet. I was still in the building at the time and went up on the roof of No. 10; from there, you could clearly see areas on fire beside the Renault plant and a tall column of smoke to the right as well, although I could not pinpoint its location at first. I learned later that it was the racetrack at Longchamp that had been hit. As they went by, Allied aircraft bombed an air defense gun emplacement in the middle of the racetrack. There were many victims, because there were races that day. The Erdelys had just rented an apartment at Porte Saint-Cloud. Their windowpanes were blown to bits, the entrance door torn from its hinges, and the dishes came clattering down from the kitchen shelves. Madame Erdely told me later that she and her husband took shelter in a corner, and she plugged her ears and started screaming. As soon as there was a lull, they wanted to go down to the basement, but it was full of water because the pipes had been hit. The four-storey house right beside theirs was completely destroyed and all its residents buried under rubble. Erdely told me that he saw some children in Boulogne pick up a lip with a piece of mustache still attached.

Allied planes dropped tracts recommending that the inhabitants of Boulogne leave the vicinity, because they are going to be back every weekend to bomb Renault.

The dye-works only dye three colours anymore – navy blue, black and brown; apparently the dyes always used to come from Germany.

9.4.43 Colette, one of the waitresses at No. 10, got pregnant by the former *Küchenmat*, the cook subsequently transferred to the coast, who is married and has children. She denied her condition to me for a long time and brought me numerous doctors' certificates stating that she was just anemic. She finally came to me to admit her pregnancy and asked me to keep her as long as possible. The *Hausoffizier*, Engert, is a fine man and allowed me to keep her by relegating her to the linen supply room. Her co-workers feel sorry for her and predict that her future will be complicated; still, they took up a collection for the unborn child. Engert also told me to give her some old sheets and a blanket. The new cook is already under attack by several waitresses who all aspire to the title of "sultan's wife." He is a handsome young man who keeps the kitchen in perfect order.

Tract dropped by Germans on Paris, mocking Churchill, 1943

However, he has already come to tell me, "I know how to make men obey me but it's different with women; I don't know how to control them. I always end up giving in."

Rautsmann brought me an Allied tract he picked up in the yard. In it, it says that an Allied landing is imminent and German troops are invited to join the Allies and not fire on the French.

11.4.43 The civilian official so devoted to the Party, W., came by No. 10 and gave us another political lecture, assuring us that Africa and the South of France are of no interest to the Germans.

Yesterday, I was entertained listening to the mysterious messages on British radio: "The train at 7:43 in the morning will stop en route" and "A door must be open or closed. I repeat twice." I was told they were messages for Resistance fighters announcing parachute landings of arms or people.

13.4.43 Everyone says the Germans have lost the war. On all sides, we hear, "When the Germans leave Paris..." and even "When the

Communists take power..." Madame Glouchevitch thinks France will surely go through a period of Communism, but it will not be serious because the French are anti-Communist by nature. What is serious is that so many people see only the possibility of two victors, Communism or National Socialism. Many young people, carried away by anti-Communist ideals, are enlisting in the militia.

14.4.43 Madame S. is a telephone operator at the switchboard in the Hôtel de la Tramouille, occupied by German typists. She told me that her husband had called her on the telephone one evening. She immediately called the *Heimleiterin*, who asked her who the gentleman was she just spoke to. Going into the office, she heard all the telephone conversations taking place at that moment, despite the fact that the receiver was not off the hook. She thinks the *Heimleiterin* must have a microphone attached to the switchboard.

17.4.43 Apparently there are many Frenchwomen who have "been with" Germans. When you cross Parc de la Muette in the evening, you see many French–German couples sitting on benches engaged in conversation in pidgin French. Former Suchet guards often brought me letters they had received from their French girlfriends and asked me to translate them – naïve letters and apparently sincere because, after the war, all a German soldier has to offer is the risk of reprisals.

19.4.43 Olga Galitzine appeared in front of Suchet in a horse-drawn carriage, had me called, and asked me to accompany her to Bougival, where she was going for lunch. The weather was so beautiful and I was so tired that I could not resist... On the way, L. joined us on a bicycle. We took roads bordered by charming villas covered with flowering wisteria. Also in season are lilacs and paulownia, exotic trees with large purple bell-like flowers, named in honour of the sister of Alexander the First, Anne Pavlovna, queen of Holland. All the flowers have turned the whole landscape a shade of purple. The suburbs of Paris, which I knew only from the windows of trains and cars, appeared in a completely different light. Our grandparents must have appreciated it more. It seems to me there was also more elegance in their day. The sight of Second Empire belles languishing under their parasols in victorias must have been more attractive than the young sportswomen one can barely see piled the way they do now into their low Simcas. A fashion magazine from the late nineteenth century came into my hands recently, showing the clothing found in shops, outfits meant for the racetrack, like the ones seen nowadays at English Court garden parties.

We had lunch at the Coq Hardi in a delicious setting on a terrace bordered by forget-me-nots and hydrangeas, a pre-war lunch, without coupons of course: roast beef, puff pastry, eggs, and so on. A garage for bicycles at the entrance, which means the patrons were from Paris. Not more than two German cars.

26.4.43   Russian Easter. Despite all the restrictions, I do not know of a Russian who did not have *koulitch* or *paskha*. The white cheese for the *paskha* was the hardest to find and varied in price from twenty-five to two hundred francs per kg, depending on supply sources. I went with my brother and his family to the rue de Lourmel church for the twelve Gospels. I was struck by the poverty of the church's parishioners. For Easter Mass, we went to rue Daru as usual. People there could be divided into two distinct groups. There were the profiteers, the sharks, or *pescicani* as the Italians nicknamed them after the First World War, whose wives wore enormous fur coats and garish hats. That group talked loud and was very popular. The other group, common mortals more modestly dressed, kept to themselves and looked thin, pale, and tired.

The religious service started at seven-thirty in the evening instead of at midnight, because of the blackout. It was strange to see the lighted candles held by the faithful in broad daylight!

All the press talks about is Katyn, where the Germans have discovered mass graves with thousands of bodies of Polish officers, most with their hands tied behind their back.[77] The newsreels showed au-

---

77   The Katyn massacre is generally thought to be the massacre of high-ranking Polish officers in the Katyn forest near Smolensk, Russia, in April–May 1940. In reality it was also the execution of thousands of civilians, scientists, journalists, doctors – the best and brightest of the Polish intelligentsia. For many years Russia and Germany blamed each other for this crime. Only recently, after the declassification of Stalinist documents, has Russia admitted responsibility for the slaughter. A sad postscript to this story is a plane crash in the Katyn forest in April 2011, which killed 103 high-ranking Polish politicians, generals and Olympic officials on their way to a joint Russian–Polish service of remembrance for the victims of Katyn.

diences the sad spectacle. An International Red Cross commission is to go investigate on site. The Germans seized on the incident to proclaim that such atrocities could only be committed by "barbarian beasts"; however, the French whisper that there are mass graves of that kind in Kiev, where ten thousand Jews have been executed by the Germans in reprisals for attacks that took place when the German army entered the city. I mentioned the Khatyn[78] situation to Admiral Kinzel, who commented, in the gruff tone he uses when he wants to avoid a particular issue, that the Germans would be better off not to raise that incident because they themselves have many things to reproach themselves for, but it is better not to talk about.

30.4.43 Saw Kouglovsky, who is back from the Russian–German front. He is very satisfied with his activities there. He told me that White Russian émigrés are welcomed by the Russian people, who share what provisions they have left with them. Many churches have been reopened, factories have been set up to manufacture church candles and workshops to make icons, but it is nearly impossible to find priests to say Mass or get liturgical accessories. In one of the churches Kouglovsky was in, the ciborium was an old jam jar and the priest's vestments were made from an old greyish-brown canvas bag. The priest told him that he is baptizing up to two hundred babies a day now. He is the fifth priest in the position since the arrival of the Germans; partisans assassinated all his predecessors. I asked Kouglovsky who exactly the "partisans" are and he answered, "Members of the local GPU[79] who did not follow the retreating armies but took refuge in the surrounding forests and often led raids into occupied territory. The people are afraid of them." While cutting through a forest, Rotoff was injured by partisans who had been on the lookout for him for a long time. Kouglovsky described the conditions of the inhabitants of the regions where he was as "absolutely miserable." He also assured me that the Germans requisitioned less food supplies than the Soviet

78 In 1943, inhabitants of the Belarus village of Khatyn were herded into a barn and burned alive. 149 people, including 75 children, perished. The massacre was in reprisal for the ambush and killing of four Nazi officers.
79 Translator's note: secret police

authorities did. The people were impressed by the German soldiers' cleanliness and concern for comfort; they had to relentlessly battle the lice, bugs, cockroaches, and so on that fill the houses.

1.5.43 Statutory holiday. Employees only worked until noon.

12.5.43 Tunis and Bizerte have been occupied by the Allies. Rommel has gone back to Berlin. The African campaign is ending in disaster for the Germans. There is no news of von Paulus, because the Soviets are not part of the International Red Cross and do not give any information about their prisoners. The Germans tried to threaten the Soviet authorities with the summary execution of Russian prisoners if they were not given the information they wanted on Marshal von Paulus and his army, but the Soviets replied that the fate of their prisoners was of no interest to them. They consider them traitors to their country.

There were air-raid warnings during the night from eleven o'clock until twelve-thirty and then from two o'clock until five o'clock in the morning.

According to British radio, Churchill has left for Washington to finalize a plan for the invasion of the continent.

25.5.43 The *Komintern* has been dissolved by the Soviets. Many Russians say bitterly, "Now that there is no longer an *Internationale* or Communism in Russia, there is nothing left but a nation like any other, which Germany wants to conquer." Personally, I think that, alas, the dissolution of the *Komintern* is just a political manoeuvre and will not change the regime in any way.

27.5.43 The Allies are bombing Italy incessantly and consider its fate sealed. Admiral Kinzel told me that the Germans have no illusions about the resistance of Italy; he personally thinks Germany will not be able to continue to fight under these conditions. However, he doubts that the Americans will ever reach an agreement with the Soviets and it could all wind up being a thirty-year-long world war.

Went to see Fyodor Oom by bicycle. When I got off my "little queen," I attached the bike with a lock and chain to a tree on the hospital grounds and then put a lock and chain through each of the two wheels. I am still never sure of finding it there when I come back out again. I brought Fyodor half a rabbit prepared by Josephine, thinking he would eat it in several sittings, but he threw himself on it like a savage and devoured it right then and there. I found him in bad shape, rambling on in a way that was comical at times, despite the tragic situation. For example, he showed me a poor old gentleman who lives in an outbuilding of the hospital that has been converted into an asylum, an old man who has completely regressed to childhood, saying he is a very rich man with a very important position and I must be particularly kind and respectful to him. He also complained that he cannot sleep at night because the walls of his room open and powerful projectors hidden in the walls light up the room *a giorno*.[80] He also made me open all the cupboards and wardrobes in his room to make sure his enemy was not inside them, a Soviet agent with the mission to watch him...

28.5.43   The German propaganda "line" about Russia has changed a little recently and no longer refers to *Bestien*. Newspapers and posters no longer show pictures of Soviet soldiers that look like they come from a mug-shot file. The Vlasov army is being promoted. Photos published of ROA soldiers look as good as the Germans did in 1940. However, Russian workers brought to Germany by force, the *Ost*, are paid nine marks a week, compared to foreign workers paid two marks an hour.

6.43   Marina Klugenau had a tooth pulled yesterday and then went to her friends' home. Around eleven o'clock in the evening, her friends called me at Boulevard Suchet, where I was spending the night, to tell me that she was hemorrhaging. They did not know what to do. They could not send her back home, because she lives in the suburbs. I told them to send her to me at Suchet at once, because it was getting close to curfew. I ran to No. 10, where Dr. Vogel and Dr. Hausser, the dentists, live. Unfortunately, they had gone out, and I could only leave a note for them at the guardroom. Meanwhile, I tried my best to take care of Marina, without any real results, however. I was really worried. Around midnight, the two doctors knocked on my door. They took Marina to the German dis-

---

80   Italian for "as if it were day"

pensary at the Rothschild villa; they brought her back within half an hour and told me the hemorrhaging had been stopped, and there was nothing more to worry about. Marina could no longer return home, so I put her to bed as best I could on the floor of my room. The next day, I wanted to thank the doctors for their services, so I asked them to come for a cup of coffee, since I had a small reserve left. Dr. Vogel is a fine man, helpful, calm, what the English call a "decent chap." Dr. Hausser is gifted with a much stronger personality, however, and a great deal of self-assurance; he is a politician and probably belongs to the Party. I cannot say that he is not helpful or kind, but one has the impression that he is always on his guard and, personally, I watch what I say to him. I asked O.W. to keep me company. Hausser had barely come in when he started giving us a political lecture, this time on the future of Europe after the war. The Atlantic coast of France will be joined to Belgium and Holland and become part of the Great Reich, and so on. He looked convinced, despite the current military situation. It really is mysticism, as Baron Nolde said.

Every morning, we see Lieutenant Niedner, who comes to get the products he is entitled to and then gives them to the custodian at the château de Bagatelle, who does his cooking for him. Niedner always walks around in civilian clothes; he is really a sculptor and painter, whose mission is to sculpt busts of submarine unit officers who have died for the Berlin Navy Museum. He works from photographs of the deceased and information provided by the family. He uses the little château de Bagatelle for a studio. I suppose he was sent to work in Paris to be safe from the bombings and to use French stocks of bronze and marble. He is well brought up, always dressed to the nines, and speaks very good French sprinkled with slang he has been taught by his girlfriend, who is a prima ballerina with the Opera.

Gypsies are being rounded up by the police and put in camps surrounded by barbed wire. The authorities – which ones? – want to settle nomadic tribes to facilitate control of their identification cards. Meanwhile, however, they are separating children from their mothers and placing children with the nuns; it was officially explained that the mothers do not suffer from the separation...

No vegetables in the markets but lots of wild strawberries in... the woods. I gathered a large basket in the space of two hours when we went with Barbos and Bicha to M.K.'s at Sainte-Mesme. The return trip to Paris reminded me of travelling by stagecoach. We were tightly packed in between baskets containing chickens, rabbits, strawberries, and so on, but everyone was good-humoured and no one complained. There was no check on arrival.

3.7.43 Slept at Suchet and was woken up around two o'clock in the morning by air-raid warning tests. The guard went to all the floors shouting, "*Alarmprüfung! Die Herren, die zum Ministerium und Einsatzgruppen gehören, nach unten! Das Auto kommt in 10 Minuten*" – "Practice drill. Men from the Ministry and the Special Forces are to meet downstairs. Cars will arrive in ten minutes." All the Germans hurried downstairs, completely dressed. I heard them come back around six-thirty in the morning.

Inspector Köttgen, who is to leave for three months' duty in Germany, came to ask me to keep his things during his absence, because his house in Cologne has been destroyed. And yet there is talk of "settling" nomadic tribes like gypsies! Are the Germans currently living a non-migratory life?

15.7.43 The Allies have landed in Sicily.

The French did not work on the national holiday, but the employees of German installations did not have the day off. I think they must have consoled themselves by thinking that this state of affairs is not going to last long. People talk only of the departure of the Germans. The linen keeper at No. 10, who is going on holidays in the next few days, asked me for her pay in advance – she is so sure of finding the building empty on her return. My hairdresser assures me most seriously that we will soon be eating *gâteau Saint-Honoré*[81] because, as soon as the Germans are gone, we will again have everything, the way we did in the past.

16.7.43 A whole group of inspectors at Suchet have had their homes destroyed by bombings and have left on special leave.

81 A time-consuming and extravagant cake named after St. Honoré, the patron saint of pastry chefs

20.7.43 Rome has been bombed. British radio said that the pilots' mission was to target strategic spots and spare historical monuments, but the newspapers here said that St. Lawrence Outside the Walls was hit, and there were deaths and injuries.

The Germans do not even try to hide the seriousness of the military situation anymore but always add, *"Immer den Kopf hoch halten"* – "Keep your chin up!" I must say that, generally speaking, they have guts. Naturally, I know nothing about German politics. I can only note the conversations I hear around me. What are Hitler's real goals? When I hear Hausser talk about the dismemberment of France or the soldiers on guard duty or Inspector Siewert tell me about pushing the Russian people east and repopulating the territory with German people, when I hear it whispered that the Jews taken to Germany are exterminated there, it all seems so senseless to me and so inconsistent with the attitude of the majority of the Germans I see, that I end up not really believing it.

In spite of everything, against all odds, the routine of German life continues as in the past. Pospichil is making a thousand plans for the organization of a newly requisitioned property at Nointel: bars, fridges, stoves, "harvest festivals"… When she heard that, Madame S. cried, "The poor unfortunate! Does he intend to set up all those comforts for the English?" Nointel is a lovely place, by the way. I took the opportunity to join Rautsmann and a group of employees who were going there to examine the possibility of a canteen at that location for women staff in the German navy who have to spend the weekends there, much against their will because they prefer to spend their Sundays with their escorts far from all *Heimleiterin*, female supervisors. I walked in the woods and even slept under a tree for a few hours! The château is a Louis XIII classic, a narrow rectangular box. From the château, however, run two alleys broken by stone retaining walls and terraces that rise to a clearing bordered by dark pines. In the middle a large pool has been installed with clear blue water. The air was full of the scent of pine sap warmed by the July sun, and the calm that reigned there made you forget the proximity of Paris, the war, and all the cares.

27.7.43 Sunday evening, the radio broadcast the news of Mussolini's resignation! The King has taken command of the armies and, at seventy years old, Badoglio is going to replace Mussolini. They say the war is going to continue, but I have trouble believing that the Italians, who did not want to fight in Mussolini's day, now want to fight for Badoglio. The radio, I mean London radio, did not give any details. One has the impression that negotiations are underway on all sides and the Allies are still waiting to cry victory. The same people who shouted "*Duce, Duce!*" and went to drop their wedding rings in the urns in Piazza Venezia in 1936 noisily demonstrated their joy at the announcement of his resignation.

The German press often alludes to a secret weapon, not gas, with devastating effects that will be terrifying. The Germans are working on its development and it will soon be completed, the famous *Vergeltung* – retaliation – promised by Hitler. Submarine activity has stopped completely. Apparently the English have found a way to locate German submarines, even at a great distance. This evening, when I was walking Inspector Kliem's little dog, which he leaves with me when he goes on a mission, near the Square honouring veterans who died for their country, I clearly heard the BBC broadcast, which was not even jammed. Two officers standing in a corner of the Square were listening to it with great interest, too.

29.7.43 The press does not mention Mussolini anywhere. He left the political scene to disappear into nothingness. The most conflicting rumours are going around about his fate. Arrested? Executed? Safe and sound in Germany? No one knows. The Chamber of Corporations has been dissolved.

Phosphorous bombs were dropped on Germany. People jumped into the water to avoid the flaming liquid falling from the sky and flowing in the streets.

Engineer Koch, who is usually very reserved, just came back from Germany, from Kiel, and told me, "*Wir haben den Krieg verloren*" – "We have lost the war."

Despite the race to the abyss, the course of human relations follows the path set by nature and circumstance. I have a lot of trouble navigating around the intrigues and love affairs between Germans and staff.

Recently two waitresses were pulling each other's hair and accusing each other of sharing the favours of the *Küchenmat*. I told them that they would be dismissed if it happened again; in truth, however, I really have no authority to do so. All it would take would be for the sergeant to go to Pospichil and intercede for his favourite and he would succeed. Marthe, the Alsatian saleswoman in the canteen who sells German cigarettes with tickets and black-market goods without tickets, is not only impolite but rude to everyone because Engineer K. is her boyfriend. Jeanne is a very beautiful and very stupid Basque woman who is a chambermaid in Block "M" and the girlfriend of Wiedemann, the head engineer. She takes advantage of that fact to lock herself in his room all day instead of doing her work. When I spoke to Pospichil about it, all he found to say was, "It is a very sensitive issue. Wiedemann has a very important position. I would not like to annoy him."

1.8.43   Yesterday I looked for a pair of shoes with a dress shoes coupon: leather shoes, that is, with a wooden sole. The streets were almost deserted. The women were dressed the way they usually dress for the beach: hatless, with bare feet in sandals made of cloth with wooden or cork soles, wearing Tyrolean dresses with full skirts in printed or checked fabric with straps and white blouses, their faces tanned. Saturdays and Sundays the metro is invaded by young people in camping clothes, backpacks on their backs, heading outside the city to spend the weekend in the country. That is a new sight for Paris and gives the impression of a "New Europe."

Hamburg has been bombed again. In a room at No. 10 Suchet today, I found five cleaning women with their arms raised to heaven, tears in their eyes, frozen in front of a photo of two children surrounded by a wreath of fresh flowers. They explained to me that they were the children of Inspector Hôfle from Hamburg, who were just killed in the latest bombing. Hôfle asked his cleaning woman to be sure to put fresh flowers in the wreath and give him the bill afterward. These Frenchwomen had forgotten for the moment that the children were German and just sympathized with a father's pain. How easy it would be to understand one another with a little good will and have pity on each other, but no, the law of nature is inexorable. All living things devour one another, on every level.

3.8.43 I succeeded in finding a pair of shoes with my coupon. The upper is made of leather, the leather of bedroom slippers, and the sole of joined wood, which makes the shoe flexible enough. I was even caught in heavy rain and came home with my shoes on!

9.8.43 Inspector Hôfle has just come back from Hamburg. His house was destroyed and his wife and children sent to a camp in Eastern Prussia.[82] He told me that eighty-four thousand people were killed or charred in the bombing. Barbos has also told us revolting details about the German occupation of Russia. First of all, the word of the day is that there is no Russian civilization or culture. In Germany, he came upon a hotel where two maids were taken when they got out of bed to go to work on a nearby bridge, they were told, but in reality were thrown into a truck and taken to a camp in Germany. From there, they were "rented" to whoever requested them. Like all their compatriots, they wore an armband with the word *Ost* and were not allowed to go into a restaurant or other public place of business.

10.8.43 From now on, you have to register with a supplier to be able to buy vegetables and fruit, which have disappeared from the Paris markets, although the suburbs have plenty.

Last night, the anti-aircraft guns made a hellish racket. You could not even hear the sound of the aircraft. The whole building on rue de l'Université shook.

11.8.43 British radio announced that the Allies have entered Catania, Italy. The people welcomed them with shouts of *"mangiare, mangiare!"*[83] The spokesman for the Commander in Chief announced that bread would be distributed without tickets in the marketplace. Propaganda methods are the same everywhere! Who does not remember the free bread and soup distribution organized by the Germans in the early days of the Occupation?

82 This note about Inspector's Hôfle's children being sent to a camp in Prussia seemingly contradicts the note on 1.8.43 that they had been killed in a bombing. It is likely that they were initially believed to have been killed but managed to survive.

83 Translator's note: Italian for "to eat"

12.8.43 Professor Fecht came to see me. He told me that the Fascist regime's time is up; it would disappear even if military events did not precipitate its fall. He has no fear of Communism in Italy, because the Allies will not allow it. The only victor in this war, in his opinion, will be America. England will lose all its dominions and France its colonies; even if France appears to keep them, America will have economic control. Likewise, the colonies of small countries, Holland, Belgium, and so on, will break away from the mother country.

14.8.43 Inspector Hôfle came to bring me his white military jacket, from which a "patriot" – his word choice – had cut out a large square piece of fabric without him noticing. Hôfle thinks it happened in a crowded metro.

15.8.43 Rome has been declared an "open city." Spoke at length with Inspector Häring, an Austrian, who tried to convince me that everything is not going as badly as one might think. One must judge mainly on the basis of the facts. Ukraine is still in German hands. The Soviets are starving and only holding on because of American aid. The loss of Orel, Belgorod, and so on, is unfortunate but not catastrophic. England does not know what is coming; anyone who has not seen it should hurry and go see it while there is still time.

I had the impression that, like a coward singing his head off to give himself courage, Häring was trying to find reasons to believe what he was telling me but, in his heart, already has doubts...

Schw. just came back from Hamburg; he arrived there immediately after the bombing. He told me about the bombing of the city. Of the seven people in his family who lived there, only two were spared. The streets were strewn with charred bodies, unrecognizable, either shrunken or extremely swollen. Common criminal prisoners wearing rubber gloves were clearing the streets, but not fast enough to avoid the smell of the bodies filling the entire neighbourhood. Allied aircraft dropped bombs with liquid phosphorous that flowed right into shelters where hundreds of people who had taken refuge there died, suffocated by the smoke. The inhabitants of Hamburg were evacuated en masse to other centres. I think that, after this war ends, few people will still be living where they were born and have lived all their lives. In Russia, the civilian population of some cities and villages has been transported a thousand leagues from their homes for military or political reasons. The population of entire regions of Poland and the Italian Tyrol changed in a few weeks. One of the sailors on guard duty told me a few months ago that the inhabitants of his village had been designated for Ukraine, according to a post-war plan. He greatly regretted having to leave his house, in spite of promises that his new house would be nicer than the previous one.

22.8.43 Sicily has been occupied by the Allies. The German newspapers commented on the operation with the usual slogans common to every country: "voluntary retreat by the German army" and "stunning proof of their perfect discipline" and so on.

Vlasov appears to no longer be *persona grata* to the Germans.

9.9.43 I just tuned in to British radio and heard that Italy has surrendered unconditionally... That is the first step toward the agony of the giant Germany... Even the day before yesterday, the Italian press officially denied any rumours of an upcoming armistice. Tracts were dropped by the Allies in Italy, encouraging the people to sabotage orders from the Germans, who must be considered "public enemy No. 1."

Last Friday's bombing shook several sections of Paris. Many buildings near Montparnasse railway station were damaged. Yesterday evening, when I was waiting for the train at Montparnasse station, a neighbouring building several stories high suddenly collapsed with a crash. The employees at Suchet hung on the telephone all day long, calling cafés near their homes to find out if the neighbourhood had suffered in the bombing.

10.9.43 Received a letter from Ella giving me our niece's address in Switzerland, which means that it will soon be prohibited to correspond with Italy...[84]

The French press, or rather the French press controlled by the Germans, is publishing articles on King Victor Emmanuel, reminiscent of what could be read in the newspapers at the time of the

84 Ella Shirkoff, Countess Hendrikoff's sister, lived in Rome. The niece in Switzerland was Marchesa Irina Rangoni-Machiavelli (neé Shirkoff).

Belgian Armistice.[85] The Traitor King is Victor Emmanuel now, and a cartoon showed him at a bank teller asking for payment in dollars of the "thirty pieces of silver."

A new Republican Fascist government has been proclaimed in Northern Italy; however, there has still been no news of Mussolini.

Madame Mojaïski, one of the telephone operators who is interested in astrology, assures me that she sees Hitler's end in the cards. She also sees a brilliant future for Russia, for *all* Russians, which seems to include a lot of different ideologies.

Germans are not allowed to go out after nightfall. If they go into the city during the day, they must leave their address and telephone number at the guardhouse. If there is no telephone where they are, they must call the guardhouse every two hours.

A friend of Vladimir's who just came back from the coast told him that the entire population there is armed. The weapons were provided by paratroopers who are dropped regularly in the region. The peasants set fire to farms that sell their produce to the Germans. You can get everything you want without tickets. For 20 francs, he had a meal in a bistro with 2 lbs of white bread, a bottle of beer, all the butter you want, and deli meats. He also saw bones covered with meat lying in the street; even the dogs did not want them.

13.9.43 In a dramatic turn of events on the Italian scene, Mussolini has been arrested and taken in various stages into the mountains, where he has been watched closely by anti-Fascist guards, and, as we now learn, was liberated in spectacular fashion by a group of German paratroopers. Hitler was nicer than the crowned heads were about the internment of the Russian Imperial family in Siberia. The daring action certainly merits admiration, although if Germany and Italy lose the war, as everything seems to predict, it would be better for Hitler and Mussolini to disappear from this world as soon as possible.

Saw Father Jean from the Russian Church in Auteuil. He spoke to the Russian priest in Hamburg, who told him that the first bombs fell on the zoo, right on the administration and guard buildings. Every-

---

85 King Victor Emmanuel III was king of Italy.

one in the buildings was killed on the spot. The animals escaped and, terrified, went to hide in the shelters with the human beings. The heat in the shelters was so intense that many people could not stand it any longer and went out into the street thinking they would find a bit of fresh air there, but got stuck in liquefied pavement and died.

One of the engineers in Block "M" left on a mission in a big hurry, as always. We have noticed that he is always sent on duty when important events are being prepared. I think his group must prepare the sea route for the fleet units; however, none of us, apart from the Germans, that is, really know the exact nature of those duties. This time, Engineer Herbert looked very worried. He only told me that the main phase of the war was going to carry on unceasingly; every resource was going to be put into action; "the world was going to tremble." I asked him, "Will it be gas?" and he answered, "Something like that but much worse." What is the liquid phosphorous poured by the Allies on Hamburg, after all, if not liquefied gas? The Führer promised "reprisals and that's what they'll get."

14.9.43   Engert, the *Hausoffizier*, asked me to prepare him a list of staff who could potentially stay at Suchet in the event that it becomes an "entrenched camp" – a charming prospect! Personally, I would not have much confidence in a list prepared in advance. Princess W. told me afterward, "You stayed calm, but I could read on your face what was going on inside you."

Long conversation with Inspector Struhal, an Austrian with polished manners and gentle speech. He married late and is the father of a little girl and is always in the process of buying something or having something knitted for her. He is not a Nazi by any stretch, more of a monarchist. He speaks very bitterly of the war in Italy: "*Italien ist nicht gross, der Rückzug wird nicht lang dauern*" – "Italy is not a big country. The retreat won't take long." He has no confidence in Mussolini's new government. He compares it to a poor salesman who launched into one business after another without building a solid base for the operations undertaken and waiting for them to bear fruit. He admires the social reforms made by Il Duce, but thinks his major fault was to get involved in unpopular wars. If he had been able to keep the peace, he would still be in power. In closing, he added, "I prefer dynasties because they have more time ahead of them to get rich, so they do so at a slower pace."

17.9.43 Bombing in Paris. The air-raid warning was sounded at dinner time, that is, around seven-thirty or eight o'clock. There was no anti-aircraft artillery fire, so no one budged. However, when a loud explosion was heard, everyone rushed to the large glass door in the restaurant at No. 10. An air battle was taking place in the grey sky. Small clouds of smoke were forming around the combatants, then three planes started going down in circles. One of them was in flames. Its golden nose zigzagged in the grey-blue sky like one of the coins travelers throw into the sea in the Indies then have the natives fish them back out. Except, in this case, we were powerless witnesses of the destruction of a human life...

Anti-aircraft guns could finally be heard. Squadrons of aircraft flew very low over the building at Suchet, which was shaken as if by an earthquake. The lights went out and everyone who was standing near the window rushed into the hall like a cloud of startled sparrows. All the lights went out and darkness reigned with no electricity until the evening of the next day.

Renault was hit again; so were the gates at Saint-Cloud, Auteuil, Bécon, and Asnières. Young Wolkonsky was killed on the tennis court by aircraft flying by Combertin stadium.

Thank God, it is raining today. Certainly this is the first time I have rejoiced at seeing rain fall...

21.9.43 Professor Fecht came to see me today. He is even more pessimistic than usual and told me that he has foreseen everything since 1939. At that time, they "blacklisted" him. He commented to me that Mussolini has not yet announced the list of his cabinet, and it will be impossible for him to rally many people around him.

23.9.43 Communist tracts were stuck on walls in various districts. Parisians are invited to join the Party to deliver the country from the oppressor.

1.10.43 Ritter, the General Labour Office representative from Germany, was killed in Paris. There were no reprisals, at least officially, but for two days French officers have been posted in front of all the buildings occupied by the Germans.

Tuned in to English radio; the station was not jammed. The announcer was giving instructions to Resistance fighters on how to act when carrying a secret message, how to conceal identity, how to sabotage work in factories, and so on.

Last Sunday, I was at Bellevue. Going past Renault, I could see the workshops; metal twisted every which way, stretches of wall collapsed. The Sèvres Bridge is open to traffic but the guardrail has been torn off in places, and the middle of the bridge is a pile of rocks, gaping holes, and debris. Everywhere are signs with a skull and crossbones painted black and the inscription "Danger of Death." As I was cautiously crossing the bridge, a clap of thunder was heard; people mistook the origin of the sound and immediately began running in terror in all directions.

In Bellevue, the Tête Noire district was also heavily hit. There were casualties, because the suburbs have no shelters, nothing but basements. There was an air-raid warning again in the evening despite the cloudy weather. I went to get bread and had the Hitrovos' two bassets on the leash; they immediately began to howl and pull so hard on the leash that they nearly made me trip. There was no electricity on rue Massenet; Olga's elderly mother was sitting in a corner shaking, with an icon of St. Seraphim of Sarov clutched in her hand.

Maroussia de N. came toward the end of the evening and talked to us about the bombing of Montluçon, where her daughter lives. The air-raid warning sounded during the night, and the town had no shelter, so Sofka Tr., her husband, and her baby took refuge in a field outside the town. They stayed lying down, flat on their stomachs, in a ditch for nearly an hour. They had run outside in their bathrobes and wrapped the baby in blankets.

3.10.43 K., one of the telephone operators at Suchet, told me lately, "God, you're innocent and don't know how to set yourself up. You could have earned thousands of francs with the position you are in. Look at what's happening around you. Do you know there are people who would pay dearly just for the job you have?"

9.10.43 Winter time came into effect again on October 4. Blackout is set for six-thirty in the evening. From that time, the city is plunged into blackness. To get around, you have to use flashlights; their light also has to be concealed, painted blue or covered with cellophane that colour. It is extremely difficult to find flashlight batteries. All the stores that used to sell them have a sign posted in the window saying, "No batteries left." Of course, one can find them on the black market, for example, in metro corridors or from illicit street vendors; however, they are usually inferior quality and only last a few hours.

Rag collection has been announced for October 6 to 16. Special collection centres have opened at various spots in the city. A special scale has been posted in the streets announcing the number of textile points given in exchange for rags: one point for every 0.25 g of woolens, one point for 3 kg of upholstery fabric, and so on. Points can be used separately, that is, not combined with a textile card. So I was able to get sixty-six points, which will be most useful to me, because I have spent all the points I was entitled to. Naturally, one can always "make an arrangement" by paying the salesgirl ten francs a point, a transaction that is illegal but very common.

13.10.43   Yesterday someone gave me back a twenty-franc note, which has an illustration of a sailor pulling on a rope. Hitler's head had been cut from a German stamp and inserted in the noose at the end of the rope. I was told that the notes are circulating throughout Paris.

Twenty franc note: Hitler's head in a noose

Maroulka Tchernychew was arrested on charges of espionage but released fairly quickly. She was the head of a purchasing office for the ss and was said to earn a good deal of money. Rumours were going around that she got a young Russian Jewess across the French–Spanish border: a certain Madame Ostrowska, a former customer of the Hitrovos, who was accused of being an Intelligence Service agent.

Dined at Admiral Kinzel's. He did not talk politics but discussed the principles of "fatherland" and "border" at length. He assured me that the destruction of the Tower of Babel was the worst punishment God has sent the human race. As long as men spoke the same language, they were unaware of the idea of a fatherland, with its latent threat of war.

Saw Liakhoff, who is back from the Russian front. He told me that the inhabitants of territory abandoned by the Germans willingly follow them in retreat, because the Soviet authorities subject anyone remaining in occupied territory to horrible reprisals. A peasant woman from the village Liakhoff's detachment just left joined them at the first halt and told them that her neighbour had been beaten with a revolver by her husband, who had returned with the Soviet troops. The husband also beat her aging parents, whom he blamed for not forcing his wife to leave. So the peasant woman did not wait for her son to return, but fled. Liakhoff added that, in Kiev, people were keeping a distance from both Germans and Russian émigrés.

Today, I saw scenes in the newsreels of the German retreat in Russia, endless lines of wagons, herds, horses, and so on following the German army, a real migration of people leaving behind their homes, memories, traditions, roots.

20.10.43 Herbert and Wiedemann returned from Rome. They saw Ella. Knowing that I had a sister in Rome, Wiedemann had suggested that I give him her address and, if he ever went that way, he would get news of her. This is the first time I have had news from Ella since the Italian armistice, because mail service with Italy, occupied or not, has been suspended. Rations are better in Rome than in Paris, and more goods are generally available. Wiedemann thinks that Rome will not be bombed by the Allies, but he does not have many illusions about Italian military resistance. He advised Ella not to budge from the city, that she would be better off there than anywhere.

31.10.43   The R.'s, both husband and wife, had dinner at my place. He told me that he was looking for a Russian, a completely honest man who speaks fluent German, for... the Security Services, the *Sicherheitsdienst*! He explained to me at length that, up to now, the Germans have had a bad experience with former émigrés and seem to have more confidence in the ROA. He thinks it would be "in the interests" of émigrés to take the ROA place.

1.11.43   Hellenschmidt, the *Baurat* – head of the planning department – in Wiedemann's group, died yesterday as a result of injuries he sustained in the bombing of the Paris–Caen train. Hellenschmidt was an ambitious man who thought his career had been blocked; he cordially detested his chief and all Russians generally. He had put me in real danger. Wiedemann's girlfriend, his housekeeper Jeanne, was afraid that I would interfere in her love affair with him and, I think, more out of stupidity than an actual desire to endanger me, had gone to Hellenschmidt and told him that I was a spy working for the Allies, and that I had found out in advance that Wiedemann was leaving for Italy by looking at his plans and maps, and had even given him a letter for someone in that country. I continue to think that she did it out of stupidity because she did not realize that she was compromising Wiedemann much more than me – certainly not in her interest. Delighted to play a dirty trick on Wiedemann, Hellenschmidt hurriedly sent an official report to the responsible authorities, and the report was sent to Pospichil and Engert, the *Hausoffizier*, for investigation. I suppose poor Wiedemann also had to spend a bad quarter of an hour and regretted many times that he did me a little favour by going to see Ella and giving her a few lines from me, even though I had not sealed the letter. I was questioned by Pospichil and Engert and explained to them that I had, in fact, given Wiedemann a letter for my sister. I had left the open letter on Wiedemann's desk in his room, and Jeanne was there at the time. It never occurred to me to hide it. Wiedemann did not specify when he was going to Rome or even tell me that he was going there soon. I gave him my sister's address in the hope that he might eventually see her someday and give her news from me, because I could not send her a letter by mail. Pospichil and Engert both told me that they were going to arrange things so that there would be no unpleasant outcome for me, and Pospichil added that, as soon as Jeanne went on vacation, he was going to take the opportunity to dismiss her on the pretext of staff cuts. I then called Jeanne in and asked her if she realized the seriousness of her accusation and her actions as a Frenchwoman, but she stubbornly kept repeating the same refrain, "Yes, I told Hellenschmidt that you are a spy." I finally gave up on any explanation.

Yesterday Minister Schleier gave a big reception. The former concierge of No. 6, who still lives in the building, was in the coatroom, while an honour guard of sailors was posted near the elevators and at the entry. All spit and polish, smart in full dress, they looked like they came fresh out of the box. An officer from the German embassy gave out bags of candy, cigars, cigarettes, and beer to the guards on duty and then went to tell the two French officers on guard in front of the building to come in and have their share as soon as they had a free moment.

3.11.43 Italians living in Paris have been registered and are now called by the various German placement offices. One of the waitresses, Anita, a poor Italian girl with an illegitimate child on her hands, who is always the butt of jokes by her fellow workers, came sobbing to find me and showed me her notice to appear. I promised her that I would go with her, because I knew that she would never be able to defend herself. I asked Pospichil to prepare a certificate for her as evidence that she works in a German installation, and we went to the office on rue Lafayette to take our place in the line going up a spiral staircase. Two Italian officers were maintaining order with the self-satisfied *gentilezza* characteristic of Italian administration. One of the people in line complained, saying to one of the officers, "All the same, I would rather be in your place than mine."

The officer answered, "Oh, you know, my place is no better than yours, no more certain."

While we moved one step at a time toward the room where the board, made up of a German, an Italian, and a Frenchman, was in session, I thought about how lucky Russian emigrants were to avoid being sent to Germany when war was declared with Russia. I watched the people leaving the room after seeing the board, which was *gentilissima*, according to the officer, only requiring 50% of the Italians called to appear. The men went for a medical and the ones declared fit for Germany were given a card by an employee, signed a contract and were told to report the next day to the railway station, the Gare de l'Est, where they would be paid a bonus of a thousand francs on departure. The faces around me were worried, and conversations were mainly about the health conditions that would allow them to stay in Paris. One of the men near me shouted out loud that he had syphilis and wanted to know if that was sufficient reason to avoid being sent to Germany.

When our turn finally came to go into the "Holy of Holies," I saw a German official in uniform sitting at a table beside an Italian, who looked gentle and friendly, and a Frenchman. Behind them stood a German civilian with the insignia of the Party on his lapel, probably a Gestapo representative. We were told to sit down and, without waiting to be questioned, I immediately addressed the official in uniform, in German, and gave him the certificate from Pospichil confirming my words. The German examined the document, passed it to his colleagues and, after questioning Anita and a brief consultation, told me that Anita would not be disturbed and we could go back home. The poor girl was so shaken that I had to take her arm and help her go down the staircase.

Conversation with Troubetzkoy, who was on duty yesterday at the telephone switchboard in No. 10. One of his friends came back from the Russian front and described to him in great detail massacres of Jews in Russian Ukraine. In one of the small towns occupied by the Germans, the entire Jewish population, men, women, and children, were assembled in the main town square, taken to the woods nearby, and herded into a clearing. Troubetzkoy's friend was one of the guards who had taken those unfortunates there, but did not see the massacre personally because he was posted at the entry to the woods.

However, German soldiers who witnessed the murder told him later that the men in the group of Jews were ordered to dig narrow ditches and the Jews were told to lie down in them in rows of six. The German police shot them in the back of the head with revolvers as they lay in the ditch. Meanwhile, the rest of the condemned were lying flat on their stomachs a little ways away from the ditches and were called in groups of six to undergo the same fate. Although Troubetzkoy's friend did not see the massacre with his own eyes, he remained convinced that the soldiers told him the truth, because not one of the Jews he had accompanied to the entrance to the woods came back out. However, he also told Troubetzkoy that hatred of Jews is so great in Russia that executions of that kind do not raise much protest among the non-Jewish population!

He also talked about going with the German army to another town where the entire Jewish population had been executed, except doctors, dentists, shoemakers, and tailors. The shoemakers and tailors were put in a concentration camp and, when the local populace needed their services, they asked the Commandant of the camp who had the orders filled by the prisoners. The doctors and dentists suffered the same fate as their unfortunate fellow Jews. Troubetzkoy's friend personally saw a Jewish dentist, who had treated him, taken away by German soldiers. When she spotted him, she started shouting and begging him for help. He tried to intervene, but the soldiers pushed him away, claiming they were carrying out an order – *Befehl*.

That is the first time I have heard a description of massacres of Jews by someone who saw them up close. One often hears talk of raids in the Jewish quarters, entire streets deserted from one day to the next. It is well known that the inhabitants were taken away by train to an unknown destination, but nothing is known of their ultimate fate. Only once did I hear the BBC refer to a concentration camp for Frenchwomen in Germany; judging by the names cited, I understood that the deportees had to be Jewish women. I cannot imagine the Boulevard Suchet "boarders" taking part in murder like that. I have even heard many of them refer to the SS with apprehension. Are those decent bourgeois Germans aware of the massacres? If so, what is their reaction? I do not venture into that terrain in my conversations with them. Since the incidents with Dr. Schark and with Jeanne, I have become more cautious and restrict myself to listening.

8.11.43 I went to rue d'Aboukir hoping to find fabric at affordable prices because of my dressmaking connections. The street was completely silent, deserted, all the shop fronts and windows closed – a dead city, one might say. Finally, seeing a butcher shop open, I went in and naïvely asked if it was a day the shops were closed every week. The man gave me an ironic look and asked me if I had lived in Paris long and was I not aware that I was in a Jewish neighbourhood? In fact, examining the storefronts more carefully, I read only names like Lévy, Nathan, and so on. He added that all those merchants had been deported...

One of the engineers at Suchet, a certain Ilzig, who had recently arrived, was suddenly recalled. I said in passing to the head engineer, Koch, that Ilzig must have received an order that saddened him because I had never seen him so depressed. Koch asked me point-blank if it had ever occurred to me that Ilzig might not be "100% Aryan." Then he added that Ilzig was half-Jewish; moreover, he had never concealed it. Ilzig had fought very bravely on the Russian front but could never get his officer's stripes because of his Jewish background. "Now," said Koch, "some zealous type at the Ministry must have found out about Ilzig's pedigree and brought the matter to light again. I admit that is the law, but why send him here if clearly he could not stay? Personally, I regret the incident, because Ilzig was a *netter Kerl* – a nice chap."

My number one friend, as O.W. calls him, came to Boulevard Suchet. He is a black marketeer. I do not know either his name or his address. I do not even remember how he introduced himself at Boulevard Suchet. He usually brings meat ordered the week before, which he transports openly on his bicycle rack. His prices are lower than in the Russian canteen in No. 6. He pulls samples of material, oil, cocoa, and so on out of his pockets. However, he is not the only one selling black market goods at No. 10 and No. 6. Lately Rautsmann laughingly said that a person could dress himself from head to toe and eat well without ever leaving the two buildings.

12.11.43 Grand Duke Boris has died of a heart attack. A large crowd attended the funeral services at his residence and, the day of his burial, the cathedral could barely hold all the people who came to pay their last respects. Grand Duke Boris was the only one of the members of the Imperial family in Paris who still had a little of his fortune and, on holidays, gathered some of the Russian émigrés at his home.

16.11.43 Armed attack at the liquid air plant in Boulogne. A woman came at nightfall to ask to speak to her husband, a worker in the plant, claiming an urgent matter. The guard let her in. She aimed a machine gun at him and let in fifteen or more armed individuals after her. They made all the workers leave and set explosives in the plant. The attempt did not succeed because the fuses burnt out too soon, but the terrorists were able to escape unmolested.

17.11.43 Went to the ballet at the Opera. It was the first time I had seen Serge Lifar on stage, and I found him admirable, as a director and dancer.

26.11.43 London radio announced that the bombing of Berlin was going to continue "until the heart of Germany stops beating."

A machine gun nest is being built on the roof at Suchet. At Bellevue, the left side of rue Massenet has been evacuated. The whole street is blocked with zigzagging cement walls, making it difficult for pedestrians to get through.

3.12.43 Yesterday there were manoeuvres around the Suchet block. Machine guns positioned on the roof shot blanks. Troops occupied the interior of the houses and, from outside, one could see rifle barrels through windows half-covered with sandbags. The gates and the entrance to Parc de la Muette were surrounded with barbed wire. The whole scene made a fairly gloomy impression. Tongues are wagging because no one knows for sure whether those precautions were being taken in anticipation of a landing or an armed revolt.

German coupons called *Reichsmarken*, circulating in occupied countries, have been withdrawn starting the first of this month. That will reduce the purchasing power of the Germans, who found the coupons easily in Germany where they were imported by foreign workers – hence a great fuss among "black marketeers."

Conversation with Inspector Klebe, an anti-Nazi, who said of Hitler, "A building painter, even a genius, cannot become a political leader within a few years." He also assured me that all Hitler's so-called social reforms existed well before he did.

5.12.43 Two young Vlasovs were brought to the canteen in No. 6, barely nineteen or twenty years old, in German uniform with a different colour of epaulettes and braid, nice but uneducated. We wished them good luck when we said good-bye and they immediately replied, "Above all wish us a speedy return to our dear homeland." But how can they go back to Russia after wearing anything even resembling a German uniform?

Yesterday Pasha M. brought small backpacks to Suchet and asked the Russian employees to make packs like them and fill them with items from her list for Christmas presents for Soviet prisoners and conscripts. One of the women at Suchet, a Frenchwoman, was curious to know who the backpacks were for and, after my explanation, cried, "Oh, how kind of the White Russians!"

Léon Grecoff is back from Germany, where he had gone to work. He told us that the working conditions were comfortable, heated rooms, adequate food, showers, and so on. In spite of that, workers who go on leave do not return – neither will he, for that matter – and the Germans now designate someone to answer for each worker who leaves. If that worker does not return, the guarantor can no longer go back to France. Léon informed the plant that he had enlisted in one of the units of Cossacks departing for the Eastern front, which is not true, and got all the food ration tickets he needed in exchange for... a large quantity of cigarettes.

12.12.43 Went to Madame Keller's, where one of her friends who just came back from Berlin talked to us about the city. He told us that he was unable to find the *Leipzigerstrasse* among all the surrounding debris. When he asked a *Schuppo* for directions to that street, the policeman obligingly answered, "But you're on the site of the *Leipzigerstrasse*, sir." Around him, however, was nothing but rubble. He spent a whole night putting out fires in houses burning after a bombing, aided only by women.

Rumour has it that the concierge at the Navy Ministry on Place de la Concorde, currently occupied by the German navy, is in the process of buying his fourth house, the fruit of his "transactions" with the occupants.

All the Germans in Paris at this time adore the city and dream only of coming back after the war!

Went to the *Odéon* to see *Souvenez-vous, Madame.* The German censor must not have read the script very carefully or else did not understand a thing! France, personified by a beautiful woman with blonde hair, has forgotten her past, even her name. A villainous doctor wants her "neither completely dead nor fully alive" and, as payment, gently removes an earring, saying, "See how skilfully I did that; she didn't even notice." Throughout is the refrain, "Victorious or vanquished, France can never die!" The ending portrays France in a blaze of glory.

22.12.43 At No. 10, Christmas dinner is being prepared for a hundred and twenty-six people. Admiral Kinzel will preside but has asked that "*O du fröhliche, O du selige [O Sanctissima]*" not be sung, as little in keeping with the current situation as it is.

English radio announced that the Americans are in the process of building eighty thousand landing craft.

Russia now has a national anthem. Up to now, the *Internationale* has served as its anthem.

Many attacks, train derailments, and so on. It is dangerous to venture into the back streets after nightfall.

23.12.43 Saw Skertz, who just came back from Berlin. He said that the first bombing of Berlin was the worst, because nobody expected it. The weather was poor that day, the sky overcast. Afterward, English radio praised the technical level achieved by the RAF that allowed an air raid to be carried out despite the weather conditions. Skertz was at a restaurant that evening, and the warning sounded so late that he barely had time to go up to his apartment, get the suitcase he always kept ready for such an eventuality, and go down to the shelter. He praised the discipline of the Germans. He saw women in the shelter, their teeth chattering in fear, get up at the signal of the zone head and go upstairs without a word to put out fires.

When the end of the raid was signalled, he went up to his place to eat a bit of sausage and drink a glass of beer because the emotion had given him an appetite. Then he went to see a neighbour, an older lady he found sitting calmly in her armchair; she had not gone down to the shelter and greeted him with these words: "As you see, I am still alive; my time has not yet come."

25.12.43 Here it is, the fourth Christmas we have spent under German occupation!

At two-thirty in the afternoon, the managers of the requisitioned buildings were called in by Pospichil, who offered port and cakes. At four o'clock, the *Küchenmat* at No. 10 served dinner to all the building staff, forty people in all! On the menu was soup, a slice of veal with potatoes and carrots for each person, and apple fruit cake. When the non-commissioned officer (NCO) came in, the staff applauded him by clapping. There had been a gift exchange to start. I was given an azalea from the staff and a bottle of perfume from the NCO. The staff gave him a complete smoking set in varnished wood. The NCO asked me to explain to the staff in French that the ingredients for the meal did not come from the canteen; he had bought them outside with the savings the Administration had managed to set aside. I did not understand his explanation very well, but it satisfied everyone.

There you have it. What would Mr. Churchill and Mr. Roosevelt say if they had the gift of second sight? I am far from thinking that these Frenchwomen are unpatriotic. Familiarity does not always breed contempt, however; human nature prevails over everything else. In any case, if the Allies ever occupy Germany, I am convinced that the Germans who have to work *volens nolens* for their former enemies will also end up establishing friendly relations with the ones who treat them with humanity.

OCCUPATION AND LIBERATION

"Parapets on the banks of the Seine have become observation points for Parisians, who watch the 'Great Departure' from front row seats. Apparent calm reigns in the city; however one senses that the calm is only on the surface..."

4.1.44 Allied aircraft again on New Year's Eve. Asnières, Courbevoie, and Neuilly were hit; two hundred and seventy dead and as many injured, not to mention victims of the devastation. The air-raid warning siren sounded at around eleven o'clock in the morning. With the carefree attitude of their age, Hélène and Marina tried to convince me that a warning without bombing was particularly annoying and they preferred "the real thing." A few minutes later, however, they were caught under air defence fire, just as they were crossing the little glassed gallery that goes from No. 6 to No. 10. A piece of shrapnel landed right at their feet, and they ran to the office, pale and frightened, with pieces of broken glass in their hair. Since that day, there have been warnings several times daily.

Mademoiselle Langheld, Admiral Kinzel's secretary, just got back from Berlin; she has lost all her belongings, which she had taken down to the basement as a precaution. Allied aircraft dropped phosphorous bombs, and the phosphorous flowed through the vents into all the shelters. However, her apartment on the first floor of the building was untouched. There you have it – everything is a question of chance! Her friends cook on... an electric iron. They no longer have gas or water, but still have electricity.

One of the engineers at No. 18 Boulevard Suchet told me that an Allied landing is imminent, because the much-heralded weapon of

German reprisals is going to be developed by February or March at the latest, and surely the Allies are aware of the progress of work.

Meanwhile, the Germans act as if they expect to withstand a siege in Paris and the surrounding area. They are building bunkers at Suchet. Walls with pieces of broken bottle are being erected in outlying areas. Huge slabs, which, I am told, cover anti-tank equipment, can be seen embedded in the ground in some streets in Paris.

This afternoon, I saw a train of carts carrying hay and straw pass Suchet. The soldiers driving them were all older and let themselves jolt back and forth, perched on their high seats, looking glum. Traffic stopped for a few minutes to let them pass, and people watched them go by with ironic looks on their faces.

The battleship *Scharnhorst* has been sunk by the English, a grave loss for the German navy, already short of naval units.

7.1.44 Departure of a large number of the officials from No. 6 and No. 10, including Inspector Lichy, who was still preoccupied at Christmas with making his room more *gemütlich* – comfortable; Inspector Siegmund, the son of the German Potin, who tried every way possible and impossible to avoid departure for the front; Inspector Sperling, the young philosopher, who fled the society of men, preferring to wander in the Bois de Boulogne with a book by a classical author in his pocket and his dog for his only company. In the end, however, his dog betrayed him and went over to the SS, who offered more plentiful fare. Sperling continued his pretentiousness right up to the last minute, but that was not the attitude of most of his comrades...

Berlin was bombed again. London radio said, "A few more raids and Berlin will disappear from the face of the earth."

Bicha's sister-in-law came back from Nice. She said that the whole coast is covered with barbed wire and anti-tank equipment. One of her Croatian countrywomen brought her news of her father and told her that Yugoslavia is in the grip of civil war. The English have abandoned the cause of General Mikhaïlovich and are now supporting a man called Tito, whose real name is Brosz; Tito is just the initials of his party.

10.1.44 Hofer, the head of German navy accounting, has been recalled to Germany because someone in high places remembered that he is married to a Jewess. Moreover, he did not hide it. His co-workers told me that Hofer had to fill out an official questionnaire at the time of his mobilization in Germany, like everyone else. His answer to the question "Are you and your wife Aryan?" was "No." I have wondered many a time whether Hofer himself is Aryan. Someone filed his questionnaire without reading it, and it was not until five years later that the omission was noticed! Hofer is to be assigned immediately to a civilian industrial firm, to a job much inferior to the job he currently holds. His wife has not been deported but placed in an armaments factory as a labourer. Hofer's recall was loudly criticized by all his co-workers – also a sign of the times.

13.1.44 Dinner at Admiral Kinzel's. He spoke of Hofer and regrets his departure. A year ago, the Admiral received an official letter bringing to his attention the fact that Hofer was married to a Jewess. The Admiral simply removed the letter from the file and did not pursue the matter. However, one of his co-workers saw the letter and tried to find out where it went. The Admiral thinks that co-worker, whose name he did not reveal, probably played that nasty trick on Hofer.

Engineer Koch told me that he and all his co-workers have been given an official card with the address of a location where they are to seek shelter in the event that their residence is bombed. The card also includes the name and address of a family required to provide accommodation in that eventuality.

Yesterday, a non-commissioned officer came to check the number of rooms that could potentially be occupied by the German embassy staff, if they move to Suchet. I sincerely hope I am no longer there in that event.

Serge Hitrovo just came back from the coast, from Saint-Brévin, which is guarded by the ROA, the Russian Liberation Army, former Russian prisoners who agreed to join a legion of volunteers formed by the Germans. Merchants now display bilingual signs, Russian and French. The French people are starting to speak a few words of Russian and say, "We were waiting for the Russians; well, they're already here." Serge said that the soldiers lack discipline and drink too much. He found it really strange, in the French landscape, to see Russian *telegas*, carts with typical Russian harnesses, like a *douga*. The soldiers wear a red star on their belt, and their machine guns are also marked with a red star. Serge spoke to them, and the soldiers told him that, in the event of a landing, they will not move! They also told him that everything is better at home. The officers are more reserved and do not speak readily. There are often tests of artificial fog on the coast; the fog is so dense that you cannot see two steps in front of you. Livestock flee in every direction in panic. Apart from that, the peasants and farmers do not complain because they have made a pile of money from occupiers and occupied. Serge stayed with a farmer who wanted to go with him to deposit a *million* francs in a Paris bank, but the fear of being robbed en route made him change his mind later.

Went to *Galeries Lafayette*. Despite all the restrictions and lack of raw materials, Parisian industry still manages to produce ravishing items. Objects are displayed just as carefully and artistically. The fabrics, ersatz though they may be, are just as attractive to the eye and soft to the touch. However, wrapping is no longer provided; you have to supply the paper and string yourself. There is no longer home delivery either.

25.1.44 Michel Zweguintzoff and Irène Shebeko got married on Sunday, January 23, at the church on rue Daru. Michel and our family arrived modestly by metro, which, fortunately, was running at that time. Most of the male and female friends of both families arrived at the church by bicycle.

I was the substitute for Michel's mother – *посаженная мать* – and had to go into the church with the groom. According to an old tradition, the bride's parents do not attend the ceremony at the church but wait for the married couple at their house with ritual "bread and salt" to welcome them! So I had gone to pick him up at home, where I found a nervous and agitated family, especially Michel who did nothing but yawn nervously. Serge Zweguintzoff arrived with young Nicholas who was to be the icon bearer – *мальчик с образом* – and was dressed in a Russian blouse with an embroidered collar. We waited for a fairly long time at the church for the arrival of the bride, who lives in Neuilly. The bride came with her old *Niana*, nanny, in a padded, closed, horse-drawn carriage, like the kind one sees in engravings from the last century. I entered the church on Michel's arm, following the child with the icon, who walked in ahead of us carrying the icon Michel had been blessed with. Michel was so emotional that when the priest asked him the ritual question, "Do you take this woman and so on?" he could not get a "Yes" out, and I heard the priest whisper to him, "Say yes."

Liouba Grecoff has just arrived from Cannes, demoralized and stunned. After living a comfortable middle-class life in Cannes – small villa, children's maid, cleaning woman, intimate circle of friends – she ended up stranded in a tiny room in a terrible district in Paris.

Tsarskoye Selo and Pavlovsk have been recaptured by the Soviet Army; there were battles at Anzio and Nettuno. Who would pay any attention now to a Hitler–Mussolini interview? There was a time, however, when an interview of that kind could change the face of the world.

More departures of German officials for the front. They will not be replaced.

London radio complimented Englishwomen on the restraint they show in their dress. That certainly does not apply to Parisian women; never have so many gathered, flared, draped dresses been seen, so many turbans that require a metre and a half of fabric, so many furs...

A couple of street vendors were given permission to bring their merchandise to No. 10 Boulevard Suchet and sell it without tickets to the Germans. They have some of absolutely everything – fabric, stockings, perfume, lingerie, shoes, chocolate, and so on.

Minister Schleier, who occupied the upper floor at No. 6 with his family, has left permanently for Germany; the movers carried out not only the family's luggage but also the furniture that belongs to the apartment's owner!

28.1.44 Had lunch at Madeleine de Ganay's. Her brother-in-law, Jean Gradis, is in a camp for Jews near Paris. He is subjected to the same regimen as his fellow internees and required to do various jobs. His daughter goes to see him, but can barely speak with him; however, she has permission to send him packages. The close quarters in the camps are not the least of the ills prisoners complain of; young Gradis told us that his father suffers from being in the company of "yids from rue du Sentier." Madeleine de Ganay has no fear of Bolshevism, which according to her is only a German propaganda weapon and will never become established in France; however, she thinks we will go through a "slightly Communist" period after the war, that is all, which will re-establish the balance between war profiteers and... others.

3.2.44 Admiral von Fischel was passing through Paris and tele-phoned me, or rather, had Lieutenant Lange telephone me – the famous Lange from *Abwehr* III, the German intelligence agency, who interrogated me so sensitively at the time of the Dr. Schark incident – to invite me to have tea with him at the Ritz, where he was staying. I vaguely knew von Fischel when I was working at the *Zahnstation* and he came several times for treatment. I was somewhat taken aback; the Ritz is surely the place I would least like to be seen in the company of a German. Nevertheless, I ac-cepted the invitation out of a mixture of curiosity and... I frankly admit, fear, because I never spoke to von Fischel much and his invitation astonished me.[86]

The Ritz, now almost fully occupied by the Germans, was fairly deserted. Two German sentries were posted at the entrance; how-ever, inside, the staff I knew by sight has not changed. I was taken to von Fischel's suite; he immediately rang for tea, which consisted of... tea and water, nothing more. Von Fischel then opened a locked cupboard, from which he took out cookies and sugar. Apparently I was the only guest. Von Fischel then began a monologue that lasted until my departure. He described life in Berlin nowadays. There is no longer water, which is distributed to people by truck, no gas or

---

86 Admiral Hermann von Fischel (1887–1950) began his long naval career dur-ing World War I. During World War II, he was the Commanding Admiral of the Channel Coast and later head of teaching staff for the German Air Force. He retired in November 1944 but was captured by the Russians in 1945. In 1950, he died in a POW camp near Moscow.

electricity. The first thing he did on arriving in Paris was to take a bath. His apartment in Berlin has been completely destroyed. After each bombing, mobile kitchens distribute hot soup to the people, and sometimes a small glass of brandy. Bombing victims are fed at kitchens of that kind as long as necessary.

He then told me that he was one of the first members of the National Socialist party and, since 1918, was in anti-Communist or anti-Spartacan units made up of volunteers, in which captains and simple sailors enlisted without any concern for rank; forty-year-olds were led by young lieutenants. I stayed for about an hour, listening attentively to von Fischel's monologues, which did not enlighten me as to the reason for his invitation!

The next time I saw Admiral Kinzel again, I told him how surprised I was at seeing a "von" show so much enthusiasm for the Nazi cause. To that, the Admiral replied, "Oh, but von Fischel has only been a 'von' for one generation."

5.2.44 Langenberg is back from Berlin. He spent two days in Paris. He told me that all means of communication have been destroyed in Berlin and it takes him three and a half hours to go from his residence to his office on foot and just as long to return. He has matured and aged – he is twenty-seven years old. In spite of and in response to everything, he repeats every German's stereotypical statements: "*Nur den Kopf hoch halten*" – "Whatever happens, keep your chin up!" and "*Der Krieg* muss *gewonnen werden*" – "We *have to* win the war!"

All empty apartments are going to be listed, and Parisian bombing victims housed in them, by order of the German authorities. Germans are certainly good administrators and organizers who know how to deal promptly with any eventuality and get the machine running again, orderly, and physically clean; on the other hand, they lack flexibility, grace, finesse, and the quick reflexes that seem to me to be essentially characteristic of the Latin race.

6.2.44 Air-raid warnings without interruption from eleven o'clock in the morning to three o'clock in the afternoon. The first warning signal caught me by surprise in a train near Alma metro station. When the end of the air-raid warning was signalled, I came back up to ground level and decided to continue on my way on foot. However, I had barely reached the Trocadéro station when I had to go back down to the metro because aircraft formations were flying overhead and the anti-aircraft guns were firing noisily. I had to wait half an hour for calm to be restored. The woman sitting on the platform beside me was talking loudly about how she admired the distinctly geometric order airplane squadrons maintained in the sky, while the person she was talking to reproached her for seeing beauty in "birds of death," whether German, French, or English.

All the services at Suchet were, of course, disrupted.

I went to the bakery in La Muette to get a 1 kg loaf of *white* bread, which you can order with tickets for 1,200 g and pay 12 francs 50 – if you have friends there! However, you cannot take it out unwrapped; you have to hide it under your coat, or ask the salesgirl to wrap it carefully in paper you supply yourself. We only had 50 g of butter for the month of February and no tea; up to now, you could choose between ersatz coffee, undrinkable, and 25 g of tea per month.

One sees few German soldiers in the streets; all who are able have been sent to the front and replaced in the rear by women and civilians. Boulevard Suchet, however, is really a centre of requisitioned buildings, and three soldiers armed with rifles, German military police, march back and forth day and night. The streets and squares are streaked with bright-coloured road signs in German. The occupied buildings are surrounded by fences painted white and guarded by sentinels; passersby are asked not to come too close. In front of some of the buildings fly National Socialist flags, a white swastika on a red background; SS residences fly flags with two white letters, "S" in the shape of a lightning bolt, on a black background. Most of the big hotels, such as the George V, the Plaza-Athénée, the Majestic, and so on, are occupied by the Germans. The Ritz, however, is only half occupied by the Germans; the Cambon side is reserved for the public, as is the bar and tearoom, for reasons it is easy to guess!

Along Avenue Henri Martin are the buildings requisitioned by the Torpedo Arsenal, the *Stabsquartier*, which is Admiral Kinzel's residence. The headquarters of the security zone commander for the West, the German Admiral in command of coastal defence, the

BSW – *Befehlshaber Sicherung West* – is on Avenue Maunoury, behind No. 6 Boulevard Suchet. The U-boat command headquarters, the BDU – *Befehlshaber der U-Boote* – was in the vicinity; however, the building is now empty, because Admiral Dönitz' staff was transferred to Angers and, in part, to Berlin.

Various hospitals, the new Beaujon, the Percy in Petit-Clamart, and part of La Pitié, have also been occupied by the German authorities. Some big theatres, such as the Rex and the Marignan, have become *Soldatenkino*, theatres reserved exclusively for German soldiers, who have to show ID when they go in.

Part of the Uni-Prix department store on rue des Ternes has become a *Soldatenkaufhaus*, reserved for German soldiers, but the other half is still open to the public. In the part open to the public, prices are the same as everywhere else, while in the requisitioned part reserved for German soldiers, black-market items are sold from French stock at prices slightly below black-market prices. The administrators remained the same; they are French – or French Russians! If you know them, you are sometimes able to quietly purchase black-market products officially sold at the *Soldatenkaufhaus*.

Germans, both military and civilians, travel free on the metro and are supposed to occupy first-class cars exclusively. However, for reasons I do not know, they are supposed to pay for their seats when they travel by bus.

11.2.44 Today one of the cleaning women at the BDU came to the office at No. 10 with a very strange request: to have a certificate prepared stating that she had given birth to a baby whose father is German. By the way, the woman is married to a Frenchman. The request awoke my curiosity and I asked her what profit she thought she would gain from a certificate of that kind. She assured me that her grocer told her that, with a certificate of that kind, she could get more food supplies than children of French fathers are entitled to get. She was very disappointed when I told her that we could not prepare a certificate of that kind.

15.2.44 Hélène Beningsen (née Bilderling), who is Russian in spite of those names, has been arrested as a hostage for her husband who escaped. She is expecting a baby in five months. Vera

Obolensky and Sofka Nossovich have also been arrested and even deported to Germany. They were caught distributing Gaullist tracts, so say they.

18.2.44 Swiss radio, which generally gives very accurate information, has announced peace negotiations between Finland and Russia.

Little Professor Fecht has been demobilized and recalled to Germany. He is a very cultivated man with a highly developed sense of humour, which is rare for a German.

Lieutenant Niedner came to tell us that he was almost sent to the front, but is going to succeed in avoiding that catastrophe. It was not very courageous of him, but he is not a soldier at heart at all; he is an artist who does not have the bohemian nature of an artist. He is very careful with his tips; apart from that, he is well brought up and educated.

22.2.44 Anti-terrorist courses have been started, where young people learn to handle machine guns, grenades, and so on, in order to fight *against* the Resistance. Marina Klugenau's brother Michel joined the organization and came to say good-bye to his sister at Suchet. I asked him if he had thought about it carefully before enlisting in the anti-Resistance militia. He answered that, above all, he is anti-Communist and, in his opinion, the Resistance forces are mainly made up not of patriots but Communists. The English support the Resistance because, to them, any way to fight the Germans is good; they do not think about the danger of a policy of that kind. Personally, Michel Klugenau detests the Germans but wants to combat the danger of Communism at all costs, which is personified by the Resistance in his view. He quit his job, which provided him an adequate salary, and overcame all his family's objections. He is also a member of the COSI, an individual workers' aid committee, a volunteer organization whose members go to bombing sites to lend assistance to people. Yet his older brother is with de Gaulle in Africa! Young people, as a whole, are in a hurry to give of themselves unstintingly, groping and searching for an ideal and often embracing conflicting causes with fiery passion!

23.2.44 Protective measures around occupied buildings are being reinforced. The outside fences at Boulevard Suchet are being recovered with barbed wire. The little garden where I planted tomatoes has been completely demolished. I missed my tomatoes, then consoled myself thinking that, in any case, I would no longer be at Suchet for the harvest... Despite that certainty, I followed the example of the Germans and replanted tomatoes in another corner of the garden!

24.2.44 Theft is increasing at Suchet. What can be done about it anyway? The temptation is so great, control is so difficult, and there is a shortage of everything in the markets. Everyone at every level steals, and everyone knows it. In the evening, kitchen staff walk out with any supplies they can get their hands on concealed on their person. When employees are hired, they are required to sign a contract committing *on pain of death* not to misappropriate anything for their own profit. Yet each time I do inventory near the end of the month, I find only a quarter of the cutlery and dishes. No one has been shot yet, thank God, and everyone knows that, too.

Young Colette came to show us her little girl, whose father is the former *Küchenmat*. The baby is beautiful and her mother proud and radiant. Her co-workers surrounded her; some exclaimed excitedly, others nodded their heads. Colette came to ask permission to live in one of the maid's rooms at Suchet. Engert smiled and said, "Well, since we started, we must continue," and told me to give her one of the best maid's rooms. The officials at Suchet took up a collection for Colette and gave me the money saying, "*Für unser Kind.*"

25.2.44 Churchill's speech announcing that the war might not end in 1944 had an immediate impact on the black market; supplies that had reappeared disappeared as if by enchantment, and sugar, which had dropped to one hundred thirty francs, went back up to two hundred twenty francs.

28.2.44 Madame S. came back from Berlin; she told me that you cannot find a single toothbrush there, not to mention other basic necessities. In restaurants, cutlery is only set on your table if you pay a twenty-mark deposit and, even so, most customers prefer to pay that amount and take away the cutlery, which cannot be found on the market. However, the government does what it can to provide assistance for bombing victims, who are given immediate assistance, one hundred marks for Germans and fifty marks for foreigners, and five hundred marks to purchase clothing. Bombing victims who had an apartment are reimbursed by the government for the value of its contents if they previously had an inventory certified by a special commissioner.

Merchandise is becoming increasingly rare here, too. The German Supply Corps no longer delivers tablecloths to occupied buildings. Engert considered the possibility of buying paper tablecloths but paper also cannot be found on the market.

2.3.44 Conversation with Inspector R. Before the war, he was director of a *Grands Magasins* consortium and member of an international labour commission. He spoke to me about the international conferences he attended and the problems he always had making foreigners understand National Socialist labour legislation. Members attending the conference listened to him with a great deal of good will and curiosity, but the questions they asked him proved that they had not understood anything from his explanation. He also added, "If international labour representatives can't grasp the meaning of our laws, what can you ask of people who are indifferent to social problems and do not want to change the status quo? How can we try to impose our ideas and laws on those who are content their own way? To them, our way of life is the same as prison." However, he is convinced that many of the laws will survive the regime and even be adopted by other countries. He anticipates the end of the war with apprehension, because he does not believe in the possibility of compromise. At the time of the collapse of France, England was in a worse position than now and, in spite of that, categorically refused any peace overtures from Germany. The evacuation of Dunkirk so ridiculed by the German press was a major military success and should have given Germany pause for reflection.

He doubts that Germany will come out of the war victorious; even in that case, however, he has concerns about the soldiers' return to their homes and the demobilization of women. What are the majority of German cities? Ruins piled on ruins. The country's entire population has been displaced. Children from Berlin were gradually evacuated to Luxemburg; now they have been brought back to Germany and evacuated to the rear. There will inevitably be social repercussions.

Went to the BSW infirmary to get the results of the blood tests all employees in the Suchet restaurant and kitchen were required to have, and 10% of the staff had positive Wassermann reactions![87] The German nurse told me that he was going to repeat the blood tests for greater certainty; however, everyone who has a positive reaction will, of course, be dismissed. The test is compulsory in Germany for restaurant staff.

The Suchet block was like a beehive this morning! I could clearly see that there were a lot of Germans burning to know the test results but did not know how to get them without compromising themselves, and tried to find out by devious methods. The non-commissioned officer from the kitchen nevertheless took advantage of a free moment to corner me and ask, blushing and stuttering, the results of the test for a waitress, Louisette... who will have to have her test repeated, a bad sign, alas!

5.3.44 I slept at Suchet last night and was woken by very loud anti-aircraft fire. Then, around four-thirty in the morning, the night watchman came and knocked on my door because the lights were left on in the restaurant at No. 10 and had to be turned off at all costs; however, the door was locked and the keys that should have been hanging in the guard room could not be found. I hastily got dressed and ran across the space separating No. 6 from No. 10, admiring as I ran the air defence rockets streaking across the sky. When I got to No. 10, naturally I immediately found the keys hanging in their customary place in the guard room, in clear view; however, the current German guard is already not very wide awake in the daytime and becomes completely useless at night. Then at six-thirty in the morning, the coffee maker came to ask me to open the cupboards for her because, this time, they really could not find the

87 The Wassermann test was an inaccurate blood test used to detect syphilis. It also produced positive readings for tuberculosis and malaria.

keys. I have duplicates of all the keys as well as a master key. The coffee maker is not a very intelligent girl and scatterbrained; however, one has to accept anyone sent by the German Supply Corps and not be too difficult.

A. A. Polovtsoff has died.[88] "One of the last Europeans," someone said of him, meaning by that "one of the last representatives of European culture." He had been the curator of the Imperial Palaces at the time of the Revolution, and it was a pleasure to hear him explain such-and-such a style, describe in detail such-and-such a room in a palace, talk about its history...

10.3.44 Madame Aslanoff, who works in the linen room at Suchet, is in despair; her daughter left last year for Germany where she was called by an uncle and worked there as an architect. Of course, she had to sign a contract. Now the bombings have affected her morale to such an extent that she no longer wants to go back there. There is nothing to be done, however; the German authorities require her to return to Berlin.

14.3.44 All the telephones in the buildings at No. 6 and No. 10 have been removed and sent to the front. Only four were left behind: two for the guard rooms, one in the office at No. 10, and one for the *Hausoffizier*. Reflecting mirrors have been put up in the guard rooms. At the building entrances, the doors are locked at nightfall, and the guard opens the door with his revolver aimed at whoever rings the doorbell. One of the guards told me that he had bought civilian clothes and intended to hide in Paris if he was sent to Germany.

Movie houses, concert halls, and theatres are closed several days a week because of the shortage of electrical power.

18.3.44 The metro will only run until ten o'clock from now on. Twenty-one stations are going to be closed. Industrial plants will not have power from eight-thirty to eleven o'clock in the morning and from two to six o'clock in the afternoon. Theatres will be open from six to nine o'clock in the evening.

88 A Russian diplomat to India, an expert in Russian art, who tried to save the art in the Imperial Palaces at the time of the Revolution. His extensive papers are housed in the Yale University Library Archives.

London radio is encouraging Parisians to carry as many packages and bundles as possible in the metro to make it more difficult to search for weapons, which are often carried camouflaged on the metro. Madame L. told me that she had a terrible scare recently; she was in a moving metro car when French police officers started checking the packages carried by travellers. Madame L. suddenly felt a heavy weight on her shoulders; two people behind her had machine guns aimed at the officers and were resting them on her shoulders. The officers pretended not to notice, and the individuals with machine guns jumped off the train at the first station it came to and got lost in the crowd.

Inspector M. told me that a woman he knew had been completely undressed on the street. A passerby lent her his overcoat and accompanied her home.

25.3.44 Hungary has been occupied by German paratroopers.

Some of the sheets and blankets at the Suchet buildings have to be returned. There will now only be two sheets and two blankets per person in the linen room. Employees who were living at No. 6 and No. 10 will have to leave the buildings, because they are going to be returned to the military authorities and defended "if necessary."

I was at Anne-Marie du Pontavice's, who gave me dresses and clothing for Hélène Bilderling; Hélène can no longer get into her dresses because she is expecting a baby, and had to cut and reattach them with laces. Hélène is still in prison; however, lately she was allowed to see her mother. Marie-Carmen du Pontavice, who is Spanish by birth, was also at Anne-Marie's; Anne-Marie strongly advised her to get involved helping Spanish anarchists who were arrested as a result of an operation against the Resistance and are not getting any help from anyone. Marie-Carmen categorically refused, saying that she knew her countrymen better than anyone; the abbot she would have had to go with to visit detainees will never find the necessary words to reach those fanatics, who were fighting in the middle of winter barefoot in sandals and shirtsleeves, without a jacket or sweater, and were none the worse for it. She added that she prefers to use her time and money to help children in the area.

I went past Avenue Kléber yesterday; all that can be seen are barbed-wire fences, bunkers, and German sentinels. The public has to take a detour via Avenue Victor Hugo. I saw a passerby come through one of the barricades and asked him if I could go through. "Oh, no," he answered. "Only the unfortunates privileged to live on the avenue, of whom, alas, I am one, are allowed through."

7.4.44 Hélène Bilderling has finally been released.

It is rumoured that all big dogs are going to be recorded and requisitioned to be sent to the front where they will be used to detect mines. It may be ridiculous to pity dogs when so many human beings are deported or killed every day, but I cannot stop myself.

11.4.44 The Easter season was as sad as the times. The Villeneuve-Saint-Georges area has been bombed. Employees who live in the southern suburbs did not come to work. Trains that were to depart from one station, the Gare de Lyon, were sent to the Gare de l'Est then finally to the Gare Montparnasse. Barbos, Bicha, and I went to visit Chaville. The woods have huge craters here and there; the neighbouring village was half-destroyed; twisted gates hung in the air; shutters off houses, chairs, gas heaters, and so on lie here and there, half-buried in the craters.

Coal, which is used to manufacture synthetic gas, will no longer be delivered to Suchet. From now on, wood will be used for cooking. There will only be hot water one afternoon a week. Several canteens will be closed, and the employees who ate there will come to the canteen at Suchet to eat. There have been no potatoes distributed for weeks.

Odessa has been evacuated by the German army. The release announcing the evacuation was highly original and can be summarized as follows: the Russians thought the Germans were going to defend Odessa. Well, they were indeed caught out – the Germans simply abandoned it.

Michel Klugenau just got back from a military operation against Resistance fighters. He recounted to us enthusiastically how his unit fought against an alpine regiment commanded by a general who had occupied an almost inaccessible plateau in Savoy since the armistice. The militia found supplies and weapons dropped by parachute at that location. Michel is so wrapped up in what he calls his "mission" that it is absolutely impossible to talk to him. It is really sad!

23.4.44 A tragicomic incident occurred at Suchet. I slept at Suchet that night and was woken up at five-thirty in the morning by shouts and the noise of a door being smashed in. I hastily got dressed and opened my door. The whole corridor was full of smoke; all one could see were grey silhouettes moving in a kind of fog. Someone shouted in German that the landing had taken place and American paratroopers had taken the building. Being caught in a fight was certainly only half appealing. Nevertheless, I decided to go down to the guard room using the service stairs, where I passed shadows dragging suitcases and bundles behind them. At the guard room, I found two inspectors unconscious; the guard was trying to resuscitate them and explained that the two inspectors had fallen asleep holding a lighted cigarette after drinking too much. All the materials are now artificial, so the whole room caught on fire in no time. Siewert's room was next door; he noticed a strong smell of smoke and punched in the door and pulled the two drunks out in time. The panic that took over the building shows how worried the Germans are about the possibility of a landing.

The northern part of Paris was bombed from midnight until two o'clock in the morning. The racket was so loud, one could not close one's eyes.

The next day, London radio announced that a thousand aircraft had taken part in the raid.

26.4.44 There are said to be seven hundred victims of the bombing. Inhabitants of the seventeenth arrondissement think fearfully about the proximity to the railway station, the Gare des Batignolles, and are now going to spend their nights in metro stations. As a result of the raid, watercress and leeks are no longer found in the markets.

April 16 was Russian Easter. The service began at seven-thirty in the evening, because of curfew, and ended at nine o'clock, in broad daylight. I spent the evening at Barbos and Bicha's and had dinner the next day at Serge Zweguintzoff's. A Russian woman was there whose husband is of Jewish origin; he had himself adopted, for a considerable sum of money, by a Caucasian prince. Despite legally changing his name, he has been arrested and deported. No one knows where. I came home around nine-thirty; the last metro is at ten o'clock, so there was a huge scramble to get on the metro. Two Germans beside me were surprised by the good humour that reigned in the crowd, saying that, in Berlin, people were less patient and grumbled and got mad, because the Germans' nerves are raw.

Anyway, I missed my connection and had to head down the Champs-Élysées on foot in the dark. Women were selling their services to passersby. Two young women whose faces I could not make out asked a German for a thousand francs each; he answered in French with a strong Teutonic accent, "No, that is too much. It will be a thousand for both."

Went to see an amateur Russian troop performing a series of sketches, *Chauve-Souris* style. The stage was lighted by lamps, the seats hastily thrown together, nearly no scenery except a background painted by one of the performers, practically no costumes; in spite of that, it was all charming, talented, and tasteful.

27.4.44 One of the waitresses at Suchet came to say good-bye. She told me she earned more selling little packages of caramels on the boulevard than working at Suchet.

3.5.44 Now the only railway stations that provide passenger service are the Gare Montparnasse and the Gare de Lyon.

Saw Dr. Käfer, one of the German dentists, who is currently posted at Le Vésinet. He told me that there were a lot of victims of the last bombing there, but also a lot of lucky people because a bomb fell on the railway station, where there was a train carrying a load of cigarettes. While half the people, assisted by German soldiers, cleaned up the wreckage, the other half, also assisted by German companions, pillaged the railcars. *Fourteen million* cigarettes disappeared in no time! The price of that item has dropped significantly on the black market.

New restrictions on gas, which will only be transmitted from five to eight o'clock in the morning, eleven in the morning to one o'clock in the afternoon, and seven to eight-thirty in the evening from now on.

It is nearly impossible to find a laundry that takes in washing. Those establishments no longer get any coal.

According to what the Suchet guard told me, yesterday at around five-thirty in the morning, air-raid warning tests were run by the ss, who stood, watches in hand, at entrances to the occupied buildings and noted how long it took officials to get dressed and come out. I was on the street around nine o'clock in the morning and, at that time, saw a motley troop in uniform, *feldgrau*, parading along Boulevard Suchet with Engineer Ahorn on the right flank. He always looks like Punchinello but looked even more comical in his soldier's uniform, which did not fit him very well. Traffic had been stopped for the parade; rolls of barbed wire were placed at the entrances to Parc de la Muette and armed sentinels were posted along the boulevard. I must say that the peaceful, not-at-all-military appearance of the troop of officials was in funny contrast to the warlike measures.

The Germans have built imposing bunkers at several locations in the city, one of them on Avenue Montaigne, an enormous concrete structure with a roof said to be 6 m thick and walls 3 m thick, with little portholes for guns. Rumours are going around that near the Majestic is a camouflaged building with an exterior that shows nothing unusual but inside is also a concrete bunker. They also say that those shelters are built so solidly that it will be difficult, if not impossible, to get rid of them once the war is over, because of the risk of blowing up the whole district. Maybe they will be preserved as an attraction for future American tourists.

8.5.44 Dinner at Admiral Kinzel's. Present were a certain Mr. Winkler (a bank manager), von Knesenbeck (a corporate manager at the Siemens Company), a Naval official, Mademoiselle Langheld (the Admiral's secretary), Lieutenant Pospichil, and Madame Keller. The apartment the Admiral currently occupies belongs to the great Jewish collector Wertheimer.[89] The apartment is more reminiscent of a museum than a private residence; Renaissance furniture stands next to peasant armoires, nineteenth-century paintings beside mod-

---

89 Pierre Wertheimer was a major shareholder and a financier of Chanel.

ern paintings. The walls, glass display cases, and pedestal tables are covered with Church ornaments, Etruscan statues, and so on. I have often wondered whether the Germans are at home in their requisitioned apartments, whether the war has made everybody accustomed to living in a foreigner's home.

Getting back to dinner, at which the appearance of potatoes was greeted with a unanimous "*Ach, Kartoffeln*" because even the German canteens have shortages of that precious food. The whole time I had the impression of living in a "state within a state" and better understood the control the Germans have over every sign of life in the country.

First, I learned that all German women and children, with the exception of mobilized women, have been sent back to Germany. Their departure took place in such short order that it created a fair amount of panic among the Germans and great rejoicing among Parisians, for whom the order is only an advance sign of the "Great Departure." Winkler explained that the measure was due to the difficulty of maintaining the food supply in France; it was better organized in Germany. He added that the Allied bombings had succeeded in disrupting rail transport in France. Von Knesenbeck did not share his opinion and said, coldly, that the order had been given in anticipation of the invasion.

Winkler then went on at length about the improvements in the French economy made by the Germans. The output from farmland cultivated by the *Luftwaffe* has tripled since its occupation by the Germans – a detail I did not know. Talking about labour, he commented that there are still ample human resources in France; a lot of unnecessary staff can be seen in restaurants and hotels, such as grooms, wine stewards, porters, and so on, who no longer exist in Germany. However, German labour offices lack German personnel; the administration of those offices is almost entirely in the hands of the French. That is why the number of people required for Germany is far from reaching the necessary figures. Control over workers designated for Germany is so slack that for every thousand individuals declared fit for departure, only a hundred or so usually go; the rest disappear without a trace.

9.5.44 I went to the Russian theatre again. I was seated near the Rog.'s. They had a Japanese diplomat with them who spoke fluent Russian and two big Germans in civilian clothes – ss officers, as Madame Rog. obligingly whispered to me. The two showed insatiable curiosity and never stopped asking Madame Rog. the names of people in the audience, who their relatives are, and so on. Madame Rog. had asked me in advance to come and "have a little something" at their place after the show. When I got there, the Japanese diplomat and the two Germans were there; all three made a very disagreeable impression on me. Madame Rog. took me aside at a certain point and asked me how I liked her guests. I answered, "Frankly, I find them appalling." She assured me, "I do, too, but we are obliged to see them and have them over." I fear the Rog.'s are caught up in events they will not be able to extricate themselves from easily.

10.5.44 Bombing of Argenteuil. Allied aircraft drop little strips of silvery paper as they pass, which are said to disguise the sounds intercepted by German detection equipment.

15.5.44 Everyone talks of nothing but the "landing." English radio described the review of the landing troops by Churchill. The newspapers even explained that the systematic bombing of cities in the West is the prelude to the landing operations.

Places that had been pro-German up to now have changed allegiances. Germans are avoided there and everything bad possible is said about them. *Sic transit...*[90]

The electricity is going to be cut off from seven o'clock in the morning until eight o'clock at night, except for "priority users" that will have electricity from one o'clock in the afternoon until eight o'clock at night, including the Suchet buildings, because they contain medical and weather services. Kitchens, offices, and so on in the basement at Suchet seem like mine pits; the cooks use battery-operated portable lamps for light and carry them from one room to another. Barbos has no gas in his building and told me that the only chance of making a hot meal during the day is when

90 Part of a Latin phrase that translates to "Thus passes the glory of the world."

there is an air-raid warning, because the power goes back on then to enable people to go down to the shelters.

Twenty-nine more metro stations have been closed, and the metro is soon expected to stop running completely.

Today a truck came to pick up the belongings of officials at Suchet, which they have to ship to Germany. There were only thirty-three boxes in all, for one hundred and twenty-six people who live in the two buildings. Many of the officials have no address to ship their belongings to because their homes and all their relatives' and friends' homes have been completely destroyed by bombs.

17.5.44 Xénia Bouboroff Bilderling and her daughter Hélène – she has finally been released! – very kindly came to thank me for the things I sent Hélène at Fresnes.[91] Hélène talked about her prison stay. The cell she shared with two other women was really intended for only one detainee. There was only one bed, where the oldest woman slept. The other two slept on straw on the floor, including Hélène, who was pregnant. The toilet was in a corner of the cell; they draped a coat over a chair to act as a screen. It was very cold and damp in the cell, and the windows were never opened. During her stay in prison, Hélène received several packages from unknown individuals and organizations, including packages sent by the Quakers.

22.5.44 I often wonder whether the Germans really believe that posters can convince a French person. Right now, the walls are plastered with a poster showing a collapsing wall with a worker doing his best to support it; the text reads, "Every hour of work in Germany is a rock in the rampart protecting France."

German soldiers are no longer allowed to go out unarmed. Soldiers walk around with rifles strapped on. Last Friday, O.W., Marina Klugenau, and I went to the Bois to get some fresh air; the sunshine

91 Fresnes, built in the 1890s, was and still is one of the largest prisons in France. During World War II, British agents, members of the French resistance, Allied airmen, and other political prisoners were held here. Fresnes was feared because of its horrific conditions and known for the torture that took place there. Some famous inmates were the French Resistance courier Odette Samson and the auto industrialist Louis Renault.

was magnificent. A lot of people were out walking, among them German sailors carrying huge rifles, accompanied by young women.

Thorez spoke on Moscow radio and gave the French people instructions, in case of a landing, to occupy all the town halls, railway stations, electrical power plants, and so on. I would have preferred it if those orders had been given by someone other than Thorez![92]

Today I heard a member of the Supreme Allied Command on BBC radio speaking to the people on behalf of General Eisenhower. He recommended carefully studying the roads, rivers, approaches to cities, and so on, in case the Allies need guides. He also recommended studying the movements of German troops, recording the numbers of cars, even examining the features of the figures in the German High Command to be able to recognize them later.

Personally, I have no doubt the landing will take place and will succeed.

24.5.44 Spent the evening on Avenue Henri Martin at the time of the departure of the employees of the Torpedo Arsenal at Houilles. That installation now works at night, because of the power cuts. The unfortunate employees live like termites without ever seeing the light of day, sleeping in the daytime and working and eating at night.

31.5.44 Lovely weather and, of course, air-raid warnings, up to six a day!

Water no longer comes up to buildings' upper floors. The Hitrovos have to go fetch water in pails at the bottom of the bank of the Sèvres. Large reservoirs on wheels of water have been placed in the basement at Suchet; the Germans call them *Wasserwagen*.

5.6.44 Rome was occupied by the Allies yesterday. The population cheered them and threw flowers as they went past.

6.6.44 The BBC announced that the invasion operations began last night. Paratroopers were dropped in Normandy behind German troops. Just after midnight, at twelve-thirty, General Eisenhower announced to the French people that the Allies had landed on French soil. Tracts with that news were dropped on Paris and the surrounding area.

92 Maurice Thorez was a French Communist leader who lived in Russia at the time.

8.6.44 The BBC announced that the Allies have occupied Caen and the coast between Cherbourg and Le Havre for 40 km inland. They have four hundred naval units and eleven hundred aircraft under their command. The Germans have given assurances that they have pushed the Allies back to the sea, but admit the occupation of Caen.

The atmosphere in the city is tense and worried. Guns on track vehicles go by along Boulevard Suchet, making a terrible metallic sound.

Officials at Suchet are divided into two camps; the "purists" assure others, whether sincerely or not, that they are delighted that the "abscess" has burst, and now "we'll see." The others, the majority, are concerned but always repeat their *"Den Kopf immer hoch halten"* – "Keep your chin up!"

From now on, Germans are prohibited from going out after nightfall. Apart from that, daily life in the buildings and air-raid warnings continue as if nothing had happened. Workers are at work on the apartment formerly occupied by Minister Schleier, knocking down walls, building partitions; probably once the administrative machine is set in motion, it continues to run by inertia.

In Rome, Prince Umberto has been declared Lieutenant General of the Kingdom, which reminds me a great deal of the year 1917 in Russia, when the Emperor abdicated in favour of his brother. The results will probably be the same.

The Germans are recruiting nurses from the Russian émigré community to be sent to care for ROAs. Special courses have been started at Lariboisière, run by a German doctor with the assistance of an interpreter. Candidates will do a three-month practicum in a hospital and, from the outset, receive a salary of twenty-five hundred francs and meals in the canteen. The offer has not met with a great deal of success, because the fate of Russian volunteers, émigrés whom the Germans had promised the moon and the stars, is still on everyone's mind. The émigrés who enlisted for the Russian front were soon declared "unreliable" and sent back home where, of course, they could no longer get their former jobs back.

9.6.44 The Allied news broadcast I listen to every evening, at very low volume, reports that German resistance has increased. But it seems to me that cannot be of any importance because the German army is now in the same situation the Allies were in 1940, "man against machine" as the Germans said of the Allies at that time. Now the "men" are the Germans!

13.6.44 The BBC describes the enthusiastic reception given to the Allies by the people in cities the Allies occupy.

Air-raid warnings have become so frequent that one no longer knows when they start and finish.

Starting today, there will be an inspector on guard every night in each of the two buildings. The guard in No. 6 will sleep in one of the maid's rooms on the service stairs. How I pity him! The guard in No. 10 will spend the night on a couch in the office at No. 10. The two rooms will be linked to the guard rooms by a signal in case of an air-raid warning.

All radio receivers have been removed from the buildings and only two sets are left, one in each of the guard rooms at No. 6 and No. 10. The officials gather around the two radios when it is time for the German news broadcast, which must not be very reassuring, judging by their expressions.

Apart from that, life continues as in the past; from one to three o'clock in the afternoon and toward evening, the terraces of the buildings at No. 6 and No. 10 are occupied by Germans in short shorts, their upper bodies bare, baking in the sun.

Parisians are very calm, on the whole; one might scarcely believe the landing has taken place. I suppose everyone is convinced that the "Great Departure" is only a matter of days away. A lot of people have torn up their ration cards in anticipation of the upcoming return to pre-war food supplies. My hairdresser predicted that we are going to be eating *gâteau Saint-Honoré* before the end of June, because that is how it went in the other war. As soon as the armistice was signed, shops were bursting with provisions.

Fernand, the driver from No. 10, had a bad moment to get through, however. A ferret-faced individual came to the guard room in No. 10 one morning and insisted on seeing Fernand. The guard came to call me because the man was speaking French. The man then told me that he was from German surveillance services and at once showed me his papers. It appears that not only was he employed by the Germans, but he was French. According to him, Fernand had loudly proclaimed his joy in the metro at the announcement of the Allied landing and generally spoken in a "subversive" manner. The man wanted to take Fernand away right then and there. I was not too reassured because I suspected that the individual had to belong to intelligence or security services, the ss or sd. I asked him to wait and went to speak to Fernand, who was showing off and assured me that he was not afraid of anything. In spite of that, I asked him to stay quietly in his corner and, knowing what a fine fellow the *Küchenmat* Fritz was at heart, I went to find him and ask him to resolve the matter. Fritz simply shrugged his shoulders and said that one could not really demand that Frenchmen weep at the news of the landing and went up to the guard room. A few seconds later, Fernand came to tell me that I did not have to worry anymore; the non-commissioned officer had shown the man the door. The next day, however, officers from the sd, Germans this time, came twice to ask to speak to the *Hausoffizier* about Fernand. Engert was away each time and, I suppose, having other fish to fry, the sd ended up not bothering Fernand any further. However, if Lieutenant Prange had still been here, Fernand certainly would not have gotten off so lightly.

The Germans naïvely imagine that they can still win the sympathy of Parisians; they have set the curfew back to one o'clock in the morning "as a reward for the population's dignified conduct during the landing"!

16.6.44 Spent the evening at the Rog.'s. They told me about the German authorities' offer to the Gerebkoff committee; the Germans would take under their protection people who collaborated with them. All they had to do was sign certain papers to be given a special passport that would allow the bearer to benefit from a preferential system in exchange; for example, bearers of that passport would have priority in case of an evacuation of the Parisian population, anticipated by the Germans. The passports, according to the Rog.'s, would protect the bearers from forced repatriation to Soviet Russia in the event of an Allied victory. They assured me that many people took advantage of the offer. In any case, the Rog.'s will leave after the Germans do, and they may not be wrong; Rog. will certainly be criticized afterward for his activities on the Gerebkoff committee – I was told he handled Jewish cases.

20.6.44 The Allies have cut the German army defending Cherbourg in half, and the newspapers are preparing the public for the announcement of the occupation of the port by the Allies.

The famous secret weapon the Germans bragged about for so long has finally been developed and launched against England – rockets launched from some point on the coast, which the English think is around Calais. The BBC gave a fairly detailed description. The robots bombed London and the south of England and caused a great deal of damage.

I was in Engineer G.'s room settling a laundry bill when the German station announced the appearance of the rockets over England. G. is normally one of the most uncommunicative and reserved of men, but he suddenly began acting like a madman, cheeks flaming, running around the room, shouting, *"Endlich, hier kommt die Vergeltung!"* – "Finally, here comes retaliation!" I understood at that moment all the doubt and uncertainty hidden by his mask of calm assurance.

King George VI visited the Normandy front with General de Gaulle; yet we are assured that relations between de Gaulle and the Allies are not too friendly.

Someone stole my courser! Or rather Marina let my bicycle get stolen. While I was out, she took it from my office, where I usually kept it, and went to the post office, leaned it against the side of the counter beside her, and a second later my bicycle had disappeared forever! When I came back, I found Marina sobbing and she apologized. All the Germans knew what had happened and came to express their sympathy!

27.6.44 Cherbourg has been occupied by the Allies. The Germans are retreating in Italy. Vitebsk has been re-occupied by the Soviet army.

I spent Sunday at Bellevue. There was an air-raid warning. Waves of bombers flew over our heads; anti-aircraft artillery shot down two. Liouba Grecoff grabbed her little girl and ran to the basement; from there, she shrieked loudly because she was so frightened!

4.7.44 Pospichil left last week with a *Quartiermeister*, they say, to prepare accommodation in the event of evacuation from Paris. Yesterday, Inspector Klebe came to tell me confidentially that the Staff of the Navy yards, *Oberwerftstab*, is leaving Paris in two weeks. He had his wife and daughter leave for Germany; he married a young Russian here and has succeeded in passing her off as an ethnic German – *Volksdeutsche*.

Yesterday, Inspector Breitenbach came to requisition three hundred blankets from Suchet. When I pointed out to him how that reduced the entire stock to nothing, he replied, "Don't worry! You don't seriously think we'll still be here in the winter?" He then added, "As for Paris, not much will be left, because we won't leave without defending ourselves." That was the first time I heard a German frankly state that the "Great Departure" is a matter that has already been decided. One must only hope that the Germans leave so fast that they do not have time to destroy the city.

Henriot has been assassinated by a phony militia group who disarmed the guards on duty in front of and around the Ministry of Information, rang the doorbell, showed false documents, and went directly to Henriot's bedroom.[93] They woke him up, shouting that they had come to defend him because someone was trying to kidnap him. As soon as Henriot opened the door, they shot him with a revolver, right in front of his wife. Henriot was on the radio daily; his unquestionable talent as an orator made one listen to him more than one intended, like Lord Haw-Haw, although he did not have the same tongue-in-cheek humour. He spoke with passion and conviction; it was not the radio reporting style of Jean Paquis, who ended his broadcasts with the slogan "England, like Carthage, must be destroyed," mocked by listeners. He was certainly a dangerous adversary.

93 Philippe Henriot was a French politician. At the time of his death, he was Minister of Information and Propaganda in the German-backed French government.

After that, for several days, the radio played recordings of his voice and movie theatres showed a close-up of Henriot's head on his deathbed on the big screen, accompanied by recordings of excerpts from his former speeches. It made a fairly macabre impression.

5.7.44 Air-raid warnings without stopping from eight until eleven o'clock in the morning. All Suchet services were disrupted. Parisians were asked to do their shopping in the morning, because the metro only runs at three-quarters-of-an-hour intervals from two to five o'clock in the afternoon. The power is cut off starting at six-thirty in the morning, so I prepare my cup of black-market tea in the evening and keep it until morning in a thermos I am lucky enough to still have because they are nowhere to be found now. Mademoiselle Théobald, my landlady, found an old coal heater in the attic and takes care of it as if it were the most precious thing in the world; she does her cooking on that relic by piling several pots on top of each other. My little seamstress, a Frenchwoman born in Russia, thanks heaven every day for allowing her to bring her samovar from Russia, which she operates with twigs.

Wiedemann saw me holding flowers brought by one of the gardeners who works at La Muette and commented ironically, "Well, Monsieur de Rothschild is soon going to be enjoying the sight of the flowers we planted in his garden." The Germans now speak openly of their departure.

7.7.44 Little Dreier, one of the calmest, most silent residents currently at Suchet, heard that my bicycle had been stolen and came to tell me that he could get me a used bicycle, in good condition, from friends, if I could pay a thousand francs for it. A bicycle of that kind costs several thousand francs everywhere, so I accepted with pleasure, because it is becoming increasingly difficult to get around in Paris. Dreier gave me a receipt in due form for my thousand francs and, the next day, gave me the address of a French family where I could have the bicycle picked up. The bicycle is already in my possession; its front brakes do not work very well but it is very light and I can once again "swallow space." I take care of it as if it were the most precious object in my possession. If I go out on foot during the day, even for a moment, I lock it with two padlocks and keep the keys around my neck, and wrap the chain around a table leg.

Liouba Grecoff came to get me with her little girl and the young Bilderling girl. We went to Parc de La Muette, where the children went for a donkey ride. A calm, sunny afternoon – one might have thought we were back in pre-war times.

A trench shelter has been dug in Rothschild park, with an exit on rue de Franqueville. New German contingents have arrived in the buildings around us, men around fifty years old, who look like honest villagers.

11.7.44 Soviet radio announced the upcoming capture of Königsberg, and the Americans announced the occupation of Florence, "which, they say, is one of the most beautiful cities in Italy." I love that "they say."

Runstaedt has been replaced by von Kluge. The BBC said that Runstaedt fell into disgrace for saying that the battle is now hopeless.

Butter can be found more easily now – I mean, on the black market, of course. German soldiers who come back from the coast sell it for two hundred francs; the black-market price is eight or nine hundred francs. So German trucks are assailed by the crowd at truck stops. Bicha recently went by La Madeleine church and asked what the gathering was. "It's the butter market," an onlooker told her, laughing.

27.7.44 There was an attack on Hitler, masterminded by soldiers, but the plot failed. The news only reached Paris late in the evening. Rumours were going around that there was an attempted military "putsch" in Paris; the Gestapo were arrested for a few hours on the orders of Stülpnagel, who later committed suicide. I was sleeping at Suchet that night on the pull-out couch in my office when two employees came to wake me up around two o'clock in the morning to announce that the whole building was empty, all the Germans had left. Although I am usually a very light sleeper, I heard nothing; they must have all left on tiptoe. I got dressed hastily, trying to think what I was going to do. Go back to rue de l'Université? What about the curfew? Stay at Suchet? What would be the outcome? Then I took the service stairs down to see what was happening. It was very dark and I could only see the shadows of a few employees who sleep at Suchet. Then someone came to tell me that the guard had remained at his post, his helmet on his head, and the telephone operator told me that she was not permitted to reveal where the Germans went but everyone was going to come back soon and everything would return to normal. So I went up to my room; in fact, my neighbour in the next room, Engineer Koch, was already there. When he saw me, he came over and said in a low voice, "They just telephoned and gave us orders to go to bed, fully dressed, though. The warning was given as a result of the attempt on the Führer." That is how I heard what had happened.

The next day, one of the Germans told me that there had been a "terrorist" attack on one of the occupied buildings. Rautsmann later explained that the German army had tried to arrest the ss units.

Other sensational news was the arrest of Olga Galitzine. I think that news made a bigger impression on Russian émigrés than the attempt on Hitler. Not only did Olga see a lot of Germans (often big shots) and had them to her home, but she was also seen with them in public and professed her devotion to Hitler and National Socialist doctrine out loud, which was rather laughable, given her lifestyle. People even went to her when they needed the Germans. Now rumour has it that the Germans discovered that her real name is Rose Shapiro, she is Jewish, and her first husband, Bonnell, was Jewish, too. I thought for a moment that she had herself arrested to clear herself in the eyes of the Allies. However, our cousin Kostia Shabelsky, who got the news from Olga's husband Boris Galitzine, described to me the regimen she was subjected to – handcuffed, with ss officers threatening her with their fists and addressing her familiarly as "*tu.*"

I saw Vera N. Dumesnil at a charity bridge. Vera saw Olga Galitzine often and told me that the Germans interrogated her, as they did all the people entered in Olga's address book – thank God I was not listed in it! A German officer came to Vera's and asked her if she ever thought Olga was Jewish and whether she spoke Russian with a Jewish accent. Vera answered that she always thought Olga was Polish. The officer even told Vera that Olga's son was circumcised. Now that I think about it, I recall that Olga often said, "You know, there are people mean enough to say I'm Jewish. Do I really look like a Jew?" I am sorry for her, as I would be sorry for anyone in those circumstances; it is doubly hard, especially for a person like her, to fall from the scaffolding she took so much trouble to erect for herself. However, I also think that few people will be sincerely sorry for her.

The charity bridge where I saw Vera was a total flop, by the way; only ten people responded to O.W.'s invitation. One of them explained to me that profiteers during the occupation are now afraid to show their faces and are trying to get to Switzerland. Young R. told me that she and her husband quit their jobs because working for a kilogram of butter a month was not really worth the trouble. She did not reveal to me their current occupation but just told me that they had lunch and dinner in restaurants and paid a hundred francs a person for their meals.

An English airplane dove down over Parc de la Muette and machine-gunned the park, where children were playing as usual, and Madame W. was sitting placidly on one of the benches. She threw herself flat on her stomach in the dust, going behind the trunk of a tree to avoid the hail of bullets, and came running to Suchet saying that she had never been so frightened in her life. I suppose the airplane's intended target was the Rothschild château.

1.8.44 Went to Bellevue by bicycle. The metro was not running, and Paris was like a dead city. The Hitrovos told me that, during the last air raid, a lot of tracts were dropped on Bellevue. A large unopened bundle landed on their neighbours' roof; afraid of unpleasant consequences, they hurried to go and give it to the local *Kommandatur* in accordance with the orders posted on walls. When they got there, they were sent away, told that no one cares about those tracts anymore and the French could dispose of them however they wished.

AU NOM DES GOUVERNEMENTS

DES ETATS-UNIS D'AMERIQUE

ET DE LA GRANDE-BRETAGNE

AVIS
au Peuple Français

Au moment même du débarquement du Corps Expéditionnaire Américain en Afrique française du Nord, le texte suivant a été radiodiffusé aux populations des deux zones de la France Métropolitaine

AU VERSO ➡

American and British leaflet

3.8.44 The lightning advance of the Allies increasingly tightens the narrow circle in which the German army is fighting. Rennes, Nantes and Florence are now in the hands of the English and Americans. The Soviets are at the gates of Warsaw.

I heard a radio report from occupied Rennes, describing reprisals by the population against collaborators. Women who had slept with Germans had their heads shaved and were marched around the streets of Rennes like that.

Hasty departure of officials from Suchet. They are leaving in small groups. All day long, one hears the pounding of hammers hurriedly nailing boxes closed. Klebe left with the first group and told me that the last departures would be on August 15.

Engert, the *Hausoffizier*, is gone for ten days. Before he left, he gathered up whatever provisions he had in his possession – lemons, coffee, chocolate, and so on – and told me to take what I wanted and give the rest to his cleaning lady. He also asked me what my plans are for the near future. I told him that I have no plans but, in any event, I am going to stay in Paris if possible. To that he answered that I am absolutely right; many people who worked in German installations were afraid of reprisals and tried to leave for Germany, but what would they find there? To start with, there will neither be work for foreigners nor organizations to take care of them. Here, internal events may take a serious turn but it is always better to stay in the country where one has friends than to throw oneself into a foreign country in ruins. He thinks the only way for Germany to avoid civil war is to be occupied as quickly as possible by the Allies. Otherwise, one can anticipate the reaction of people who were promised the moon and the stars and will return home to find nothing but ruins and poverty. He was in a conversational mood and talked to me about the French occupation of La Sarre, where he is from, after the first war. One day, a French officer ordered him to take off the ribbon he wore in his buttonhole, a war decoration. Engert answered him that he had earned it, the same as the French had earned theirs, and had the same right to wear and be proud of it. The officer gave him a military salute and did not bother him anymore.

In Paris, the metro will no longer run from Saturday at one o'clock in the afternoon to Monday at the same time.

5.8.44 The Americans are in Le Mans and, they say, even Chartres.

Kremer came to the office to speak to me. He spoke freely. He is dismayed and disgusted. The future of Germany appears grim to him, a dead end. He accused Hitler of lack of military vision and experience and lack of tact; his speeches were always coarse and boastful. It was easy to predict that, if Germany was able to prepare itself from 1933 to 1939, America and England could, too, from 1939 to 1944. America also has all the money and raw materials anyone could want and is outside the reach of enemy aircraft. How could Hitler have thought he would come out of this battle victorious?

Then Inspector Bachmann came to find me to say that, if I ever found myself forced to leave France, he was placing his apartment in Leipzig at my disposal, on condition, of course, that the apartment still exists at that time. If he was not personally there, his parents would welcome me in his place. I was truly touched that someone in Bachmann's position could still think about others and concern himself with their fates, especially since I have never spoken freely with Bachmann the way I often did with some of the other officials at Suchet, such as Klebe, Struhal, and so on, and I never had much to do with him, even professionally.

I was at the Glouchevitchs'; they are in a state of joy. They told me that a lot of officers have already left by bicycle, in the direction of the front, to join the troops led by General König, who is not German, as one might think, but the General-in-Chief of the Resistance Army. Madame Glouchevitch was there and created a little chill by saying that she was sorry for the Germans.

8.8.44 Inspector Inselmann still wanted to hold a farewell dinner. The guests numbered thirty. Inselmann belongs to the German Supply Corps and provided all the food. He gave a tip of two hundred francs to each of the waitresses and came to bring a sack of potatoes to O.W. and me.

Weekly meeting with Pospichil. Someone asked him what will become of the occupied buildings if the Germans leave. He answered,

"It's absolutely impossible that we would leave!" then added that precise instructions would be given in good time.

The employees have now started cleaning out the occupied buildings; drapes, blankets, rugs, and so on disappear as if by magic.

Engert came back to Suchet for a few hours. He asked me to go up to his room to settle a few bills and because he wanted to tell me about his trip while he was making his final preparations for leaving. The roads are swept by airplanes that fly at very low altitudes; you can only travel after nightfall and still have to avoid main roads. He went past a railway station during an Allied air raid and within five seconds there was no longer anything left but a layer of dust where the buildings and trains had been. The neighbouring village was lit up by an explosion several kilometres away. He gathered up injured soldiers along the road but most of them died in the car. One of them kept repeating like a refrain before he died, "And my request for a transfer is going to be wasted now." Engert said, "It's strange what occupies a human brain at a time like that." His wolf-hound was sick, and I took care of it in his absence, but he took it with him anyway, saying that he preferred to shoot it himself, if need be, rather than know it was killed by someone else.

Engert is a very honest, frank, and fair man, an excellent administrator; it was easy to work with him. He was extremely emotional when he left.

The three dentists have left, and the *Zahnstation* is no longer operating. One of them came to bring me packages of coffee before he left that Madame Mutafolo, Dr. Lutowski's girlfriend, sent him regularly through his Paris co-workers. So I sent a message to Madame Mutafolo asking her to come and get the packages of that so-rare commodity, and she appeared two days later, in tears and ravishing, and did not stop repeating, "Luto, Luto, what is going to happen to him now?"

10.8.44 One of the German engineers from the *Lotsenkommando* just got back to Suchet from a mission in Saint-Nazaire, his uniform in tatters, his face drawn. He told me that no one's nerves can withstand that hell! The sky is constantly black, literally covered with Allied aircraft that meet no resistance. Trucks bringing German soldiers back to Paris were stopped at the entrance to the city and the Germans made the soldiers hanging in clusters onto the outside get off before they reached Paris to avoid making too bad an impression on Parisians!

12.8.44 Intense movement reigns on Paris streets; cars, trucks, German tanks go by constantly from the front, camouflaged with freshly cut branches. Soldiers are often lying on the fenders of cars, as they did in the early days of the Russian revolution. Rows of trucks are parked under the trees along the avenues at night; in the morning, one sees soldiers in shirtsleeves washing with pails of water and shaving in front of the trucks' little mirrors. Parapets on the banks of the Seine have become observation points for Parisians, who watch the "Great Departure" from front-row seats. Apparent calm reigns in the city; however, one senses all too clearly that the calm is only on the surface and an incident could erupt from one minute to the next. I now keep my bicycle in my room at rue de l'Université and do not take it out anymore because rumours are going around that the Germans are requisitioning bicycles.

17.8.44 All the German officials left Suchet during the day yesterday. The order to leave was given to them at two o'clock in the morning the night of August 15 to 16. They were divided into two groups; one left for the Plaza and the other for the Regina; however, I was told later that they were all simply directed to a barracks. Around one o'clock in the afternoon, Inspector Recht approached me and quickly told me in a low voice, "It's the end. Can you come to see me in half an hour in my room?" When I came to his room, he had me sit down and told me, "This time the Americans really are in Chartres. All the railway lines have been cut; only the main roads remain, and they are under machine-gun fire day and night. I'm not sure we will be able to get through. We are leaving Paris tonight. No one will go to the Regina or the Plaza. Most of us will be directed to a barracks like simple soldiers. I advise you to leave Suchet as soon as possible." I told him that in the morning Pospichil and Admiral L. had come to Suchet to reserve rooms for the Admiral's staff. Recht replied, "That has all changed already. The Admiral is getting ready to leave, too. Do you remember our conversations? You see that we were right." He, Klebe, and Kremer had often criticized Hitler's policy and saw the end of the war very pessimistically. He offered me a small glass of liqueur and gave me a large box of cigarettes as a farewell gift, repeating that he foresaw only ruin and disaster for Germany and it was all Hitler's fault. He was extremely nervous and did not succeed in hiding it.

Officials from both buildings then came to say farewell. Many of the cleaning women were crying. They had basically been treated well by the occupants of No. 6 and No. 10 and, at this moment, saw them only as human beings in misfortune. If only those humanitarian feelings could prevail in the future and make new wars impossible!

On a comical note, the carpenters working at No. 6 came as usual and would have continued their work renovating the fourth floor if Rautsmann had not sent them back home.

The German guards left the buildings on August 17, in the afternoon. From then on, kitchen services were no longer running. The non-commissioned officer had distributed the provisions he still had in stock to the employees before leaving and had not forgotten to leave me a share, too. At that time, I was at Lieutenant Pospichil's waiting for the employees' pay; they were to be given two months' salary. Around five o'clock, I brought back the pay for the cleaning women at No. 6, the kitchen, and the restaurant; floor staff at No. 10 were usually paid by the German Supply Corps. I closed myself in the office with O.W., and we began preparing the pay envelopes. They were paid cash, and it was a fairly large amount of money. While I was waiting, I started paying the employees on the list who were on site and recommended that the ones I paid leave the buildings as soon as possible. It was all I could do. At that time, Rautsmann was paying the male employees at No. 6.

As soon as the employees heard that they could go home after they received their pay, scenes that reminded me of the Russian Revolution took place on every floor. The employees fell on the sheets, blankets, and so on. In half an hour, three floors at No.

10 were completely cleaned out of anything of value. The Alsatian cook, a big, strong woman, who was accused even in normal times of carrying provisions out in her underwear – one day she let a kilogram of butter that was hidden on her person fall out in the guard room – had heaved three large rugs onto her shoulders and could barely move under the weight of that burden. All that could be seen everywhere were large bundles tied up in bed sheets that women from No. 10 were dragging behind them. A crowd of onlookers had gathered day and night in front of the buildings, across from them, on Boulevard Suchet, with a somewhat questionable attitude. Fearing things might get out of control, Rautsmann telephoned Pospichil, and German sentinels from a barracks nearby came to guard the doors of No. 10 at around seven o'clock in the evening.

Three inspectors, Breitenbach, Erhardt, and Köster, whom I later learned were guarding Navy funds, came to spend the night at Suchet again.

18.8.44 In the morning, I came in to continue handling payroll. The cleaning women from No. 10 were in a state because the money for them had still not come in. Two of the kitchen employees who lived on the other side of Paris and had not been coming to work anymore lately because they would have had to come on foot suddenly appeared and during the day made as many as three trips on foot with linens and rugs. The German guard was opposed to taking bundles out, in principle, but it was easy for anyone familiar with the building to find an unguarded exit. The barman at No. 10 was doing a lively business with employees, selling them the stock of wine and cognac, which he said Inspector Köster gave him as a gift. He even went so far as to give O.W. five hundred francs for her charities, which, in my opinion, she was wrong to accept. Similar things went on at No. 6. The bar was emptied, not only of wine and the like, but also all the dishes, cutlery, and so on. The buildings' offices were in indescribable disorder, the floors covered with shredded and burnt paper and such. From all the requisitioned buildings arose a cloud of smoke; the Germans were destroying lists and documents by the armload. Pospichil had also given me orders to burn all lists and correspondence of any kind, and they were being carried out. I kept only the employee pay list. Coming to Suchet on foot in the morning, I went past requisitioned buildings and saw crowds sharing the booty there as well. In some buildings, German soldiers were throwing the crowd provisions, bedding, furniture, and so on through the windows. The crowd snapped up those gifts with shouts of joy. Women sitting on the sidewalk argued as they compared their loads. Along the streets, all you could see were individuals bent under the weight of bags, packages, and the like. That is all too human and, alas, reminds me so vividly of scenes of Bolshevik Russia that it cannot help but leave an unpleasant impression. The sight of a crowd unleashed always scares me, too.

What a surprise I had toward evening when I saw two German inspectors, Wiedemann and Küchenmeister, appear from the *Lotsenkommando*, dirty, looking like they had not slept for several days. They came to ask me whether they could occupy their rooms at No. 6 Suchet again. They looked dazed seeing the emptiness and disorder around them; they did not seem to expect it. I think they had lost all contact with their base. I told them to go and wait for me in my office at No. 6 and went looking for sheets and blankets, which I ended up finding in the linen room at No. 6. I still had a small stock of tea and a few eggs in my room, which I offered them, because there was no longer a kitchen at No. 10, and I could clearly see that they had not had anything to eat. Wiedemann then asked me point-blank, "What are they saying about the military situation?" I hesitated to answer, so he added, "Go ahead and speak frankly. Tell me what they are saying on English radio." Then I told him that, this morning, London radio said that the Allies have surrounded Paris and are approaching its outskirts. Wiedemann then said quietly, "*Es ist höchste Zeit, dass wir abhauen*" – "High time we clear out!" He and his comrade said their farewells and said they thought it was more prudent for them to leave immediately, especially since they still had a car at their disposal.

Meanwhile, a German *Feldwebel* came to Suchet with a requisition order for lodging for his troop of a thousand men, who were to stay there that very night. They brought a mobile kitchen with them;

however, the *Feldwebel* asked me if I still had some plates and cutlery. The troop arrived toward evening. In spite of the chaos, in spite of the fact that the unit was in retreat, absolute order was maintained. A higher-ranking officer went upstairs with his men to the floor assigned to him and, within a few minutes, without any pushing and shoving, the men were crammed in, three or four to a room, so they had to sleep on the floor. The kitchen set to work at once, while boxes of provisions and ammunition were lined up in the courtyard. Onlookers were standing along Boulevard Suchet, seated on folding chairs in the front row as if they were at a show; they did not take their eyes off what was happening in the buildings. As I was going by the restaurant, the troop's non-commissioned officer approached me and asked me if I had eaten; when I answered in the negative, he signalled me to follow him, had me sit down, and brought me a plate of *Eintopf* – stew – and a cup of coffee, apologizing for the poor menu and adding that if I needed to spend another few days working at Suchet, as long as he was there, the other employees and I could always come and eat at their canteen.

The employees who had been lodging at Suchet were now making preparations for leaving. I called young Colette and encouraged her to leave without delay, because everyone knew that her child's father was a German and she had to fear reprisals. She did not appear to listen to my advice, however, and told me that she was acting as an interpreter for the troop and still had plenty of time ahead of her.

19.8.44 As of today, all the employees at No. 6 and the restaurant and kitchen have now left Suchet. The cleaning women from No. 10, who are still waiting for their pay, are the only ones left. The employee who had been sent to get the money at the Prefecture, which supplied the money for those employees' pay, came back around twelve-thirty to tell me that the Prefecture offices categorically refused to pay the necessary amounts for the payroll, claiming orders were given by the Resistance. So I gathered the staff from No. 10, explained the situation, and told them I was going to try to find Lieutenant Pospichil to see if I could get the necessary amount for their pay from him. According to the information

I had, he was at the *Führungsstab*, one of the Rothschild family homes that was used as headquarters for the German Admiral L., located in the Bois de Boulogne, about a twenty-minute walk from Suchet. I did not have my bicycle with me, and none of the women from No. 10 who had bicycles were willing to lend me one, so I had to go on foot. On the way, I passed cyclists who shouted at me, "Hurry, Madame, curfew at two o'clock. The town halls are all occupied and decked with flags." The *Führungsstab* was surrounded by barbed wire and guarded all around the perimeter by sentinels. Rumours had been circulating this morning that the Admiral was in the process of negotiating some kind of armistice with the Allies and the surrender of the capital.

When I reached the entrance, I showed my pass, called an *Ausweis*, to the sentinel and told him I had to speak to Lieutenant Pospichil on a service matter. A soldier accompanied me to a large empty room, and Pospichil soon appeared, looking defeated and tired, in the company of other officers. He told me he could no longer do anything, because he no longer had funds at his disposal, but was going to give me a message for the Supply Corps paymaster, and I could try my luck with him.

Then I went to the Supply Corps paymaster with his message, still accompanied by the soldier, and was pleasantly surprised to find myself face-to-face with Inspectors Breitenbach and Erhardt, whom I knew. There was yet a third inspector there, but I did not know him. I explained the purpose of my visit to them and showed them Lieutenant Pospichil's message, saying that he had succeeded in finding the money to pay the employees he was responsible for, and only employees of the *Standortverwaltung* were left unpaid. There was then a brief consultation among the three inspectors and the one I did not know asked me, "And what proof do we have that you have not already collected the pay of those employees?" I had not, in fact, thought of that possibility and could not provide them with any proof. However, Breitenbach and Erhardt immediately said, "We know this lady well. You can trust what she says. Her word is enough for us." I must admit that this testimonial gave me great pleasure. Breitenbach then told me to come back in an hour and the payroll money would be ready. I left him a copy of the list of employees. When I left, the soldier who accompanied me asked what was happening in Paris, because he and his comrades found being there like being in a fortress; they had no communication with the city.

Around two o'clock in the afternoon, I asked O.W. to go get the payroll money, which would already be prepared; I had warned Breitenbach that she might come in my place. Not only was it ready, but the exact amount of each employee's pay was in a separate envelope! She soon came back, accompanied by German soldiers, rifles at their shoulders, which made her look like a prisoner. In fact, she herself had asked to be accompanied by an armed soldier because she feared being robbed en route. The German non-commissioned officer guarding the buildings still occupied at Suchet lent O.W. two German soldiers who accompanied her there and brought her back with the pay, safe and sound. We then began to pay the employees and have them leave as quickly as possible in small groups, because none of us wanted to stay any longer than we had to at Suchet. That day, I left Suchet for good, never to return.

On my way home to rue de l'Université, I saw that the town hall in the sixteenth arrondissement was, in fact, flying tricoloured flags; young men in helmets with yellow armbands on their arms were on guard and shouted at passersby, "Immediate, indefinite curfew." There was no longer a single officer in the streets.

A tricoloured flag was also flying over the Trocadéro.

During the day, I often heard gunshots fired in the street. Someone came to say that German cars and motorcycles were going up and down the streets firing right and left to disperse the groups that were forming in the streets; fights had broken out in Place de la Concorde and on the Grands Boulevards but the Alma district was fairly calm.

Late in the afternoon, I had a visit from Lida M., one of the employees at Suchet, who came to bring me my radio and a few small objects that I had forgotten at Suchet and to tell me that I was unreasonable: everyone took away furniture and things that did not belong to them and I, on the other hand, forgot to take objects that belong to me. She was caught in gunfire coming to my place and took refuge under a carriage entrance, but the building's concierge noticed her and shouted, "Get out of here. Those are probably things you stole from the Germans. I don't want to shelter a thief." That is the reward you get for a good deed!

20.8.44 I had lunch, as best I could, at rue de l'Université and went to Barbos' by bicycle. Then we went out on foot with Bicha. The city, that district at least, was perfectly calm. Young people in swimsuits were baking in the sun on the riverside quays. A group was playing ball. You would have thought you were on a peaceful beach a few hundred kilometres from Paris, not in a city whose fate was to be determined in the hours to come.

On our return, we lined up at the butcher shop. The people in line were discussing events animatedly. Apparently posters have been posted in Paris saying that an agreement has been signed between the Germans and the Resistance forces, the FFI. Both sides commit to not shoot at one another. Cars with French officers and German soldiers went by on the streets, the officers announcing on a loudspeaker that the Germans were leaving the city and recommending that the public let them leave peacefully.

The town halls are still occupied by the FFI. Returning home, I noticed that the building on rue de l'Université was full of flags. My concierge told me, "FFI orders."

Olga Hitrovo telephoned me from Bellevue. The Germans blew up the villa they were occupying on rue Eiffel when they left. The explosion was so powerful that a window casement flew off the Hitrovos' villa and broke into a thousand pieces.

21.8.44 The sound of distant firing could be heard all day long on Monday. London radio announced the Allied presence in Fontainebleau and quoted the German news release reporting that the Allies were at the gates of Paris. Marshal Paulus spoke on Moscow radio, declaring that he had rallied to Seydlitz and encouraging the German army to cease fighting.

Rumours are circulating that the agreement signed between the Germans and the "French authorities" has been broken – no one seems to know exactly which authorities that means. The flags have been removed from the Trocadéro and rue de l'Université.

Rautsmann telephoned me from Suchet and told me that the troop was still there and keeping the house clean and in good order. He also told me that two of the employees from Avenue Henri Martin went underground yesterday, taking with them the cash confided to them for paying employees...

22.8.44 Many tricoloured cockades are displayed in shop windows; however, there are still many Germans in Paris. German trucks and cars go by at crazy speeds, and the soldiers keep their rifles aimed at the crowd and grenades in hand. Madame Aslanoff, who worked in the linen room at No. 6, telephoned me from Courbevoie to ask me how I am and to tell me that all the bakeries were pillaged by the crowd. I told her to come and see me when the city calmed down, because I have her pay.

23.8.44 Posters have been put up in Paris reminding the people that rationing has not been abolished and, at this time, food products and supplies are not yet reaching Paris. Another poster, signed by Thorez and Cachin, Communists, calls male and female citizens to arms and orders them to occupy railway stations, gas and electrical power plants, and so on and to open prison doors. I read the posters stuck on columns in the elevated Passy and Grenelle metro stations.

During the day, I went to Bicha's and, since there were rumours going around that Paris had been liberated, we turned on the radio and heard London radio announce the liberation of Paris. Listeners would hear the Marseillaise[94] and the bells ringing in Paris. So we opened the windows but, instead of the Marseillaise and bells, we were disconcerted to hear distant artillery fire and, from time to time, the rat-a-tat-tat of machine guns!

There was fighting in the streets around the town hall in the sixth and seventeenth arrondissements, Place d'Italie, and Place de la République. Otherwise, other neighbourhoods in the city are quiet. One no longer sees almost any Germans in Paris or German vehicles going by along the riverside quays. Bicha told me that she was waiting in line lately when there was a burst of gunfire and women in

---

94 "La Marseillaise" is the national anthem of France.

line grumbled, "Listen to that! Can't they just let them leave undisturbed; that's all they ask." Certainly Parisians will be happy to be rid of the occupiers but that does not come without some fear of Communist excesses, so everyone wants to see the Allied troops enter Paris as soon as possible. There are often fights around vendors selling newspapers with differing opinions or people putting up posters. One political group barely succeeds in putting up a poster before an opposing group tears it down. Lately I saw someone trying to put up posters who first barricaded a street in order to be able to work in peace.

24.8.44 Yesterday Bicha and Irène were involuntary witnesses of a public punishment. A crowd had surrounded a sobbing woman sitting on a chair in the middle of the sidewalk. Hands held the ends of her blond hair up in the air as they shaved her head. Bicha thought for a minute that what she was watching was a free hairdressing demonstration, the kind one used to see before the war; however, Irène saw that a swastika was being marked on the woman's forehead and started pulling Bicha by the sleeve. They hurriedly backed away. That type of punishment is now applied to women who were "with" Germans.

Collaborators, Paris, 1944

I often wonder what became of Marina Klugenau. Grade left on August 16 with his group. Marina tried everything to follow him, but all the German organizations she approached refused to take her. Finally, in the evening on August 17, one of her friends, a fanatic spinster, came running to Suchet saying that she had finally found a convoy that would take Marina. Marina was not at Suchet; she had gone downtown looking for transportation to Germany. I tried to make the "benefactor" leave before Marina got back, but Marina appeared in the meantime, hastily gathered up two small backpacks she had packed in advance, climbed on her bicycle, and left, without even taking the time to go and say good-bye to her parents. She just left them a message, which she asked me to give them in person.

Alas, she never wanted to listen to anyone, not even Grade's friend who came to talk to her frankly, warning her against the object of her passion. Will she even find him again in the chaos? I hope not.

Yesterday two armed youth entered Levsh.'s and took Natali, the grandmother, who was taking care of her sick husband, to the police station, accusing her of participating in the interrogation of patriots. Fortunately, the police officer knew her personally, and she had no trouble clearing herself.

The *Kommandatur* is still in Place de l'Opéra, and the Germans still occupy some of the villas in Bellevue.

Our cousin Kostia Shabelsky telephoned me and told me that Olga Galitzine has been taken to Germany in an armoured railcar.

27.8.44 The Allies have entered Paris!

I am going to try and recount the events of the past few days.

On Thursday evening, August 24, I was at rue Saint-Saëns, where my brother Barbos lives. When I was getting ready to return home to rue de l'Université, sustained gunfire broke out near the Passy passageway, followed by machine-gun fire near the Champ de Mars, which I have to cross to get to rue de l'Université. The concierge stopped me as I went by and told me that I could not go out because there was shooting from every direction. There were an endless variety of rumours about the source of the shooting; some said the Germans were holding the bridges of Paris and shooting at the crowd, who returned fire. Others said "collaborators" were firing on the crowd from the rooftops.

At first, we thought that the Germans had finally left Paris during the day because, before going to rue Saint-Saëns, I had taken a detour toward Avenue Henri Martin and found the avenue blocked off. From a distance, I could see a group of German trucks in front of the Rothschild building and the occupied buildings on Suchet, and soldiers with packs on their backs getting ready to leave. Irène also told us that Pospichil had telephoned her around three o'clock in the afternoon to say that they were leaving for good. Apparently, however, isolated units were left at several spots in the capital: the École Militaire, the Hôtel de Crillon, the Continental, the Majestic, and so on. So I called my landlady to tell her that I was going to stay at my brother's overnight. There were constant comings and goings all evening; each family member in turn went down to the concierge to glean some information.

In the evening, the radio announced that the first detachments of Leclerc's army had entered the capital and, this time, we really did hear the sound of bells in the streets. People were still guarded, however, and although they had already started to deck the buildings with flags, there were not very many people in the streets.

The morning of Friday, August 25, we saw out the window a dense crowd occupying Boulevard de Grenelle and the smaller neighbouring streets. We went up to Michel's apartment on the fourth floor, from where we could see that corner of the neighbourhood clearly. A magnificent sun shone on a joyful crowd cheering the first French tanks at the top of their lungs as the tanks slowly made their way through the mass of Parisians throwing them flowers, clinging to the sides of the tanks, and so on. In trucks following the military units stood young men in a variety of clothing, shirts unbuttoned over their chests, police caps over one ear, and rifles in hand – members of the FFI, the *Forces françaises de l'intérieur*, as people now call the French Resistance forces.

My brother suggested that we go down to the street instead of staying at the window but, when we were getting ready to go, rifle fire broke out followed by a burst of machine-gun fire from the direction of the Grenelle metro. The crowd rushed into the smaller neighbouring streets while bullets whistled around them, and the trucks and tanks headed in the direction of the Passy Bridge. We just had time to close the windows and take refuge in the back of the apartment.

The afternoon was calm. The crowd gathered again along Boulevard de Grenelle. Motorcycles and military trucks started to move again in the streets adjoining the boulevard; young women had already climbed in to sit beside the soldiers.

At rue Saint-Saëns, tenants gathered on the stairs and at the entrance; anybody who came in brought the latest news and everyone listened avidly.

Madame Rennenkampf, a Russian who lives in the building, told Bicha that she had gone out with her husband and spoken to a soldier in the street who looked to her like an American. Hearing her speak Russian to her husband, he immediately answered in fluent Russian. When Madame Rennenkampf asked him if he was a White or Red Russian, he answered laughing, "Oh, we don't make those distinctions in America; all Russians, White or Red, joined the army."

Afterward, I telephoned the Hitrovos to ask them what was happening in Bellevue. They told me that when they went out in the morning to shop at Sèvres, they had to turn back because the bank was covered with the dead bodies of Germans. It seems that, on Thursday evening, German detachments in the Bois de Meudon headed for the bridge in Sèvres, unaware that troops wearing the colours of General Leclerc, Count Philippe Leclerc de Hautecloque, occupied the bridge, and were completely exterminated by his troops.

Toward the end of the afternoon, rifle fire was heard again. I telephoned Mademoiselle Théobald, my landlady, who told me that she had gone out to see "all the interesting spots" and had witnessed the surrender of the Hôtel de Crillon; German officers were coming out right when she went by the hotel. The crowd threw themselves on them, wrenched the suitcases they were carrying from their hands and scattered their belongings, pyjamas, photos, and so on, all over the street. "The crowd really manhandled those Germans," added Mademoiselle Théobald.

The newspapers published these days were mostly started during the occupation and distributed clandestinely to the public. They are aimed at patriots and urge them to start identifying traitors and collaborators without waiting for courts to be established and without bothering to get warrants for their arrest. In the troubled times we are going through, alas, the spirit of personal vengeance is naturally given free rein. Armed FFI bands walk the streets, enter houses and cafés and arrest "suspects" solely based on denunciations by neighbours. Bicha and I were just getting ready to go out to buy bread when tenants of the building came running back in, shouting at us to stay home. There had been a raid in one of the small neighbouring streets. The FFI were taking away any passersby they encountered in their path, with no explanation. The tenants told the concierge that they saw the FFI take away a tenant of the building, an ex-serviceman disabled in the First War, whose right arm had been amputated at the shoulder. While we were waiting on the doorstep, we heard shouts and hisses. Trucks were going by with German prisoners standing with their hands behind their heads, and the crowd was throwing rocks at them, often succeeding in getting close enough to them to strike a few blows.

Sonia G. came to see us in the evening and told us that she had seen Germans taken in trucks to the École Militaire and the crowd was throwing stones at them, as we had seen in rue de Grenelle, kicking them and shouting insults. Some of the people in the crowd did not approve of such actions and said, "Don't forget that our prisoners are still in Germany. What if they treat our men like that?" But other voices shouted, "They're dogs. There is no law for them."

I slept at rue Saint-Saëns again that night. On Saturday morning, we heard firing again. Bicha went down to the concierge and came back in a panic, saying that two Russian tenants had been arrested and taken away by the FFI. Other tenants told her that notices had been posted on pillars in the Grenelle metro station saying that it was Germans, militia, and White Russians who fired from the rooftops on the crowd, and there had been a shout from the crowd, "Death to the White Russians." After telling us that news, Bicha ran back to station herself at the entrance to the building, which had become a real listening post, and I went down with her. We saw a building tenant named Nelidoff, a White Russian, who looked frightened, being led away between two Turks, black under their red caps, armed with rifles. Behind them ran the concierge, gesturing and protesting animatedly. At that point, Michel appeared, took Bicha by the arm, and led her forcibly into the apartment.

After dinner, I decided to return to rue de l'Université where, in contrast, I found absolute calm. The whole neighbourhood was draped in French, American, English, and Soviet flags; the Soviet flag is a hammer and sickle on a red background. I observed that the Grenelle district, much more democratic and "leftist" than the seventh arrondissement, was flying only French flags, with a few English and American flags here and there!

Mademoiselle Théobald told me that her niece, who has always been a member of the Resistance, was very busy these days conducting investigations.

I fell asleep around eleven-thirty but did not sleep long. Anti-aircraft fire was making a deafening noise. The sirens started wailing after the fact. Doors and windows trembled, and the sky was lit up with bullet flares. It was a bombing but, this time, the aircraft were German. Tenants came running downstairs from the upper floors again. From my window, I could see tenants from the building across the way, which has no basement or shelter, running to the nearest shelter. The bombing lasted approximately three quarters of an hour. The next day, we found out that a squadron of German planes had, in fact, flown over Paris and the twelfth, seventeenth, eighteenth, and sixth arrondissements had been hit. No one expected anything of the kind, and people were caught unprepared.

General de Gaulle also spent some unpleasant moments. He was supposed to go to Notre Dame for a thanksgiving service and had barely entered the cathedral when there was a burst of gunfire. By chance, we were listening to the radio right then. The power is not always on, except with frequent cuts. We heard the announcer describe the incident with emotion. You could hear gunshots mingled with religious songs. The announcer said that people took shelter under pews. General de Gaulle showed a great deal of courage, listened to the prayers until the end, and left at a calm pace to the shouts of the frenzied crowd, who tried to kiss his hands and even his feet.

When I telephoned rue Saint-Saëns around noon on Sunday, Michel answered briefly and excused himself, promising to call back later, because a home visit was underway at that time in the building. He called me back later to tell me that they had come to Barbos' and he would tell me the details in person when I came over.

I went to see them around four o'clock in the afternoon and found the whole family still highly emotional. They told me that, around eleven o'clock in the morning, Bicha was about to go out and was stopped at the entrance door by a group of armed civilians accompanied by a gendarme who immediately ordered the concierge to close the entrance door and watch that no one left the building. Bicha went back home and, after an unpleasant hour of waiting, someone knocked loudly on the door. The power was off at the time. Barbos did not open up quickly enough to suit them, so the FFI forced the door, which gave under the pressure. They then ordered Barbos to put his hands up, searched him, and asked him fairly rudely if he had any weapons. Barbos showed them the old pistol and sabre hanging on the wall. One of the FFI then asked to see Barbos' identification papers while the others lifted the cushions off the couch, as if to ensure there were no hidden weapons. They then appeared to consult with the gendarme, saying, "Still, it really was here we were told to search," and asked the gendarme if he did not think it was necessary to take Barbos to the commanding officer. However, the gendarme, who was probably doing this job reluctantly, answered, "No, let's hurry; we have no time to waste." When they were gone, my brother went to speak to the concierge, who told him that one of the tenants had gone and denounced Barbos and Bicha, saying that they had Germans there during the Occupation and that their oldest son had left for Germany, when he is currently at scout camp. She defended them as best she could but thought she might go crazy with FFI groups coming anytime to search the building; again this morning, they took five tenants away.

28.8.44 On Monday, notices signed by Colonel Roll have been posted in Paris ordering the execution, without a conviction, of anyone who allegedly fired on patriots. General König, for one, is trying to instil a little discipline among FFI members, and rumours are going around that they are going to be mobilized and assigned to regular Army units.

Stores, offices, restaurants, and theatres are still closed, and trains and the metro are still not running.

Crowds of people are wearing tricoloured cockades. Many young women stick tricoloured bows in their hair; nearly all young women go bareheaded in the street since the Occupation. Or else they arrange to have the three colours in their outfit: a white blouse, blue skirt, and red belt, for example. Shop windows are also decorated with the national colours.

Black automobiles marked with the letters "FFI" are driving around the streets at crazy speeds. American anti-aircraft guns are stationed on all the bridges. The features of the American soldiers are hard to make out because they wear helmets that come down to their eyes. They are surrounded by young women; one often even sees them sitting right on the guns – a picturesque sight but hardly military. As I was crossing the Grenelle bridge, I heard a soldier repeating very slowly to one of them, "You must not always ask: cigarettes, cigarettes."

There was an air-raid warning during the night, but the anti-aircraft artillery did not fire. The power is always on during air-raid warnings to allow Parisians to get down to the shelters, so I was able to iron my linen suit between one and three o'clock in the morning.

29.8.44 It is Tuesday and there is still no gas, and no bread in the bakeries. Yesterday I lined up for an hour and a half, and the bakery closed suddenly before my turn came, so I was left without bread. Merchants are afraid to sell on the black market, and normal supply has not yet been restored. We are still far from seeing the *gâteau Saint-Honoré* my hairdresser promised.

30.8.44   It is Wednesday. Yesterday I went to see the Rauts-
manns, W.A. and his legitimate wife, that is – political events arrange things nicely. I went by bicycle because the metro is still not
running. Rautsmann told me how the Suchet saga ended. The troop
left on Thursday, August 24, at around seven o'clock in the evening, taking young Colette with them. She did not intend to leave
but, in the last few days, she received many threatening letters.
Since head-shaving executions had begun, Rautsmann strongly advised her to leave Paris for a while. So she went and gave her baby,
whose father is German, to friends to care for and left with the
German soldiers in a truck, to end up God knows where. The troop
left in such great haste that ammunition, provisions, and even some
of their packsacks were left behind on the sidewalk. The crowd
watching in the area around the buildings immediately rushed in to
pillage, but a member of the French Red Cross appeared and said
that the buildings and all their contents had been requisitioned by
that organization and gave the order to close the entrance doors.
Rautsmann barricaded the doors with tables and carpets rolled up
against the inside of the double doors, and stayed in the guard
room at No. 6 all night. He was woken in the middle of the night
by the lights suddenly coming on and decided to do rounds to
check. When he got to the kitchen in No. 10, he heard footsteps
and someone cried out in a frightened voice, "Who goes there?"
It was an armed FFI member who had managed to enter the block
of buildings at No. 6 and No. 10 but did not know how to get
out. Around six-thirty in the morning, FFI, police officers and Red
Cross representatives came in. They immediately began to search
the buildings and asked Rautsmann several times whether the bunker on Avenue Maunoury had been mined. During that time, two
Germans came down Boulevard Suchet on motorcycles misfiring
and making a lot of noise. They stopped in front of the entrance to
No. 6 and got off their motorcycles without being bothered by the
French forces, then realized what was going on, got back on their
motorcycles and disappeared.

The arrests continue. The Winter Velodrome is the centre where
prisoners are being held. They sleep on the track, and a cordon

of officers guards the approaches. They say Sacha Guitry is being held there.[95]

31.8.44 I lined up for half an hour at the bakery today, then for an hour for meat at the butcher, where they offered canned meat for sale. The butchers were alerting customers that the canned goods were German and could therefore be eaten without fear!

The FFI is going to be incorporated into the Army, which raises some difficulties because the Resistance Army gave its members ranks that do not match regular Army ranks.

Went to O.W.'s by bicycle to get the rest of the employees' pay and then took it to the women who had not been able to come and collect it at Suchet. It would be hard for me to describe their surprise when I brought them two months' pay. They probably imagined that I would run away with the cash! I sent money orders to several kitchen employees from whom I wanted an official receipt, for greater security, and wrote to two cooks, who are both fine people, to come and pick up their pay in person at my place.

1.9.44 On Friday I passed close by the Winter Velodrome on my bicycle and had to take a detour because the neighbouring streets were blocked off by a cordon of officers, and lines of buses were parked at the entrances to the Velodrome. I found out later that prisoners were being transferred to Drancy prison, a former concentration camp for Jews during the Occupation.

I was going to see Mademoiselle Romanoff when I met the Izied.'s en route to the Swiss Consulate to try to have their uncle Wolkoff, who is an English subject, released. Mademoiselle Romanoff greatly fears a Communist uprising. That is essentially what a large number of Parisians fear, mainly because of the Alliance with the Soviets and the potential role they could now play. The Gerebkoff committee offices are occupied by the Union of Russian Patriots, a pro-Soviet organization. Their newspaper, *Le Patriote Russe*, is highly reminiscent of the newspapers in Moscow.

3.9.44 On Sunday, the anniversary of the declaration of war, the city is calm. The newspapers do not come out today. Since trains from

95 Sacha Guitry was a French actor.

outlying areas are not running yet, Vladimir Hitrovo telephoned me and asked me to draw his ration of tobacco; he had sent me his card some time ago because they hardly ever come into town any more. I arranged to meet him at Liouba's at Porte Saint-Cloud, halfway from Bellevue. I went there by bicycle. What would I have done without my brave courser? Vladimir hitchhiked with American trucks.

They came to question my landlady about a certain Madame Z. who lived in the apartment's maid's room for a few weeks. Madame Z. is accused of espionage. In reality, she is a very innocuous person, not very intelligent, her mind a bit deranged.

4.9.44 Went to see Kostia Shabelsky. His place was also searched for the "rooftop shooters," but seeing him in the late stages of tuberculosis – apparently his condition has worsened – the FFI themselves apologized and withdrew immediately. Alek Galitzine was there with his wife, Hélène; I had not seen her since the war started. When Olga Galitzine was arrested, the whole family, including the children, was arrested and sent to the camp at Drancy. Alek and the two children were put in the "Aryan" section, while Hélène was in the Jewish section. However, they were released five days later.

The power was on for a quarter of an hour and I was able to listen to the news. The Allied advance is so rapid that maps of Germany had to be sent by air to the fighting units.

Colonel Roll published an order prohibiting shaving women's heads and marking their forehead and cheeks with a swastika. Yesterday, leaving Barbos', I saw a gang of children armed with sticks, which they were pretending were rifles and revolvers, surrounding a little girl. They had her against the wall, hands tied behind her back, and when I asked them what they were doing, they answered, "We're pretending we're shaving her."

6.9.44 An hour of gas a day has been promised, from seven to eight o'clock in the evening during the week and from noon to one o'clock in the afternoon on Sunday. The metro is still not running.

One of the Suchet employees came on foot to bring me vegetables from his garden. He told me that the first few days of the Liberation were very tumultuous in his neighbourhood; women's heads were shaved and German prisoners and militia were executed on the spot by an unleashed populace. He witnessed a summary execution: a German prisoner was laid down on the sidewalk and a tank went over him several times. It was the women who were most cruel.

Went to the Guil.'s place. P. Guil. recounted how American officers came to Fahrman to look for parts and plans the Germans could have left in the offices. Afterward, the manager came to warn the engineers to be very cautious, because the American officers could be Germans in American uniforms, coming to recover their plans and projects.

One of the Dad. sisters was there. She talked about the visit they had from General König. The husband of one of the sisters was in the African army and was killed there. General König told them that the FFI had pre-empted the Allied plan; the Allies intended to enter Paris later. The FFI uprising made it necessary to send the Leclerc division to maintain order, and it had to get there by forced march. The FFI could not have held out for long, because they did not have enough ammunition. Social unrest was also feared. Apparently the order for the liberation of the city of Paris was given by General de Gaulle without prior agreement with the Allies, because he wanted it to be the French, not foreigners, who liberated the capital.

7.9.44 Went to Barbos' for dinner, on foot this time. American trucks were parked along the sidewalks by the riverside quays; soldiers and young women were sitting in the trucks or on the sidewalks, wrapped in each others' arms, in the most tender poses. Many blacks were among the Americans. One of them gathered a dozen children in the Champ de Mars and took them to an ice cream shop and bought ice cream for each of them.

Lida Mis. came to see me; she made the whole trip from Meudon on foot. She told me that, when the Allies came, many German soldiers were in the woods at Meudon. When they came out to give themselves up, the FFI shot them right in front of the people. The building where she lives was searched from top to bottom because there were rumours that two soldiers had taken refuge there. Lida said, "I often wonder what I would have done if Germans had come to ask me for shelter. Could I have closed my door on two hunted animals?"

Many women have had their heads shaved and been marched through the streets like that. A young neighbour of the M.'s, eleven years old, came in one day sobbing because she saw a man and a woman with her head shaved being marched naked through the streets of Meudon to the hisses of the crowd.

Soviet troops have entered Yugoslavia.

Mail between America and France has finally been re-established.

Old "carriages" of all kinds, pulled by horses, are temporarily providing service from La Madeleine to the Bastille.

Two cooks from Suchet came to pick up their pay. They are already working again, one at the Plaza, as in the past, and the other at an Allied military club. One of them told me that, in Colombes, women were dragged through the streets naked, brushed with tar, and rolled in feathers. Would those not be fantasies seen through "the eyes of Moscow"? They remind me of routine procedures in Russian "pogroms." It seems to me that the Germans had a great deal of success with the feminine population of Paris, at least judging by the number of women having their heads shaved. The two cooks then talked about de Gaulle; they consider him a weak man who will not be able to restore order in the country. They bemoaned the foreign tutelage that France, alas, cannot do without for the time being.

M.N. Czernychev has been arrested; she is answering for the misdeeds of her daughter, who was arrested by the Germans a few weeks before the Liberation and taken to Germany. The daughter was running a purchasing office for the ss during the Occupation and, they say, made a sizeable fortune, which enabled her to buy the Schiaparelli château, a house in Boulogne, and so on. The newspapers describe her as a "torturer," "the lover of the killer Laffont," and so on.

10.9.44   Sunday I had dinner at Barbos'. A cousin of Bicha's named Gagarine, who was there, escaped from Belgium in 1940 and went to England, where he joined de Gaulle's army. He often talked to Soviet officers, who told him that no one in Russia distinguished between White and Red Russians anymore; however, of course, that does not apply to anyone who bore arms against the

"Union." In Caen, the city was draped with flags showing Allied colours, but he noted the absence of Soviet flags and insisted that they be flown beside the Allied flags.

12.9.44 The metro started running again yesterday.

Went to Bellevue. Olga Hitrovo and I went into the woods to hunt for berries. The woods are full of underground shelters, sheet-metal boxes, and so on – vestiges of the Occupation. We went past the cemetery in Sèvres, where German soldiers who were shot by the FFI are buried. "It's fortunate," Olga said, "that their families still don't know how they died." Passing the fence of a property, we were stopped by young English pilots who were standing inside the fence and wanted to know whether it was far to Paris and how the Germans were. "What were they like to talk to?"

The newspapers published a list of people who have been arrested: among them are Alice Cocéa, a very well-known actress and the director of *Les Ambassadeurs* theatre; Germaine Lubin, an opera singer;[96] Pierre Fresnay, a well-known actor; Bernard Grasset, the publisher; the Marquise de Polignac; and Sacha Guitry.

All the theatres are still closed.

15.9.44 Went to Meudon by bicycle to get vegetables and fruit from the plentiful suburban markets, whereas in Paris one can no longer find the tiniest radish. On the way, I met two women who were Suchet employees; they told me that they had asked a postal carrier on the street for information. She asked them their nationality; when she found out that they were Russian, without inquiring further as to their "colour," the postal carrier took them into a bistro and bought them an aperitif. "You are our Allies now," she said. She must not have read the posters in the fifteenth arrondissement!

Parisians are already turning the tragic events of recent times into jokes. L. told me that, in Meudon, a street singer gave a comic performance about Jews returning to Paris, pretending to greet Monsieur or Madame Schmoll in the audience at each refrain, and also turned the entry of French troops in Paris into a joke about one room being enough to house them, pretending to shoot without bullets in their rifles.

96 In 1940, the Countess attended a performance by Germaine Lubin and wrote that "the Germans liked it very much."

Then, when I went to rue Saint-Saëns, I found that Barbos and Bicha had four young Russians staying with them for three days, children from eleven to fifteen years old; they had been in a German camp for foreign workers at Cherbourg. One of them was the "godson" Barbos adopted during the Occupation. When the Germans left the coast and left the camps unguarded, the deportees escaped into the countryside. The four youngsters decided to go to the only address they knew, which was Barbos'. A French colonel picked them up on the road and dropped them off at Barbos' at around five o'clock in the morning. Barbos told me that they were in rags and complained a lot about their mistreatment in the camp, particularly by a Polish guard who beat them mercilessly. They had been taken by the Germans to the village square to play soccer and the most fleet-footed fled into the woods, but that little group did not have time. None of them had ever heard of a church or a prayer; however, they remember seeing their parents make the sign of the cross. They found France much less "cultured" than Russia.

Meanwhile, the radio announced that a Soviet repatriation commission was currently in Paris, and Soviet nationals were to report to the centres indicated on the radio. The four youngsters then took their leave of Barbos and Bicha, who had at least succeeded in finding clothing for them.

Bicha is still working as a telephone operator in the same hotel where she worked during the Occupation. General König's staff occupies it now. She says that the officers are very nice. One of them even gave her an orange lately, a very rare gift these days.

16.9.44 When I was at dinner at Liouba Grecoff's, a Russian woman whose name I do not remember told us that an ROA in American uniform came to see her. He told her that they are going to be sent to London and, from there, to Japan! It is just like the Royal German and Royal Swiss regiments under the Old Regime in France, who went from one master to another. There are also Russian émigrés from the First World War in their barracks, but they are kept apart and do not mix with the Soviet soldiers.

Liouba told me that she saw German prisoners going by under guard by soldiers in American uniform. When some women tried to attack and beat them, the "Americans" intervened; one shouted to his comrade, "*Эй, Митька, дай ей в морду, если не можешь с ней справиться!*" meaning something along the lines of "Hey, Michel, give them a punch in the mouth if you can't get around those women!" Liouba thinks the "Americans" were ROAs again.

17.9.44 While I was at the hospital in Boileau, where I went to see our stepfather, a nurse came to ask me to act as an interpreter for two women in "the FFI." Two elegant young women wearing tricoloured armbands then took me to the bedside of a young Soviet who had been taken prisoner by the Germans. He escaped when the Americans were coming and was taken in by a Frenchwoman, whose mother is Russian. The FFI women brought him coffee and a small Soviet flag, and the hospital gave him a bottle of champagne.

Then, when I went to Barbos', two young Soviets were there; one of them was a *Komsomoletz*[97] and spoke in clichés. He did not say "a German" but "the enemy of the human race." Both were not very educated. Bicha asked them if they had ever gone to church and they answered that they did not even know what she meant, because in Russian that word means "workshops." Bicha then asked Vladimir to take them to rue Daru and told them, to tempt them, that the singing was very good there. However, Vladimir told her when he got back that his companions only stayed inside the church for a few minutes then waited for him in the courtyard.

Power has been restored at rue de l'Université. The weather office across the street earned us that pleasant surprise, because we are connected to the same plant. In other neighbourhoods, power is still only on from seven-fifteen to eight-fifteen in the evening. At mealtime, the courtyard of the building on rue de l'Université is filled with thick smoke from the charcoal stoves the tenants use to cook their meals; the only fuel one can get is charcoal.

19.9.44 At Kira Kozl.'s, we talked about the Khroush.'s arrest; they were taken away by the FFI without even having time to take a coat. They are accused of collaboration because they did not leave their building, which had been partially requisitioned by the Ger-

---

97 *Komosomol* was the youth division of the Communist party, for ages 14 to 28.

mans. They are in Drancy, which now has six thousand prisoners. Kira tried to go see them but was not allowed in.

Then I went to Sofka Polotzoff's. I found her in the kitchen, holding a spoon in one hand and a flashlight in the other for light near the stove; flashlights can still be bought from hawkers in metro corridors. Sofka had me stay for dinner. We ate in the dark, definitely a Rembrandt scene.

Vladimir Zweguintzoff made friends during his stay at scout camp with the military "cleaners" of the American army – that is, the Negro divisions employed to do the dirty work. The good-natured soldiers were willing to sell all their military equipment, so all the scouts were dressed from head to toe in American military clothing. R. told us that an American recently came to buy a hat at Schiaparelli for his wife; he did not have any French francs, so he paid with military rations. Boulevard de la Madeleine has become a real black-market centre. American soldiers walk "from la Madeleine to l'Opéra" selling cigarettes, rations, and so on by the armload, without even taking the trouble to seek shelter in a carriage entrance. The newspapers report sales of trucks full of American military equipment.

22.9.44 Koukol has been arrested. Bobrinsky nearly was; he was accused of speaking German on the telephone during the Occupation. The conversations had been recorded on records. He succeeded in proving his innocence, however, because he does not speak German; it was the tenants from downstairs who used his telephone.

24.9.44 Babysat little Macha Grecoff while her parents were out. In conversation with the child, I asked her, "Will you take care of your mother when she gets old?" She answered at once, "Yes." "And your father?" She thought, then said, "No, I couldn't feed two people; it would cost too much."

In contrast is this comforting human anecdote. Serbian neighbours of the Hitrovos were arrested as a result of a denunciation. The police locked up the house and fences, and the animals, dogs, chickens, and rabbits were left without food and care. A working-class family named Bourgeois who also lives in Bellevue – the husband is a foreman at Renault – succeeded in getting the keys to the

Serbian neighbours' house from the Town Hall and are now taking care of the animals. They send their son by bicycle every day to take food packages to the Serbian prisoners, who are in prison in Versailles. They continue to do so despite threats from some neighbours of being implicated if they continue. I must say, the Serbian family has lived in Bellevue for twenty years and has always been respected by the neighbours.

Lida M. went for a walk around Suchet, like a criminal drawn back to the scene of the crime! She saw the former head plumber again; during the Occupation, he always had a smile on his face for everyone and submitted invoices for astronomical amounts to the Germans. The man now says he was a Resistance fighter and threatened Lida with being arrested, along with all the White Russians. Lida retorted that they will be in good company because, in Meudon, everyone who was arrested was French. I have a thousand times more esteem for the employee Robert C., who resisted throughout the Occupation and always kept his distance and independence, when he would have profited much more from other tactics. At least he showed his anti-German sentiments during the Occupation, not after.

Went to the Klugenaus. Those poor people make me think of the broken trees one sees on bomb sites. Everything is in ruins around them. Their daughter Marina has disappeared; they do not even know if she is still alive. They have not heard from Michel, the youngest, who must have been shot by Resistance fighters. The oldest is currently fighting on the Alsatian front. The father told me, "Anyway, I think Michel is no longer alive; maybe it's better that way. Our neighbour's son, a member of the militia, was shot before his parents' eyes the first day of the Liberation. Michel probably suffered the same fate, because armed men came looking for him at our place. They aimed their revolvers at us and wanted to know where our son had gone, but ended up believing we were telling them the truth about having no news from him, and have not come back."

30.9.44 Saturday, I was at the Gl.'s, who live across from Villa Rothschild. Around the villa are red signs with the name "Barbara" written in large letters. The Gl.'s explained to me that is the name of the unit encamped at Villa Rothschild; the Americans choose a name or a silhouette of a woman as a motto or insignia. One often sees bathing beauties or other little female figures, more or less dressed, painted on their military jackets. The French newspapers have even dedicated a few columns to descriptions of these clothing fantasies "that would make a French non-commissioned officer fall over." However, they hastened to add that modern behaviour of that kind did not stop the Americans from winning the war.

We talked about Renault's arrest. Some accuse him of assisting German military industry by staying open during the Occupation; others defend him, saying that he prevented many workers being deported to Germany. No one defends Laval; however, everyone disapproves of how his trial was conducted.

They say the English General D., on a visit to Paris, was struck by the elegance of Parisians; in London, women nearly all wear uniforms and, when they do not wear uniforms, they dress as soberly as possible.

I have been looking for a job and failed with the Americans, where I was guided by Irène K., who works for them. I was warned that, even in offices, the work is purely mechanical and mind-numbing. However, business in Paris is still in waiting mode. The French themselves have run to the Americans, and "beggars can't be choosers!" I then followed a real way of the cross. American organizations naturally cannot, or at least should not, allow themselves the luxury of individual hiring. In conjunction with the French Ministry of Labour, they have established an "assembly line" system for hiring. A placement office for American organizations has been opened on Avenue de l'Opéra, where the American authorities go when they need staff. However, that office does not do the hiring, at least in principle. It is supposed to act as intermediary, sending requests to the French placement office on rue de Jussienne. If the regulations are followed to the letter, people looking for work with the Americans should go only to the office on rue de Jussienne, which would then direct them to Avenue de l'Opéra. In practice, however, the crowd besieges the Avenue de l'Opéra office, lining up there night and day. Avenue de l'Opéra employees are the first to "break the chain" because the American system is incompatible with French temperament. As they receive a request for a certain occupation, they ask the crowd, shouting, for example, "Are there any drivers among you?" and only then do they send the candidates to the rue de Jussienne office, to avoid being too out of line with American regulations. Candidates come back to the Avenue de l'Opéra office with a card from the rue de Jussienne office, then go to another office at the Majestic Hotel to get a hiring sheet and submit it to their workplace. That is not all. They still have to be interviewed by the American G-2, the Second Office, located at yet another address. That may seem long and confusing to write about but it is much longer and more confusing to carry out. The offices ignore one another and try to push their candidates first. The office hours are the same everywhere, which means you often have to wait a whole week before you have all the necessary papers in hand.

5.10.44 I have been working at A.G. Casualty for a few days at 54 Avenue d'Iéna. The building is a private home that belonged to a Jewish family and was requisitioned at one time by the Germans. I went through the G-2, where I had the good fortune to run into a Russian in American uniform. Comparing the interrogations that friends and acquaintances were subjected to, I see that I was indeed fortunate. Olga Bagr., for example, was told, "So, you went to work for the Germans to go to bed with them, didn't you?" She worked as a chambermaid in a hotel occupied by the Germans. She very placidly answered, "Oh no, if I wanted to go to bed, I would have had enough Russians to do that." Still, my little G-2 agent did ask me sly questions, following the routine used by the police in every country. For example, he did not ask me whether German groups or "circles" existed during the Occupation but asked, "Which German circles did you belong to during the Occupation?" I had never heard of the existence of such circles – кружки. Or he asked me, "Do you by any chance know which committee was located at No. 4 on rue Galliera?" – the Gerebkoff committee. The fact that someone has started working for the Americans still does not mean he or she has been accepted or is *persona grata*. The investigation continues for weeks, and you are only sure you have been accepted when you get a permanent card from your workplace.

8.10.44 A sergeant explained the abbreviations that appear on the lists that will be distributed to us when the Army files arrive from London; for the moment, we are doing absolutely nothing.

Butter rations have been increased to 250 g per month. Electricity is now on from seven o'clock in the evening to seven o'clock in the morning and gas from noon to one o'clock in the afternoon and seven to eight o'clock in the evening. Shoes with wooden soles are being sold freely. The flour at the bakers' is whiter. Films of any kind are still prohibited; only newsreels are shown. We will be able to see films again starting Saturday.

Was at the R.'s and saw a fellow named Nelidoff, who had been arrested in the first few days of the Liberation. The concierge's daughter had accused him of firing on the crowd from his window. Fortunately, he was able to clear himself by pointing out that his apartment looks out on the courtyard and he has no window on the street. He thinks the concierge's daughter was trying to get revenge because he had intervened several times when he saw her beating her children. Nevertheless, he thought it was more prudent to move.

N.N. Koukol, P.'s assistant, is being held at Drancy. He spent six days on a bench at the police station in the company of a French officer. Khlebnikoff has also been arrested; he detests the Germans but his company had to do business with them. The crooner, Tino Rossi, has also been incarcerated. Since he has always been the idol of fourteen- to sixteen-year-old girls, they line up in front of his prison with food packages and protest against the purge by loudly shouting out his name night and day.

10.10.44 Our boss at A.G. Casualty is a man named Lieutenant Gordon; his Jewish parents are originally from Kiev. He gave us a little speech to start that must have flattered most of our troop, which was made up mainly of middle-aged women. He asked us not to distract the American soldiers who are to work with us from doing their duty; they have an inaccurate idea of "Gay Paree." He then briefly explained the mechanics of our work. Daily reports are sent from hospitals; the indications they give about the injured are recorded on cards that are transmitted to the authorities in America, who inform the families. We were interviewed individually by Lieutenant Gordon. A big issue was made of the interview, but all he asked each of us was to recite the English alphabet for him. That surprised me and seemed so innocent. It had a strange effect on me and I skipped the letter "Q" at first. He reminded me of it, smiling.

12.10.44 There is now a magnificent MP,[98] wearing a helmet and white gloves and gaiters, who stands at the entrance to the office and checks passes.

The building is not heated, and it is bitterly cold inside. We work in our coats all day, with our legs rolled up in robes or blankets; those of us who have them have to bring them with us from home. The WACs[99] who are sitting among us grumble while they work; they wrap their heads in scarves and work wearing gloves. We have an hour for lunch, or rather to go searching for lunch. Place d'Iéna is not a district with small restaurants; the few that exist in the vicinity give priority to their usual customers and are closed several days a week anyway. I made a list of the days restaurants are closed, and the employees constantly come to ask me for it toward lunch time. Restaurants are afraid to deal on the black market now and avoid serving meals without tickets. You are just as hungry after lunch; you see employees snacking all day long, a carrot here, a crust of bread there.

Our cousin Kostia Shabelsky died on October 11. A whole page of our youth disappears with him! I remember that when his mother, Aunt Maroussia, died, he told me, "When she was alive, she was the wall hiding the precipice that awaits us all sooner or later. But now that she has died, I realize I am alone on the brink of the precipice. Now it's my turn."

I had gone to see him the night before he died, but he did not recognize me. He suffered terribly and fought; he was suffocating. However, the next day in death he had regained calm and found peace; he looked like he was sleeping. I went part of the way home in the dark with his daughter Sofka after the prayers for the dead. A drunk American soldier grabbed us by the arm; when I spoke

98 Military Police
99 Members of the Women's Army Corps

English to him, he let us go and apologized. Sofka told me the preposterous story of Olga Galitzine's escape from the armoured railcar taking her to Germany. According to Sofka, she pulled open the door of the cattle car she was in and jumped from the moving train, hitchhiked, and finally turned up in Paris. Kostia hid her for twenty-four hours, then she took refuge in the country. She has not changed and still has the same self-confidence, the same way of treating people. She is truly one of those beings who, as the Russian saying goes, do not drown in water or burn in fire.

15.10.44 The work at A.G. Casualty is soul-destroying; you barely finish something when you start again at the point where you left off. We sit at tables in front of filing cabinets. I have the letter "S," with all the "Smiths" in the American army! We pass one another the reports and take out the cards with the names that appear in the reports, and attach them to them. That is all. An hour later, you get all the cards back and have to file them in the cabinets again. You do not even need to speak English for this job. We work on an assembly line, so if one of the employees is slow, she stops the whole team. The sergeant is always hurrying us up, because he has to cover a set number of cards a day. He is surprised that the employees sometimes ask him, "What does this or that mean?" He then asks us with undisguised curiosity, "But why does that interest you? These things are unimportant." The Europeans then explain to him that it is easier to work when you realize what you are doing and why you are doing it.

The WACs are astonished by the Parisians' appearance, their elegance, the high prices – the dollar is at fifty francs. They had been told that the most profound poverty reigns in Paris and ask, "If you have nothing to eat, why do you have permanent waves?" It is an amusing difference in mentality.

16.10.44 All the Americans call one another by their first names. Our sergeant does the same with us and, by dint of hearing him call in turn, "Irène, Marie, Olga," and so on, without any age distinction, we ended up just calling him "Harry." One of the employees said that she could not get used to it because "it's as if one is speaking to servants."

Most of the WACs enlisted in the army thinking they would be employed as drivers for generals and so on; instead, they have been left hung out to dry over cards for six months. They grumble and the sergeant has to point things out to them all the time. One of them is particularly sulky and said to him one day, "When we were asked to join the Army, they told us, 'Sign up, it's your war.' Well, if I had known 'my war' would be like this, I would happily have stayed home in peace and quiet."

Nearly all the sergeants and American officers and civilian employees are Jews. I suppose that is because our services are in the "rear" of the Army. Most are of Russian origin. Sofka V. spends her time entertaining us with her reflections. She works in the next room; lately she came and whispered to me, "Come and watch our sergeants for a minute; they're telling the employees they are all Russian 'Cossacks.'"

We Europeans are struck by the casual dress and manners of American soldiers. Soldiers speak to their officers with their hands in their pockets, one foot leaning on a chair. One of Sofka V.'s "Cossacks" suffers from what he calls "athlete's foot," and he constantly takes his shoe off and puts his bare foot on the table where the cards are and picks it. Right now I am going through a similar "process" to what our grandmothers must have gone through when the first strange automobiles appeared, locomotives spewing smoke, in place of the old horse and carriage. The American Army is so different in its structure and mentality from all the armies I have known up to now. One has to get used to it slowly. Since that Army won the war, however, it is the Army suited to our times.

22.10.44 Sunday today, but I worked from nine-thirty to four-thirty. I chose a weekday, Thursday, for my day off because otherwise I would never have the opportunity to go to a store. Friday now seems like Monday to me, and Sunday is a black hole, like every other workday at A.G. Casualty.

Discussions between WACs and employees. One of them, a Frenchwoman, whom I suspect has been a maid for an English family because she always talks about life in a castle there and I strongly doubt she was there as a guest, said it was a good thing for people to shave the heads of women who had children by German soldiers. The WAC, who had seen that sight in newsreels in England, retorted that she found it revolting and, if she had a child by a German, she would have kept it and demanded that everyone respect her.

Yesterday morning, the "Corporal" called attendance by spelling our names. No one recognized their name and she marked us all absent. Then, seeing us all sitting at our tables, she asked why no one answered. We explained to her that we are not accustomed to spelling our names and did not recognize them. We asked her to read our full names, at the risk of mangling them.

The WACs often pass around chewing gum. At first, no one knew what to do with it, but now the Europeans chew gum like veterans.

We sometimes have to check messages of good cheer. Each wounded soldier's family is entitled to send a telegram of comfort to the wounded soldier once a month free through the War Department. One can easily imagine the paperwork created by those telegrams. And, in spite of that, America won the war!

The Soviet Embassy is trying to rally refugees from the First War to its cause by offering to give them Soviet passports and permission to return to their country.

The execution of Admiral Platon and Minister Daquier de Pellepoix was announced, denied, and finally officially confirmed. They were both executed by the FFI.

A new wave of arrests. A list of writers who have been blacklisted was published by *Le Figaro*. Those writers will not be able to write for newspapers or have their books published. Among them are Montherlant, Frondaie, Suarez, Desmaisons, Pierre Benoist, Béraud, and so on.

26.10.44 The writer Georges Suarez, editor of the newspaper *Aujourd'hui* that came out during the Occupation, has been condemned to death.

Théodossienko, the head of propaganda in ROA camps, who they say made plans for the Germans' Russian campaign, had better luck – just seven years in solitary confinement. Admirals Marquis, Laborde, and Esteva, the airman Detroyat, and the directors of the Caudron–Renault companies have been arrested. Louis Renault died in prison.

V.P. recently witnessed a very lively discussion between two customers of a bookstore, where she had gone to find a book. One of them was attacking de Gaulle, saying that he would never manage to restore order in the country by his own means. The other threatened to denounce him. The first customer replied that, since the motto "Liberty, Equality, Fraternity" has been reinstated – it had been replaced by "Work and Country" during the Occupation – he was taking advantage of that freedom to say what he thought. Moreover, he was already on leave from captivity, arrested in principle but released pending trial because of the shortage of space in prisons.

One of the former waitresses at Suchet came to see me. She is now working in a hotel requisitioned by the Americans. She and her co-workers are not only required to take blood tests regularly for the Wassermann reaction, but have to be examined every two weeks by an American female doctor, a rather reasonable measure. They are examined four at a time in the same room. "Luckily," she said, "my companions are nice girls. They told me, 'Don't worry, when it's your turn, we'll look away.'" They are not notified in advance, and she added that the doctor must not be amused every day because most of the waitresses are really dirty! Male employees are also thoroughly examined.

Recently, after missing the last metro, I was walking home in the pitch dark. Someone I did not know whose bicycle broke down walked part of the way with me. He told me that he had just been to the Normandie theatre to see a Soviet film, *Twenty-four Hours of War in the USSR*. Seeing the soldierly appearance and impeccable dress of the Soviet troops, he realized why that Army had been victorious. In response, I cited the example of the American Army, which does not have a soldierly appearance and whose soldiers wear poorly polished shoes, and it was also victorious. That did not convince him, because he retorted that, in his opinion, there were only two great armies in the world, the Russian Army and... the German Army. In spite of that opinion, he is a member of a Resistance group in the eighth arrondissement and immediately asked me to join it, without even knowing who he was dealing with.

29.10.44 Sonia Bilderling and her mother have been arrested.

Olga Hitrovo and I were stopped in the street by two Soviet soldiers, who heard us speaking Russian. They asked about the address of a restaurant they were looking for, then asked us to sit with them at a café and have something to eat. One of them was intelligent and remained guarded; he told us he was the Soviet representative in repatriation camps at Versailles.

Olga asked him a lot of questions, which he answered evasively or not at all. When she asked him what he did before the war, he answered, "You have before you a soldier, which has to be enough for you."

To her question, "Where are you staying in Paris?" he answered, "I am at the disposal of the Soviet Embassy," then told us that he had escaped from a German camp and went underground with the French, which had earned him a "partisan card" so he could now eat without tickets. He did not like France. He found Frenchmen petty, greedy, and not very courageous. "They're all rich in this country," he said, "but they are afraid to part with a cent, while we take pleasure in spending money when we have it and having a bit of fun. The French prefer to be bored. Look at the villages, how sad they are. As soon as their work is done, the farmers all go home and bury themselves in their houses. Where we live, the village is lively and gay after work, which only lasts eight hours; we get together at the club in the village. There is a club in every village where there are newspapers, books, a reading room, games; we play music, dance, and play chess. None of that existed in your day," he added in a slightly ironic tone.

"Of course it did," I replied, "but in a different form, naturally, because that was about thirty years ago. In my day, the villagers got together in the evening at the homes of those who had a more spacious *izba* or in the village Town Hall. There was no electricity in the villages at that time, and they lighted the room with a wooden torch – лучина. The women and young girls were spinning or cracking sunflower seeds; people sang and played the accordion. They were called посиделки – chat parties – and were usually held in the winter when the work in the fields was done." But I could see that he was convinced that everything that currently exists in Russia was invented entirely by the Soviet government and also that everything in Russia is better than anywhere else – a narrow point of view but comforting for Russian national pride, which so often suffered during emigration.

"Wait five years," he said, "and you'll see, we'll surpass America in everything," which already impressed me less.

Olga Hitrovo was astonished that farm work could take only eight hours because, as she remembers it, farmers worked from sunrise to sunset during the summer months. "That was in your day," retorted the fellow with a great deal of self-assurance. "We have changed all that. We have mechanized farming, and now eight hours are enough." The two soldiers then criticized the conduct of Frenchwomen, particularly their relations with American soldiers. "It's impossible to imagine something like that happening at home! All those women kissing American soldiers in the street, hanging onto them with their arms draped around their necks – it's disgusting. That's the Americans' fault, too. If we were the ones who occupied Paris, we would not have tolerated such disorder. It's a crying shame – *подобное безобразие.*"

I asked them where they were from. The "tough guy" told me, "Leningrad, or if you prefer, St. Petersburg." The other one was a native of Kursk, a provincial city where I lived during the First War. "Has Kursk changed?" I asked him.

"Certainly," he said. "You wouldn't recognize it anymore." He then admitted that the streets in the *Streletskaia Sloboda*, a faubourg of Kursk, still flooded with water in the spring and the inhabitants had to get around by boat when the snow was melting.

2.11.44 It is Thursday and yesterday was All Saints' Day – cold but lovely weather, an exception to the rule that it always rains on this date. We worked today, because Lieutenant Gordon said he had not received instructions to the contrary from the Ministry of Labour, which severely chilled the employees' zeal. They now find the Americans tough; they do not show enough concern for employees' well-being. It was not just today or an initiative of one employee that the matter of a canteen for employees was discussed.

Professor Gosset, the head surgeon at St. Joseph hospital, died in prison. He was arrested for operating on patients with German surgeons present, which was considered an "act of collaboration."

Olga W. also told me that, at tea at her friends' home, she met a very elegant woman wearing a very pretty turban. Olga was looking at her, and the woman admitted to her that she had had her head shaved. Her husband, a plant manager, had been accused of industrial collaboration, and the FFI rushed to her home in the early days of the Liberation and shaved her head. The next day the head of the plant's Communist cell came to express his sympathy and regrets, assuring her that the incident took place without his knowledge and also without the knowledge of the workers, who had always appreciated all that she and her husband had done for them.

There was an air-raid warning, followed by explosions. News about it has been censored, which did not prevent rumours from spreading that V1s had been launched at Paris.

7.11.44 Received our first paycheque, plus compensation for one day of leave per month, because we will not have leave in kind. We were lined up single file in alphabetical order to collect our paycheques, which greatly astonished the employees, and were warned that it was forbidden to ask questions or make claims. Those who were not happy were to go to the office at the Majestic Hotel to complain.

Today is the sergeant's day off. It would seem *a priori* that distributing cards to sixteen employees and checking their work is not all that difficult. Well, every Tuesday, when the sergeant is off, appalling chaos reigns in our room. The sergeant's second-in-command gets nowhere and, when it is the corporal, a woman who is a farmer by trade, it is even worse. We have to redo all the work the next day.

Some of the employees have already received a blue card, a permanent pass, which means that they have been cleared by the G-2.

We still do not have heating at work. The cards we handle are yellow and beige and it is often difficult to distinguish them from one another, because we work in electric light. Even when the sun is shining brightly, the sergeant insists that all the lamps be turned on. When some of the employees went to protest to the lieutenant, he replied, "If you can't work, we'll replace you."

8.11.44 Today I was sent to work in "verification." That office contains all the cards of all the soldiers who were in hospitals, while our filing cabinets contain only the names of those who are currently in hospitals.

The newspapers announced the distribution of one bottle of champagne for every three people. You have to bring two empty champagne bottles.

Last Sunday, when I was at rue Daru, there were many Soviet soldiers there with a red star on the front of their caps and officers wearing an armband with their rank in large letters. I bought two Russian newspapers for five francs a newspaper; French newspapers cost two francs. On the front page of one of them was a picture of Stalin. The newspapers contained articles by émigrés who had returned to Russia and described life in that country in the rosiest light.

There is a great deal of talk about amnesty for émigrés from the First War. Many of my countrymen imagine that everything has changed; naturally, there will be less comfort there than in France, but perhaps one will be happier there. How I wish that were true and how I cannot believe it, in spite of everything!

Hairdressers are allowed to do permanent waves again. I took the opportunity to go have one done. I admired the energy of an older lady, about seventy years old, blind and deaf, who came on the arm of her maid to have a permanent wave, a manicure, and a pedicure.

Soviet representatives are surprised that reconstruction in France is progressing so slowly. The Soviet Consul told G. Gag., who purportedly wants to go back to Russia, that factories are already running in Stalingrad and delivering tractors for export.

10.11.44 It is starting to get cold. I sleep with two hot water bottles, two eiderdown quilts, two sweaters, and a pair of socks.

16.11.44 November 11 went by calmly. Demonstrations were feared, and the parade route was guarded by the police, the FFI, and American MPs, some even posted on the rooftops.

The Hitrovos were called in to the *Sûreté* on denunciations signed by ten tenants of the building where they have their store. They were accused of receiving Germans and offering them wine and cigarettes, which would have been impossible to check, even if it had been so, because of the positioning of their store. The police officer told them that they should consider themselves fortunate that the denunciation ended up at the *Sûreté*; otherwise they would have been sent to Drancy and waited months there before being interrogated.

At the home of friends, I met a young Russian woman, an actress in the theatre, who went to Germany during the Occupation to perform for prisoners. She met Soviet refugees there, professors, doctors, and so on, who had left the country following the Germans. What struck her the most was that the majority of them were toothless. They were dressed in rags and looked miserable. She met a friend she had not seen since she left Russia. The woman's husband died after living six years under daily threat of arrest. For six years, he had to report to the NKVD each day and was interrogated for two hours.[100] "He wasn't sick," her friend told her. "He no longer had the strength or the desire to live."

Inhabitants of Riga told her that, when the Soviet army approached the city, they threw tracts saying that the whole population should remain there; no distinction was made any longer between Whites and Reds. However, as soon as the Red troops occupied the city, all those fine words were forgotten and executions began immediately. That was confirmed to her by Madame Kouznetzoff, the wife of the owner of a large porcelain factory in Riga.

23.11.44 Saw three Soviet films: *Stalingrad, The German Defeat Outside Moscow*, and *Twenty-four Hours of War in the USSR*. The last one was the best from a technical point of view. It had all the characteristic camera work of Russian films, the contrast of light and shadow, scenes shot from unexpected angles, moods. In the deserted streets of Moscow in the early morning, patrols on horseback ride through the streets; the silence is broken only by the sound of horses' hooves on the pavement. Then, suddenly, the

---

100 The NKVD was the People's Commissariat for Internal Affairs, the precursor to the KGB. It was the Soviet Union's police organization, which, among other things, administered the gulag system, carried out mass executions and deportation, and enforced Stalinist policies both in the Soviet Union and abroad.

departure of the troops, the evacuation of factories, the intensified work in factories in Asian Russia to replace factories occupied by the Germans; all that effort had to be at the cost of thousands of human lives. However, it will be a heroic page in the history of Russia. Who pities the workers now who built the pyramids in Egypt? We only admire the results.

The other two films showed executions, the victory parade in Moscow in which German soldiers and officers were forced to parade with their generals marching at their head, soldiers with beards marching with heads bowed, their uniforms torn and flapping loose around their bodies, dirty, mostly shoeless, their feet wrapped in straw. The cortege reminded me of the triumphant return of the Romans, dragging the prizes of war behind them. The humiliation of the vanquished is always painful to see, whatever their nationality or the party they belong to. What struck me was the calm that reigned in the crowd standing on both sides of the parade – not a hostile gesture, not a shout – while the Parisians in the theatre audience whistled and shouted angrily as a sign of their approval.

Camps of Russian prisoners were also shown, or rather what was left of them, endless frozen cadavers lying behind barbed wire… I pity our civilization!

25.11.44 I went through some fairly frightening and unpleasant moments, a real gangster film. I was having tea with Mima Gag., who lives in a large apartment on Cours Albert 1er. The maid had gone out shopping and the butler had retired to the kitchen after bringing the tea. We were sitting calmly, chatting, when we heard a rush of footsteps, and three men burst in front of us as if they came out of a box, pushing the butler, as white as a sheet, in front of them. Two of them, about twenty years old, bareheaded, wearing military-style trench coats, were armed with revolvers, holding one in each hand. The third looked more mysterious, wearing a dark overcoat with the collar up, a fedora pulled down over his eyes, and a pair of dark glasses; he aimed a machine gun at us. One of them then said, "We are with the FFI. My father was killed by the Germans. You collaborated with them. Now you are going to give us your money and your jewellery."

Mima did not realize what was going on at all and answered very politely, "You are mistaken, gentlemen, I never collaborated with the Germans. Moreover, I never even saw a single one during the Occupation, because I hardly ever go out."

"Enough discussion," said the one who appeared to be the leader. "Get up and give us your money. You, Jo, keep those two in line," he added to the man with the machine gun, meaning me and the butler they had meanwhile thrown onto the sofa where I was sitting. Then he made Mima get up and led her to the door to her bedroom, while the man with the machine gun stayed half-hidden behind a screen, with his gun aimed at me and the butler, repeating, "If you move or cry out, there will be dead bodies in the house." I did not move or cry out, but I felt my heart beating very hard, and I could not help thinking that it would really be stupid to die like this, after coming unscathed through several wars and revolutions, the Occupation, and the Liberation. At that moment, the doorbell rang. The gangsters in Mima's bedroom rushed out and asked the butler who it could be. He said he did not know and continued saying it, in spite of the threats and promises to put a bullet into him if he lied.

The leader then ordered Mima to go open the door, recommending that she not cry out or give any warning, pointing a revolver in her back. The visitor was Gleb G., who came by for a cup of tea. He was instantly grabbed and thrown onto a chair in the salon. That was the moment I wanted to laugh. The poor man did not understand what was going on; he saw me sitting well-behaved on the sofa beside the butler, surrounded by armed men. It was not exactly a "five o'clock tea" atmosphere.

From that moment on, our bandits looked like men in a hurry. They told us to go single file into the next room. I was last in line and could feel the barrel of a revolver in my back, a most unpleasant sensation – something I had only seen in American films. They say fear sends your heart to your heels, but I felt my heart beating fast in my throat. We were locked in the little bathroom beside the bedroom and, since there was nowhere to sit except on the toilet and bidet, Mima asked if they could bring us a few chairs, which one of

Olga Hendrikoff | *A Countess in Limbo*

them most kindly did. After locking us in, they shouted at us to stay perfectly quiet and not cry out at the risk of being shot; they would come back in half an hour. We soon realized that the bandits were not going to come back and started inspecting the place. The bathroom only had one small window with frosted glass, so high up that we could not reach it, even by climbing on a chair. We therefore had to wait for the maid to come back, which took more than an hour. Finally, we heard her worried cries, and she ran to let us out when she heard our shouts. The concierge and police were alerted; the concierge had to go use the neighbour's telephone to call the police, because the telephone wires in the apartment had been cut.

The raid was reconstructed in stages. The bandits had come in the service entrance on rue Jean Goujon, rang the kitchen doorbell, and pointed a gun at the butler as soon as he opened the door. They ordered him to take them to his boss. While the man with the machine gun guarded us in the salon, the other two bad guys rifled through Mima's jewellery. They forced her to give them the key to her safe, where she had put five hundred thousand francs just the night before, and took her pearl necklace from around her neck. One of the two police officers, who arrived on bicycles after the concierge's call, told us quite candidly, "Lucky those guys left before we got here." When I asked him why he said that, he explained that the police had "lost" many weapons on Liberation, while "all those guys" are fully armed. I suppose that the bandits operating right now in Paris are aware of that situation.

Mima was expecting an American commanding officer, a friend of hers, to come over that day, but he had sent his apologies at the last minute. I wonder how the affair would have unfolded if he had been there, because he would surely have been armed. What would his reaction have been? The American employees at Iéna laughed uproariously when I told them the story of the hold up.

Two days later, we had to go to the police station to look at photo files to try to find the men who had put us through such unpleasant moments. Mima told the police officer that the three men who broke in on her were handsome young men, while the men whose pictures were on file were simply appalling. The police officer answered her good-humouredly, "Madame, it's because the individuals whose photos you are looking at were manhandled a bit in interrogation. They looked a lot better when they were brought in." He then complained that their work was made very difficult by the purge of senior members of the vice squad, who had a lot of experience in the "criminal world" and had the identities of all kinds of gangsters at the tips of their fingers.

30.11.44 Rations are being cut again. Sugar is always rationed, but in metro corridors, hawkers offer you caramels, madeleines, apple turnovers, and so on, all guaranteed "pure sugar." A newspaper even published a kind of list of black-market stock exchange prices with different exchange rates based on the neighbourhood where the commodities are sold!

I usually have lunch in little restaurants in the vicinity of Avenue d'Iéna. Well, in any restaurant, you can eat without tickets if you pay double the price, without any formalities or being a regular customer. Similarly, in stores, except *Grands Magasins* where the accounting is more closely checked, you can "make an arrangement," as it is called, with the salesgirl, usually by paying an additional five francs per point and buy fabric, clothing, or other rationed products without tickets.

The Hitrovos are now having more trouble getting fabric supplies because some chemical products necessary in the manufacture of rayon came from Germany.

General de Gaulle has formed an alliance with the Soviet government. The newspapers are full of details about his visit to Moscow: the receptions, the gifts he was given, and so on, and praise the significance of the pact signed by "the two great powers on the Continent." The Allies, on the other hand, appear to find that move distasteful.

I had to renew my work card, which was declared void by recent decrees. I had to repeat all the steps you usually take to get your first work card – that is, certificates of residence and work and endless line-ups at various counters. What is interesting is that, on the one hand, workers who worked with or for the Occupation authorities are subject to reprisals, yet on the other hand enjoy privileges such as 75% unemployment benefits, as a result of an agreement between the French authorities; French workers in Germany receive the same unemployment benefit rate.

Théa Par. has been arrested again. Her mother was able to go and see her and talk to her through the bars. Théa was sobbing and kept saying, "*Maman*, save me." It is hard to imagine the little bird, the little fashion design figure Théa has always been, in prison behind bars. She still does not know what the charges against her are.

23.12.44 The German offensive in Belgium has led to new precautions; serving food to American soldiers in public places is not allowed. The reason is that they have their canteens and mess, and they could be German soldiers in American uniform trying to eat in a restaurant. American troops are consigned to barracks from eight o'clock in the evening. The MP on duty at the Avenue d'Iéna building has been given a rifle, and he checks our passes very carefully.

The Americans put up a large Christmas tree in the hall. The employees took up a collection to buy four bottles of wine for the sergeant and I forget what knick-knack for the lieutenant. The day before, the sergeant suggested we give each other little gifts, drawing names for the recipient. The ones who were drawn by the Americans were the lucky ones, given items in rare supply such as chocolate, cigarettes, and the like.

Some soldiers sang "Stille Nacht" in English; otherwise not much was done. The quiet, somewhat sentimental atmosphere of reverence observed by the Germans at this time was totally missing.

END OF THE WAR

"'If that is progress, then we are too far advanced,' said the good wife of farmer Poupard. How many times have I remembered those common-sense words spoken by a simple woman!"

1.1.45 Welcomed the New Year symbolically at eleven o'clock in the evening at rue Saint-Saëns. Apartments are still not heated, so Barbos installed a sawdust heater in the small entryway they also use as a dining room. The sawdust is put away in sacks in the tiny little kitchen and bathroom. The pipes from the heater go through a pane of the kitchen window. Michel and Irène have moved into Barbos' apartment, because the owner of the apartment they were subletting has come back to Paris permanently. With Vladimir, that makes five people in three rooms, not counting the baby who is due any day now.

The German offensive in Belgium has been stopped. An air squadron bombed Germany Christmas night. The newspapers said that the head of the squadron was in Germany when the end of the line of aircraft was still in England.

Spy neurosis is still rampant. Armed officers accompanied by American MPs stop all cars and buses in the outskirts and search them. We were warned at Avenue d'Iéna not to give information or records to military personnel we do not know by sight, which is fairly difficult to put into practice because we do not know the military staff in the units located on different floors who come all day to ask us for information.

I had dinner with the Bilderlings, Sonia and her mother, who have just been released. They described the stages of their arrest to me. To start with, they were detained at the police station in their neighbourhood for several days, in the basement, sleeping on the ground. Fortunately they had brought blankets with them. The first night their cellmate was a very pretty and elegant Frenchwoman with her daughter, who was about twenty years old. They were accused of having German lovers. The Bilderlings shared their blankets with them. The next morning a new prisoner was brought in, the wife of a stable hand at a nearby riding school, arrested for mending the breeches of three Germans who came to ride at the ring. She was transferred the same evening to the Conciergerie, where the Bilderlings met her again later. The next night, the husband of the Frenchwoman came to take their place, offering himself as a hostage to make it possible for his wife and daughter to go back home. The Bilderlings were finally interrogated and accused of occupying a Jewish apartment during the Occupation. They had, in fact, occupied one, but as a result of an amicable arrangement with the concierge, whom they had given a written promise to vacate the apartment as soon as the legal tenants came back. They were no longer living there at the time of their arrest. They were then transferred to the Conciergerie. The gloomy appearance of the prison made such an impression on Sonia, who had held up until then, that she nearly lost all her self-control. However, they had barely entered the women's room when they found they were among acquaintances. The wife of the stable hand welcomed them and assured them that the Conciergerie was much more comfortable than the police station. Marie Sheb. and Maroulka Tchernychew were there, too, and Marie immediately took Sonia to the young women's corner and introduced her to the other prisoners.

The Conciergerie also had some distinguished detainees: Arletty, a very well-known film actress, accused of having a German lover, and Ginette Leclerc, a film actress, arrested for producing the film *Le Corbeau*, which was shown during the Occupation. The prison conditions at the Conciergerie were, in fact, less harsh than at the police station. They had a straw mattress for the two of them; the guards sold sandwiches for ten francs apiece; the male prisoners were in the room above the women's room; and the prisoners communicated between the rooms through a hole in the ceiling. Nuns were assigned to the prison; their presence and care were a great support to the prisoners. M. Bilderling and Sonia were finally released one day without ever finding out why they were arrested or released. They have changed districts but told me they tremble every time the doorbell rings.

4.1.45 We still do not have heating at Avenue d'Iéna and work with gloves on our hands. Food supplies are still poor; frozen potatoes were offered for sale, and the newspapers said that, contrary to what has always been said, frozen potatoes are not harmful to health. We did not get the 250 g of fat for December. Food stores offer only onions and *foie gras*.

I received an additional sheet on my income tax return for 1943. Under the Occupation, the German authorities had ordered that employees' salaries only be taxed at 5%. The tax department is now catching up.

Hitler spoke on New Year's Eve and gave assurances that he would never surrender. No one believes him now.

The Polish Committee in London, the former government, protested because the Communist Committee in Lublin has proclaimed itself the legal Polish government, and General de Gaulle sent representatives to it. However, that government is still not recognized by all the Allies.

Bicha works as a switchboard operator in a small hotel, and there is no heating at her job either. To go to work, she puts on Vladimir's ski pants and Barbos' toque and wraps her head in a wool scarf. The hotel manager told her she looks like a whirling dervish. The hotel where she works was occupied by the Germans during the Occupation and is currently requisitioned by the French Army. The Soviet Repatriation Commission also occupies a few rooms there. They often ask Bicha to act as an interpreter for them. Seeing her completely frozen at her switchboard, a Soviet colonel recently invited her to come up to his room and have a glass of vodka. She went to tell the manager who, with her French common sense, cried, "Was it really worth the trouble to leave your country twenty-five years ago to go drink vodka with the Soviets now?"

7.1.45 Russian Christmas. The Orthodox church in other countries, except the Romanian and Finnish church, always follows the traditional calendar, which is thirteen days behind the European calendar. Yesterday was Russian Christmas Eve. Our churches were full to bursting. We tried to get into the church on rue Michel-Ange but could never get past the porch. I could hear mysterious words all around me, such as "Since when? Three days ago" or "Three weeks ago." It was friends asking one another the date they got out of prison. Then we went to rue Saint-Saëns, where Barbos had managed to build a Christmas tree out of pine boughs.

I tried to change jobs and went to the Allied censors of correspondence from German prisoners. All the Americans there were Jewish. I was asked to read letters that had been copied many times, some in Gothic handwriting. I was told that was perfect and I could start work right after another G-2 interview; however, I do not think the job tempts me enough to redo the interview.

The social group at Avenue d'Iéna is a varied mix; among the American military personnel are a woman farmer, butcher, and cook. One of the sergeants is the owner of a funeral parlour, one of those places where the deceased is on display for the family after skilled hands have dressed him, done makeup and hair, and so on. The sergeant does not look the least bit like an undertaker though. He is big and fat and very cheerful. Sergeant Harry, our boss, is not very highly regarded by his co-workers because he did not have a car in the United States, that apparently being one of the measures for judging the value of an individual in America...

The WACs often wear coloured bows in their hair, which contrasts strangely with their khaki uniforms. The general opinion is that the American men and women lack freshness and are old for their age.

We are now used to calling the American soldiers by their first names and hearing them call us by ours, the only exception being Princess Chalikoff, a woman in her sixties; the Americans simply call her "Chali."

11.1.45 When I got home, I found a pneumatic post message from Léon de Rosen, asking me to come for tea at the home of friends where he was staying.[101] I found the atmosphere military, an atmosphere of resistance – genuine resistance, in this case. Everyone there had actively taken part in the Resistance. Colonel R. and Léon recounted to me how they had crossed the Channel, a voyage that took them two days and two nights in a fishing boat. They let Madame R. know they had arrived safe and sound by one of those mysterious messages broadcast by the BBC from London. Léon also recounted to me how friends of his had escaped to Algeria and were torpedoed by the Italians. The boat they were on, the *Empress of Canada*, sank in no time. The passengers just had time to put on their life belts. One young woman, twenty-two years old, stayed in the water four days and four nights, clinging to a floating beam with sixty other passengers. The beam was not big enough to hold all the survivors, so they had to take turns; they tried to stay afloat within oil spills, which sharks avoid. There were only four left when an Allied airplane fished them out. One of the passengers let herself go under when she saw that her husband was no longer alive. When the husband of the young woman realized he was dying, he told her to go to his friend if she survived and tell him that her husband had entrusted her to him. Léon heard that they recently got married. When the young woman was taken out of the water, she had several flesh-eating rodent fish on her back but had not felt them biting her.

15.1.45 A French police officer came to investigate me on orders from the American G-2. The concierge refused to answer his questions and sent him to my landlady, Mademoiselle Théobald. One of the questions the officer asked her was, "Did she have men visit her at home?" At first, Mademoiselle Théobald took that very haughtily and asked him, "Do you not see where you are, Monsieur?" then wanted to know why my private life might be of interest to the American authorities. The officer dutifully replied that he was very surprised himself but the questions had been dictated to him by the American authorities. He also added that he nevertheless liked Russians very much!

---

101 *Pneumatic* refers to mail delivered through pressurized air tubes. The pneumatic was used in Paris until 1984.

Le Figaro recently published the list of foodstuffs we actually get: one egg per month, 100 g of margarine, 150 g of meat per week, but not always. We did not get any butter this month, or potatoes or other vegetables or fruit. Children get a quarter of a litre of milk per day. In the country, you can get everything you want; it is the transportation that is lacking. At the little restaurants where all our employees have lunch, the menu rarely includes anything but watery "garden vegetable" soup, which means potatoes and carrots in water. No dessert or coffee or meat.

The Lublin government has been installed in Warsaw.

A Polish woman at Avenue d'Iéna very kindly told me, "Madame, I was raised hating Russia, and now I see that they are the saviours; you'll see, they are the ones who will save the world."

An English officer came to bring me a letter from Ella. They are all safe and sound. Ella, Lerik, and Nora Ruggeri work for the Allies.[102]

Boutoroff, who worked as a handyman at Suchet during the Occupation, was dismissed after working for the Americans for four days. However, his wife, who also worked during the Occupation as a chambermaid, has been given authorization to work at A.G. Casualty.

I was attacked last night in the Champ de Mars. My brother had accompanied me back to the entrance to the garden and, when he left me, said that he thought I could take the path across to Avenue de la Bourdonnais alone, barely a five-minute walk, since it was such a bright moonlit night. As soon as I started down the path, however, I heard hurried footsteps behind me. I turned around and saw a young man, who looked like a student, with a briefcase under his arm. I sped up my pace anyway and soon heard him running. I still thought he was a student running for the metro and was not alarmed. When he got to where I was, the young man suddenly pushed me and grabbed my bag, which he started to pull toward him with all his strength. I started shouting and pulled back on my bag. I suppose I was dealing with a beginner because, right when the handles of my bag were starting to give, he let go and

102 Lerik is the son of Ella, Countess Hendrikoff's sister. Nora Ruggeri is Countess Hendrikoff's cousin.

disappeared into the bushes. Then I heard women's voices and saw two passersby coming in my direction. They came up to me and asked if I was the one who screamed. They had seen me defending myself but were afraid to intervene!

Veta Kr. was also attacked near the Trocadéro, around nine o'clock in the evening, and beaten so severely with a billy club that she was taken to the hospital.

8.2.45 France–USSR committees have emerged in all arrondissements, and series of lectures on Russia are given, Soviet films shown, evening events held, and so on. One of my co-workers at Iéna brought me an issue of a new weekly, *Lettres Françaises*, and pointed out the article on the first page by J.L. Bloch, a Communist sympathizer and journalist who has come back from Russia and is currently giving lectures to the committee in the seventh arrondissement. In his article, he describes the Soviet citizen: "The Soviet is generous by nature" and so on, as if he was writing about a new inhabitant of Russia. Everything Russian is now eaten with Soviet sauce. Russian émigré choirs that have been in Paris since time immemorial are now called "Russian Patriot choirs" and French newspapers devote articles to them that would lead you to think the choirs are Soviet creations.

Pierre Brasillach, editor of *Je Suis Partout*, a weekly that led a relentless campaign against the Jews during the Occupation, was executed yesterday. Maurras has been condemned to solitary confinement in perpetuity. Prince Regent Cyril of Bulgaria was executed a few hours after his conviction.

Madame Bobr. went to tell Madame Ilov. that Théa Par. has been released; all the charges levelled at her have proven unfounded. However, Théa is afraid to go back to her apartment, because she found out that it was her concierge who denounced her.

Bakeries are short of bread, and big stores are nearly empty of merchandise. The American authorities finally opened a canteen for their employees. Only bread tickets will be collected.

Went to the theatre to see the English play *Dear Brutus*; the French title is *La Nuit de la Saint-Jean*. My friend and I wrapped ourselves in the blankets we had brought with us because the theatres are still not heated. Although the action in the play is supposed to take place in June, the actresses wore fur coats on stage, and wool sweaters could be seen under their tunics in the second act. When the actors spoke, you could see little clouds of condensation around their mouths.

The work at A.G. Casualty does not appeal to the Europeans. First of all, we are not used to assembly line work in an office. The way employees are dismissed is surprising, too, because it is inconsistent with French custom. This is how it goes. The employee involved is called in to see Captain Christie, who tells him, without further explanation, "I am very sorry. You don't work here anymore." A Jewish employee was recently dismissed like that for being away for ten days; she just got out of a concentration camp and thus expected more consideration. She had submitted a doctor's certificate stating that she was confined to bed because of illness.

Lieutenant Gordon recently called in the sergeant and pointed out to him that the female employees were going to the washroom beside his office too often. You should have heard our "delegate" – we had to elect a delegate for each room – a Greek woman who is very vociferous and volatile by nature, shouting at the top of her lungs, "If Gordon does not want us to go p— in the bathroom, let him give us chamber pots in the office."

Employees are now talking about joining the union, the *Confédération Générale du Travail* (CGT), and membership forms were passed around among the employees. However, Irène Kour. and I refused to join. First of all, neither she nor I want to enrol in a Communist sympathizer organization; then I doubt the Americans will accept the move.

15.2.45 When I was at the Iziéd.'s, I saw Sandra Wolkoff, who had just arrived from London. She described the V1 and V2 bombings. Although the V2 were more deadly, exploding without any sound in advance, the V1 rockets frightened Londoners more because their whistle announced an impending explosion, but it was impossible to predict where the rocket was going to land. The motor often broke down and the rocket went out of control, descended very low, and started doing flips in space then suddenly corrected its position and continued its course. London has suffered a great deal from bombings. Not only have many buildings been destroyed, but a lot of houses have been so shaken and disturbed that, in the building where she lives, for example, one can hear talking and laughter from the next house. Food supply is better organized in England than in France.

22.2.45 Irène Zweguintzoff had a baby girl, Hélène, on February 20 at 9:58 in the morning.[103] We went to see her at the clinic where she was born. Irène looked as fresh and rested as if she had just come back from a holiday in the mountains.

I was at a lecture at the France–USSR committee in the seventh arrondissement. A lot of people were there, medical students and doctors; the lecturer was a Dr. d'Alsace, and the topic of the lecture was "Medicine in Russia."

The information the lecture was based on was provided by J.P. Bloch, a Communist sympathizer and journalist who just got back from Russia. D'Alsace began by saying that the current status of medicine in Russia should not be compared to medicine in Western countries but instead with the status of medicine in Czarist Russia. According to his claims, there was no free medical care in Czarist Russia. D'Alsace chose to ignore municipal hospitals and Zemstvo hospitals, which were *free*. In my day there was also compulsory health insurance.

He then claimed that only 35% of the cities had hospitals, which I doubt, because there were even hospitals in the villages, and out of one hundred and sixty million inhabitants, there were only twenty thousand doctors (???). He explained that doctors in Soviet Russia are public servants, have no private clients, and cannot choose where they live or the hospital where they work. When he left medical school, he went to a centre chosen by the State. Professional privilege does not exist, and doctors are required to report any case

103 Hélène Charvériat (née Zweguintzow), Managing Director of the Union of French Citizens Abroad, was awarded the French Legion of Honour in 2007. (The French side of the family uses the spelling "Zweguintzow" instead of the spelling "Zweguintzoff" used by Countess Hendrikoff.)

of infectious disease, such as tuberculosis, syphilis, and so on. Patients do not choose doctors or hospitals. Medical care is completely free. At the end of the lecture, d'Alsace asked if anyone wanted to ask questions. A few young students stood up and asked him questions, including whether doctors were really content with State control and whether patients would not prefer to choose their doctor themselves. D'Alsace babbled an answer that any doctor was as good as any other and added, as an excuse, that it was difficult for the Western mind to grasp that concept of medicine.

The newspapers reported figures for the number of people purged in September – one hundred thousand.

We have been issued mess cards that we are supposed to show when we enter the canteen. The sergeant who punches the cards is an American of Russian origin; he surprised us one day by exclaiming in perfect Russian, *"Беда мне с этими бабами!"*, which means "Women are a curse!" The food in the canteen is not particularly varied or appetizing – nothing but canned goods – but it simplifies life substantially and is economical at ten francs a meal.

A French colonel arrived at the Hôtel de la Bourdonnais bearing letters requesting pardons addressed to de Gaulle. One was written by the wife of one of his fellow officers, the mother of three children. Her husband has been condemned to death, accused of industrial collaboration with the Germans. The colonel complained a great deal to Bicha about the absence of any order in the countryside. Bands of Spanish Communists released from German camps are terrorizing the entire population of Auch without being bothered by the authorities.

In peace time, if an earthquake had killed a tenth of the number of victims reported daily by the press, people on every continent would have risen up in horror. Collections would have been taken, missions sent. Nowadays the newspapers report that twenty thousand people perished in a raid on Cleves, thirty-five thousand at Dresden. I do not mean that it is only Allied aircraft that sow death; the Germans also sowed death in London and in Russia. I just mean that war gives human beings a hard shell of indifference; people would react totally differently in peace time.

This war has made stars of aviators, paratroopers, and women soldiers, WACs and Wrens, and the like. Nurses, the Sisters of Charity of the First War, draped almost monastically in veils, bent like angels at the bedsides of the injured, have disappeared to make room for young Valkyries in uniform who drive trucks and cars, pilot planes, labour in the fields on tractors, battle paperwork behind the lines. They wear the ranks and insignia of their male comrades, salute soldiers and officers in military style. American and French women inject a bit of imagination into their dress, perch their caps across masses of curled hair, wear make-up, and have a slightly music-hall look. Englishwomen look plainer, tidier. The Germans also enlisted women in Army services, but only the *Blitz-Mädel* – telephone, telegraph, and radio operators – wear a kind of uniform, but have no rank. Red Cross nurses wear a striped blue and white cotton dress, a white bib apron, and a starched cap that hides their hair. One sees them in medical centres and canteens for troops in transit. American nurses also wear a uniform, often slacks, but I do not think they play a very important role at the front because the wounded are picked up by stretcher-bearers, put on hospital planes, and brought to the rear by air, often even to another country.

Wounded French soldiers are not the ones who get public attention and care. There must be injured Frenchmen now, because there are soldiers fighting, but all the concerts, charity galas, and so on are always for the benefit of prisoners – "Day of the Absent" and the like. In the metro, however, one sees posters calling on the public for material help for General Leclerc's soldiers "who lack everything that usually provides fighting men with comfort." "They gave you victory. They are cold. They need shoes, gloves, blankets," and so on.

Admiral Dum., who had been arrested, was released. Seeing her sitting at her tea table, looking elegant with her hair nicely done and make-up on, one forgets that she just spent more than three months in prison. When they came to get her, they told her she was being taken to the police station in her neighbourhood to ask her for some information, so she did not take blankets or toiletries with her. Two hours later she was on her way to Drancy.

Maklakoff, Admiral Verderevsky, and Kedroff went to visit Soviet Ambassador Bogomoloff, who received them in friendly fashion but let them know they should not count on an amnesty. He said, "There are too many things émigrés will never be able to accept, such as the concept of a federation in Russia. For you, Russia is your homeland, with its Orthodox religion, Russian language, Russian population. For us, our homeland is the Union of various Republics that make it up, with their diverse religions and diverse languages, where every citizen, Buryat or Ukrainian, enjoys the same rights."[104]

8.3.45 General Roatta, Badoglio's Chief of Staff, has succeeded in escaping.[105] He was being held in Rome in a private hospital. The electricity was off for half an hour and, when the power was restored, General Roatta was no longer in the clinic; all that was left was his bathrobe lying on the floor.

The newspapers also published the story of General Giraud's escape; he had escaped a German camp during the Occupation, showing incredible presence of mind and daring in the event.

There were promotions among the American military staff at Avenue d'Iéna and our sergeants are all busy sewing stripes on their sleeves. Our boss, who, by the way, spent the whole war in offices in the rear, wears on his sleeve a large badge approximately 10 cm long with a red lightning bolt on a blue background cutting through a big gold chain – the Allies breaking the chains of Nazism. Lower down is a badge with the stripes of his rank of sergeant technician and as many small stripes as he spent six-month periods in the European theatre of military operations: in his case eight stripes. Finally, there is a big stripe that represents three years in the Army.

Madame R. told us that she saw a cartoon in the newspaper with a little soldier whose sleeves are bare of any stripe or badge, sur-

104 The Buryats are a large Buddhist ethnic minority in Serbia. During the Russian Civil War, the nomadic Buryats and the Cossacks sided with the White Russian Army; both groups were excellent horsemen.
105 General Roatta had previously been Mussolini's Chief of Staff. Premier Pietro Badoglio was asked by the Allies to remove General Roatta because of the war crimes he had perpetrated in Yugoslavia.

rounded by ranking officers covered with badges and so on with the legend, "Simple soldier or someone who doesn't know how to sew."

Furthermore, even the Soviets understand the value of those decorations. After abolishing epaulettes, stripes, and the like, they re-established them again, and their diplomats' uniforms are all bands of gold.

Our sergeant told us that, for the first time in his service, employees are allowed to speak to American military personnel and among themselves. In London, an officer was permanently stationed in the offices to ensure that absolute silence reigned. At Iéna it is definitely different. First of all, there are a lot of young women who flirt with the sergeants – and, God knows, they are not very attractive, but they have chocolate, cigarettes, and so on. Only there is one employee, by the name of Luxembourg, who took over the whole black market by mysterious means, and my co-workers have not yet succeeded in supplanting him.

The work is so monotonous that Irène and I play little games to avoid becoming completely mindless while we deal with the cards: a kind of radio game, "Guess what I'm thinking?" and the like.

Read an article in *Collier's* on Soviet politics in the Near East. Stalin has become the symbolic protector, the *Ab Sharab*, of African tribes. Every time Egyptian workers, for example, send recriminations to the authorities, they send a copy to the Soviet representative, Mr. Novikoff,[106] a tactful and knowledgeable man who shows respect for Orthodox churches, visits convents, promises them aid from the Soviet Government. Diplomats who work for him are selected from among those who speak native languages or dialects, while foreign diplomatic or industrial representatives rarely speak anything but English.

15.3.45 Metro fares increased as of today. We have not had butter for three months. This week we did not get meat. Irène Zweguintzoff is entitled to extra rations and got 50 g of meat with bones. The sergeant was interested in what rations we received and asked whether it was much more than during the Occupation. Someone

---

106 Nikolai V. Novikoff was the Soviet representative in Cairo, Egypt, during World War II. Later he became the Soviet ambassador to the United States.

replied that we have less now and it costs more. He was surprised and said that the Americans are not taking anything and brought everything with them. No one could give him an explanation.

One of our WACs explained to us that they all have to have a medical once a month. They line up and go four at a time into the room where they are examined by a woman doctor. I asked her if they were separated by screens. She replied, "You must be joking! At the beginning, I was extremely embarrassed. Now, I don't pay any attention."

I cannot reconcile the lack of discipline and outward signs of respect in the American Army and the fear all the sergeants have of their superiors. The sergeant did not want to let me leave half an hour early to go to the collector, so I asked to speak directly to the lieutenant. The sergeant looked at me as if I had said I wanted to go throw myself into the lion's den and tried to dissuade me. But I stood my ground, and Lieutenant Gordon immediately gave me the necessary permission.

30.3.45 A parade is planned for Easter Monday. The Leclerc division will take part. In Auteuil, one sees a lot of soldiers with coffee-coloured skin, wearing turbans and beards. When they saw them, women in the street cried, "Oh, look, here come the Russians!"

American soldiers came into the hairdresser while I was there and offered everyone German cherry brandy. Then one of them showed me a cross with the inscription "*Deutsche Mutter*" and asked me if I knew what the decoration was. He had torn it from the neck of the woman they evicted to stay in her house. He then told me that they liked Germany much better than France; "everything is so clean and they have such wonderful beds."

1.4.45 Bicha told me that there are eighteen Soviet officers at the hotel where she works right now. They are all very suspicious. Recently there was a power outage at the hotel and they immediately started shouting that it was sabotage. Bicha says that they often use words with a new meaning; for example, they say, "*пошли на постановку*" – we went to the "production" instead of saying to the "theatre." In my day, similar language errors were often made by people with little education. One of them brought Bicha back a jar of butter from Moscow, a touching kindness.

At the G.'s, an American officer talked about relations between Russians and Americans, in Russian. The Americans only see Russians during working hours. They have to burn their newspapers when they are finished reading them, "for fear they fall into pro-Nazi hands," say the Russians. Russian soldiers are quick thinkers and speedily learn to handle new American machines. The Americans, however, think they still make too much use of human resources where the Americans have used machines for a long time. It is true that the Germans took tractors and so on with them and, in many regions, the peasants are forced to labour with old wood ploughs.

2.4.45 As a protest against not getting a pay increase, an employee at Iéna threw all the drawers of cards she was working on on the floor. It was a way of saying good-bye, because she had already submitted her resignation. Employees who work standing in the hallway with no windows and dim lighting from ceiling lamps also said they were quitting their jobs. The sergeant gathered us all together and announced that we should not have demonstrations; the employees in the hallway were going to be transferred to a better lit and ventilated space. How can the employees who are trying to join the CGT be criticized?

Colonel Roll-Tanguy, a former boilermaker and labourer, has been put in the regular Army.[107] The current head of the FFI is "General" Revers, a former PTT employee.

5.4.45 Had lunch at the Eristoffs'; they just found an apartment, which is equivalent to winning the grand prize in the lottery. The apartment is on the second floor of a small private hotel in the sixteenth arrondissement. You get to it by a spiral staircase and come to a series of charming little rooms with a low ceiling and half-moon windows that overlook gardens and little courtyards where chickens strut, roosters sing, and rabbits jump around in their cages. You would think you were far from Paris, living in the last century.

107 Henri Tanguy was a metal worker in the Renault factory south of Paris in the 1920s. He took the name of his friend who died in the Spanish Civil War; hereafter he was known as Colonel Roll. During World War II, he was the leader of the Communist resistance in Paris and in 1944 became head of the FFI.

8.4.45 American soldiers almost solely supply the black market. Boulevard de la Madeleine "from the Madeleine to the Opéra" is its official centre. American soldiers walk along the boulevard, usually with a backpack; they are immediately accosted by French civilians with knowing looks, disappear into a carriage entrance, then come back out and head off in the opposite direction, the French civilian feverishly clutching an object wrapped in newspaper under his arm – one or more cartons of cigarettes. Paris is full of German shoes and merchandise sold by GIs; however, the GIs also sell their shirts, uniforms, military blankets. At Iéna, American soldiers got their hands on the library of the former owner of the building, Günzbourg, and his porcelain and gold tea service with the Günzbourg monogram; I do not know whether he is still alive. It is possible that they did not take it; someone else may have profited from it because American control is not very tight. Nevertheless, I was surprised.

11.4.45 The Rhine has been crossed by paratroopers. The operation, and others of its kind, were filmed and shown on the screen. A small trap door opens, men jump into emptiness, white umbrellas deploy and turn like snowflakes above miniature landscapes. Large gliders open like the mouths of antediluvian animals and out pour troops, guns, and equipment of all kinds. It looks so simple, yet how many studies and efforts it takes to achieve that result. The spectacle would be almost sublime if it was not destined to exterminate human lives and civilizations.

Saw a Soviet film at the theatre, *Kharkoff's Trial*. The film started out showing rivers bordered by sandy banks flowing through meadows, fields of ripening wheat rippling like the waves of the sea – the landscape reminded me of where I was born and flooded me with strong emotions.

The action then changed to a military courtroom. There were three Germans accused – a colonel, a captain, and a non-commissioned officer – and a Russian driver. The Germans were questioned with the help of an interpreter. They all answered in the same emotionless voice and accused themselves of the worst crimes; they described gas extermination trucks, admitted having women beaten to death and children killed after being taken to a hospital on false pretexts, and so on. They gave the impression they were robots; one might have thought they were under the influence of a drug.

We had to line up for a fairly long time to get into the theatre. In front of us was a slightly Oriental-looking gentleman with two very beautiful women. Hearing us speak Russian, he turned to us and started speaking Russian. He explained that he was Afghan but had studied in Moscow and was here with his wife and daughter. Then he added, "Aren't our Afghan women beautiful?"

14.4.45 Went to the Norwegian Legation to pick up a package sent by Zaren Wang. I was supposed to speak to Colonel Ebbesen, who had been a military attaché in Moscow from 1922 to 1925 and speaks Russian well. In our conversation, he told me that the Revolution in Russia had been necessary. Russia was two hundred years behind other countries socially. The Russian people were not well educated and evolution of the kind that took place in Norway could not have occurred. He considers Russia still behind, despite the Revolution. He also said he expects some levelling of the fortunes in England and America after this war.

There was an atmosphere of dignity and calm courtesy at the Legation. It is a democratic nation, without the noisy vulgarity of the Americans.

Roosevelt is dead. There were various reactions from the Americans. One even said that Roosevelt was the worst blackguard who ever existed! However, a Russian employee arrived sobbing; when the sergeants asked her the cause of her sadness, she said it was the news of Roosevelt's death that got her into that state!

We had to observe five minutes of silence. You cannot imagine how long five minutes can sometimes seem. Toward the end, I saw the lips of several of my co-workers trembling, holding back a desire to laugh that was out of place, it goes without saying. I admit, however, that the tension of those five minutes of silence, the absorbed face of the sergeant who was timing the minutes, wristwatch in hand, the sight of Irène sitting facing me and trying to avoid looking at me, also made me want to laugh, to my shame.

I relegated my bicycle to the seventh floor and think my faithful courser, which gave me such valuable service during the Occupation, is going to be put out to pasture permanently. Traffic has increased considerably, although has not yet reached the pre-war level. A lot of expensive cars have appeared on the streets, despite gas restrictions. The American jeeps alone, which are driven at crazy speeds, are a danger to the public. During the Occupation, a bicycle was a necessity and an object of envy. Young and old, workers and elegant Parisian women pedalled with gusto. Now one only sees very young people or workers use them. Bicycle taxis, which were the rage in Paris during the Occupation, have almost completely disappeared. The little cars of various styles, from sedan chairs on wheels to wheelbarrows, attached to a bicycle or tandem, powered by human muscle, were truly one of the characteristic sights of the war years. However, horse-drawn carriages have increased. One usually sees a line of hackney cabs at Place de l'Étoile and American GIs have their pictures taken comfortably ensconced in their cushioned seats.

One sees fewer dogs in Paris than before the war. It was extremely difficult to feed them during the Occupation, although poodles were still fairly common at that time. One often saw them perched on the rear carrier of a Parisian cyclist.

19.4.45 Went by a crowd on Place Clichy gathered along the route of French prisoners repatriated from Germany. Cattle trucks had been requisitioned for the purpose and were transporting them to the Gaumont theatre, from where they then got home to their families.

The trucks going by were decked with little tricoloured flags. The prisoners looked joyful, smiling, tanned by the sun. When the trucks were stuck in a traffic jam and their progress slowed down, women went up to them and shook the men's hands, and asked the name of the *Stalag* they were coming from or for news of their husbands or sons.[108]

Prisoners are being repatriated at the rate of approximately ten thousand a day. American planes bring them back to France. They say that food supply problems were too complicated to hand the

108 *Stalag* is an abbreviation for *Stammlager*, which were military prison camps.

prisoners over to the UNRRA.[109] Repatriation centres had to hastily be opened at the Gaumont and Rex theatres, the Luna-Park, and the Winter Velodrome. Bicha saw a prisoner on the street weeping and saying over and over, "I spent five years living for this day and now I find out my wife left and took our daughter with her."

A neighbour answered him, "What do you expect? It lasted too long."

The story is also told of the prisoner who came home when his wife was out and, finding a child he did not know in the apartment, picked him up and threw him out the window. It was a neighbour's child.

The Soviet authorities are deporting Romanian and German workers to Russia to rebuild devastated areas. There were questions raised in the British Parliament on the matter. The right of free men to make their own choices of where to go was discussed, but nothing further was done. The Allies do not want any complications between them.

Stories of German atrocities in Jewish camps and concentration camps are starting to appear in the newspapers. Photographs show crematorium ovens with partially burned bodies, survivors who are human skeletons, heaps of bodies piled one on top of the other. There is talk of medical experiments performed on deportees who were used as guinea pigs for scientific research.

It seems incredible to me now that, throughout the Occupation, neither I nor my circle of friends and acquaintances, who did not know any Jews or Communists, ever heard of the camps or what was happening there. Caspary and his wife, German Jews who lived across from the Hitrovos in Bellevue, disappeared one night and were swallowed up by oblivion. We never found out where they were taken or what became of them. Only once did Admiral Kinzel allude to something terrible that was better not to talk about. It was at the time of Katyn, when the Germans seized on

109 The United Nations Relief and Rehabilitation Administration was the idea of American president Herbert Hoover. The agency provided relief to thousands of the displaced just after World War II. Its functions were later taken on by the Marshall Plan.

the incident for anti-Soviet propaganda purposes.[110] The newspapers described the mass murder of Polish officers and published photos; documentary films were shown on the screen. In that conversation, I spoke out indignantly against the crime. The Admiral interrupted me in an almost surly tone, saying, "It would have been better not to raise that issue in the press. We have plenty to reproach ourselves for, too," and immediately changed the subject. Were those fine bourgeois gentlemen I knew during the Occupation aware of the crimes? Did they close their eyes, as Kinzel probably did, knowing they could not prevent them? Anti-Communist Russians in Russia must have been prey to similarly confused feelings during the war.

29.4.45 Marshal Pétain has returned to France and turned himself in to the authorities; General König went to get him and refused to shake the hand the Marshal extended to him. He is now at Montrouge. A number of newspapers published the motto, "All stand united against the Marshal so that his return is not a source of division for French people."

Spoke to one of the many French prisoners who, knowing I am Russian, told me, "Excuse me, Madame, but I have to tell you that your countrymen are behaving like savages in Germany. Not only do they rape German women; they rape Frenchwomen who have been deported." I naïvely believed that the Soviet military authorities would give strict orders to the soldiers to make a good impression in Europe! I have lost many of my illusions in recent times.

30.4.45 The radio announced the arrest and execution of Mussolini, his mistress Clara Petacci, and a few other members of his Party. The bodies were hung by the feet and displayed that way all day in a public square in Milan.

When I think back to the shouts of "Duce! Duce!" that used to resonate around him when he appeared on his balcony in Piazza Venezia, what an ignominious end! How capricious and illogical his fate to have been saved by Skorzeny under such peril-

---

110 For more information about the Katyn massacre, see the footnote on page 203.

ous circumstances and still not escape his destiny!¹¹¹ Why was he granted a respite?

In Genoa, people killed German soldiers who were there and hung them from the walls of the city. I remember seeing a sight like that at Madame Tussaud's museum in London. However, those scenes represent the Middle Ages. Have we really not progressed since?

French radio just announced the end of the war and the unconditional surrender of Germany. No one knows anything about Hitler yet. There are rumours that he is dead, which seems likely, because the peace overtures to the Allies were sent by Himmler.

1.5.45 The question of whether May 1 would be a day off work raised a great deal of discussion. Before the war, May 1 was not a statutory holiday, although a large proportion of workers took the day off for political reasons. During the Occupation, the day was declared a statutory holiday. In the end it was decided to declare May 1 a public holiday. At least that is going to cut short individual demonstrations.

Municipal elections, in which women voted for the first time, gave the Communists a decisive majority. Communist propaganda is very active, and the public is looking for something new, as the Russian saying goes: "*Думали так, передумали сяк, ну-ка, бабушка, на новый лад,*" which means "After thinking about various possibilities, let's try another way now."

The Allies have changed tactics toward the Soviet army. The first few days American and Soviet troops met at Torgau, "fraternizing" was in full swing; now the Allies can no longer cross the demarcation line. One of the clients at the Hôtel de la Bourdonnais told Bicha it was better that way because the Soviet authorities are carrying out "clean-up operations" in their zones that it is preferable to know nothing about.

---

111 Otto Skorzeny, a Nazi hero, set up schools to train troops in commando warfare. In September 1943, just after Rome was bombed and Mussolini was arrested, Mussolini asked his friend Hitler to be rescued from a ski resort where he was being held in the Apennine mountains. A daring raid with Skorzeny in charge, code named Operation Oak, used gliders to fly in commandos, which culminated in the successful rescue of Mussolini.

Poland was not invited to the conference in San Francisco, and the fifteen members of the Polish government who went to Moscow have disappeared without a trace.

2.5.45 Yesterday, May 1, the French newspapers did not come out, but the American *Stars and Stripes* had a huge headline on half of the first page announcing "Hitler is dead." According to that newspaper, Hitler and Goebbels died May 1 but details are not yet known. Admiral Dönitz has been named successor to the Führer. Count Bernadotte of Sweden is said to have begun peace talks with the Allies on behalf of the Germans.

The Fascist Italian army and the German army in Italy have surrendered unconditionally.

In the evening, the French newspapers also published the announcement of Hitler's death. Vendors were shouting, "Hitler has croaked."

3.5.45 Our sergeant came to tell us that he was "very sorry" but the American authorities did not agree to consider May 1 a holiday. Those who worked and expected to be paid at a higher holiday rate will, alas, be paid at the usual rate; those who did not come in to work thinking they had a day off, paid at the normal rate, will not be paid at all. Everyone protested without winning their case.

I have been working for the American army for six months and have gotten used to feeling like a small wheel in a formidable machine. Relations between employees and employers are very different from what they were under the Occupation. I say that at the risk of being called a "collaborator" or something of the sort and keep my reflections to myself. However, everyone who worked in German installations during the war years and is now working at Iéna says the same thing as I do. Lately, I was going home to rue de l'Université by metro when a young girl threw her arms around me. She was one of the waitresses at Suchet. She is now working in an American installation. "Oh, Madame," she said to me, "what a difference! How much happier we were at Suchet!" And she is French!

"Be quiet, Marguerite," I said to her fearfully, "We'll be sent straight to Fresnes." Certainly, however, the Germans took much better care of their employees' well-being than the Americans do. The *Hausoffizier* went down to the kitchen to see how the employees were fed, which enraged Rautsmann. He reminded the officials at No. 6 and No. 10 that it was right not to forget the staff at Christmas time and took up a collection among his co-workers. The bosses always helped everyone who wanted to improve their situation, always encouraging *sich verbessern* – them to improve themselves. Well, I do not want to compare, but the difference astonishes me. Is it because the Germans had suffered privations that the Americans have not experienced? All the same, everybody in America cannot be a millionaire!

Here I feel any personality is erased. I do not wish to generalize and say that Americans are nasty or tough or the like. One on one, many of them are nice, good-natured, and so on. It is the system that is tough, automatic.

Food supplies have improved slightly. The black-market price of butter has dropped, because we have been promised 500 g of butter in May in return for fat tickets. You see a lot of leeks in vegetable markets; too many even, because you are obliged to buy some if you want to get rarer items. You can now get salad, carrots, onions, cauliflower.

Strawberries cost two hundred fifty francs per kg. A qualified clerk earns one hundred fifty five francs per hour. In stores, you see dresses for two-year-old children at prices of four hundred, five hundred, and even six hundred francs. The gross monthly salary of a qualified clerk is four thousand seven hundred francs.

I have already received a care package from Zaren Wang twice: coffee, cigarettes, a pair of artificial silk stockings, boxes of matches, which still cannot be found here, chocolate, tea. Yesterday, I received a package from America from Nancy Zweguintzoff with tea, coffee, cocoa, powdered soup, and so on. It is a marvel to see such precious commodities, which one cannot find or afford in Paris.

The currency for barter now is a package of cigarettes. It opens every door for you. Your shoemaker refuses to re-sole your shoes? A few cigarettes and enough said. Cigarettes to the salesgirl to pull the object of your desire out of a cupboard – only sold to a chosen few! In the evening, when I am returning home, I see groups of young girls and youths surrounding American soldiers; instead of laughter and jokes, or words of love, all one hears are the little words, "How much?"

Recently our sergeant said to us, "Now that the war is over, you will be going to go back to Russia." When I explained to him that it was impossible, because we do not have Soviet citizenship or permission to return, he asked with astonishment what our nationality is then.

"We don't have any, at least officially; we are not citizens anywhere."

Countess Hendrikoff's Nansen Passport

"Who governs you?"

"No one." Seeing that he could understand nothing from my explanation, I continued, "We abide by the laws of the countries where we live; our passports and identification papers are marked stateless."

The sergeant shook his head and repeated, "All the same, I can't understand how you can live like that."

7.5.45 Yesterday, Sunday, was Russian Easter. Saturday evening, I went with Bicha, Barbos, and the whole family to the midnight service at rue Daru. The metro does not run after ten o'clock in the evening, so the service was held at nine o'clock instead of midnight. There was a crowd, although not as many as in pre-war years because, at that time, you could not even get into rue Daru; this time, we were able to get into the churchyard. There were many Americans in the crowd or at least many Russians in American uniform, but not a single Soviet uniform.

Was at the Chipoffs', where all who remain of the fine flower of Russian emigrants were gathered, headed by Grand Duke André. Gr. was back from Nice, now a GI rest and convalescence centre. He was talking about his sister-in-law, who has finally been released after six months in prison. She was arrested as a result of a denunciation, even though she could be accused of nothing. He expected to see a gaunt, thinner woman, but the door was opened by a big woman, all swollen. Apparently that was the effect poor nourishment and the prison diet had on all the prisoners. She told him that she suffered so much from communal living during her imprisonment that she is starved for solitude and no longer wants to see anyone.

Rumours about the surrender of Germany have been circulating all day. Finally, around three o'clock, one of the employees who had gone to the window shouted that newspaper boys were running with special editions and the MP who was on duty beneath the windows waved the papers to show the headline announcing in big letters, "Unconditional Surrender."

8.5.45 The newspapers finally officially announced the end of the war in Europe. Churchill and General de Gaulle are going to speak on the radio around three o'clock.

Afternoon. Lieutenant Gordon told us at first that the employees of American services would not have the afternoon off, but around three o'clock the sirens began to howl and the bells to ring; there was no longer any way to keep the employees there and we were allowed to leave.

In the streets, flags were flying, cafés were full, and American cars were roaring by with young women perched on the seats or the laps of GIs. In the evening, the streets were lit and Parisians did not camouflage their lights for the first time since the beginning of the war. Gangs of young people paraded during the day along the major arteries carrying little tricoloured flags.

10.5.45 Sofka Nossovich, who had been arrested by the Germans for distributing tracts, came back from Germany where she had been deported. However, Vera Obolensky, who had been arrested at the same time she was, was executed.[112]

Civilian employees leaving for Germany with the Allied Occupation troops are given a list of rules of conduct. They are not allowed to visit Germans at home or foreigners living in Germany, shake hands with Germans or foreigners, frequent German public places, or exchange gifts.

A co-worker of Michel's returned from Rome and told us that Italian youths do not want Italian girls to go out with Americans and that they shave their heads if they catch them! My niece, Hélène Shirkoff, asked, "Is it true that, in Paris, young girls ride around in jeeps? That would be absolutely impossible here in Rome." After all, it is true that, in Italy, the Americans are the victors. Naples has fallen back into its pre-war destitution, filth, and disorder. Most of the streets there are off limits to the Allies, and posters warning of the risk of venereal disease are stuck on all the walls.

George Bibikoff came back from Germany, after just missing the Soviet troops in Berlin. Marina is now at Sigmarinen, which is occupied by the French.

13.5.45 Splendid weather, 32°C in the shade.

112 Princess Vera Obolensky (also known as Vicky or Vika) was a member of the French Resistance. She was arrested and taken to Berlin, where she was executed on August 4, 1944.

The Americans are all busy counting their points. They need ninety to be demobilized. Each child, decoration, and year spent in the military theatre of operations entitles them to a specific number of points.

An official *Te Deum* ordered by Soviet Ambassador Bogomoloff was held at rue Daru! The officers who live at the hotel where Bicha works were in attendance. Bicha finds them boorish. General Pavloff reminds her of Stenka Razine, and she says she would be afraid to run into him in the woods at night.[113] The woman manager asked her laughingly if she would like to spend time with those officers normally.

On May 1, all the Soviet soldiers were drunk from morning on, singing at the top of their lungs. The French officers came out of their rooms, frightened, and asked whether it was Russian Easter. Bicha tried to keep a straight face and answered, "No, 'we' are celebrating May 1." She asked one of the Soviet colonels why they had restored wearing epaulettes. He answered that it was done at the request of soldiers who were not able to recognize the officers. "Admit it," Bicha said, "It gives you pleasure to wear them." The colonel smiled without answering.

Recently Bicha got hold of a Russian history book for middle-level classes in Russian schools: nothing but the history of revolts, revolutions, and the like, describing at length the revolt led by Pougatcheff, a precursor of the Bolsheviks. However, the history of the Czars and their reforms go unmentioned. On every page are tirades about persecutions that victimized the peasants. When Bicha drew the colonel's attention to those passages, he replied, "Don't pay any attention to all that! They're only slogans for the people and of no importance. Émigrés who return to their country will help us rebuild Russia."

15.5.45 Yesterday, Tuesday, was the "Women in War" parade. Women in uniform representing various Allied units paraded along the Champs-Élysées. Some of the female battalions formed up beneath our windows, so it was easy to watch them.

113 Stenka Razine (1630–71) was a Russian folk hero, best known for leading brutal uprisings against the nobility and merchant class.

At the head of the parade were the American WACs in khaki, wearing little military wedge caps on masses of curled hair, gloves, and butter-coloured scarves. Female officers wore a skirt the same pinkish-beige colour as male officers' pants. They were followed by the English Army Transport Section in lighter-coloured uniforms, wearing peaked caps on tightly pulled-back hair, no gloves, and by the Women's Auxiliary Air Force in very pretty steel-grey uniforms. The Frenchwomen came at the end. They were more imaginatively dressed, wearing khaki blouses instead of the suit jacket of the Anglo-Saxons and various styles of shoes. The French Navy Auxiliary wore navy blue with three-cornered hats the same colour. The Republican Guard band came last. At a given signal, the female soldiers stood still. The Englishwomen then performed the following manoeuvre perfectly: they spread their arms in a cross to ensure the same distance between them, then did a little jump landing on slightly spread legs and crossed their hands behind their back. It was a perfect movement – however, totally lacking feminine grace.

In Berlin, Russian women soldiers direct traffic.

Recently, when I was going down the metro corridor, I heard my name called but did not immediately recognize the coffee maker from Boulevard Suchet in her navy-blue uniform. The girl was really quite stupid, always the butt of jokes by her co-workers, who amused themselves by playing tricks on her all the time. She often caused me sleepless nights because she always forgot her keys or left the light on in her office. I asked her in some surprise what she was doing wearing that uniform. She replied proudly, "I occupy Germany."

Saw the surrender of Germany at the movies as well as the signing of the armistice by Keitel, Friedeburg, and Stumpff. Previously the bombing of Berlin, the surrender of the military leaders to Montgomery, and the capture of Bertesgaden and Munich were shown. Then concentration camps, mass graves, partially decomposed bodies being exhumed; the work was done by German prisoners wearing gas masks. "If that is progress, then we are too far advanced," said the good wife of farmer Poupard. How many times have I remembered those common-sense words spoken by a simple woman without much education!

The provinces voted and voted for the Left.

The San Francisco conference came to an abrupt halt. The Polish conflict has not been settled. The Big Three do not appear to look kindly on the Soviet plan for the independence of the colonies.

The *New York Herald Tribune* published an article entitled "Guide to Russians," describing the failings of the Russian diplomatic representatives, their lack of tact and "international manners" and their distrust – delegates do not get into bed before checking under tables, beds, inside cupboards, and so on – but adding that the Soviets must be encouraged to find grounds for agreement.

In fact, the USSR has won a military and political victory. The Allies are forced to deal with the USSR, even submit to its decisions. Nothing is known about what is happening behind the Chinese wall represented by the demarcation line now separating Yugoslavia, Bulgaria, Romania, and part of Germany from the rest of Europe. Despite all the insidious questions Eden and Churchill were asked, the British government was not able to obtain permission for its newspaper correspondents to enter Soviet zones. No matter how much the Allied press compares Russian diplomats to musicians who play by ear and improvise and to writers unfamiliar with grammar, the Allies need Russia and are trying to find a common language that will enable them to reach agreement with "that uncivilized colossus."

18.5.45 One of the sergeants explained to me how the wounded are repatriated to America. It only takes twenty hours by air to take a wounded soldier back to the United States. Negro stretcher-bearers are usually used, because they combine muscular strength with flexibility and gentleness in handling the wounded. Medical personnel, including a doctor, accompany the wounded soldiers and, in the event of an emergency, surgery can be performed right on the plane. Entire hospitals have been transported that way by air and started operating twenty-four hours after landing.

The assimilation of diverse nationalities in America is entirely to the country's credit. The ill-assorted mixture of races nevertheless forms a united front. I have spoken to Italian, Spanish, and other soldiers; they all feel American above all, even when they continue to speak their own language and belong to diverse religions.

Liouba Grecoff told me about a friend who visited them, Mikhail-off, who worked in Germany and found himself in the Soviet zone when Germany was divided. All Russians, émigrés, prisoners, or ROAs were parked in concentration camps guarded by women. The ROAs told him that the camps were worse than German camps. To start with, their clothing was taken and, in exchange, they were given rags; watches and rings were torn from their hands and gold teeth from their mouths. Mikhailoff was fortunate that he still had his French armed forces card and was able to obtain repatriation to France.

19.5.45 Had dinner at Liouba's. One of her former school class-mates, N.K., was there, a woman about forty years old. She had fol-lowed the German army in retreat with her two children, sixteen and seventeen years old, and had now arrived illegally from Germany. She spoke slowly and calmly about horrible, terrifying things, as if something in her was broken. Her husband suffered from ulcers and had just had an attack when the Germans were approaching Rostoff. He was given orders to leave the city, but she had no way of moving him in the condition he was in, so she decided to stay. Rostoff was taken by the Germans, abandoned, and captured again. During the short interval when the city was retaken by the Soviets, her husband was torn from his bed and thrown into prison, where he died three days later. Her brother-in-law was also arrested and went insane a week after his imprisonment. When the Germans took Rostoff again, she had decided in advance to follow them should they retreat. That is how she got to Darmstadt. When the Allies took the city, she was put in a concentration camp for Soviet nationals. The Commandant was a Soviet general under the orders of an American commander. She spoke English, so she offered to act as an interpreter. The Ameri-can commander had great difficulty understanding why so many Russians refused to go back home. One day, a group came to him and said they were all Greeks, Italians, and so on, but had lost their papers and asked to be repatriated to their country of origin. When questioned, they later admitted that they were Soviet and Russian citizens but did not want to go back home at any cost, despite all the guarantees given by the American and Soviet generals. Finally, the American commander gave them a pass to leave the camp and allow them to get out of the impasse on their own. Many French workers gave written promises to Russian deportees saying that they would marry them in France, and the French authorities agreed to "repatriate" the chosen women on the basis of the promises.

N.K. also told us that the French repatriation authorities constantly showed understanding and helped the Russians who refused to go home any way they could. One officer proposed to N.K. that he marry her fictitiously; another issued her a certificate saying that she was born in Toulouse and had lived in France until 1939. However, her children were immediately placed in another camp and sent back to Russia. She explained to us that she no longer had the strength to go back to Russia, especially since she doubted she would ever be able to be reunited with her children. She thought that her children's youth and ignorance of living conditions other than the conditions they had known in Russia would facilitate their return and life in that country.

She does not believe there will be a change of regime, nor that religion will be re-established. Naturally, soldiers have seen how workers live in other countries, but she does not think that could have a serious influence on the regime. In the conversation, she used many new and unfamiliar words, for example, *курсовка* for "vacation" and *очередь* for "metro line."

20.5.45 Storm and torrential rain. I just bought myself an umbrella – they recently reappeared on the market – and carried it proudly; to my great disappointment, it let the rain through! I went back to the merchant to claim a refund of my money; he said to me most cynically, "Of course it is not rainproof, Madame, you can't expect to get a rainproof umbrella for fifteen hundred francs!"

Deportees and prisoners have been given permission to fish in the Seine with a rod and line on Saturdays and Sundays "in an effort to improve their food supply."

Saw three deportees today with gaunt faces, heads shaven, dressed in some kind of striped pyjamas – the uniform of concentration camps – sitting at a table on the terrace of a café on the Champs-Élysées. American soldiers were photographing them from every angle.

Sunday we worked at A.G. Casualty until four-thirty in the afternoon. Since there was not much work, the sergeant who is second in charge, Bob, entertained us with "stories of the country." This sergeant is the only one who is unshakeably calm and professes deep distrust of his superiors. He is from Georgia. He and his mother have a passion for wild animals, which they tame. For a while, he had a mountain lion, a type of cheetah if I am not mistaken, which he walked on a leash like a dog and had trained to attack blacks (!), and had tamed a racoon, a white raven, and an alligator. Speaking of Negroes, he explained to me that Negroes have separate compartments on trains and separate sections on buses in the southern states. They cannot go into restaurants frequented by whites; their children go to segregated schools. It is different in the North; restrictions against blacks are not as strict. Blacks have the right to vote but, according to him, do not make use of that right because "they simply don't care." However, he thinks that, after this war, the Negro issue will cause new problems because of the participation of Negroes in the war, although always in Negro battalions, and the exodus of blacks to the North to work in war factories. I asked Bob what he would do if a Negro MP made a chance comment to him in the street. He gave me a fierce look and simply answered, "He better not try."

The sergeant is really an original; he speaks to civilians and superiors with the same nonchalance, never calling superiors "Sir." He is the only one who does no black-market trading. He has been married and is divorced. When I asked him if he intended to remarry given his age – he is twenty-six years old – he replied, "Oh, no, a woman could never stand me. I like to go out at night and drive around the streets or take off for a few weeks in the mountains without saying anything to anyone."

30.5.45 Deportees and refugees cross the French border clandestinely every day. The Soviets require the repatriation of women who married French workers in Germany because they do not recognize the validity of those marriages. Liouba met a Russian woman with a baby in her arms at the Prefecture who told her that she had married a French worker in Germany; she did not speak a word of

French but had taught her husband to speak Russian. She was very happy in France and did not want to go back to Russia.

I hear praise from all sides about the kindness and humane attitude of the French authorities toward the new wave of refugees. France has really lived up to its reputation of political tolerance and honoured the right to asylum of stateless people. It is all the more praiseworthy because France has not yet recovered from the effects of the war and fortunately is making up for the excesses of the Liberation. So many individual cases have been cited to me that they almost become the general rule – false certificates of residence, transportation of refugees to France, most of the time by the French military without waiting for official permits, refusal to deliver Soviet refugees to the police in their country, and so on.

Monetary reform – all denominations over fifty francs are to be turned in to post offices and bank tellers from June 4 to 10. The head of every family is to receive six thousand in new currency, plus three thousand for every dependant member of the family. The rest will be left on deposit until new currency is issued. Apparently the measure has been dictated by the massive number of false bills that have circulated since the Liberation. The Allies brought currency with them in the form of an American dollar printed in America, easy to counterfeit.

Himmler was taken by the Americans but succeeded in committing suicide by swallowing a potassium cyanide capsule he had hidden in a dental cavity. He was buried in a vacant lot, its location unknown to the public, but his brain was removed first and is going to be sent to a laboratory and examined by specialists.

Admiral Friedeburg, who signed the official surrender in Berlin, has also committed suicide. Admiral Dönitz and General Jodl have been arrested and taken by plane to an unknown destination.

Z.R., who works in a hotel where American soldiers stay, buys armloads of goods from them, stockings, shoes, and the like that they bring back from Germany; lately she has bought white damask covers used in Germany to cover eiderdown quilts, and is going to use them as bed sheets. One also sees a lot of German makes of cars in the streets driven by Americans. I expected the Allies to show a good example and now see that American troops are not the last to pillage, even without the excuse of having suffered destruction and requisitions like the Russians and Germans.

3.6.45 Rina Ruggeri[114] arrived in Paris and came to see me. I found her greatly changed, of course, and she must have thought the same about me. When you see one another regularly, the eye gradually becomes accustomed to the ravages of the years, but after a lengthy absence, you can see the difference in the appearance of people like us. However, she has kept her characteristic vitality. She has already obtained a residence permit; a charitable official at the Italian Embassy burned her Fascist passport and issued her a certificate stating that she was honourably known to the Embassy. She even went to a clothing centre for deportees but, when her turn came, there was nothing left to give out. A gentleman dressed in a brand new suit who was standing in line attracted her attention, and she asked him how he got a suit like that. He answered, "By helping myself. I simply went into a store, tried on a suit, and left with the suit on, suggesting to the salesman that he send the bill to the Ministry of Prisoners and Deportees."

During the war, she opened a small restaurant near the ghetto in Warsaw and had sixteen employees working for her and a three-room apartment. When the Soviets approached Warsaw, she fled with a distant relative and ended up in Germany. There she got by as best she could by any expedient, selling cigarettes, liquor, and so on. She was in Dresden the day of the dreadful bombing of the city. The air-raid warning was followed immediately by the bombing; she just had time to throw a coat over her nightgown, grab a suitcase with her most precious belongings, and run out of the city, taking shelter in a nearby field. When she went back to Dresden, she could not find the building where she had been staying; the owner had been buried under the ruins. In the street lay burned and shrivelled bodies; she assured me that was the effect of phosphorous bombs. Streetcars were stopped on their tracks with dead people sitting on the seats. In the next stage, the city was occupied

114 Countess Caterina Ruggeri-Laderchi, a relative of Countess Hendrikoff's cousin Nora Ruggeri

by the French. An Allied officer advised her to go to a refugee camp because it would simplify the paperwork. She followed his advice and spent twelve days in a camp. They were well fed there and were even allowed to take the blankets that had been distributed with them. They slept anywhere, men and women in wooden bunk beds. A convoy took them to France.

She ran into problems in Lille. She was carrying an Italian passport, coming from Germany, and arriving in France instead of Italy, which looked suspicious to the French authorities. They made her go through the showers with other detainees in the presence of black soldiers who were standing guard and male nurses, all shouting rude jokes at her, such as "Countess, show us your..." She acted as if she heard nothing. Finally a French officer issued her a permit for Paris. She finds the city much changed, disorder, sadness, lack of luxury.

4.6.45 Meat will no longer be served in restaurants, except on Sunday and holidays.

Yesterday, I saw two French young people at the Hitrovos, from the provinces judging by how they sounded; it was like reading a novel from the last century. There are nine children in the family and they live off the produce of their property. The day one of the brothers had First Communion, the parents served a meal to all the farmers in the vicinity. Big tables and benches were set up on the lawn, and everyone drank to the young man's health. Many of the peasants living in Vendée do not even know how to sign their name. They do not have radios or cars or bicycles, which were so common in the area of Le Mans. However, their coffers are stuffed with banknotes. The two young people, brother and sister, give you an impression of moral and physical freshness, in no way like Parisians. And Parisians represent France to foreigners! I myself, who have lived in France for so long, did not think there were still regions where such a peaceful and patriarchal existence is led.

14.6.45 The American sergeants said noisy farewells to one of the employees, who monopolized all black-market trading at Avenue d'Iéna. They put up two signs in prominent spots saying "Good-bye, Roger" and "We hate to see you go" and served everyone wine and doughnuts. Never has a farewell of that kind been given for any of the employees who left. Sophie V., who was standing near me, whispered in my ear, "Look around you carefully and remember who his customers were; now at least we'll know who to go to for something." Previously, the sergeants turned a deaf ear to black-market offers and assured us that they never ever sold any merchandise.

An American soldier came to the hotel where Bicha was working and offered cartons of American cigarettes at four hundred francs instead of five hundred. An American truck was waiting at the entrance, and an officer was personally unloading the cigarettes the employees and passersby were buying by the armload.

The farmer where M.B. spent the summer exchanged twenty-four million in currency. At Janson secondary school, the headmaster stopped a student at an exit and made him open the suitcase he was carrying, which held seven million in black-market profits!

Yesterday at the American canteen, a fellow speaking French with a thick German accent – I think he was a Jewish émigré – made quite a speech, singing the praises of the Communists and saying he impatiently awaited the establishment of the Soviets in France, so that French workers could live as comfortably as Russian workers. I asked him which Soviets he was talking about, Russian or French? "French Soviets," he replied, "but with the admirable Soviet Russian organization." Then he started talking disparagingly about officers at the time of the Czars, calling them "rotten." I told him then that I am Russian and think he was talking hearsay without knowing what he was talking about; I got up and he ran after me and very politely asked me to forgive him, assuring me that he did not intend to hurt my feelings or offend me...

Marina Klugenau has come back to Paris. She telephoned me and we had lunch together. She recounted her epic to me more or less in detail starting from when she left Paris. She left with a German convoy that was machine-gunned en route; she lost what little baggage she had, one suitcase that she had perched on the carrier of her bicycle. She reached the German city where she thought she would find Grade but, of course, he was no longer there. A German family took her to their home in the country and gave her clothes. As the front advanced, they all left for Berlin, where Marina worked for a while at the French Delegation. Apparently she saw Grade again, who she says had changed a great deal... She then followed the French Delegation to Bavaria and succeeded in being repatriated. She was interrogated at the border for two hours by an officer from the Second Office. The interrogation was very rude. For one thing, the officer told her she was then going to be examined in front of everyone by a female doctor to see how many men she had slept with. They made her sit down and a German woman and her husband, a French deportee, were brought in. The woman was several months pregnant and did not understand French. The officer told Marina to act as an interpreter and explain to the woman that she was going to have to undress and be examined by a doctor. The woman started to cry and the husband tried to protest, but a sergeant hit the woman and took the man to another room. Marina then had to be present at the medical examination of the woman in the presence of all the soldiers. When the woman went out, the officer told Marina that it was her turn. Marina told me that was the moment she was most frightened in her life, because she was determined not to let herself be examined at any price. She made an effort to stay calm and answered that never had anyone spoken to her like that in her life. She does not know why that simple sentence made her interrogator change his mind, but he said to her, "You can skip getting undressed. I see that you are a pure young woman."

Marina does not dare go back to her parents' home in Clamart, because her papers have been stamped "voluntary," meaning that she left for Germany voluntarily. In the fray, she supposedly got engaged to a young Frenchman from a good family, but the parents are strongly opposed to the marriage and I highly doubt it will happen.

26.6.45 I changed jobs! I am now one of two "managers" of an American Red Cross canteen in Bourget. I could not stand Iéna any longer. Not only was the work there exasperatingly monotonous – you had barely taken out cards when you had to put them back – but the electric light from morning until night in dimly lit rooms made my eyes so tired that when I went out into the daylight, I saw everything double, all the outlines of things. I put out feelers to American

Express but you are not fed there, and the food issue is an issue of primary importance right now. Then I went to fill out a questionnaire at the American Red Cross, where surprisingly my work during the Occupation not only did not go against me but was considered "a very good reference!" I was then called for an interview by the manager of the canteen that is going to be opened in Bourget and had nothing but good luck. I was called to come on Thursday, which is my day off at Iéna, and was accepted right away, in spite of the number of people who came for an interview that day.

I had the usual way of the cross to follow again to stay in line with all the administration offices for a change of occupation – apparently a canteen manager is in the hotel industry. It must be very attractive to work in the hotel industry, because they put me through every possible misery, sending me from one office to the next, from one placement office in the northern part of Paris to another one located in the south. I ended up resorting to the tactic of asking to speak to the "Big Boss," who immediately gave me the necessary permit, moreover, to the great disappointment of the employee who had to endorse it and did not miss the chance to say, "Wait until the Americans have left"! Then line-ups and more line-ups at the Prefecture and the G-2, where I had the good fortune to run into the Russian-American who had interviewed me the first time. He recognized me and said, "Oh, yes, you worked for the Germans. Don't worry about it. All that will soon be forgotten."

I left Avenue d'Iéna without many regrets, despite the very flattering certificate Lieutenant Gordon issued me.

9.7.45   The Red Cross canteen is not operating yet, but I go there every morning until three o'clock in the afternoon. I get up at five-thirty in the morning and take the metro to Porte de la Villette, where an American military truck comes to pick me up and drops me at the Caserne des Roses, a cluster of barracks painted green, where there are still German signs, such as *"Seid bereit im Stillen. Der Kampf um Deutschland geht weiter!"* – "Be ready in secret. The battle for Germany continues." The American soldiers wander here and there waiting to leave for the United States. They look fairly sloppy but clean.

I was at Bellevue. Olga Hitrovo's niece who escaped from Yugo-slavia with her little boy is now making arrangements to go back there because she is homesick and feels too unhappy here. Olga is astonished at her thinking that way given that life is so primitive and stripped of any comfort in Yugoslavia. In my opinion, the lack of comfort is not that important in this case because, after all, her niece was happy there. What is important is to be happy, and how you get that way does not much matter.

The American newspapers describe German scientific discov-eries. In peace time, V2 rockets were to carry mail to America; it would only have taken forty minutes to cover the distance between the two continents. Stratospheric stations were planned that were to capture the light and heat of the sun and fuel cities and so on. But in war time, solar heat could burn entire countries and make the oceans boil!

July 1945 The two Red Cross workers are very nice and even fairly pretty; their institutional dress is even really quite becoming – a steel-grey suit of military cut and a grey felt hat.

The Allies have entered Berlin, which up to now had only been occupied by Soviet troops. They found the city in ruins; red ban-ners and signs are everywhere, with familiar slogans from Stalin's speeches and sayings and the like. Traffic is directed by Russian "policewomen" who wave red and yellow pennants. All the street names are in Russian. One of the curiosities of Berlin is Hitler's Chancellery, now defunct, just ruins.

Yesterday I ran around the whole neighbourhood looking for a shoemaker who would agree to re-sole my shoes. All I saw were closed shops and signs on doors: "Closed due to lack of merchan-dise." Finally, I found a shop open, where I ended up getting my shoes accepted by using Italian and cigarettes.

Yesterday, at the police station in my district, where I had to go to renew my identification card, a steady stream of individuals came one after the other to denounce so and so, a worker who left volun-tarily for Germany, a prisoner who now expressed pro-German sen-timents. The police chief shrugged his shoulders and said, "When is it going to end? It's enough to turn you against everyone!"

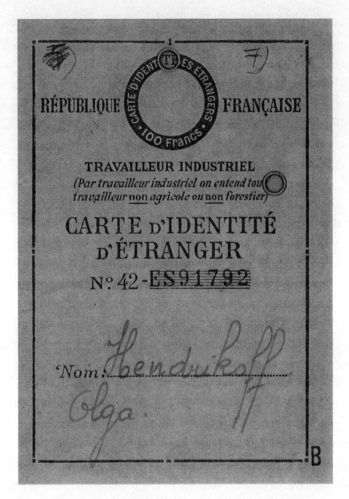

Countess Hendrikoff's Foreign Identity Card, exterior

Facing the Red Cross barracks at Bourget is the French airmen's barracks. As good quality as American uniforms look and as clean as GIs look, French soldiers look poorly dressed, almost ragged, disorderly, like Caran d'Ache cartoons.[115] At the barracks exit stands an American MP, revolver at his belt, cap on head, immaculate white gaiters. At his side is a little sprat with holes in his shoes who showed me that the soles are in tatters. His pants are torn along

115 Caran d'Ache was a pseudonym for Emmanuel Poiré (1858–1909). He was a famous for publishing political cartoons in the French newspaper *Le Figaro*. "Caran d'Ache" was derived from the Russian word *Karandash*, meaning "pencil."

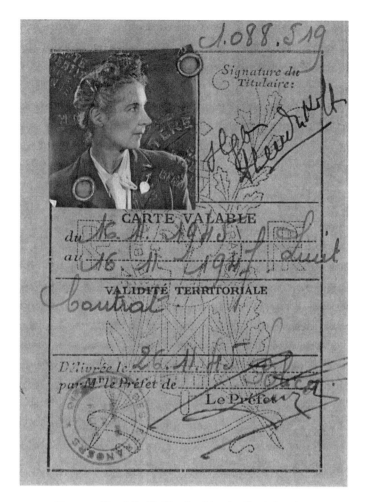

Countess Hendrikoff's Foreign Identity Card, interior

the whole length, showing his drawers. Behold the representative of French aviation! Yesterday, as I was waiting at the fence for the truck that was to take me back to Paris, I watched the changing of the French guard. A young boy in a semblance of a blue uniform, buttons unstitched and attached with nails, approached the sentinel and said to him, "Seems I replace you." The other threw his rifle into his arms and hurried away.

A French sergeant who was standing not far away said to the soldier, "Do you know what you got in '39 for those buttons? Nothing less than solitary confinement." Then, speaking to me, he said,

"Believe me, Madame, I saw the exodus in 1940. Well, the Army looked better than that then. And they want us to fight the war with that." The soldier listened, sniggering, saying over and over, "I don't give a d——."

That is why General de Gaulle's grandiloquent speeches seem a poor fit for the current situation in France. Unless he is the one who is right and, by shouting that France is a great nation and nothing will get done without France, the French end up rallying and France again truly becomes what she was, a Great Nation!

Last week, there was a French–American wedding at Bourget. A tall, blonde Frenchwoman with a law degree, she told me afterward, married a short American captain fifteen years older than her, a Jewish type. The wedding took place in the Club chapel right in the barracks used alternately as a military tribunal and a chapel for all rites. The Protestant chaplain who officiated is a gentle, sensitive man, a true priest despite his military uniform; he wears the badge of the priesthood on his collar – two silver crosses. He spoke the words of the sacrament with a great deal of fervour and, after slipping the ring on her finger – costume jewellery, not a wedding band – he addressed the young married couple, asking them to pray with him. The prayer he said was, as he explained to me later, "improvised." Afterward, he came to ask me to share the wedding meal and keep the bride, who did not speak a word of English, company...

The strict "no fraternizing" orders in effect in Germany have been rescinded by the Allies. After all, the Soviet troops were "fraternizing" before the eyes of the Allies, while young German women swayed in front of the American soldiers, slapping their thighs and sniggering "*verboten.*"

18.7.45 Yesterday I started my week of evenings, which means I have to eat in the city at noon. Class "D" restaurants have become stricter about fat tickets. Before, if you did not have any – and who has any left after the fifteenth of the month! – you had to pay six francs extra. Now, they simply refuse to serve you. Class "B" restaurants, however, which advertise menus for forty francs in accordance with the regulations, serve you a one hundred and fifty franc menu without tickets, not even for bread.

Yesterday the driver who took me back by truck to La Villette metro told me he would like to see Paris again in ten years because he is well aware that Paris now is nothing like Paris in normal times. In fact, there is no longer any luxury, or beautiful cars, or elegant women, or social gatherings. Stores perform feats to present attractive window displays, but the items on display are generally completely unnecessary objects.

Billboards and street signs in English have replaced German signs, which is why Parisians speak of the "American Occupation."

19.7.45 Had lunch at Madame K.'s. She still lives in a room on rue Henri Martin; one of the tenants offered her hospitality to thank her for the services she provided him during the Occupation. She told me about the suicide of Liza Maltzeff, who managed a building requisitioned by the Germans during the Occupation. When the Germans left Paris, she left to follow them. She sincerely admired them. She stayed in Germany until the surrender and was then put in a concentration camp with Soviet nationals, because the Allies started out putting all the Russians together and sorting them later. There she learned of all the horrors of the German camps, which she was unaware of before then. She was repatriated to Paris and, seeing her on her return, Madame K. was struck by the change that had taken place in her. She no longer had the desire to live, as if she was broken. She ended up poisoning herself.

An American soldier of Czech or Slovenian origin also described to me the camps at Dachau and others he had visited. The Americans made the locals file through the camps, and many Germans fainted at what they saw. He assured me that the inhabitants were completely unaware of what was happening in the camps, so difficult was access to them. The smell of dead bodies caught in your throat before you entered the camp. He added that, when the Germans were there, perhaps they burned the corpses and the smell did not spread outside.

With all that, he spoke without hatred of the Germans. He thinks Germany is the most beautiful country in the world; the houses there are clean, well kept, welcoming. "And why did they want war? They had everything to be happy," he told me. It was not the first time I have heard comments like that from American soldiers. He then asked me if I smoked and, a true Slav, immediately brought me several packages of cigarettes and refused any payment for them. Cigarettes are now the currency of exchange *par excellence*. Americans sell them by the armload, but Slavic blood will never be cheap. Despite the assimilation of foreign elements that shape the American nation, I always recognize a Slav under an American uniform.

28.7.45 This week I work mornings. I get up at five-thirty and get back to Paris around four-thirty in the afternoon. I drink a cup of tea or ersatz coffee and go to bed and fall asleep at once. Sometimes Mademoiselle Théobald, the kind soul, comes to my room at around nine o'clock and brings me vegetable broth.

There have been a series of thefts at the canteen, and the guilty party has finally been arrested, one of the canteen employees who threw the items or produce he stole over the barbed-wire fence that surrounds the camp. An accomplice was permanently waiting at the spot and caught them in flight. What is difficult to understand from a human standpoint is the American system of burning everything the Army cannot use. Units that are leaving make a pile of all their clothing, canned goods, and so on – everything that represents priceless treasure to starving Parisians who are short of everything – and make an auto-da-fé. Coffee left in the pots is poured out into the garbage at night. The Americans say, not without reason, that if they did otherwise, they would never know what was rightfully obtained or stolen.

Saw one of the former Russian employees from Suchet. He saw a Soviet detachment go by, went closer, and shouted, "Who here is from Ekaterinodar?" Seeing that no one answered, he then corrected himself, saying the new name of his city, Krasnodar. A young man left the ranks; it was his nephew. He invited him to his home, a small working-man's apartment in Clichy. The young man could not get over the luxury of the building. He said he had to accompany a Soviet orchestra to the ship in Marseille but would come back to see him on his return. His uncle said to him, "Say good-bye to me; you'll never come back again." The other man continued to assure him he would come back but he never did. S. told me that, to make the soldiers go back home, they are taken at night under false pretenses.

S. then told me that a young man he knows, who works as a driver for the Americans in Germany, had to repatriate Soviet prisoners in the Soviet zone. When they got to headquarters, they had them get down from the truck and line up; an NKVD officer ordered all the officers to step out of the ranks; only five men stepped out from the group. The officer was furious and said that there must be more than that. After waiting to see if anyone else stepped forward, the officer took out his revolver and, one after the other, shot the five men who had admitted they were officers. The young driver was so affected by the sight that he could barely get his truck started and was still trembling when he reached the American zone. When he recounted to his American superior what he had witnessed, the superior told him that unfortunately his fellow Americans could not interfere in the Russians' affairs.

A holiday camp for children of Russian émigrés took on two Soviets as a cook and her assistant. NKVD officers arrived and took away the two women and even the former Russian colonel in charge of the camp, an émigré from the First War, and beat him up then let him go.

Trial of Marshal Pétain. The accusers file through the courtroom – Reynaud, Daladier, Lebrun, and so on. Reynaud accuses the Marshal of agreeing to an armistice for fear of a revolution, which seemed a worse danger to him than the Germans. Rank-and-file employees discuss it in the metro. "The people they called as witnesses to accuse Pétain should be in the prisoner's dock themselves for being so poorly prepared for this war. They are the ones really responsible."

The first session was stormy. Counsel for the Marshal protested the appointment of Mongibeaux as prosecutor as well as of some of the judges because they had sworn an oath of loyalty to the Marshal in their day. Mongibeaux declared that an oath of that kind did not bind him in any way.

Many French soldiers in the street are wearing badges on their arm with the motto "Rhine-Danube" and the silhouette of a club, the French club that beat Germany. They are French Occupation troops.

Laval landed today at Bourget and has been incarcerated at Fresnes.

8.8.45 Our stepfather, Fyodor Oom, died at the clinic on rue Charonne. His nurse, a Spanish Red who wore a badge with the hammer and sickle pinned to her collar, showed devotion and provided the most sensitive care right to the last. We buried our stepfather in Sainte-Geneviève-des-Bois cemetery. The Orthodox Church rising in the middle of wheat fields, the birch trees in the cemetery, all give a Russian feeling to the French landscape and you forget you are in Seine et Oise, 40 km from Paris. In church, among the old men and women residents from the Russian nursing home in dark, worn clothing, was a small bright light, the priest's little boy, about two years old, dressed in light colours, rosy, with such blond hair you would think it was platinum.

I never felt the beauty of our funeral service as much as this time. "Oh Lord, grant peace to the soul of…" Fyodor's poor tormented soul will finally find peace in death.

We had lunch afterward at a little inn kept by a Russian, with a pre-war menu, bread, leg of lamb, apple pie, wine, and so on. Without tickets, of course, at the black-market price, but the meal was worth it.

At the railway station, Gare Saint-Michel-sur-Orge, German prisoners guarded by an American sentry were pushing railcars along a yard track, railcars of all nationalities bearing the name or trademark of the country of origin: *Deutsches Reich*, F.S. for *Ferrovia di Stato*, and so on.

Everyone is talking about the atomic bomb that destroyed Hiroshima. The Americans are rejoicing and say it is the end of the war in the Pacific. Most of the people who work with me were shocked.

Why was the use of gas prohibited? After all, it only strikes combatants, but they refrained from using it. Yet the use of benzene gel bombs and the atomic bomb was allowed – to pulverize any vestige of life in an entire city. When we were children, we all read the story of the destruction of Pompeii, but the lava was more charitable. It spared the inhabitants' corpses.

The Pope protested against the bomb, but we are no longer in the Middle Ages and his voice no longer holds any authority for anyone.

Sainte-Geneviève-des Bois, 2011

9.8.45 Bicha had an edifying conversation with the Soviet colonel who is staying at the Hôtel de la Bourdonnais. Still quite recently, he told her that very few émigrés could return to Russia. Now he is repeating to her that Russia needs the educated element of emigrants, especially emigrants living in France. He said that Bicha should not believe the tales going around about Soviet Russia. Bicha could choose where she lives, would have an apartment. Her husband would find a job as a manager of a horse stud farm, her older son would also be assured of a job in Moscow, and her younger son, who is an engineer, would have no trouble finding a job in his profession. She herself could give foreign language lessons. He again added that everyone earns a good living; he himself earns one hundred and twenty pre-war rubles a month. Bicha said to him, "But you will not trust us. You will treat us like spies."

"Oh, no," he replied, "Far from it. But since many people will want to ask you about the kind of life you were living in a foreign country, a certain discreet surveillance will be necessary at first."

Bicha told him, "You know, I am no longer so young. I want calm and peace. It is precisely that discreet surveillance I fear and would not want."

10.8.45 Japan has surrendered.

I went to the Louvre to see the collection Monsieur de Besteigui gave the museum. Each painting is a masterpiece. There is a Fragonard that is absolutely Impressionist in technique and a magnificent portrait of a Spanish countess by Goya. I went back to see the few rooms that have been reopened; *Mona Lisa* was smiling her enigmatic smile behind a large rope that protects her from the public... How far all that is from the atomic bomb and daily cares, how restful...

15.8.45 Marshal Pétain was condemned to death; however, the sentence has been commuted to life imprisonment. Jurors were named in advance, not randomly selected as is normally done, chosen from among the members of the Resistance, the underground, and so on. As a precautionary measure, the buildings where the jurors live have been guarded by officers. One of the jurors, in fact, lives right near me. Two officers were guarding the front of his building in a strange manner. They were both sitting on the edge of the wall that supports the fence around the building's garden, each with girl on his knee!

15.8.45 The *Canard Enchaîné*[116] parodied the Marshal's trial. The defendant was General de Gaulle in the event that he had lost the war, and Reynaud, Daladier and company appeared as witnesses to testify to the General's guilt with the same passion and the same evidence.

The radio officially announced the surrender of Japan.

Conversation with American soldiers at Bourget. One of them showed me a wristwatch and told me, "You know, this watch belonged to a Nazi." I thought that I would then hear the story of a stirring deed, how he took the SS officer prisoner or shot him. In reality, however, it all came about very differently. The American spent time with a German family who treated him "just like a son," to use his words. In answer to my question of whether visiting German families was allowed, he answered, "No, but everyone did it." Their son had been an SS officer at one time but was now wearing civilian clothes. He showed him the SS mark in the crook of his elbow. When the time came for the American to go back to the United States and he went to say good-bye, they gave him the watch, not sold by retailers, which only SS shock troops were entitled to wear. "Of course," he added, "they may have been glad to get rid of it, but still, they were fine people."

I asked him if the Americans were doing much black-market trading. He replied that he personally did not, but his comrades were buying watches in Switzerland to resell later to Russian soldiers. They bought a watch for five dollars and resold it for five hundred. American soldiers in general are delighted with German cleanliness and comfort, much preferring Germany and the Germans to France and the French!

Yesterday evening, the young soldier who brought me back from Bourget by truck, taking me and the others in the truck right to rue de l'Université, told me, "I think I drank too much cognac and champagne."

116 A satirical French newspaper

"Be careful," I said to him, "I wouldn't want to end up in a ditch, and you yourself wouldn't want to go before a military tribunal."

Then he told me that he drinks because he is alone and sad. His friends go out with Frenchwomen, but they are only girls for a one-night stand, and he is "just a kid" looking for something more than that. He could not tell me exactly what he was looking for in a woman. "I have it all very clear in my head," he explained, "but when I have to put it into words, I can't find the right words anymore." I felt sorry for the poor "kid"; he was so naïve. Really, I find Americans very child-like, yet they do not know how to amuse themselves. They drink and then no longer know what they are doing. The day room where they spend time is gloomy. They sit half-slouched in wooden armchairs or on benches, without speaking. Some play cards, supposedly just for the pleasure of playing because they are not allowed to play for money, then go settle their accounts outside the Club. The radio plays night and day, so one ends up not hearing it any more. They are served all the coffee they want; they just have to bring their mess mug to the waitresses who stand beside the two large pots, one filled with black coffee and the other, coffee with cream. They drink astronomic quantities of it. They can also help themselves to as many doughnuts as they want, which are a kind of fritter only made of deep-fried pastry.

28.8.45 Paris celebrated the anniversary of the Liberation. The bells rang and there was dancing in the streets, as there is on July 14. There were not very many people in the streets, however, because Paris has returned to its pre-war rhythm – offices, shops, and so on closed until mid-September, doctors and dentists gone on vacation.

The Soviet Metropolitan Nicholas arrived in Paris and visited Metropolitan Euloge at rue Daru and Metropolitan Seraphin at rue Michel-Ange, the heads of the two rival Orthodox churches that each consider themselves the heir of the old pre-war and pre-revolution Russian church. He attended religious services at Sainte-Geneviève-des-Bois church, the Russian nursing home, and Sunday will say Mass at rue Daru, concelebrating with the cathedral's clergy.

The church on rue Pétel, the only church in Paris that has al-ways recognized Moscow's ecclesiastical authority, wanted him to go there first. However, he replied that he had come to Paris not to create disunity among the parishes but, on the contrary, to bring them together. When the clergy at the church on rue Pétel prayed for *Богохранимая наша Страна Советская* – our Soviet country, protected by God, he pointed out that, in churches in Russia, they simply pray for Russia – *Страна Российская*.

One of the members of the clergy at rue Daru, who repeated all that to me, added, "I don't really know what to think about it all."

A group of interpreters, Americans of Russian origin, spent a few days at Bourget. They really revolutionized the Club. All day long there was nothing but Russian songs and dances; some of them were dancing on the tables. All the other soldiers made a circle around them. One of them told me that his name is Mitchell. When I asked him how he came to have such an American name, he started to laugh and answered good-naturedly *"Ну какой же я Митшель!"* – which means something like, "By no means am I Mitchell! My real name is Vladimiroff. Only I was advised to change my name when I got American citizenship."

Someone else added, "You have to admit, we've brought you a bit of gaiety and liveliness during our stay here. Nobody ever gets bored with us Russians!" He also told me that they were at Torgau when the American and Russian troops linked up, but were of no use because the Russian troops were all native Uzbeks and other Asians, who did not even speak Russian and had to communicate with their countrymen with the help of interpreters.

Then a group of Russian Jews surrounded me, speaking volubly. One of them repeated, "You are Russian? You are Russian? I am Ephron, you know, Ephron, you must know. Do you remember the *Grande Encyclopédie Russe*, Brockhaus and Ephron?"

When they left, the whole group came and kissed me on both cheeks, Russian style!

29.8.45 We went to serve coffee and doughnuts to a group of a thousand soldiers on a train departing for the United States. The soldiers had stayed longer than usual, so were no longer an anonymous crowd. They were individuals we knew, even by name. There was little Winslow, who had been so hurt that I did not know the location of the state of Wisconsin where he was from; he took me over to the map of the United States hanging on the wall of the dayroom, pointed his finger at Wisconsin, and solemnly told me, "You can forget Winslow but you should never forget Wisconsin" – and so many others. We were hoisted onto two trucks, the manager Miss Alice and a waitress in one and me and another waitress in the other. The trucks stopped on both sides of the train, which was stationed on a yard track, and we used a dipper to fill the split bottles the men held out to us through the doors of the stock cars they occupied, with forty horses and eight men. We had the coffee in large basins, and the truck drivers moved forward so slowly along the train that we were not even splashed. Groups of officers directing the departure were standing here and there, while French civilians sitting in the meadows beside the station were dividing up the treasures they had been able to pull out of the auto-da-fé that usually follows departures.

After that, American prisoners, soldiers incarcerated for misdemeanours, came to clean the wooden barracks where the soldiers who just left had been staying. The prisoners are always accompanied by guards armed with rifles. Other than that, it is impossible to tell which of them is a guard or a prisoner; relations between them are most amicable. The prisoners have to do all the major jobs in the camp – get rid of garbage and so on, work they do wearing thick leather gloves, which makes a big impression on the French staff.

A soldier who came back from Austria showed me his wallet stuffed with shillings, which he is going to exchange for dollars. He told me that it only takes three days to become a millionaire. He sold his watch to a Russian soldier for an amount equivalent to $800. Then he added that all Russians are savages. When I pointed out my nationality to him, he hurriedly apologized, explaining that he has to tell the truth anyway; all the Russian soldiers he saw are poorly dressed and thieves, in his opinion. They grab everything that comes to hand; they completely pillaged Germany. In the French zone, the French are doing the same thing. He saw French soldiers unharness a farmer's horses and take them away. He said that the Americans occupied Stuttgart because the French were behaving too badly there. In fact, I think I remember hearing talk of people raped by Moroccan troops. He did not mention the conduct of American soldiers, but I think all nations apply the law of retaliation and pillage with a vengeance.

30.8.45 Had lunch at Bicha's. She told me about her conversations with the Soviet officers at La Bourdonnais. One of them told her that, on their arrival in Paris, they were naïve. They thought that all the émigrés were on their side. Now they know better. They know that many émigrés hate them and "with the agreement of the French authorities" went to Russia to commit sabotage. It would be different for Bicha, however; she would be given three quarters of a hectare and a small house in the country where she would live very well! Bicha asked him if the interior layout of the houses could be changed in any way. "Yes, of course," he answered, "to improve them, not to damage them." The houses are not private property as we understand it in France. "Besides," he added, "We will soon abolish private property in France." Bicha pointed out to him that she doubted it would be easy to do in France, where the French are proprietary by nature. The man then asked her why she left Russia. "Someone probably said to you, 'Let's leave!' and you left."

Bicha said to him, "But have you forgotten the Terror in Russia at that time?"

"Oh, not for everyone," he answered. That officer later came to ask for the key to the room of one of the comrades, a former prisoner of war, who was supposed to leave that evening for Russia, which worried Bicha, because the officer involved belonged to the NKVD.

An officer, this time French, a former member of the Normandy–Niemen air-force squadron, praised the progress in Moscow, where there is a store similar to Galeries Lafayette and people can get everything they need. He even said that Communism was the only suitable regime for Russians, because Russians are lazy by nature. However, he reproached our compatriots for the lack of comfort in the country, the dirty *izbas*, the absence of toilets, stove benches for beds – *лежанки* – with rabbits and chickens nesting under them, not to mention bugs. He concluded, "Impossible to make love under those conditions."

31.8.45 Searched *Grands Magasins* for fabric for curtains for the GI Mess. I found out things have changed. Fabric is still very poor quality; nevertheless, there is some, and people buy it with points. Crockery is sold for ceramics coupons, which is also progress because there was none at all for sale during the Occupation.

General de Gaulle is in America; the French newspapers describe the ovations, dinners, decorations he is receiving. However, the *New York Times* suggests that President Truman has the same aversion for the General that Roosevelt had in his day.

7.9.45 Bicha spoke with a French officer who just came back from captivity via Russia. He had been liberated from a German camp by the Soviet Army and spent six months in Russia. When Bicha asked him questions about life there and explained to him that she and her family were burning with the desire to go back there as soon as possible, he could only say, "Madame, are you crazy?" Bicha repeated to him the conversations she had with the Soviet officers and the officer from the Normandy–Niemen air-force squadron. To that he answered that the airman had only seen what they wanted to show him. He had personally seen the Soviet occupation of Germany – drunken soldiers killing men, raping women, even deportees of other nationalities. Saying something that displeased them was enough to be shot immediately. He added, "The troops you see here are an elite corps. The great majority of soldiers are uneducated, not Communist. Russian soldiers are brave. The problem is that the regime of terror has not changed, and you could not be happy there."

He also told her that the whole German population of East Prussia had been deported to Siberia and that part of Prussia has been occupied by deportees and former Russian prisoners of war. In Berlin, the Soviet authorities raise grandiose granite monuments to the glory of the Soviet soldier, which seems to be a sign that they intend to stay there indefinitely.

The situation in Germany creates serious problems for the Allies. France and England both have food rationing and have to feed their German zones to avoid revolts and obtain better labour production. Russia is in a better position, first of all because it received the most fertile part of Germany in the partition, while the other Big Three kept the industrial part seriously damaged by bombings. It is like the Russian tale where the peasant shared the harvest with the bear. The peasant took the top of the plants – *вершки* – and the bear took the roots – *корешки*. Any change was in vain; the peasant always came out ahead. But this time the Russian bear was the most cunning.

The Soviet administration does not worry about humanitarian considerations. The American newspapers write openly that the Soviets do not allow anyone to enter their zone so that all the excesses they indulge in remain unknown; in Berlin, they behave differently because they know they are being watched.

8.9.45 In the Russian colony, there is talk of nothing but the service celebrated by the Soviet Metropolitan, Nicholas Kroutitsky, at rue Daru and the attachment of the émigré church to the mother church in Moscow. Up to now, the Orthodox churches outside Russia were divided into three irreconcilable camps: the churches that recognize Metropolitan Antoine as ecclesiastical head, who lived in Yugoslavia in peace time and was elected by the émigré Synod residing in Karlowatz, Yugoslavia; the churches headed by Metropolitan Euloge, including rue Daru, that did not want to recognize the authority of Metropolitan Antoine and, when France recognized the Soviets, became subject to the Patriarch of Constantinople; and, finally, the churches that recognized the supreme authority of the Patriarch of Moscow.

Metropolitan Nicholas arrived last week by airplane, toured the churches, visited various members of the Russian clergy, and finally said Mass with great pomp last Sunday at rue Daru, assisted by bishops and forty priests. The Soviet Embassy sent a representative for the ceremony. The cathedral could barely contain all the faithful, and a number of people fainted during the service.

Metropolitan Nicholas, a handsome, well-groomed fifty-three-year-old with a short, well-trimmed beard, and his clergy were wearing magnificent sacerdotal vestments and dazzling mitres. He addressed the faithful, telling them how pleased he was to see them all reunited with the mother church in Moscow. Then after the service was over, he went up to Father Sakharoff's apartment on the second floor of a small building on the grounds of the church and appeared at a window. The frenzied crowd cheered him while he, somewhat theatrically, shouted words spoken only at Easter: "Christ is risen" – and this is September! The crowd was electrified and shouted, "Indeed He is risen," the Orthodox sacramental response to the priest's invocation during the Easter service, and "Take us with you to Russia!" It was touching and pathetic when you think of people shouting to go back to the old country they left some twenty-five years ago! In spite of everything, they burn with the desire to go back there!

The next day, all the clergy were invited to a reception at the Soviet Embassy. Léon G. did not go, but the verger told him that the refreshments were "sumptuous" with hams, cheeses, meat patés, champagne flowing freely, and vodka served in water glasses. Ambassador Bogomoloff and his wife did the honours. Waitresses without aprons passed plates with sandwiches and so on and tried to bring Soviet colonels, who were under the influence of vodka, back to their right mind with forceful slaps on the back when they started fraternizing with members of the Parisian clergy, exchanging memories they had in common from their youth. The slaps were accompanied by energetic warnings, such as, "Be quiet, you talk too much!"

Aphonsky, the cathedral choir master, told me that he had never before felt such a strange sensation of being "photographed without knowing, recorded" – watched.

14.9.45 I have to repeat all the steps I already took to work for the Red Cross because Major Saunders, the head of the French–American Labour Office, let our director know that he was completely unaware of our presence at the American Red Cross and required evidence that we had gone through the G-2, had work certificates, and so on.

Received a letter from Nancy Zweguintzoff who, in spite of having American citizenship, complains of the boredom that reigns in the United States, which seems very "provincial" compared to Europe. André Zweguintzoff, who just got back from there, agrees completely.[117] "Men there only talk business." On the other hand, the American soldiers I see at the Club all prefer the life they live in America

117 André Zweguintzoff is the brother of Nancy's husband, Alexander (Sasha) Zweguintzoff.

and think only of returning home as soon as possible. I think one point of view does not contradict the other. American civilization seems purely material to me; the less educated classes there benefit from more material advantages than they would have in Europe. However, the educated classes find little there aside from material goods, and the refined, intellectual element turns to Europe.

16.9.45 Every time a new group of soldiers arrives at Bourget, a few always detach from the group and spend nearly all their time in the office, discussing all kinds of problems, sharing their impressions with us and, in short, acquiring a personality for us. This time, one of them is called Petro Hetman. He is of Russian–Ukrainian descent; his parents were born in Kiev. Inactivity weighs on him, so he always comes and asks us to give him a job of some kind "to keep him busy." Lately he stayed in the office for a few hours talking politics and the social order. Like most Americans, he hates the English, criticizing them for their traditionalism and their desire to rule the world. He includes in his dislike the new military doctor, Burgess, who is American by birth but has always lived in England, so he speaks with an English accent. Hetman criticizes him for "thinking like an Englishman." He also disapproves of the French for always having their hand out, and for the lack of sanitary conditions. The street urinals in Paris shock him, as does the lack of bathrooms in apartments for those with average incomes. "Frenchwomen replace water with perfume," he says. "They don't keep themselves clean." Then he talked about the Negro issue, explaining to me the position of that class of American citizens in... America, the sections of streetcars reserved for blacks in the South, schools exclusively for Negroes. He says he is distressed to see Frenchwomen going out with Negroes and adds that he is even more horrified by mulattos because they are living proof of the promiscuity of black and white individuals.

One of the companies currently here at the Club is an entire company of blacks. They stay strictly apart and do not mingle with the whites, who avoid even going to the Club the evenings the Negroes play music, jazz, a rhythm without melody. The musicians are surrounded by their fellow company members, who are enraptured, delighted, shaking on one spot to the beat of the music.

24.9.45 A young lieutenant, Campbell, came to the office several times to talk to me. He is a young man, twenty-two years old, who looks gentle and refined. The war interrupted his medical studies. Recently, Miss Alice came to tell me, in his presence, that we had to dismiss a waitress who has been sick for about ten days. Campbell immediately asked if he could pay the employee's salary out of his pocket so we could keep her; unfortunately, it is impossible. The night before he left, he showed me the photo of his young and beautiful wife and his baby, whom he has never seen, and told me, "Alas, I think I will never be able to readjust to normal life anymore or feel content and happy. I would never have thought I could kill, and I killed women, children. I saw them die from my bombs, because the plane I was flying flew very low. Often at night, their faces haunt me and prevent me from sleeping. At the time, I didn't think about it all, but now, I'm a bundle of nerves. Lately a plane flew low over the roof of our mess and I had a fit of nervous shaking. Maybe the best solution would be to continue flying."

I tried to comfort him by replying that human beings have unlimited reserves of vitality; the career he was aiming for as a surgeon would enable him to rebuild and recreate after having destroyed. How many Campbells will go back to their homes, their faith destroyed, their morale shaken, in the grip of doubts, no longer knowing how to go back to being the men they once were?

Sunday I went to Courcelles, to the camp for Russian children, who are staying in the former Kliaguine "château."[118] The owner, a big businessman, a supplier to the Russian army in 1914, then a supplier to the regular, or irregular, armies of any country, to the Phalangists[119] and the Reds during the Spanish Civil War, is now in prison at Fresnes. The "château" is spacious but very dilapidated. The children, from four to seventeen years old, sleep four or five

118 Prince Kliaguine was a friend of Tsar Nicholas II and a supplier of arms to the Russian army in 1914. He owned many châteaus and also owned the Hotel Napoleon in Paris, which he bought as a present for his future wife. It was a centre for Russian high society in the 1920s and '30s, catering to many illustrious guests such as Prince Yussoupov, Orson Welles, and John Steinbeck.

119 A term that originated from the Fascist Falange party during the 1936 Spanish Civil War

to a room. They look pale and undernourished. The Occupation really undermined their health. When I expressed my astonishment that the Committee managed to feed the children satisfactorily with the few resources available, the supervisor answered simply, "It's easier than you imagine when the funds are used for the purpose intended."

26.9.45 The Club's female staff had to take a medical at the Beaujon hospital. The canteen employees were slightly annoyed because they had not been warned in advance and were not too sure of the cleanliness of their lower parts. "A woman is always a bit dirty," one of them told me with a great deal of candour. Another who was past sixty asked me, "Do I really have to take the medical? It has been quite a long time since I had anything to do with the gentlemen."

It certainly must be acknowledged that American soldiers are very clean about their person. They are not as carefully groomed as German soldiers. Their uniforms are loose, their stance not very soldierly, their shoes not polished, not even brushed, all of which contribute to giving them a sloppy appearance. But they are clean. The dayroom does not have any smell of body odour, even on busy days. A soldier recently caught a little Ukrainian who had been picked up by American soldiers in Germany and trailed after them, and sent him back to clean up better because the cleanliness of his ears left something to be desired.

Yesterday, the nurses in the clinic set up in the same building as the Club came to the office for a chat. One of them told me that he now avoided going to the Rainbow Corner, the American Red Cross Centre; in front of it, all the black-market business is done with his Jewish co-worker Tannenbaum. They cannot take two steps without being accosted by Tannenbaum's French compatriots, *Landsmänner*, harassing them with offers of "combinations." Another Jewish nurse admits that being Jewish was a big help to him in Switzerland, the source of black-market watches. American soldiers go there just to buy Swiss watches, which they then resell in Germany or France at an exorbitant price. The American authorities tried to reduce speculation of that kind by setting the amount a soldier is allowed to exchange legally at a hundred and thirty Swiss francs. Waler, however, immediately found fellow Jews in Switzerland who obtained an ample supply of Swiss watches for him – I do not know how. He even brought me one; I paid for it in pre-war English pounds. His comrades assured me that I could trust him, because they threatened him that he would have them to deal with if he tried to cheat on the price of the watch. Apparently there is a "law of the underworld" that is respected by all these gangsters in uniform.

27.9.45 I was in the process of sewing a badge on the sleeve of an officer's jacket when a sergeant made a fairly disagreeable remark to me about the time I was wasting to please an officer. "And why don't you like your officers?" I asked him. It is a fact that most of the soldiers do not like their officers; they watch their slightest actions jealously to see that they are not served first or better than the soldiers. There is no officers' club at Bourget, so the officers who go through the repatriation centre sometimes come to have a cup of coffee at the soldiers' canteen. The sergeant then began a long tirade; soldiers do not like officers who were making less money than they were in civilian life. A man who knows how to make a lot of money, in the sergeant's opinion, is a man with a head on his shoulders and is better suited to holding a higher rank. I asked him in what category he put learned men who work for the love of it or ambitious men who work for the glory. He wants to simply ignore that class of men. "As for me," I told him, "I have never known how to make money in my life; yet, you often say you respect me, and it seems to me that you consider me worth something."

"It's different in your case," he replied. "I admit you may be handicapped in France. But if you had lived in America and didn't know how to make money, I would not have respected you."

Another soldier, of Croatian origin, expounded the same theory to me. He is an architect by trade but has no higher education. He told me he is completely ignorant of all the history of architecture but that did not prevent him from earning a living, earning a good living, and creating a pleasant, easy life for his wife and child. I said to him, "Yet you give me the impression you have to aspire to learning."

He replied laughingly, "You may be right. There are probably some atavistic cells in me that are thirsty for learning because lately I've been saying to myself that, when I get home, I'll have to start taking courses at the university, despite the fact that I'm married and despite the fact that the courses last five years." He told me he feels and thinks "American" to the point that the fate of Yugoslavia during the war left him completely indifferent, while his parents followed the course of events there with passionate interest. He does not realize that he nevertheless remains a Slav, gentler, more refined than an Anglo-Saxon. It is strange how strong that blood is and how hard to dilute.

8.10.45 Yesterday, one of the blacks assigned to the base came to talk to me. He is intelligent, relatively well educated and, most of all, thirsty for learning. He is taking our French courses and studies zealously. He has an innate gift for spelling and writes the most difficult words correctly naturally, even the ones he does not understand. He is very nervous, extremely sensitive and touchy. Seeing me alone, he asked me, "May I talk to you? I have no one I can talk to about things that obsess me." He then began to describe his post-war program. He wants to fight for the rights of his people, the black race, a nation within a nation. In some states, they outnumber whites but do not have the same rights. The poll tax, a tax that entitles a person to vote, is too high for blacks to exercise their right to vote. There are not enough schools for blacks, so they cannot get the education whites do. Blacks have been freed but are still industrial slaves, and whites knowingly keep them in that position to have a cheap labour force. During the war, people preferred to use animal blood for transfusions instead of using black donors. I later asked Doctor Burgess the reason for that measure; he explained that it was because of the large proportion of blacks with syphilis. He went on to talk about Germany, telling me it should be "treated like a child, first punished, then re-educated." Oh, the irony of fate! A black from Ohio talking about re-educating the *Herrenvolk* race![120] Hitler must be turning over in his grave.

---

120 *Herrenvolk* refers to the idea of a "pure," not racially mixed Aryan race.

Laval's trial continues. The jurors again have been selected, not drawn randomly. I do not think there are many people who like Laval personally; he was never popular, even before the Occupation. But there are still protests from the public against the way the trial is being conducted, and many newspapers say that the judges' moves are irregular. The judges ask questions and answer them, without giving Laval time to answer. Mongibeaux and Mornet accused Laval of promulgating "Vichyist" decrees, yet they themselves enforced them during the Occupation. Public opinion does not defend Laval, but would have preferred to see him judged by a military tribunal. It is just the illegal form of trial that raises criticism, which is surprising in itself in the times we are living in, when any settlement of accounts is tolerated. Often it is dangerous to criticize. The fact that voices are raised against injustice to a public figure no one likes or respects seems to me entirely to their honour.

Execution of Jean Paquis, radio commentator during the Occupation, who ended all his broadcasts with the statement "England, like Carthage, must be destroyed." He went to the firing squad following Joseph Darnand, the head of the militia during the Occupation.

The situation in Indochina is worrying the government. A wind of separatism is blowing worldwide. "Vietnamese" tracts have been dropped in the Paris metro, accusing the French of trying to "occupy" Indochina after being occupied themselves by the Germans.

American soldiers returning to the United States have their pockets stuffed with Occupation marks. They only get the equivalent of $500 exchanged for them. However, a GI is full of initiative and makes an agreement for a 10% premium with his less fortunate comrades, to whom he gives the surplus of the allowed amount, taking care to stay close by while the little financial transaction is concluded. One of the sergeants in the Finance Office told me that, in the last group of soldiers returning to the United States, many of the soldiers admitted they had as much as $40,000 on them, insisting that they won the money at cards. One of them, carrying $70,000, was even arrested because his superiors found he had really pushed the limit. The Americans mainly make that kind of money selling items of all kinds to Soviet soldiers, who drag potato sacks behind them stuffed with bank notes as wallets.

Scott, the sergeant who heads the clinic, came to tell me about his financial successes. When I asked him what could have changed the big, round-faced, pink-cheeked boy he had been until just recently, always laughing, into a pale, harassed individual who always looks preoccupied and absent-minded in such a few weeks, he told me that he had just earned sixty thousand francs in a day. He later explained the mechanics of the transaction. He and a few comrades quietly took the head doctor's car and drove as far as Villacoublay, from where military planes leave for England, and entrusted their "savings" in francs – the fruit of former black markets – to trusted friends. The pilots exchange the francs for English pounds at the preferential rate they benefit from as soldiers, then when they leave they exchange them again, to dollars. Scott accepts that currency and sells it on the Paris black market then... starts over. Scott does not speak a word of French but he assures me he manages very well in his way; all he has to do is show a Frenchman a dollar and ask him how much: "*Combien?*"

20.10.45 Tomorrow the election is supposed to take place. Voters have to answer "yes" or "no" to two questions. Do they want to elect a new Constituent Assembly? Should the Assembly be sovereign or limited in its authority? Moderates, which currently means socialists, are voting "yes-yes" and Communists, "no-no." A satirical newspaper published a cartoon showing a poor voter who tried all the combinations and ended up voting "yo-yo" and "nes-nes."

Laval has been executed. He tried to poison himself but was brought back to life by pumping his stomach and the like. However, he could not be transported to the fort at Châtillon, the place intended for the execution. He was shot in the prison yard at Fresnes after refusing to have his eyes blindfolded. Some of the newspapers wrote, "A dead man has been killed."

The Soviets have occupied Poland. The move recalls the occupation of Czechoslovakia by Hitler; troops entered at the request of the Polish government to re-establish order in the country.

24.10.45 The honeymoon between England and Russia is coming to an end. The English newspapers are now reporting the Terror that reigns in occupied Poland, the re-opening of the camp at Auschwitz, and so on.

Saw Gavrilof at church on rue Daru. He is a gardener by trade, working for the Americans now. In accordance with the regulations, he had to go through the G-2 and the Ministry of Labour and was refused a work permit, because prisoners of war have priority for any job opening. The American captain to whom he had to give the Ministry's answer asked him, "Is prisoner status honourable or dishonourable in France? In America, it's rather dishonourable to be taken prisoner." To that, Gavrilof replied to him, "I suppose it's honourable, because now there is a Ministry of Prisoners headed by a Minister." The captain told him he was "requisitioning" him and he could work as in the past.

28.10.45 Civil marriage of Miss Alice, the manager of the Club. We left for Paris: the engaged couple, Dr. Savage the dentist, the groom's witness, and I, the bride's witness. At the town hall, a young woman liaison "officer" came to meet us and had us go into a room where the couple signed paper after paper then, in very good English, she explained the section of the Civil Code that would be read in French to the couple and suggested that they offer cigarettes to the usher and clerks! The ceremony that followed was rushed through in five minutes. I had to sign the register in my maiden name. Then all the staff was invited to a dinner given by the young married couple in the barracks of the Officers' Mess. I forgot to say that a wedding ceremony was held in church previously, even though the groom is divorced; at the ceremony, the organ played the singing saw in Symphony mode. Miss Alice expressly requested it and asked me after if I recognized the melody. For that ceremony, Miss Alice wore a white dress made of silk from parachutes her fiancé gathered from co-workers.

30.10.45 The Club at Bourget is going to be closed permanently on the twelfth of next month. There are a lot of blacks among the soldiers right now. Dressed in khaki uniforms, they can barely be distinguished from the dark woodwork covering the walls of the

Club. Only when they laugh and show two rows of white teeth does one notice their presence. There are also many blacks among the prisoners. Their one-piece overalls have large squares painted white on the back and legs, probably to find them in the dark.

The soldiers assigned to the base run a brisk black-market business. Dr. Burgess came to ask me if I could sell cigarettes, bars of soap, chocolate, and so on for him that he had brought from England, supposedly at the request of his wife who was afraid he was short of necessities! Now I understand why Sergeant Scott, who drank a bit too much at Miss Alice's wedding, accused him of spending barely an hour at work and disappearing to Paris for the whole day. At least he talks about his little transactions with diplomacy! Mademoiselle Théobald immediately jumped at the offer and told me that her brother would buy everything the doctor gave me. The doctor accompanied me by car to the metro, where he gave me a large package of black-market items – the young Red Cross ladies and staff rhapsodized about the doctor's kindness!

1.11.45 The Club is already nearly deserted. An evil wind of plunder reigns over the whole base. Everything is disappearing as if by magic; there is no longer a single sugar bowl, and the housekeepers' smocks disappeared from a cupboard locked with a padlock, and the padlock is intact!

Our manager, Miss Alice, is still on her honeymoon. Her two assistants are less concerned about the Club than the officers on the base. One of them has a lover, Lieutenant W., who she describes as "not very intelligent but very sexy." Thanks to those two, I had my baptism in the air. They took me to Villacoublay, where Lieutenant W. has his airplane. While the airplane was rolling on the ground, we were shaken as if we were in a car with poor suspension, but as soon as he took off, we felt nothing at all, no sensation of speed or motion. I had the impression of soaring that I have in my dreams.

A little incident that could have had fairly serious consequences occurred during the flight; I could clearly feel that we were descending but did not understand the reason why. I was sitting near a panel with switches and levers. Lieutenant W. started signalling and shouting something to me but I could not hear because of the drone of the airplane. Then he bent down and grabbed a lever and switched it; he finally regained calm, settled back in his seat, and smiled at me. Only after we landed did he say, "It's a good thing you're both novices. You didn't realize I ran out of gas. I trusted the mechanics who assured me everything was in order, but the gas tank we were running on was half empty. Fortunately, the other one had been filled with gas." When I told the officers at the base about the incident, they chimed in that, if I had told them I was going flying with Lieutenant W., they would have opposed the idea immediately, because Lieutenant W. is known for his lightheartedness – and carelessness.

Yesterday I observed the little business run by kids in Paris. They stand in front of the metro map and wait for American soldiers to come over to it. They offer their services at once, explain the direction to take, and accompany them to the connection. Naturally, they are given a tip and chewing gum.

15.11.45 Went to the Orly airfield to introduce myself to the Club manager there. Miss Alice was the one who very kindly took the trouble to direct us, me to Orly and my co-worker to Villacoublay. Orly looks like an American city, an enclave in French territory. My nephew Michel, who works at the Air Transport Command, an American organization that rebuilt the aerodrome, told me that, after the Germans left, the airfield was a muddy mass strewn with debris. The Americans brought in special machines that scraped out landing strips in no time, covered them with cement, and restored the whole area. Small barracks painted green or cream have been built beside the aerodrome, one of which will be the Club. For the moment, the Red Cross is using a château in the vicinity of the airfield, and a shuttle bus provides service between the airfield and the château.

20.11.45 The Red Cross workers took me to lunch in the Officers' Mess. The second day after my arrival, two civilians flanked by four MPs armed with rifles went by the room where we were having lunch. The Red Cross workers told me they were German "criminals" being taken to Nuremberg for trial.

Saw Bogdan L., my sister Irina's brother-in-law. Serbs have now become "displaced persons" like we were in our day. L. had a house, property, and a fortune in Belgrade and worked there as a lawyer. Now he has only the clothes on his back, a Serbian uniform with epaulettes on which the Royal Crown can still be seen. He is a fine man, a bit naïve, who will have trouble adjusting to life as a refugee; he is ashamed of being poor.

22.11.45   Books by Sven Heddin and Knut Hamsun and Grimm's fairy tales have been placed on the index by the Allies in Germany, as have all fairy tales describing crime and torture, because the Allies think that literature could have influenced Nazi leaders.[121] Freud's "nursery influence" theory is being cited in American newspapers in support of this measure. German youth will also not be able to practise all sports; canoeing, boxing, and bicycling are prohibited but they may play tennis and football and are allowed to skate. I would be curious to know how this regulation will be enforced.

The Nuremberg trials have begun; generals, marshals, and the like are accused of promoting a war of aggression and will be judged by representatives of countries on the side that dropped atomic and incendiary bombs on enemy cities, pillaged and raped, and ran concentration camps the same as the Nazi camps. In my opinion, since the accused have been brought to trial under the auspices of justice, they have to be judged by their fellow citizens or by a neutral court. What reaction can a conquered people have? I doubt that they consider any sentence pronounced anything but a settlement of accounts. No one can suspect the French of sympathizing with former Nazi leaders but I heard two French officers in a restaurant criticizing the new principle that the Nuremberg tribunal seems to establish: the obligation to question orders from leaders, that is, the right to disobedience. One of them said, "I admit they all deserve hanging but when I see Soviet judges accuse Germans of crimes they committed themselves, I want to laugh."

30.11.45   The Soviet government has called for the return of a hundred and sixty-seven Balts who were refugees in Sweden during the War. The Swedish government has agreed to turn them over. The incident has raised a highly emotional response in Sweden; re-

---

121   The index was a list of banned books and activities.

ligious services in their honour have been ordered in churches, flags flown at half mast, and Swedish women have offered to marry the refugees if it could improve their fate.

Went to the theatre to see the play *À l'approche du soir du monde*, which was well done, and the costumes were magnificent. The audience was very poorly dressed. Where have the fur coats gone, and the extraordinary hats one saw during the Occupation? I think everyone is afraid to show any "outward signs of wealth," to use an expression dear to tax officials.

12.12.45 The Club barracks were prettily decorated by a French architect; however, the practical side has been totally neglected. The plumbing froze the first day and burst the second. The doors and windows do not close, and there is no place to store provisions.

I leave Paris at eight-thirty in the morning. It is still dark. At noon we take a shuttle bus to go for lunch. The food is copious, based on American rations, and prepared by French chefs. Alas, there is already talk of prohibiting civilians from going to the Mess. The room is heated to American taste; you would think you were in an oven.

Went shopping for the Club and was dumbfounded by the prices and the poor quality of things.

Spoke to Maïka Ch. who works at the UNRRA. He told me that Soviet citizens are all passing themselves off as Romanians, Poles, and so on. That is not too hard because no one has papers anymore. UNRRA interpreters are usually émigrés from the First War, and Soviet representatives say ironically, "Here come the ex-princes again to drink vodka." According to Maïka, Madame Joukoff is fairly "presentable" and has beautiful furs and diamonds. Maïka agrees with the Nuremberg verdict because he thinks all nations will be afraid now. He was able to bring Irène K.'s daughter and her cousin from the Soviet zone. L. was in a clinic because of pain in her leg. The Soviet doctor who came first forcefully insisted that the two young girls get away "even if they have to crawl." He told them, "We are nothing but you do not know what to expect if others come." They were getting ready to leave when Maïka arrived, put them in his car, and dropped them off safe and sound at L.'s older sister's in the Allied zone.

22.12.45 New restrictions on electricity; stores will close at five o'clock and can no longer light their window displays. Many stores now light their displays with candles; the soft lighting of the past takes you back to the nineteenth century. Cafés and restaurants are going to close three days a week. The last metro will now run at ten forty-five in the evening, instead of one o'clock in the morning.

Another "restriction" that has prompted a lot of ink to flow and sparked plenty of jokes is the plan to close "houses of ill repute." The accommodation thus freed up will be made available to homeless students. I suppose that will lend itself to many misunderstandings. People in the Orly–Paris bus were discussing the measure and the man next to me said, "Madame, really, it does not stand up to scrutiny! How can you abolish an institution that has existed from the time of the Greeks and Romans?"

Plus stoics have suggested nothing less than recourse to the guillotine to cut off the black market. One of the things I did yesterday was have lunch with Serge Zweguintzoff in a little restaurant near the Champs-Élysées. The room was full to bursting for a pre-war meal with no mention of tickets; all you had to do was ask for what you wanted to eat and it was brought to you right then and there.

Mima Gag. now lives at Assomption convent, a kind of boarding house run by the nuns for high-society ladies. She did not want to continue living in her apartment after the visit from the so-called FFI. Naturally, she never got her jewellery or her money back, nor were the guilty parties arrested. At the convent, at least, not just anyone can get in. You ring at the entrance and an extern sister asks your name and the name of the person you are going to see. You are announced and only then cross the threshold of the convent. Rue de l'Assomption is quiet. There is a fairly large garden along the inner wall of the convent. The whole scene reminds me of convents where noblewomen retired in centuries past.

26.12.45 On Christmas Day, we had three hundred and thirty children from Orly at the Club. Miss Mae, the Red Cross girl, went with me to the Mayor's office to extend the invitation. The town hall, the papers, the dust, the assistant himself – the Mayor works in the city – looked like they dated from the last century. Each time Miss Mae asked the assistant a question, he thought for a good ten minutes. One would never have thought we were in the outskirts of Paris but rather in the depths of the provinces.

In the afternoon on Christmas Day, presents were handed out to the staff: cartons of cigarettes, candy, toothbrushes, chewing gum, and so on, items that are, in a word, priceless! Each box and every item was wrapped prettily in printed paper and tied with red or green ribbons. Americans seem to attach a great deal of importance to how "Xmas presents" are wrapped and do so with great care. Furthermore, the result was truly charming.

The soldiers had decorated the Club themselves: paper garlands around the doorframes, pine boughs, and so on. A large Christmas tree, decorated with electric lights – not as pretty and cozy as candles, however – and glass balls with German labels, was set up in one of the rooms. Cake, ice cream, and chocolates were piled on a long counter. The soldiers wanted to take care of the children themselves. The children started to arrive around four o'clock. The distribution of treats went as smoothly as on roller skates, using an "assembly line" system. The children filed by one after another and, as they came into range, the soldiers threw apples, candy and all kinds of treats into the bag each child was given at the entrance. The Mayor and a few teachers came. The children were delighted because most of them had never before in their lives seen the precious food items they were given.

On Christmas Eve, Miss Mae had the candles lit – they had been placed in logs of wood garnished with pine boughs and set on the small tables in the Club. She had the lights turned off, and Miss Barbara distributed sheets with Christmas carols and tried to get the soldiers to sing. However, they did not get any further than "Jingle Bells." The waitresses, who had all worked for the Germans, were listening and said, "I must say, the 'others' sang better."

Personally, I found that, despite the anti-Christian spirit of Nazism, the German Christmas celebration retained a more religious and "family holiday" feeling than the American Christmas celebration.

I went to the soldiers' Mess to ask the staff sergeant if he could not provide a few items to improve the ordinary fare of the staff on Christmas day. Staff members eat their meals, which they pay for, in the French Mess without tickets, but complain, and rightly so, that the food there is execrable. The sergeant very generously gave the order to the head cook – a Russian, by the way – to give some cold turkey. When my countryman found out my nationality, he immediately added apples, cake, and white bread for me personally. The white bread is very different from French bread, basically tasteless and soft as a sponge. I gave it to Mademoiselle Théobald, who is going to make toast with it.

POST-WAR

"I think it is a lack of suffering that makes people so indifferent and blind to the suffering of others; one really has to suffer to understand the suffering of others."

2.1.46 New Year's Day brought the re-establishment of the ration card for 300 g of bread a day. Counterfeit bread ration cards are already for sale on the black market at a price of one hundred fifty francs a card; a "real" card costs three hundred francs on the black market. The newspapers officially publish both prices.

The weather is cold. Boys and girls go out in the street in ski suits, dressed like real sports enthusiasts; women wear shawls on their heads; men and boys wear short jackets made of rainproof material with a fur collar, called a "Canadian." The streets really look very different than pre-war streets.

Nuremberg prisoners were required to take an intelligence test. The number of points for average intelligence is one hundred. All the prisoners subjected to the test were above that average. Hess had the lowest score of all but still got one hundred and twelve points! Schacht ranked first, then Seiss-Inquart. Göring and Dönitz followed with one hundred and thirty-eight points each.

Had dinner yesterday at the Lasts'. Dédé was wearing a second lieutenant's uniform with a Rhine-Danube badge; he is occupying Germany. He told us how the French occupation authorities are following the example of the Germans in everything in occupied countries and, when it is necessary to solve problems of any kind, the French say, "Let's see, what did the Germans do in a case like that?" He saw an "Aunt Sally" game underway in Place Pigalle with figures representing Hitler, Göring, and Mussolini; the crowd delighted in trying to hit them.[122]

9.1.46 Finally, I received a letter from my sister Irina in Yugoslavia, who writes, "We are both alive, because we have never done anyone any harm. Nowadays everything depends on the neighbours."

Paris has been without meat for four days; butchers are refusing to sell meat for tickets. On the black market, however, you can easily find all the meat you want.

These are some examples of the problems that arise when you place an order at Orly. The American refrigerator that just arrived at the Club does not run on the voltage from our power outlets. Miss Barbara went to ask the American Post Engineers to send a worker to change the voltage. However, work of that kind has to be done by French labourers. The Americans have to send the order *in writing* to the French, although the two administrations are right across from one another. A day passes, then a second; the third day, a young man arrives, sent by the French administration. He walks around the refrigerator then says that he is not an electrician. Everything has to start again. A heavy oil water heater was installed in the kitchen but the parts needed to run it were missing; someone forgot to order them. When they finally arrived, someone forgot to install the diesel fuel exhaust pipe! If that had happened during the Germans' time, it would have been called sabotage.

17.1.46 The weather at Orly is very cold; it is a plateau where the wind blows wherever it wants. All the barracks there are connected by a giant underground heating system that heats the whole camp. The result is amazing, because it even gets too hot in the barracks. Centralization also has disadvantages, however; yesterday, there was a breakdown at headquarters and the whole camp froze. We had to resort to makeshift heating using Field Rangers, dangerous heaters that run on gas and are intended only for outdoors.

Soldiers come to the Club to drink coffee, chocolate, and the famous Coca-Cola they drink in industrial quantities. Ice cream is

---

122 "Aunt Sally" games are a pub or fairground game of British origin. Targets that are often political in nature are set up to be knocked down.

often distributed to them, which has been prepared in nearby barracks with ice-cream mixture produced in America. The soldiers are
very fond of it, even in such cold weather.

This job is interesting for me, putting me in contact with so many
different people. I talk to the soldiers, who teach me about American
customs and lifestyle. I am getting to know their thinking, the mix
of races, types, social classes. One little soldier comes to the Club as
soon as he has a few hours free. He stands guard at the entrance. He
is a natural musician; he has never studied music but lives for music
alone, so to speak. He brings classical record albums with him, chamber music, and plays them, sunk deep in an armchair listening, apart
from the crowd of soldiers around him, not seeing them, not hearing
them. He told me that he is a bus driver by trade and often drove two
hundred miles by car after work to go to a good concert. Another MP
has me read verses he has written that are not bad at all.

The sergeant in charge of the kitchen is a Slovak who talks to me
in his language and I answer him in Russian, but we understand one
another very well. He adopted a young Russian child, thirteen years
old. An American army unit had picked the boy up in Germany and
he escaped to France after them. The American unit that looked after
him had then gone back to America, and the child remained abandoned at Orly. Miss Mae, the Club manager, who is Finnish, had
taken care of him while the Club was at the château; then, when the
Club was transferred to the aerodrome, she came to ask me to take
care of my young countryman and find him a place to live and work,
no less! All my efforts remained unproductive until the idea finally
came to me to ask the Slovak sergeant. He immediately told me to
send him our protégé. A few days later, the boy came to thank me,
dressed in American military clothes. The sergeant gave him a bed to
sleep in, in his room, and a job in the kitchen, and he has more to eat
than he can swallow. He hopes to be able to follow the sergeant to
America, but Miss Mae does not think that is possible.[123]

123 Countess Hendrikoff later added here: "Later I received a note from the child
written on the ship that took the soldiers in his unit back to America. The letter
was written in Russian and addressed to the Russian lady 'who works at the Red
Cross in Orly.'"

Spent my day off at Bellevue. Serge Hitrovo told me he is working at Versailles, at the American office that handles German prisoners of war. They are placed in offices, shoe repair and clock repair shops, and the like. One prisoner works as a barman and wears professional garb, a white jacket, and so on. The other prisoners wear former American uniforms dyed black with big letters "PW" for prisoner of war painted white on the back and pants. They all get American rations, which means that they are better fed than French civilians, and flirt with the female civilian employees.

Liouba Grecoff ordered a telephone installed at her home a long time ago. Lately, when she went to enquire about her order, an employee told her, "Bring us a certificate saying you are Jewish and you will have the telephone right then and there."

24.1.46 France has been without a government since Monday. General de Gaulle resigned, giving his reasons for taking that action in a farewell letter that, by the way, has been criticized a great deal by the press. The man in the street grumbles and says, "If everything is as good as he says, why is he quitting?"

At Orly, nearly all the cars one sees on the road are German, made by Opel. The records Special Services sent the Club are German, too.

The Red Cross asked me to get information from stores about the price of dishware. Everything made of porcelain is sold freely. Seeing the price of eight hundred fifty francs on a teacup, I naïvely asked the salesgirl, "For how many pieces?" She looked at me disdainfully and responded, "Where have you been all this time? Naturally, this price is for *one* cup."

Items made of china are a better buy, but one can only get them with a coupon, and coupons are only issued to young married couples, disaster victims, and deportees.

31.1.46 Félix Gouin has replaced General de Gaulle. The devaluation of the franc continues.

A group of soldiers from the Pacific front arrived at the Club. They tell me there are many Poles in the Indies! When and how did they end up there?

It is very difficult to keep the Club clean these days. It is raining, and the soldiers bring in mud on the floors and tables, because they have a habit of putting their feet on the furniture. All in all, though, they are fine fellows, clean about themselves and in their conversation. I have never heard them make questionable jokes or swear. They are primitive; they spend their time half-stretched out in armchairs flipping through illustrated magazines, listening to the radio or the gramophone, mainly to jazz – all in absolute silence.

5.2.46 Returning to Paris by bus, I found myself sitting next to a woman who told me her name and nationality – Russian. She had just come back from Germany, where she was working as a doctor in a women's hospital. The hospital was in the Soviet zone. She described the arrival of the Communist troops, whom she compared to Huns – all the more so, she said, because most were Mongolian. She alone of all the members of the medical staff, who were all completely terrified, went out to meet the soldiers and told them that she is Russian. No one did her any harm personally; they even reassured her that as a Russian she had nothing to fear. Apart from that, however, the soldiers behaved like real savages, vandalizing everything around them, raping all the women, young, old, women who recently had operations, and so on. "I'll never forget the sight," she said. "I nearly passed out. I really saw those scenes with my own eyes; this isn't hearsay."

The Soviet authorities then replaced the German nurses with Russian nurses and set the German women to washing floors. But that did not last long, because the Russian nurses totally lacked experience and soon it was the Russian women washing floors and the German women taking care of patients again.

One fine day, she was called to the bedside of a colonel from the NKVD, the Soviet secret service, who was sick. He had already had several doctors called in, and the woman I talked to on the bus was finally pointed out to him as a specialist in the illness he suffered from. She had to go to the colonel, accompanied by a guard. She treated him for a while and succeeded in curing him in the end. The colonel was always very friendly to her and, when he said goodbye to her, thanked her profusely; he even told her that he owed her his life and, if she were ever bothered by anyone or had a problem of any kind, she could contact him and he would always come to her assistance. Meanwhile, she and her husband had decided to escape from the Soviet zone and seek refuge in France. They were negotiating with "human smugglers" who were to get them across the demarcation line the next day. Then she decided to go for broke and confided her plans to the colonel, asking him to honour his promise in the event she was caught. The colonel thought for a moment then asked her to tell him the spot where she and her husband were to meet the smugglers. She told him. When she repeated the conversation to her husband, he was frantic. He told her that she was crazy, and now they were going to be arrested. He refused to even make the attempt, but she managed to reassure him by telling him that she trusted the colonel's promise and was convinced that he was sincere and would honour it.

The next day, she left the hospital at the agreed time, dressed in her doctor's coat, without taking anything with her to avoid attracting the attention of any onlookers. She met her husband at the appointed spot. How frightened she was when she saw an NKVD officer coming toward them. He came up to them and asked them their names and... gave them a package of food provisions from the colonel with his best wishes. They were not bothered and crossed to the American zone without incident. "You see," she said later to her husband, "I was right to trust that man."

"Yes, I agree," her husband answered, "but you didn't see how you looked when the officer approached us. You were as white as a sheet. I thought you were going to faint."

14.2.46 Letter from Belgrade from my sister Irina. She is working for a French insurance company. They heat their place with coal purchased with a "community coupon." They eat their meals at the "community union" – all highly reminiscent of life in the USSR. Among other visitors I had recently was her brother-in-law, a fine man, a Serbian, from Montenegro to be precise, naïve, honest; what he talked about and his thinking reminded me of conversations with Russian émigrés in the first few years of exile. He still wears his Yugoslavian uniform, with Royal crowns on the epaulettes, and places all his hopes in England, who has supported them financially up to now. There are still many Yugoslavian soldiers and officers in camps in Germany but his countrymen do not want to be expatriated individually, because they hope to be called soon to fight against Tito![124] Poor innocents!

Visit from a new relative by marriage, Nadia Zweguintzoff's Canadian husband Brazif, who is very nice and made the rounds seeing all of Nadia's relatives in Paris. He is horrified by our prices. In London, rations and items of all kinds are distributed more effectively and are more accessible to the average purse. In Paris, there are many luxury items but only very rich people can buy them. He does not fear Communism for America but, in England, he saw many municipal employees, bus drivers, and so on wearing Communist pins in their buttonholes. English soldiers, on the other hand, were liberated by Soviet troops and are profoundly anti-Communist; they proclaim to anyone who wants to listen that they would much prefer to be taken prisoner by the Germans and end up in a German camp than be liberated by the Soviets again. They took everything they had and fed them poorly.

In answer to my question, Brazif told me that he felt more American than English. The English treat Canadians like "poor relations" and "colonials" when Canada is a big, independent country. In the eyes of Canadians, the British Governor General is only an Ambassador of the King of England, rather than a Head of State. Foreigners know nothing about Canada, which only brings to mind the mounted police and the prairies.

21.2.46 Scandal in Canada.[125] The secret of the atomic bomb has been sold to the Soviets. The world watched with surprise as Great Britain swallowed the offensive speeches of Molotoff and Vychink-

124 Marshal Josip Brosz Tito (1892–1980) was a popular Communist leader of partisan groups in Yugoslavia during World War II. He later became a unifying force as Prime Minister and President of Yugoslavia.

125 The connection to Canada was that Igor Gouzenko was a Soviet spy in Canada during World War II. He defected in Ottawa in September 1945, with lists of Soviet spies that included scientists, a member of Parliament and civil servants. This scandal contributed to Communist paranoia and the Cold War. Canada gave him asylum, and thereafter he always wore a hood in public to conceal his identity.

si. Lek., who is an inveterate Anglophile, keeps on repeating, "Wait, be patient, England is backing off to leap more effectively to the attack." For the moment, however, England is not leaping but continuing to back off.

Alek Obolensky telephoned me to tell me that his mother wrote him an anxious and confused letter asking him urgently to bring her to Paris, because she is threatened by danger. Olga spoke on German radio during the war, the Soviets are looking for her, and she will be no safer here than in Germany, because the Soviets have extradition rights over their nationals, rights granted by the Allies during one of the international conferences, and the Allies even have to give them information and assistance. Alek has a wife and child and, as he said to me many times over, he is completely devoid of any filial sentiment for his mother; he does not forgive her for staying in Russia for purely personal reasons, and does not want to run the risk of having her in his home.

Demonstrations were held in the streets on the occasion of the execution of eleven "patriots" by France, with bands of young people running through the streets shouting, "France, murderer!" Yet no one protests against settlements of accounts that take place daily.

Red Cross employees are going to be put on the Army payroll and, unfortunately, I will no longer be allowed to eat in the officers' canteen! That privilege is not covered by the regulations but losing it is the result of the enmity that exists between the Army and the Red Cross, which wants to be absolutely independent of the Army. The order makes my life very difficult, because there is no canteen for employees in the camp. Red Cross employees live in all the neighbouring towns and villages and bring their lunch buckets to work with them. I do not know yet how I am going to solve the problem, because I live in a room in Paris where it is not possible to do any cooking.

A lot of stencil shops have opened recently, supplied with parachute silk by American soldiers who can buy yardage at the PX[126] for three hundred francs and resell it on the black market for three thousand francs.

126 PX is an abbreviation for Post Exchange, a store run on US military bases for the exclusive use of military personnel.

Yesterday a Red Cross director came to Orly and announced that German prisoners are going to replace part of the staff, because the prisoners work hard and do not cost anything. Miss Barbara, the manager, who thinks of all Germans as savage Huns who throw themselves on women and rape them, immediately asked to be given a military guard to protect us, which made the Director laugh heartily.

14.3.46 Despite Churchill's speech declaring that Communism is a threat to universal peace, fifty thousand Vlasovs have been delivered to the Soviets. The American authorities in Munich had to use tear gas during the forced repatriation, which was followed by shouting, suicide, and the like.

Russia is going to deliver five hundred thousand tons of wheat to France, right after asking America for credit. The newspapers came out with headlines in large letters announcing, "Russia is going to feed France! Russian wheat is already on the way!" The Slovenian sergeant has been supplying me with food.

Joukoff informed the Allied authorities of his intention to reopen the University of Berlin, which is in the Russian zone. The Allies began to confer without reaching a decision, and finally were informed that the university has been reopened and running for several days. The Allies are now asking whether or not the Soviets are going to use the university for propaganda purposes.

Speech by Stalin protesting against the Anglo-Saxon isolationist policy. The Allies, all the Allies, rose up against the principle of the omnipotence of German-speaking nations; now a similar principle seems to be established. The world belongs to English-speaking nations. There is another nation, however, that occupies a third of the world, does not speak English, and is entitled to figure among leaders.

19.3.46 Three German prisoners were waiting for me yesterday in the kitchen. The staff stood silently staring at them with some fear. No one had been let go yet, so I did not know exactly what to have them do. So I gave them fabric, thread, and scissors, and set them up in the American Mess to cut curtains. When I was getting ready to explain the measurements and so on to them, one of them said, "Just give us a centimetre ruler, and we'll figure it out."

"Do you even know how to sew?" I asked them.

"If it is necessary, we will know how to sew," they answered, and immediately set to work.

23.3.46 The German prisoners sew and make curtains without asking for anything whatsoever from anyone. They determined the measurements for the various curtains in a wink with absolute German precision. Relations with the French staff are courteous, especially with the seamstresses, because they have already repaired irons and sewing machines, and adapted Coca-Cola bottles to dampen clothing and help them iron. The Mess sergeant brings them coffee, but the French cook grumbles, "At first, I didn't say anything to them, because it would be me who gets caught again." You would think the French still believe they are living under German Occupation.

Young Boba Makic arrived from Belgrade and brought me a letter from my sister Irina describing her life in Yugoslavia. They call each other *Tovarish*, which means comrade, and use the familiar "*tu*" form to address one another. To find a job, you have to go to the Committee in your neighbourhood, who sends you to the Committee on your street, and an investigation is conducted among your neighbours. You are then given a sealed envelope to take to the Committee in your neighbourhood and, if the information is satisfactory, you are given a job. She advised me against sending Irina our mother's Bible and the photo of Hélène and her husband in Canadian uniform.[127] "The Bible would be frowned upon and, as for the uniform, one cannot be seen in the street in the company of Canadian, English, or American officers. At first, Soviet troops were welcomed effusively, then everyone had soon had enough, because they pillaged and behaved more like conquerors than allies."

I asked her if there were many executions. "I don't know," she answered. "The Germans killed openly, but now people are quietly disappearing without leaving a trace. Many people have been sentenced to 'civil death.' You're informed that your father or brother is 'civilly dead'; you will never see him again."

127 Hélène is Helen Carscallen (née Shirkoff), the daughter of Countess Hendrikoff's sister Ella.

She came to the Beaux-Arts on scholarship as a fine arts student and is staying at the Hotel Lutetia, which has been requisitioned. She has to watch everything she says, because the "eyes of Moscow" are among her compatriots. Lekich wrote to Irina to ask her why she was not living in his house and selling his furniture and things. Boba says, "Doesn't he know that his house was requisitioned long ago and he himself declared a 'war criminal'?" Boba's mother wept a great deal when she left for Paris but told her that she would have wept even more if Boba had stayed.

28.3.46 A new group of soldiers has arrived at Orly. They are students and have different manners and intellectual levels than their predecessors. In spite of that, one of them started the eternal argument about officers again: "Why are their uniforms made of different material than soldiers' uniforms? Why do they have separate Clubs where soldiers aren't allowed to enter?" I pointed out to him that the presence of officers among the soldiers made them pouty and morose, but he was unconvinced. How strange relations are between officers and soldiers in a democratic army!

4.4.46 Yesterday Miss Barbara came to tell me that she wants the German prisoners to eat their meals at other times and at other tables than the French staff, because she has observed too much "fraternizing" between them. Yesterday she saw one of the prisoners joking with one of the waitresses, and he gave her a friendly slap on the lower back. "I am surprised at the French," she told me. "They should know better." The newspapers are full of articles as well on "fraternizing" between American soldiers and the Japanese. McArthur even had to issue an order prohibiting "the public display of affection" between occupiers and occupied. The result of that order? "One-night inns" have been opened where GIs can "display their affection" from now on without being bothered by McArthur.

Yesterday Madame Keller came to say goodbye to me. She is leaving for America, via Brazil, because apparently one gets there faster that way. There were so many people at the Consulate that she despaired of ever getting to see the Consul, when she noticed a blond, Slavic-looking individual, who surely was not Brazilian and looked like he worked there. She approached him and bravely addressed him in… Russian; she was not surprised to hear him answer her in that language, too. He was an émigré from the First War working at the Brazilian Consulate and he helped her arrange all her papers in a jiffy.

It reminds me of a story I just heard. Two Russian émigrés meet after a few years' separation. The first one asks the second one what he is doing now. "I'm an interpreter for a seafaring captain," answers the second.

"But how?" asks the other. "You never spoke anything but Russian."

"And who says I speak anything else now? When we arrive in a foreign port, I shout loudly at the crowd on the dock, 'Hey, Russians! Whoever speaks Russian here, come aboard!' Well, even on the most deserted island, I have always found Russians, and the captain never knew I didn't speak any foreign language!"

7.4.46 Met X. in the street, who worked for a while at No. 2 Boulevard Suchet, which was occupied by the Germans. He just came back from Austria, where he went as a volunteer during the Occupation. He has the best of references and no one bothered him because he was in a punishment camp in Germany. He told me that Germany and Austria are full of "displaced persons" who do not want to or cannot go back home. He finds Paris very changed. In the French zone, Moroccan troops buy weapons of all kinds to send to Morocco.

The German prisoners show so much initiative that I would not be surprised to see them running the Club some day. Not to mention all the tools the French workers did not manage to repair that the Germans repaired in a jiffy! They now supply the Club with a lot of items presumed impossible to find: scissors, electrical equipment – they recently brought in bolts of fabric for curtains! The American captain laughed and said he did not want to look into the source too carefully, but he very much appreciated the Germans helping the poor Americans.

12.4.46 Saw Marguerite Grierson who just arrived from England.[128] She says that the quality of English goods, although much inferior to pre-war quality, is definitely superior to the quality of French

128 The sister or sister-in-law of Ruth Ogareff (née Grierson), whom Countess Hendrikoff knew in Taganrog

products. The black market does not exist in England, except for the sale of textile points. Restaurants are not rationed at all.

Bicha saw Mak., who just got back from America, which really disappointed him, and he told her, "A European cannot be happy there."

17.4.46 Went to Confession and Communion with Bicha at the little church on rue de la Tour. The church was opened the last year of the Occupation, set up in one of those charming little eighteenth-century buildings one only discovers with great difficulty because they are usually hidden behind a wall or in the depths of a courtyard. The former *salon* has been divided in two by the iconostasis, a wall hung with icons separating the sanctuary from the nave; a large bay window opens onto a garden where a little eighteenth-century pavilion can be seen in the back. You would think you were 100 km from Paris. How charming the little building must have been to live in!

23.4.46 Easter Mass was celebrated earlier than is customary again this year, at ten o'clock instead of midnight. The Mass that follows the Easter service was postponed until the next morning. There were a lot of people, and beautiful cars, but the crowd was smaller than before the war.

25.4.46 Waited a fairly long time at Place Vendôme for the bus to Orly and listened to the conversations of the drivers around me. Naturally, the government was the topic of conversation. First, they talked about the black market and what little effort the government was making to eliminate it. "What a shame to be reduced to begging! We have our hand out for wheat here and coal there, when we have all that in the country. Only the lousy government isn't restoring order in the house." They then went on to more general topics, saying that the "leftists" had barely come to power before they changed horses. "They hold on for a while, then give in. What do you want? It was too much for them. Take Blum for example, how he changed. And now, if it's Torrès, you'll see, it'll be the same story."[129]

---

129 Leon Blum (1872–1950) was a French Prime Minister associated with the moderate left. He was imprisoned in Buchenwald and Dachau, and rescued by Allied troops in 1945. Henry Torrès (1891–1966) was a Communist lawyer and politician. After the German invasion of France, he fled to South America, Canada and the United States. He returned to France after the war.

27.4.46 The Club at Orly is going to be transferred to the Army and managed from now on by a sergeant who came to talk to me and said, "First I want to warn you. The fact that a woman has five children to feed is of no importance to me. If she is not very young and active, I won't keep her."

28.4.46 Yesterday while I was in the sewing room, one of the German prisoners who was helping with the irons said to me, "Two of our men left yesterday on 'special leave.' An American they did black-market business with supplied them with American uniforms, identification papers, and so on. If they are smart, they'll cross over to Spain. Another one of our comrades left in the American chaplain's car, dressed in his suit. He left him a very polite note apologizing for the inconvenience he was going to cause him. Chaplains' cars are rarely checked at the camp exit. He has already reached home and wrote to us that everything went well and he has already been demobilized."

The position of the three German prisoners is absolutely original; they have become indispensable to Club life. They suggest improvements and simplifications to Club routine and are called upon constantly to solve a problem here or make something work there. Some padlocked cupboards were recently brought to the Club. Miss Barbara immediately called one of the French employees and asked him to open them. After lengthy, unsuccessful attempts, he called a comrade to the rescue; then another employee came to take his turn trying, while the waitresses stood around encouraging them with advice. But the cupboards still remained closed. Finally, Miss Barbara lost patience and said to me, "I can't stand watching this any longer. Please go and get one of the German prisoners." So I went to them and said, "Is there a locksmith among you?"

They answered at once, in unison, "If need be, we can all be locksmiths." And, in a wink, one of the prisoners opened the cupboards for me using a hairpin.

Recently the Mess sergeant called for one of our prisoners and ordered him to take his letters to the post office. The prisoner, however, refused point blank, saying that, according to the Geneva

Convention, sergeants are not obliged to work. He had voluntarily agreed to work at the Club but did not want to be anyone's servant. One day, when I brought them some ping-pong balls, which are fairly hard to find, one of them, delighted, cried, "*Wenn wir noch einmal in Paris einmarschieren, dann nehmen wir Sie mit!*" – "Next time we march into Paris, we'll take you along!" I made the comment that I did not care much for that type of joke, and he retorted, "Are you really sure it's impossible? It wouldn't surprise me!"

29.4.46 Went with Miss Betty to buy a little dog, which she paid for with cigarettes, soap, and chocolate.

Miss Mae got a note scribbled in Russian by young Ivan, her little protégé; he writes from the boat that according to him is on the way to America!

30.4.46 The Club is now managed by a sergeant who invited me to his *salon*, arranged and decorated by the German prisoners' efforts, and offered me a small glass of cognac to celebrate his appointment as manager of the Club. Three sergeants from the Mess were there, a Czech who must be the sergeant's girlfriend, and a German prisoner, an educated young man – a "college boy" as the sergeant told me – but overly familiar and arrogant, who seemed to think he was still the occupier. I doubt that I will be content in the new atmosphere and will stay there long.

The German prisoners assure me that at many installations where their countrymen work, they are in charge of the French teams. I did not want to believe it, but yesterday the young German, the sergeant's friend, came to take measurements at the Club accompanied by French workers to whom he was, in, fact giving orders in French. The French supervisor of the American soldiers' Club recently said to me, "It's fortunate that we have those guys (meaning the prisoners). I don't know how they do it but they manage to do everything, always come up with everything, and their work is done in five seconds."

1.5.46 Statutory holiday. Stores, offices, and so on are closed; not even the buses are running.

Paris is covered with posters with the words "Yes" and "No" – "Yes" means approval of the Constitution recommended by the Communists and Socialists. Many shops have flyers with "Yes" or "No" posted in their display windows.

Many French employees quit the Club when the sergeant changed their schedule giving them only half an hour for lunch. Can you imagine a Frenchman eating a sandwich and a cup of coffee, even if they are supplied by the army, in half an hour? Will the French ever adapt to the American pace, and will they be happier for it? In fact, while criticizing the "laziness" of the French and praising the Germans' ability to work, the Americans recognize that no nation in the world knows how to enjoy life the way the French do and envy the good life in France – *la dolce vita*.

26.5.46 I quit my job at the Club. The two radios alone, with two different programs roaring all day long at top volume even though they are in the same room, would have been enough to drive me crazy in the end. The American mentality is really so far from European thinking. Despite the reputation the French have in other countries as "lovers," I do not think French barracks have ever been decorated in the same style as American barracks. The Mess sergeant ordered one of the German prisoners to paint little pictures of barely dressed women on the Mess walls and most obligingly gave him models to copy torn out of American magazines. For his bedroom, the sergeant asked to have a woman painted completely naked, life-sized. The German prisoners commented about it, guffawing; however, the French staff members were deeply shocked.

Went to the Champs-Élysées theatre to see the newsreels, a real horror show, sensational drama in the Grand Guignol tradition. The film was *Where is Italy Headed?* It started out with a retrospective – Hitler, Mussolini on the balcony with the King and Queen, the march on Rome, Mussolini on the balcony in the Piazza Venezia, getting off the plane after he was kidnapped by Skorzeny, then sitting in front of a fireplace, sunk in an armchair with a sombre air, reminiscent of Napoleon at Fontainebleau. Then came horror scenes, one after another: the exhumation of hostages shot by the Germans, the execution of Caruso and

Caretto,[130] one torn from his hospital bed, walking on crutches, his execution sitting on a chair, shot in the back; his comrade ripped from the hands of the guards by a delirious mob, dragged outside, later thrown in the Tiber with his eyes gouged out, pounded with rocks as he tried to struggle back to the surface. He is seen hung from the fence of the Tribunal. The bodies of Mussolini and his mistress, Clara Petacci, swing head down, surrounded by a screaming mob barely contained by the police. Finally, Republican Party representatives are seen declaring that Italy is headed for an era of freedom. The sight of an unchained beast is never edifying.

29.5.46 Saw Mimi Launitz at Schourka Gol.'s. She just arrived from Germany. She escaped from Russia with her four daughters but lost track of the oldest daughter in Germany, whom she thinks is now in the Soviet zone.

I would never have recognized her; she is a very old woman, toothless, and looks like a peasant. Naturally, she was assailed with questions, which she answered jumping from one subject to the next. She told me, "If I had met you by chance in the street, I would have pretended not to recognize you. Why? Because I might perhaps have been under surveillance by the NKVD, and I would have dragged you into disgrace with me, or maybe you were spying for the NKVD. When they come to your home to pay you a visit, they are often accompanied by a friend of yours who has been forced to come with them. After that, you never trust her again, no matter what she says. When friends get together, no one introduces you to the people you don't know. They tell you, this is Vera, this is Ivan. Who are they? You don't know their names. You never know who you are dealing with. My children never knew my maiden name." She was the daughter of the chief of police in St. Petersburg, who was killed at the beginning of the Revolution.

130 On March 23, 1944, 33 SS policemen were killed by a partisan bomb in Rome's via Rasella. Hitler decreed that ten civilians for each of the 33 would be rounded up and executed. The next day, 335 civilians, many of them Jews, were rounded up off the street and taken to the Ardeatine Caves, where they were executed. Pietro Caruso, Roman Chief of Police, was responsible for the roundup. Caruso was executed by Italian firing squad in September 1944.

"When the Soviet Army entered a city – during the war, cities were continually taken and retaken – I locked my daughters in a little cubbyhole with no windows and kept them there until calm was restored."

Mimi was in a DP[131] camp when Soviet repatriation missions arrived in the city. She was told she was going to be sent back to Russia, too. She went to find the Commandant of the camp, who had often used her as an interpreter, and said to him, "You know me. I do not speak lightly. Well, if you send me back to Russia, I will kill myself and my children before your eyes."

The Commandant ended up saying to her, "Go for a walk in the woods with your children. I'll send someone for you when the mission has left."

After that, the officers at the camp came and asked her, "We understand that you, an 'ex,' don't want to go back, but the others, the soldiers, the farmers?"

"Now they understand, but it took time," she said.

Saw M.N. Bez. at the Lags.'s. She describes her visits to her daughter, who is in prison at Fresnes. In the cell next to her daughter is... Madame Mutafolo, the girlfriend of Dr. Lutowski; she had divorced her husband with the intention of marrying Lutowski someday. Political events arrange things nicely. Now her Russian husband comes to see her regularly, brings her packages, and is doing everything he can to have her released...

10.6.46 Veta Zinovieff[132] told me that what struck her most about post-war Paris is the sadness in the streets. It seems to her as if everyone is sad and preoccupied. She also told me that the most critical time for the English in the whole war was the V2 period.

The English celebrated the anniversary of the Victory; however, the Poles from Anders were not invited to the official ceremony. The Serbs, Soviet Russians, and the Poles who are Soviet sympathizers in turn refused to take part. That is why the French newspapers called the celebration "a family party."

131 Displaced Persons
132 Elizabeth Zinovieff, née Princess Elizabeth Galitzine, is related by marriage to Countess Hendrikoff.

Pillot, the company that supplied shoes to the German army during the Occupation, has been authorized to supply the public with "dress" shoes. Apparently it has not been purged.

The *New York Times* said that the two "major operations" of the post-war period were the swift demobilization of the American army and... the pillaging of Germany by GIs. Army post offices had to close on certain days to allow employees to ship the packages sent from Germany by American soldiers.

22.6.46 The Soviet authorities have published a call to Russian émigrés inviting them to become Soviet citizens. A poster to that effect, with a picture of Stalin, Molotoff, and Shvernik, has been posted on the fence of the church at rue Daru.

N.A. Levshine received a letter from the head of a Russian school in Yugoslavia. The four hundred young girls who were studying there, daughters of Russian émigrés, have been deported to Russia and are now in a little Russian village. Bicha spoke to Herzog about it, who told her, "Those children are unbelievably lucky! They have been sent back to the Mother Country and removed from the morass of emigration. Naturally, it's hard for the parents to have to be separated from their children. But what do you want? When you chop down trees, the chips fly!" He ended with that quote from a Russian proverb. Herzog is a former émigré who went over to the Soviets.

1.7.46 Huge meeting in the conference hall at Iéna chaired by Soviet Ambassador Bogomolov. Meetings of that kind will be held every week to familiarize emigrants with life in the USSR. Bogomolov announced the opening of a school and hospital in Paris for Soviet nationals. He also added that he would advise émigrés against returning unless they have relatives who will offer them hospitality, because the issue of residential accommodation is rather complicated right now. The audience was so electrified by Bogomolov's speech that people were clamouring for a *качать* – a popular old Russian custom where an enthusiastic crowd celebrates an individual by throwing him up in the air and catching him again before he hits the ground – but he managed to slip away, using his kidney trouble as an excuse.

I think of what a real amnesty might have been, allowing émigrés to return to Russia freely. However, the iron curtain is still drawn in the country; one cannot always correspond openly with its inhabitants or go see what is happening in Russia or the Soviet zone in Germany.

10.7.46 I have been working since the first of the month at the British Library. I read in the newspaper that it had opened under the auspices of the British Council, a British government promotional agency, and went to fill out an application without much hope. I was called ten days later by the unit head and… accepted immediately. He did not even want to glance at my American references.

I seem to be flipping backwards through the book of my life again. I find the English just the same now as when I got to know them in Russia in 1920 working as a translator at the English Military Mission, still from the same mould! There is certainly more variety among the Americans, but what a difference in demeanour and manners! The English around me walk on tiptoe and speak in hushed tones, in that stifled English voice. They are polite but not affable and create an atmosphere of dignity, reserve, and calm around them. After the noise and coming and going of the Americans, it seems like I am continually in a church. I also feel plunged back into a European setting. I cannot say why, but Americans always seem slightly exotic to me.

17.7.46 General Mikhaïlovich, head of the anti-Communist Yugoslavian resistance, has been tried by a Titoist tribunal and sentenced to death. Glouchevitch knew him personally and deplores the decision. He considers Mikhaïlovich a hero, a pure man, and predicts that sooner or later the Allies will regret supporting Tito.

1.8.46 The prospect of expatriating myself to America terrifies and saddens me. It is just the material difficulty – two hundred fifteen francs a day and one meal alone costs one hundred francs – for which I see no solution that pushes me to accept the offer.[133] I catch myself hoping for a miracle to intervene at the last minute and that I will be able to stay.

---

133 Nancy Zweguintzoff, who lived in Philadelphia, had suggested that Countess Hendrikoff emigrate to America. The Countess was fond of Nancy's children, Nata and Sandy. They had all lived together at Château des Touches in 1940, just before the Countess helped them leave France for the United States.

9.8.46 I had a visit from a certain Vetchenko, whose daughter married Putnik, the son of the famous Yugoslavian Voyevode.[134] They fled Yugoslavia after the installation of the Tito government. They paid a lot of money to cross the Italian–Yugoslavian border – fifty thousand francs per person. Pre-war life in Yugoslavia was sweet for Russian émigrés; when they came to Paris, they compared the life of Russian émigrés in Paris with their own with surprise and some horror. But now poor Vetchenko no longer knows what to think of our *modus vivendi*. He is astonished that I do not have a library stuffed with Russian books. When I told him that I work every day until six o'clock, he exclaimed, "But then your whole life is spent working!" He finds that the years of emigration in France have hardened the hearts of Russians; no one has time for a private chat; no one manages to see any of their friends. I tried to explain to him how difficult the struggle to live has always been for Russian émigrés, who usually arrive in a highly civilized country with no occupation useful to that civilization. The "tough" ones survive. At heart, however, I think he is right. The ones who succeed lose in gentleness, amiability, goodness, and leisureliness what they gain in "efficiency."

11.8.46 Dined at the young Andr.'s with two young Frenchmen and a Yugoslavian married to a Russian. Big discussion about French and German culture, and so on. One of the Frenchmen was spouting fine phrases, "Without France, the flame of European culture, there is nothing left. Cartesian thinking,"[135] and so on. He assured us that in the camps the prestige of the French was so great that the Yugoslavian prisoners shared their rations with the French. He concluded with "Long live the German ruins." The other Frenchman protested, saying that the destruction of German culture and cities in Germany destroyed European heritage and opened the door to the American and Soviet cultures, similar in their "machinism." The Serbian added that the Yugoslavians would have shared their rations with any nationality.

134 Vojvoda Radomir Putnik (1847–1917). Vojvoda (or Voyevode) is the highest rank in the Serbian army. Mount Putnik, in Peter Lougheed Provincial Park in Alberta, Canada, is named after him.
135 Cartesian thinking, the psychological school of René Descartes, separated the mind and body as two completely separate entitites.

I read a book about the Gobi Desert, written by two English women missionaries. I found the book fascinating and saddening at the same time. Fascinating because the authors describe an unknown world, vestiges of a culture and civilization that have disappeared, relegated to caves and grottos known only to a limited number of native people and explorers. Saddening because such a culture could disappear without leaving memories for common mortals, and it could easily happen to our culture.

The two authors of the book describe their campsite in an oasis, where one of the inhabitants who had never left the place showed them ancient plates and jade vases. His unfailing artistic sense amazed them, and they explain it only by a cultural heritage inherited from previous generations – the very heritage that is so lacking in today's "self-made men."

18.8.46 Had lunch in a little restaurant on the quai de Tokyo. At my table for four, first, a Negro driver sat down, then two young Yugoslavians. Before he sat down, the driver very politely asked, "May I sit beside you, Madame?"

"He certainly has no inferiority complex," criticized a young woman at a nearby table who spoke out loud pretentiously. She said, "That woman looks hard. A woman should look sweet. That is how a woman should be."

He introduced me to the two Yugoslavians. One of them said, "I'm Yugoslavian – Tito" and I answered, "I'm Russian – but not Stalin." Despite the difference in politics, the "Tito" gave me bread tickets when he saw that I did not have enough.

Metropolitan Euloge is dead. Great emotion in church circles and the Russian colony, because the death raises administrative issues. Who will name the new Metropolitan: Moscow–Paris or Constantinople?

20.8.46 Went to get information at the American Consulate about the approximate date of my departure. I should not count on being able to leave before next summer. Will I last until then? I rarely have dinner in the evening. If I do not go out and do not go to Barbos', I just have a cup of tea with bread and butter. I have lunch in dairy stores and am selling the things that belonged to my stepfather little by little, along with the contents of the packages Nancy sends me from America, but is that going to allow me to live until next year?

The tax department is also claiming two thousand five hundred francs in back taxes. The Germans had lowered the scheduled tax rate from 10% to 5% and now the tax department is claiming the difference.

Went to the bookstore on rue de la Pompe, where I had left books for sale. The owner is a Russian woman. While I was waiting for her answer, an English Navy officer came in and asked for a book. Struck by his very pronounced Russian accent, the owner of the bookstore and I looked at one another with the same silent question, "Could it be a Soviet uniform?"

While they were looking for the book he asked for, the officer was about to smoke and immediately offered me and the owner a cigarette. All that was so little English that the owner could not hold back any longer and said to him, "Monsieur, I am going to be very indiscreet, but you appear to me to be Russian, and your uniform is English."

He smiled, showed us the Polish eagle on his cap, and told us in French, "I'm Polish. It's the uniform the English gave us. We wear an eagle there, where they wear a crown." He said to me, "Do you speak Polish, Madame?"

He still seemed Russian to me, not Polish, so I answered him in Russian, "No, but I speak Russian, because I'm Russian," then added, "White Russian, of course."

Then he cried out joyfully, "I'm Russian, too, born in Moscow. I finished Naval School in St. Petersburg."

When Madame B. asked him what the Polish Fleet was going to do now, he shrugged his shoulders and answered, "That's what we are all asking."

21.8.46 Went to see the Putniks. The father is in the hospital; he was hit by a car in the street. The young woman has completely lost courage. She is bitter and lumps both the Allies and Germans in her resentment.

23.8.46 Tchernoff[136] and Barbos were at my place this evening. They talked about the tragic epic of Russian groups who fled their country following the Germans and ended up in Italy. Apparently the Germans had pushed the native population back into the mountains and installed the refugees in their place. On Liberation, the Italians came down from the mountains and expelled the DPs. The Allies then gave them orders to get ready to be transported to another region. The first to leave were officers. They were never heard from again. Rumours soon reached the ears of the rest of the group that the officers had been turned over to the Soviet authorities. A delegation of refugees went to plead their case to the Allied Commanders, explaining to them that by turning them over to the Soviet authorities, they were signing a death warrant for them all. The Allies turned a deaf ear and consoled them by saying that the refugees would be much better off at home and, anyway, orders had been given and could no longer be changed. The delegation then asked permission to celebrate a religious service before leaving, which they were allowed to do. Priests of different religions and nationalities said prayers and the kneeling crowd joined in. The group was then sent to Germany (or Austria?) and placed in a camp behind barbed wire. When they came to get them to repatriate them, the refugees refused to leave the camp. Exhortations, threats, nothing worked. So they turned their machine guns on them. The first ranks fell. Their comrades gathered them up but still did not move. It was not until the next day that the Allied Commander changed tactics and stopped the forced repatriation.

23.8.46 Surprise dinner at Olga W.'s. She had sent a pneumatic to invite me and, at the same time, promised me a surprise. When I arrived she told me that I would never, absolutely ever, guess what the surprise is. This is hard to explain. I absolutely did not know that Grade had been released and was far from expecting him to show up at Olga's with Marina. In spite of that, I suddenly

---

136 Possibly Louda (Juda) Tchernoff (1872–1950). Tchernoff left Russia before the Revolution to study law in France. He became a professor of law, a prolific writer and lecturer.

had a clear sense that they were exactly who Olga was expecting. I told her that I was going to write down on a piece of paper what I thought the surprise was going to be and put it in the pocket of my suit and would read it to her when the time came. A few minutes later the door opened and in came... Marina and Grade. I took the piece of paper out of my pocket on which I had written, "Marina and Grade are coming here for dinner this evening." Explain that if you can!

Grade told us the following story. On Liberation, or rather Germany's surrender, he slipped into France with false papers; he was recognized by a waiter in a café, arrested, and sent to Fresnes. According to him, everyone there bent over backwards to spoil him and make his prison stay easier. The doctor sent him to the infirmary as soon as tramps shared his cell. A "collaborator" befriended him and gave him the address of a relative who ran a hotel and welcomed him with open arms. He looks as well-groomed as usual, with rings on his fingers and a gold watch on his wrist, and so on. What is he living on and what is he doing in Paris? A mystery. Is he an intelligence officer or working for the Second Office? I doubt it. I would be more inclined to think he belongs to a freemasonry of black marketeers.

27.8.46 Militza Z. recounted to us the scene she watched at the Town Hall in Meudon. A young émigré from the First War and his fiancée, an émigré from the Second War, were in a corner, while the *Commissaire* shouted into the telephone, "And I am telling you that, as long as I am a Free Frenchman living in a Free France, I will not turn this young woman over to the Soviet authorities." The *Commissaire* then went to the Popular Republican Movement Mayor of Meudon and got him to advance the publication of the bans, and the young people were married right then and there! But how many Soviet citizens do not escape forced repatriation and how many dramas are the result? One of the priests at the church on rue Daru, Father Oleg, told us that he had a maid, a Soviet citizen, who had already tried to throw herself into the Seine with her child before he took her in. When she got the official order to report to the Soviet Embassy with her child, she went to tell Father

Oleg that he would never hear of her again and disappeared that very day. He does not know what became of her. He also told us that a French–Soviet couple and their child went to the Embassy when the woman was called in. When they got there, the woman and child were called into an office and never came out again. An official came and told the French husband that he could go back home; the Soviet government does not recognize marriages between their nationals and foreigners, and his wife and child were going to be repatriated to Russia. The man started shouting and making such a racket that they finally gave him back the child, but he never saw his wife again.

30.8.46 I just saw Militza again at the Hitrovos; she told us how her mother-in-law was "medically" examined at the American Consulate. Previously French doctors did the examinations of applicants, but there were abuses and they were replaced by American doctors. The emigration applicants are completely undressed. The mother-in-law, who is seventy-five years old, went through it like the rest and later said, "I had seven children but never has a doctor made me stand completely naked in front of him like that." Militza had to be present at the spectacle because her mother-in-law does not speak a word of English, and was fairly embarrassed herself. I think Americans have very little sense of privacy.

1.9.46 Left to spend my vacation at the farm where Liouba is currently staying. She made an arrangement with a friend who owns a farm; Liouba agreed to take care of the farm and feed the animals, and the friend took Liouba's daughter Machou with her to the seashore. The farm is very primitive, with an outhouse in a cabin in the farmyard that is the preferred spot, I do not really know why, for the chickens to lay their eggs. There is no running water; we have to go to the pump in the yard to fill our water jugs. Mice are everywhere, scratching and squeaking so loud at night that they prevent you from sleeping. They also run over your blankets at night. The stables are fairly poorly maintained. But the animals are beautiful: a large cow that a Polish refugee comes to milk, because neither Liouba nor I are able to make her give milk – I think she is making fun of us! A gorgeous goat, as strong as two men, refuses to stay tied up in its assigned meadow. We have barely come back to the house when a malicious head with horns appears in the window of the *salon* on the ground floor and two front hooves are placed on the window frame. The huge pig gives us a great deal of trouble, because we have to prepare a kind of slurry for him every day and clean his pen. We have to go cut alfalfa for the rabbits and feed the geese and ducks that come and knock on the door with their beaks at six o'clock in the morning. They are never late by a minute; one would think they have an alarm clock. The cow gives twenty litres of milk a day; since we cannot use all that milk, we give some to the dog, the cat, and the pig and even throw some away because no one wants it. In Paris, children only get half a cup a day. We make butter ourselves by beating the cream with a fork and live almost exclusively on dairy products. No newspapers, no radio – a real oasis of calm, which is restful... for a short period of time!

5.9.46 We went with the Polish farmwife to visit a few neighbouring farms. Fields of wheat and beets stretch right to the horizon. We passed carts of grain pulled by beautiful oxen or work horses. One of the farms we went past looked like a little village all by itself with a respectable number of brick and fine sandstone buildings. Through the gate of another farm a large table could be seen, set up in the farmyard with jam tarts, sliced bread, and so on. Farmers here are very rich, according to the Polish farmwife; they made a lot of money from Parisians during the war and the Occupation. As we go by farms, the Polish farmwife points out which ones' current owners were farm hands at the beginning of the war and have since bought farms and livestock with black-market profits. She refuses to believe that there is a shortage of everything in Paris, when here there is almost too much in the way of food supplies. We passed the charred remains of an airplane; I was not able to find out where it came from. She said that the peasants rushed to the site of a disaster to recover "valuable" items such as canned goods, ammunition, the pilots' watches, and so on. "Like vultures," she said. But in the countryside, there is nothing but the bitter struggle to eat and live, to live by eating others. One becomes hard on oneself and others. The condemned are fattened – poultry, livestock. A baby bird falls from the nest to be gobbled up by the chickens, and on it goes at every level.

7.9.46 We nearly lost the whole flock of geese. Someone left the gate open and out went the geese followed by the white duck, their faithful companion. We went from farm to farm; finally, a little boy led us to a large pond where, he had heard, strange geese had arrived this morning to enjoy the water. A separate flock of geese was indeed swimming there in dignified fashion, not mingling with the others. The farmers in the vicinity confirmed that the geese did not belong to anyone. But how to recognize our white duck among the flock of ducks that colour floating on the pond? We grabbed one at random but, once we got to the farm, we saw that we had made an error; the hens, ducks, and geese immediately prevented the intruder from approaching the dishes of corn and ponds of water and the poor stranger spent the whole day huddled sadly in the back of the farmyard until a farmer came to claim her the next morning. Apparently winged folk unmistakably recognize a white duck who is a friend from among others of their kind, although such signs escape the eyes of humans.

13.9.46 Saw Olga Alferoff again after a separation of... thirty years! At that time, she lived in the city of Kursk, where her father was the director of a boys' school; she was a member of the volunteer committee I organized during the First War. She later married then divorced her husband, who became a Communist. Her second husband, Plevitzki, who by the way was the first husband of the singer Plevitzkaia, was twenty years older than her and had opened a dance studio in Riga.[137] She fled to Austria when the Soviets were approaching Riga for the second time, but her husband preferred to stay. She spoke to me briefly about her life under the Communist regime: how they were obliged to attend lectures after work or be

137 Edmund Plevitzki was the first husband of Nadezhda Plevitzkaia (1884–1940), a Russian singer from the Kursk region. Loving luxury, she and her third husband, General Skoblin, became NKVD spies for the Soviet Union. They were instrumental in the abduction of General Evgeny Miller, who was taken back to Moscow and tortured for two years before he was executed. Plevitzkaia died in Rennes prison in 1940.

blacklisted, the lack of culture among the masses, and the lack of freedom of the press. "I never read the newspapers," she said. She is now waiting for a seat to become available on a flight to join her sister in Nairobi. Now that everyone distrusts everyone else, I remained constantly on my guard during the conversation. How can I be sure she is telling the truth, that she is really anti-Soviet? When she asks me for news of my family, can I tell her that my sister-in-law escaped from Russia and is hiding in Germany? Now where is the freedom people fought for?

There are only two Russian-language newspapers that come out now, and both have distinctly Soviet tendencies. The first of the newspapers, *The Russian News*, claimed that no one went to the church on rue Daru anymore since the clergy refused to accept Metropolitan Seraphin, who is pro-Soviet, as leader, whereas more people than ever go there. The other newspaper is named *The Russian Patriot* and, if not red, is at least quite pink. An anti-Soviet newspaper, *The Free Voice*, was sold clandestinely for a while but soon disappeared from circulation.

The *New York Herald* published articles by Hershey on the bombing of Hiroshima. Why was that military operation not considered a "war crime?" I do not see the difference. The civilian population was killed without any warning, and the survivors continue to die from internal injuries. I wonder if the pilot who carried the bomb was able to continue to live his little life afterward without ever thinking of the horrible destruction he was involuntarily responsible for.

15.9.46 Saw Alexandre Bilderling, who just got back from Brazil. He was sent there to propose a French aircraft model to the Brazilian government. The deal was not made because the aircraft lost its wings during a demonstration. Barbos says the fault lies with the French government, which did not have the airplane accompanied by French mechanics out of false economy. So the plane had to be assembled by inexperienced Brazilian mechanics, while the English and Americans had sent not only teams of mechanics but even cooks and food supplies so that their nationals did not suffer a change in diet.

Bilderling was struck by the abundance and wealth in Brazil. He found that the Brazilian standard of living greatly surpasses the standard of living in pre-war France. Avenues twice as wide as the Champs-Élysées are lined with thousands of imported cars. Brazil has no industry to speak of. The streets are very elegant, as they are in most Latin countries. No one carries any packages by hand; the tiniest handkerchief is delivered to one's home.

I also just saw Maka K.'s sister, who is back from Morocco. According to her, Russians live better there than in Paris from a material and social standpoint. Going there, she had to stand in interminable line-ups to get space on the deck of the ship. Coming back, a single telephone call from her brother immediately assured her of a stateroom.

In a word, it appears that Russian emigrants everywhere live better than in Paris. In spite of that, no one wants to leave Paris. It is rare for anyone to accept a position, even better paid, in the provinces or the country, much less in another country. Russian émigrés live very modestly, often poorly, in Paris; with rare exceptions, their jobs are limited to taxi driver jobs, ushers, saleswomen, fashion trade workers, with wages that do not allow a high standard of living. They live in small buildings that they often come to occupy entirely because, as we say in Russian, they are attached to the "herd" mentality and settle in groups. The fifteenth arrondissement is almost entirely inhabited by Russians. Around the houses and buildings they live in, shops and restaurants emerge at once, run by their countrymen.

21.9.46 Summer ended without anyone noticing because, up to now, the weather has been bad and really cold. Prices continue to rise at a frightening pace. The newspapers publish figures every day for the increase of banknotes in circulation. Medication that I paid seventeen francs for last spring has gone up to seventy-one francs.

On September 18, the usual *Te Deum* was held at rue de La Tour to commemorate the occasion of the anniversary of the Chevaliers-Gardes, the Saint Elizabeth, a cavalry guard regiment. The "last of the Mohicans" gathered to pray for members of the regiments still living and commemorate leaders who have died, starting with the

Empress Anna Ioannovna in the eighteenth century.[138] The regimental standard, successfully brought out of Russia by unheard-of luck, was set in the middle of the church surrounded by a garland of red and white flowers, the regimental colours.

A former cavalry guard, Guichka Cantacuzène, who lives in the country and rarely comes to Paris, came up to me and said, "God, how everyone has aged and how miserable everyone looks. One would think you had been devoured by mites!"[139]

23.9.46 Had dinner at the M.'s in Meudon. W. Rautsmann was there, patched and shabby. Would that be prudence on his part?

24.9.46 Saw Kira Kozl. who is back from occupied Austria. She told us that one of her Austrian acquaintances had an "occupier" in her home, a Soviet officer for whom she had nothing but praise. He came every day to have tea with her and behaved like a gentleman. When he came to announce his impending departure, she was so sorry that she even gave him the cup he usually used to drink his tea as a souvenir. What a surprise she had when teams of soldiers appeared the next day and began to move furniture, clothing, and the like out of the apartment, right down to the nails, which they carefully pulled out of the walls. When she ran to complain to the officer, he answered her very kindly that he lived in an area of Russia that had been totally devastated during the occupation, and he would not find everything he would need there, so he was obliged to take her furniture with him. Furthermore, he would always have good memories of his hostess and would think of her every time he drank tea from the cup she had given him.

---

138 The precursor to the Chevalier-Gardes (located in St. Petersburg) was the Imperial Guard begun by Peter the Great. It was composed of men of noble birth and its initial purpose was to protect the royal family. Later this cavalry group took on a more military role and grew to include separate units of Cossacks, Dragoons and Lancers. During World War I, this combined group consisted of three infantry and two cavalry divisions (a division having between ten and twenty thousand men). Almost all of Countess Hendrikoff's male relatives and ancestors belonged to the Chevalier-Gardes. After the Russian Revolution, members of the Chevalier-Gardes had regular meetings and reunions in Paris and New York, hence the reference to "the last of the Mohicans."

139 Cantacuzène is a very old and distinguished diplomatic, noble Russian family.

1.10.46   Had tea with Vera Pi.; yesterday was her birthday. She served me pie, cake, and the like made by her aunt. It is easy to find sugar, butter, and other rationed products now by asking shopkeepers directly and paying black-market prices. You no longer need to go to the trouble of searching for addresses like you did during the Occupation when your hairdresser sold you tea and the locksmith, meat. Grocery shopkeepers have now become the "Two Hundred Families"[140] and their wives wear designer fashions from big haute couture houses where they order the most expensive styles.

2.10.46   Verdict at Nuremberg – the newspapers came out with headlines several centimetres high. Sentenced to death by hanging were Göring, Keitel, Jodl, Rosenberg, Sauckel, Frank, Ribbentrop, Kattenbrunner, Frick, Seiss-Inquart, and Streicher. Life sentences were given to Admiral Roeder, Hess, and Funk; twenty-year sentences to Baldur von Schirach and Speer; fifteen years to Neurath; and ten years to Admiral Dönitz.

The charges in the indictment were four counts of conspiracy against peace, crimes against peace, preparation of a war of aggression, war crimes determined by the Geneva and Hague Conventions, and crimes against humanity.

The public bought massive numbers of newspapers, but I heard no comment. Only from two officers sitting at my table in a restaurant who talked about it and one said, "I agree they all deserve to hang, but still, when you hear the verdict read by the representative from Soviet Russia and think about the war in Finland and Poland and everything the Soviets did after they entered Germany, it seems like a comedy."

It seems to me that convicting soldiers raises doubts among the public, and I am not sure that soldiers fully agree with the new principle established at Nuremberg, the *de facto* obligation for the Army to discuss and accept or reject orders received. Everyone approves of sentencing civilians, especially those who were in charge of concentration and extermination camps.

140   Translator's note: The two hundred largest shareholders of the Bank of France. The families were said to run the country.

7.10.46 Vassilchikoff and Khlebnikoff have left for the US, where they are going to give a demonstration of simultaneous translation, a new system used for the first time at Nuremberg.[141] The interpreter wears earphones and sits in a cabin in front of a microphone and translates the speech as it is given. The audience is also equipped with earphones and can tune in to different translations and thus is able to follow every speech in the preferred language.

Went to rue de Passy to order a pair of shoes from a Bulgarian shoemaker. He is an odd fellow – says he is a Communist but does not approve of Tito's regime. In his free time, he belongs to a spirit circle where he takes his young French apprentice with him. After a short debate, he gave me a fairly good price and explained to his daughter, "Madame is Russian. I am Bulgarian. I have to do something for her."

8.10.46 There is always talk of a Third War, and the lucky ones who can pay commissions of ten thousand francs to airline employees are flying off to the Americas.

Had tea at the Gl.'s, who think that only another war can settle things. Madame Gl. got her French citizenship back. It is an odd situation when husband and wife opt to keep a different nationality, yet have the same name. At the British Council, there is even an employee who has dual English and French citizenship, which always creates difficulties for English rations.

12.10.46 The temperature outside is five degrees above zero, and buildings are still not heated. At the Library, we work in coats, with our legs wrapped in a blanket.

Mrs. Quinn, a co-worker, attended a session at the Peace Conference yesterday. She was disappointed by the lack of solemnity of the session. "You would never have thought they were deciding world peace. Maybe they weren't very convinced themselves of the importance of the meeting," she told me.

---

141 George Vassilchikoff and George Khlebnikoff, along with Eugenia Rosoff, were the most highly qualified interpreters of the post-war period. Many Russian émigrés went on to work at the United Nations in New York as a result of their proficiency in French, German, English and Russian. An interesting sidenote about the simultaneous translation system mentioned here is that Aurèle Pilon, a Canadian, the inventor of radar, perfected the microphones.

15.10.46 At Bellevue, a French–Soviet couple that Olga Hitrovo had met in a hospital came to see her. The man, a Breton gardener, not a polished man, a prisoner of war, met his wife, a Soviet deportee, on the farm where they both worked. She told us that she is a nurse – *медсестра*; she is young, even pretty, with no education, speaks very vulgar Russian, is abrupt, and has a hard expression in her eyes. At first, she had to take care of seventeen cows on a German farm. Then she was transferred to a smaller farm, where there were only three cows. We asked her about how well fed she was. She answered that she always had enough to eat, because she always found a way to gobble down some raw eggs or drink milk. How was she treated? She did not "let anyone get away with anything." Once the farmer turned off the light while she was taking her bath. She swiftly went downstairs, grabbed the farmer by the back of his jacket and started to shake him with all her might, shouting, "Turn the light back on for me immediately."

The farmer's wife was crying and said, "Let him go. He's old. You'll hurt him." The grandchildren clung to her skirts crying and begged her to leave their grandfather alone, but she continued to shake him until he promised to turn the light back on. While she was talking to us, her eyes were as hard as steel, shooting little flames.

Every few seconds, she repeated, "I'm not afraid of anything." She was a real daughter of the Revolution; I could easily picture her leading partisans or on the barricades. She told us that her mother is a well-known Communist and raises pigs – *свинарка* – which is a very important job in Russia today. She is entitled to free passage on the entire railway network and had even been received by Stalin at a private audience. However, her father was a *kulak*, a well-to-do farmer opposed to collectivization, who was dispossessed of his land and livestock and vegetated in misery from then on. The woman had also taken in her companion's two little girls; their mother had abandoned them and they had been placed in an institution. She went to the mayor and, by pounding on the table with her fist, got the children sent to a free vacation camp in the summer and an apartment for the family. She had brought the two little girls with her; they looked like they love her and she herself was holding them close to her and kissing them every few minutes. She told us, "Now, when I go by on rue de Sèvres, everyone greets me and respects me because they know that I take care of the two children like a real mother."

19.10.46 The execution of those sentenced to death at Nuremberg was carried out the night of October 15 to 16. Göring succeeded in avoiding the rope; he committed suicide at around eleven o'clock in the evening with a cyanide capsule he had hidden, no one knows where yet. The guard who was watching him night and day through a peephole saw him put on his pyjamas and go to bed as usual with his hands on top of the blanket, as required by regulations, then twist and moan. The guard alerted an officer and the prison doctor who could only report his death.

Göring left three notes, one for his wife, one for the prison Commandant, and the third addressed to the German people. Their contents were not revealed. A suicide seemed so impossible to carry out that several newspapers had prepared the story of the execution in advance, including Göring among the prisoners hung.

"All those condemned to death died courageously," wrote the French, English, and American newspapers. Jodl said, "*Ich grüsse Dich mein Deutschland*" – "I salute thee, my Germany" as he mounted the steps to the scaffold. Only Rosenberg did not say a single word.

However, the *Manchester Guardian* wrote, "Under the Nuremberg indictment, there is not one of the judging powers, unless it be France, which could not be accused of one or other of the counts. Britain and America share Hiroshima between them, the Russians even if with the best defensive intentions opened an aggressive war against Finland in 1939 and were expelled from the League of Nations. If law is to be respected, it must be administered equally against all and not by fits and starts..." The public reacted calmly. There was no crowd around the newspaper kiosks, no comments in the metro.

The bodies of the condemned men were then incinerated and their ashes dispersed in the wind so that, in future, partisans cannot dig up their bodies, as happened with Himmler and Mussolini.

22.10.46 The *New York Herald* quoted the *Army and Navy Journal*, which said that "the condemnation established a precedent under which the President and entire personnel of the Staff and Army and Navy Chiefs would hang if the USA were ever defeated."

I do not deny the need for a trial; all the commandants of concentration camps and prisoners who committed atrocities, promoters of anti-Jewish legislation, and so on should be tried. But does a sentence enforced by a conqueror achieve its moral purpose? It seems to me that a conquered people will always consider such an act "the law of the victor."

23.10.46 Read *Wars I Have Seen* by Gertrude Stein, in which she reports her conversations with people in France. The French asked her why the Allies "are not making progress." They cannot understand, in our era, when we can handily destroy the enemy's whole territory by bombing, while we stay put, the fear the French have of English dominance, because they had no doubt they could rid themselves of the Germans in the end, but are not so sure of ridding themselves of their Allies as easily.

24.10.46 Paretzki died insane after his stay in France. The doctors determined that the cause of death was blows he had received in prison; he and his wife had been arrested several times on charges of collaboration.

30.10.46 C. came to Paris for a few days, a visit made out of curiosity. And here I, who always criticized people whose friendships suffered when there was a difference of opinion, acted the same way! The English have a "one-track mind" – everything is so clear and unbending there – which is their strength yet may end up their downfall. Whereas, as St. John Damascene says in the poem by A. Tolstoy, there is "more than one path through the fields."[142] C. was at Nuremberg as a spectator; to him, a German is nothing but a barbarian who must be annihilated. No exception to the rule. He also told me that the English despise the French; they consider them "earthworms" but are obliged for the time being to ally themselves with those earth-

[142] Alexsey Konstantinovich Tolstoy (1817–1875) wrote the poem "St. John of Damascus" in 1858. The poem's theme of individual freedom initially caused it to be banned.

worms because politics dictates it is in their interest. I told him that every country has something to reproach itself for in this war, and no country has the right to set itself up as judge, but Danzig shouted, "Maybe all, but not England." He invited me to lunch at the Crillon, where he was staying. We ate lamb chops at five hundred francs apiece and he was very surprised when I told him that our rations do not allow such luxury and what we were eating right at that moment was pure black market, which he must have realized when he paid the bill. I could not convince him, however, because he wanted to take the menu with him to show in England how well we eat in devastated France. I think it is a lack of suffering that makes people so indifferent and blind to the suffering of others; one really has to suffer to understand the suffering of others.

Went to see the Putniks; they are Yugoslavian and told me that, during the bombing of Belgrade, the safest place was the cemetery. They took shelter there in empty caves. One night, during very heavy bombing, Madame Putnik received a message from one of her friends, who wrote, "Come quickly, I have reserved a very beautiful tomb for you, row such and such, number such and such." Madame Putnik admitted that, at the time, she could not repress a small shiver when she read the note.

7.11.46 Received a letter from my sister Irina in Belgrade. She is working for the government, because all companies have been nationalized. She had to wait for a month to get the *nulla osta*.[143] Information on applicants is gathered from neighbours in their district at the headquarters of a committee that has a file on every inhabitant. She writes to me, "Fortunately, we have always lived in peace with everyone." If the information had been unfavourable, she would have been classified in the *lichenetz* category and denied work and ration cards. She is obliged to attend political lectures on Marxism and Leninism, often held right at her workplace so it is impossible for her to avoid them.

11.11.46 Anniversary of the Armistice of 1918. How much longer will it be celebrated?

143 Meaning "no impediment"

France voted for a Communist majority. In spite of that, people in cafés, restaurants, the metro, and so on rightly claim that the French are not Communist. In fact, it seems to me that a dictatorship of any party would have trouble getting established in France, where everyone criticizes and discusses everything freely and has his or her own opinion.

Power restrictions mean electricity is going to be cut off from seven-thirty in the morning until seven-thirty in the evening two days a week. The city will be divided into sectors that will take turns without light.

I like my work at the Library and find it interesting. The Director, Mr. Milner, is a real font of knowledge. I have never yet seen him caught at a disadvantage by the many different questions he is asked. And God knows they vary in subject. Lately someone asked him for details on the pension paid by the English government to descendents of Nelson, which has just been abolished, on insects in Great Britain, on the country's relations with India, and so on. Mr. Milner has the modesty of a wise man, combined with the reserve of the Englishman. He can be in the same room with you for eight hours without saying a word. That English aloofness is called *superba* by Italians, and is why Sofka Polotzoff was taken for an Englishwoman in Italy. Children on the beach called her "Miss, Miss," and when she asked them why they thought she was English, they answered, "Because you have so much *superba*." That character trait never bothered me. The English people I knew in Russia in the twenties were members of the English Military Mission during the civil war who, at the time, showed a great deal of heart and were full of concern for all the people who worked for them. I found it an intimate, friendly atmosphere and made friends among the English people I met and got to know. In London, the man in the street and in administrative offices is helpful and polite. It is true that I have often heard it said that to appreciate the English you have to see them at home. I add "or in Russia" because foreigners who lived there were usually assimilated quickly, acquiring the best of Russian character traits; the French became bigger hearted, the English more expansive.

The *New York Herald* published an interview with J. Duclos, who said that the Communist Party would only come to power five years after the establishment of a stable government in France; that period was necessary to "prepare" the public.[144]

29.11.46 A robber broke into the Hitrovos' villa at night, probably a "beginner" because he fled as soon as the Hitrovos woke up. The Hitrovos called the police, but the officers told them that they have major problems doing their duty. First of all, they have a limited amount of gas; then, if it is a Communist who is arrested, the Party immediately demands his release, and gets what it wants.

6.12.46 Zaren Wang just spent a week in Paris. She left again very disappointed. "Paris is no longer gay, no longer carefree," she told me. But it has no reason to be, and I even think that is completely to the credit of the French. A country that fought a war, lost it, and was occupied, partially ruined and disorganized cannot really be gay or carefree. It seems that Paris' reputation as an elegant city where everything is easy and amusing is so engrained in the minds of people in other countries that Zaren did not want to believe what Americans returning from post-war Paris told her. The occupation in Germany, where she "occupies" Stuttgart, has also distorted her thinking. She has gotten used to giving orders to a conquered people. When she went into a café, she rather rudely ordered the waiter, "Café au lait." The French do not like to be given orders, especially by foreigners. The waiter shrugged his shoulders and answered, "No coffee, no milk."

I asked her, "Zaren, didn't you know that we have had neither coffee nor milk in Paris since 1940?" She also complained that the waiter at the hotel brought her breakfast ice cold and refused to reheat it, claiming that there was no gas at that time and then that he could not serve breakfast piping hot even if there was gas, because the elevators were not working and he had to walk up seven floors. A taxi driver refused to take her to the address she gave him because he did not have enough gas to go that far. And, at first, the prices in the stores seemed to her to be a joke.

144 Jacques Duclos (1896–1975) was a prominent French Communist politician.

She went to Dachau, the camp where her nephew was a prisoner and died of typhus, and told the guards, who are now guarding German prisoners in the camp, that she was disgusted to see the Germans in such good physical condition. The guard answered her that the German prisoners were treated according to the Geneva Convention. I understand her bitterness but regret the form those feelings take. Perhaps I prefer the way of thinking of old Madame G. after all, a client of the British Council Library who was interested in a book and, when she found out that the Germans and Italians were mocked in it, she said, "Then I prefer not to read it. Everyone is so unhappy now."

At the Library we work by the light of kerosene lamps, which are lit at around four o'clock. The reading room reminds me of a Rembrandt painting at that time of day; everything is plunged in shadow with oases of antique yellow light here and there that illuminate heads bent studiously over big books. Then, around six o'clock, the electricity abruptly comes on and people, suddenly blinded, greet it with a long, joyful "ah" of admiration.

10.12.46 Serge Hitrovo told me that, in the most recent repatriation of German prisoners who were working at his office, prisoners from a neighbouring camp hid among the baggage on the repatriation train. Of twelve escapees, the police only recaptured five and told Serge that they had been prisoners themselves and had not been too zealous for that reason.

17.12.46 Cold wave. Women go out in the street wearing ski pants, and little Hélène Zweguintzoff, who is not yet two years old, even wears them in the apartment, because it is not heated. The family nests in three rooms. Vera Shebeko, Irène's sister, takes care of the children[145] as soon as she gets home from work and even finds time to feed Hélène and put her to bed during the hour and a half she has off work to go for lunch herself. She works in the Opéra and Irene lives in Neuilly. So I said to her, "Vera, hurry up and get married, otherwise you have all the disadvantages of marriage and motherhood without the advantages."

---

145 Michel and Irène Zweguintzoff's second daughter, Anne, was born in 1946.

31.12.46 On Christmas Eve, the police raided nightclubs and took down the names and addresses of diners there at two thousand francs for a steak. Le Bal Tabarin refused to let the inspectors in, so was closed down for fifteen days. Surely the authorities must have a way of identifying "signs of wealth" among taxpayers other than checking the dinner bills from their *réveillon*.

Vladimir Zweguintzoff recently had a relapse of the mysterious illness that made him so sick this fall.

We greeted the New Year symbolically at eleven o'clock at Barbos', and I went home on the stroke of midnight. In keeping with an old superstition, I started listening to bits of the conversation of passersby... They were talking about America!

DEPARTURE FOR AMERICA

"In essence, I am leaving with a very heavy heart. Nothing draws me to America and Americans. My decision was dictated by fatigue, by the hope of no longer having to struggle to eat or keep moving..."

1.1.47 I went with Barbos to the Club on rue Tokyo with Mak. and André Zweguintzoff[146] and his new Russian wife – very vulgar. All four are delighted to be back in Europe. What is it about America, which offers every opportunity, that Europeans, at least a certain class of Europeans, cannot be happy there? Everyone who comes back from there says that the "New World" satisfies the uneducated classes, offering them material well-being, but it seems that America does not have enough cultural resources to offer those who are looking for something more in life than simply material comfort.

Bread is still rationed, but one sees a lot of cakes, *petits fours*, and the like in the bakeries, made, they say, without sugar, eggs, or butter, but made with good, really white flour in any event.

5.1.47 A "5% price cut" campaign has been introduced by Blum. We are assured it will create a psychological shock. The planned price increase of three francs for a metro ticket, to five francs instead of two francs, has been cut back to just two francs. The "psychological shock" is really working – everyone is happy.

First class has been abolished in the metro. The red cars that were formerly first class are still part of the train but are considered second class. Nevertheless they are still occupied by a more select public; the

146 A relative of one of Countess Hendrikoff's uncles

usual second-class public hesitates to occupy them. Just the difference in colour alone apparently constitutes a psychological barrier.

Rina Ruggeri read me a letter from Aunt Sania[147] in New York. A dinner with eighteen people was given in her honour. She wore a low-cut dress to it, despite being more than seventy years old. The table was decorated with a hundred and fifty white and blue ostrich feathers – oh, horrors!

Sophy B. told me that Grade is not only still in Paris but has even obtained a work card, although he is not working! For a German, fresh out of prison, that is really not a bad "performance."

12.1.47 Spent the evening at Serge Zweguintzoff's. The two oldest children, Nicholas and Olga, are adorable; the boy is eight years old, handsome, gentle, frail, and always looks pensive. The little girl is five years old, not really pretty, but lively, intelligent, and affectionate. She got up on my lap, put her arms around my neck, and said very amusingly, "Since I haven't seen you, I love you so much." She will be a support to the family in a few years; at three years old, she was setting a table taller than she is, all alone. However, none of us will be there to see it. Serge called me into the next room and, with sincere emotion, hesitating and starting over at every word, announced his intention of leaving for Russia at the first opportunity. He has already obtained a Soviet passport. I asked him if he had weighed the decision carefully. He assured me that he had; he had chosen farming and had always specialized in it with the idea of putting his knowledge into practice in Russia. He had spent time with many Russian officers in Berlin, and realized that many things would be hard for him to accept to start with. The intellectual and cultural level of the officers he spoke to was lower than at the same rank in France, but he wanted to leave now and not wait, because now he was being offered all the travel expenses paid for himself and his family, a job in Moscow, and so on. He thinks that Russia is headed for a change as a result of the contact with other countries; he does not think it is going back – history always goes forward. The Soviet Metropolitans he spoke to here assured him that

147 Countess Alexandra Ruggeri-Laderchi was the sister of Countess Hendrikoff's mother.

he could raise his children in the Orthodox religion, as he is accustomed to doing. The future alone will tell whether Serge was right or wrong. He created confused feelings in me; I am not comfortable about his fate and do not trust all the promises that have been made to him. On the other hand, however, I envy him seeing our country again soon, our plains, rivers, forests, and cities, which I have not been able to forget and will certainly never see again.

On the long metro ride home, I listened to the complaints of Serge's mother-in-law, who is accompanying them because she does not want to be separated from her only daughter. She confided her fears to me; she is sick at heart about leaving...[148]

18.1.47 Called to the American Consulate for the second time... The closer the date of my departure gets, the unhappier I am at the idea of leaving.

19.1.47 Sacha H. recounted to us how the Germans executed a hundred children in the village where he and his family were living during the occupation of Yugoslavia. It was done in reprisal for the death of a German child killed in a fight at school. He also said that the Germans burned hostages on pyres... Mimi Launitz described to me the executions ordered by the Soviet authorities; "suspects," men and women, were locked in an empty building by the NKVD and burned alive. One would think we had gone back to the customs of the Middle Ages. Mimi thinks that Serge Zweguintzoff has many illusions and will regret his decision. Even simple peasants deported by the Germans do not want to go back to Russia anymore. Despite all that, Mimi is not happy in Paris. She finds Russian émi-

---

148   A relative, Nicholas Zvegintzof, explains what happened to Serge and his family: "The Zvegintsov family had a terrible journey back to Russia, losing most of their possessions, and on good advice settled not near Stalin but at Askania-Nova, which today is part of southern Ukraine where Sergei was an agronomist. He took his wife, and three children, Nikolai, Olga, Sergei, and his mother-in-law. A fourth child, Natalia, was born in there. She became a veterinarian and lives and works in Askania-Nova. Nikolai died in a tractor accident on some student work. Olga successfully pleaded French citizenship and returned to Paris. She died on December 4, 2011. Sergei is still living in Askania-Nova and is the father of the young world-class pianist Kirill Zvegintsov. He placed sixth at the Honens International Piano Competition in Calgary, Canada, in 2009."

grés hardened and sees us as separated from them by an impassable wall. When pressed to explain, she told me that the conversations here mainly cover mundane subjects. She had hoped to find a moral refuge in her sister but only hears her talking about business or her own daughter; with Veta, whom she had been so close to in Russia, she no longer knows what to talk about.[149] I think Russian émigrés have, in fact, lost some typically Russian characteristics in the harsh daily struggle, such as the passion for psychological and philosophical discussions and often slightly hysterical displays of professions of faith, what we call in Russian "*надрыв.*" Yet I have observed those traits so common to pre-revolutionary Russia in many Russians from Russia today. Perhaps the changes observed are due to the necessity of adapting to ordered Western life – only the "tough" survive; the "soft" or unstable perish.

Carried away by our discussions, Mimi and I sat down for lunch at three-thirty in the afternoon! It is quite possible that, in Russia, where the State is the only boss and solves all the vital problems in life as it sees fit – work, canteens, nursing homes, vacation camps, and so on – and has regimented the whole population, individuals have more leisure time for "soul-searching" and there is more of a "herd mentality" – *стадное чувство* – than there is here. They are all happy or unhappy together; whereas here everyone lives for him or herself.

Here my poor Mimi is living far from the centre of town in a truly miserable room above an automotive accessory warehouse. The room is virtually unheated; there is nothing but a salamander heater that burns paper and charcoal. She has lost contact with her childhood friends and does not even have time to go see them. Her two youngest are at Russian school because they do not speak French, and their schooling and lunches are paid for by unknown benefactors. Her oldest is looking for work, and her other daughter disappeared in the Russian zone during the exodus. Her wishes and aspirations are basically normal. No one should live the way we do, harassed, concerned about what tomorrow has in store for us and whether we will eat, making an effort to go to the movies, to

149   Veta refers to Elizabeth Zinovieff, née Princess Galitzine.

an exhibit, or to see friends. Work should give us the opportunity to enjoy our leisure. If we have to work hard just to do nothing but work, maybe we should live another way or be content with less. But is that a satisfactory solution to the problem?

Recently I went to see Olga Hitrovo and was going back up the hill in Bellevue in the dark when a passerby approached me and asked me if she could walk with me because the road was poorly lighted and deserted. She immediately started to recount her life to me, the way travellers often do on trains because they know they will never see each other again. She just got back from Russia, where she worked as a teacher for a Russian family near Smolensk. When the Revolution broke out, she was with her two pupils in the country, while the parents were in Moscow. She had to take refuge with the two children at the gardener's, because the house that belonged to the Russian family was immediately broken into and pillaged by the peasants. She lost all contact with the children's parents and did not hear of them again until 1924. Only then did she receive a notice from the International Red Cross informing her that the children's parents were in another country and claiming them. Meanwhile she had supported the children with the income she earned giving lessons. She said, "What do you want? I couldn't abandon those children." Why did she stay in Russia after the children left? I did not ask her and she did not say. She just complained that she felt like a foreigner in her own country, where she no longer had any family ties. Would we feel as disoriented if we were to return to our country now? When I told her that I am Russian, she cried, "Oh, how happy I am to talk to a Russian. I like all Russians. They are so broadminded!"

26.1.47 A Communist is the head of Defence. The food supply problem is more serious than ever. Meat and deli meat have completely disappeared from the market.

Rautsmann, Tchernoff, and Rina Ruggeri had tea at my place. Rautsmann told me that he was refused a worker card because he could not produce consecutive certificates of residence for the thirteen years he worked and had a card. The people who could give him certificates have all been deported or have disappeared. I had the same problem getting my card, but I simply had a false certificate made up for an address where I lived to make up for what was missing. That is how you are forced to become dishonest against your will!

Yesterday, I was at Barbos' and young Kauf. was there. He works for a publisher that just received a visit from Soviet representatives who came to have books reissued for foreign sales. The Paris publisher has to improve the format and design, correct the margins, change the font, illustrations, and so on. What is amusing is that, according to Kauf., the firms that personify "French taste" are staffed by Russian émigrés. The Soviets asked him how he could assess what was missing in the formatting of their editions so quickly. Kauf. explained to them that, when he was preparing mock-ups or sketches, it was not just his technical knowledge that helped him but all his cultural background, everything he had seen, studied, read, all the memories he drew on without even realizing it.

17.2.47 The police, PTC, and PTT took part in strikes. The traffic jam at Place de l'Opéra was so bad that a group of young people, which A. Lastours was part of, stood at the intersections and directed traffic, despite cries of "fascists, collaborators" and the like.

22.2.47 You are only entitled to a single pair of shoes a year, with a coupon issued – a touching attention – the month of your birthday.

Had dinner at Bicha's with a hotel "client" of hers, a Persian officer – not "Iranian," he corrected us, because Persia is only a province of Iran and "Iranian" should be used the way "British" is used. Very much a Germanophile, "The Germans were so sensitive, such a fine race!" That is definitely the first time I heard Germans praised for their sensitivity. He detests the English, whom he considers enemy number one, and assured us that the Shah divorced his first wife, Farouk's sister, because she was in the pay of Intelligence Services. He is in Paris to take French courses. As any good Oriental would, he responds to his classmates, young English women who talk about their future Queen Elizabeth, "How is that pretty young girl in the photograph you're showing me going to be at the head, in command of several hundred thousand men in the Indies? No, come on, you're joking!"

23.2.47 The English officially announced that they are leaving the Indies. Queen Victoria must be turning over in her grave. It is difficult for our generation to realize that the Great Empire no longer exists, except in name, and is vacillating on its pedestal. England has lost its prestige for the man in the street. It is no longer spoken of the way it was before and even during the war. I read Stephen Spender's book *European Witness*. He went on a mission to Germany in 1945 to interview German intellectuals and seek out anti-Nazi writers who were still alive. Despite the fact that he prides himself on his objectivity, he approached each German with the preconception that he was interviewing a candidate for Fresnes. Hence his astonishment that representatives of a "guilty race" were not pleading guilty.

The ruins and misery he saw made an impression on him, because he realized what could happen to all of Europe someday.

If I had not worked at the British Council Library, I would have been unaware of Spender's existence. But one day, the door opened and an ageless, pink-cheeked, blond man came in and said, "I am Stephen Spender," as if he was saying, "I am Shakespeare." And I said to myself that I must get to know this author's work.

25.2.47 Visit from a Yugoslavian engineer sent to me by my sister – a Slovenian, thirty-five years old, nice, although a confirmed Titoist. He described the dictator's reforms and achievements, the reconstruction of the city and the bridge in Belgrade, which had formerly been built by French engineers and was rebuilt by the country's engineers after it was destroyed. Life is cheap because everything has been nationalized; the government encourages young people and wants them to earn a good living. He was in Dachau for a year and lost forty pounds; he had every illness possible but survived, thanks, as he says, "to my strong will to live." The French did not fight and let themselves die. He thinks France is finished as a nation and has no future, because no one wants to work here, and there is too much difference between the luxury in the shops and the standard of living of a large part of the population, and also because three years after Liberation, the country is still in complete chaos. He predicts that England will no longer play the same role as before the war. "Believe me, Madame," he said consolingly by way of conclusion, "there are now only two countries making progress, and they are Russia and Yugoslavia." How I regret that such enthusiasm, which is almost contagious, is only generated by the Communist victory!

3.3.47 Letter from Yugoslavia from Irina, trying to make me understand, in carefully chosen sentences, that life is not as easy there as we are given to believe. Christmas is no longer celebrated, but May 1 and the anniversary of the Russian Revolution are statutory holidays.

An article by Lippmann in the *New York Times* foresees the disintegration of the British Empire and predicts that the political void it creates will be filled by Russia. If America wanted to take England's place, it would require huge expenditure and the immobilization of armed forces in other countries for an indefinite period of time.

7.3.47 Paris is still without newspapers, except English-language newspapers. No one complains; it is true that nearly everyone has a radio.

Herzog, the French officer of Russian origin whom Barbos suspects is a Soviet agent, told Barbos, "I don't understand why Russian émigrés are so slow to return to Russia. Communism will soon become established in France, too, so wouldn't it be better to be at home?"

The young Doms. have left for Venezuela. They were offered the trip free and a guaranteed job. The parents are still here. The whole family lived in Yugoslavia since they left Russia. They were well off there, had a house and livestock; they abandoned everything at the approach of the Soviet troops and came here after a stay in Austria. They are not happy here. Life in Yugoslavia was slow and easy; they look at us here with amazement and admiration. Once again, I wonder if they are not the ones who are right.

18.3.47 The *New York Herald* devoted an article to Parisian fashion. While admitting that it is refined, artistic, and cannot be equalled, the author of the article suggests that it no longer suits the style of life of the modern woman, especially the American woman, who has to take care of her home and family – and build empires and no longer has time for fittings and appointments to consult with her dress designer. The article's author describes Parisian style as "the lady of the manor welcoming the joyous villagers" but now there is no longer either a lady or joyous villagers. In America, women are looking for practical elegance more than anything.

He is right, but it is regrettable that everything is becoming standardized, the "polish, the selectiveness are disappearing." Lately I was going down the street on Faubourg Saint-Honoré. Some of the window displays are still truly small masterpieces of taste. Does one see displays like that in America? I doubt it.

31.3.47 I was called to the American Consulate. The employee who examined my papers thinks southwestern Russia, where I was born, is now part of… Norway. The medical examination was very superficial. You are required to take off your shoes and stockings and dress; the doctor looks down your throat, listens to your lungs, and sends you away with a big slap on the lower back – the charge is one hundred twenty francs. Then I had an interview with Consul Osborne, who interrogated me just as if I was a war criminal. I found him most impolite.

We went with Liouba to see the Soviet film *Souvoroff*. The Hitrovos are descendents of his through the women. There was a large audience but not one familiar face, except Serge Zweguintzoff and his family and Olga and Serge Ignatieff.[150] A representative from the Soviet Embassy read a kind of introduction to the film. We were disappointed in the film, which was full of propaganda and really nothing from an artistic point of view. We left in the middle of it because three people sat down behind us and Liouba imagined, rightly or wrongly, that they were Soviet agents who were listening to what the spectators were saying; she was in a panic.

13.4.47 Russian Easter. The service was held at ten o'clock instead of midnight because of the lack of transportation. Before the war, the city provided special bus service for churchgoers. Now bus service of any kind stops at nine o'clock in the evening. There was a crowd, as usual, and we could not get in any further than the churchyard. We then went to Barbos' and Sonia G. walked home with me around one-thirty in the morning.

150 Serge Ignatieff was related to Countess Hendrikoff, both through her husband Peter Hendrikoff and her sister Ella's husband Kyril Shirkoff.

April 6 was Catholic Easter; I took advantage of four days off work to go to Les Touches with André Nolde to get the things Nancy and I had buried in the basement of the château before her departure for America. It felt strange to be back there, after an absence of seven years. Nothing had changed, but everything looked older and more ramshackle. I searched by the light of a candle for the silver that had been hidden in the basement and, despite all the occupants who had lived in the château over the years, I was surprised to find everything, even the silver spoons and forks Nancy had simply put in a cookie tin lying on the ground in clear view.

17.4.47 At Liouba's, I met a Russian priest who lives in Belfort. He had been very involved with Soviet DPs, often accommodating them by issuing certificates so they could pass for émigrés from the First War. He told us about a soldier who had obtained the papers of a Frenchman killed on the battlefield and succeeded in having himself "repatriated" to France. The man worked in factories in the Urals alongside members of the LVF, the legion of French volunteers. They worked six days underground and only came back up to the surface on the seventh day. He tried to plead the case for the French in the LVF, but the French authorities were completely disinterested.

18.4.47 Had dinner at Serge Zweguintzoff's in the company of Olga Ignatieff. Already it is another world. They were exchanging impressions about the Soviet trade legation and other similar organizations with names I do not even know. On the table were many American canned goods from the ECITO, an international organization that has a Soviet section where Serge is working at the moment.

Olga went to midnight Mass at Sainte-Geneviève-des-Bois and described to us the impression it made on her. The procession went past the little cemetery adjacent to the church. The light from the burning candles carried by the faithful sparkled in the darkness, mingled with the light of the candles burning on nearly every grave in a desire for communion with those who have gone… Rising in the warm night, religious songs rivalled the songs of the nightingales in nearby bushes…

19.4.47 Bellevue. The fruit trees are in flower. The moist per-
fumed air is totally different from the air in Paris. A sign of better
times, the vegetable garden planted in front of the Hitrovos' house
where the lawn used to be has finally been removed, and the gardens are gradually regaining their customary appearance.

The British Council Library has acquired a whole collection of
reports from English experts on German factories. The reports are
very detailed, with sketches, maps, industrial secrets, and so on. The
experts were struck by German techniques and the industry effort
during the war, the construction of new factories, the improvised res-
toration of bombed factories, and the like.

Library clients threw themselves avidly on the brochures like vultures. One of them would not even give me time to classify them, but
tore them from my hands and kept on saying, "It's wonderful that
you have them. Do you know they're worth a fortune?"

22.4.47 A young Englishman came to borrow books from the
Library for lectures in occupied Germany. One of the clients then
came to tell me that she knew the young man: he has no experience,
he is only twenty years old, and he confided to her that his only goal
is to live "like a prince" for a while, all expenses paid, and be able
to make a lot of money. We discussed the demoralizing effect of any
occupation on the occupiers.

I recently saw Marina T., who has gained weight and is full of
self-assurance, along with something new I could not define. When
I confided those observations to her friends, right away they said,
"What? Don't you know? She made a fortune in Germany. Her
parents are delighted. And everyone envies her. *They* did the same.
Now it's our turn."

But I said to them, "If you do what *they* do, you are no longer entitled to criticize the Germans for their conduct, or you have to think
they did nothing wrong." Of course, I did not convince anyone.

Went to the theatre to see an Italian film, *Four Steps in the
Clouds.*[151] Everything in it was charming. The acting was natural; the actors were even ugly, nothing like the Hollywood type.

151 The 1995 movie *A Walk in the Clouds,* starring Keanu Reeves, was a remake
of the 1942 Italian film *Four Steps in the Clouds.*

The audience was enthusiastic and, as they went out, said to the crowd lining up to go in, "Be patient. You won't regret coming." Then General de Gaulle appeared in the newsreels. I admit that his gestures and facial expressions are often a bit ridiculous but, still, to laugh uproariously every time he appears on the screen! Truly, he deserves better than that, even if one does not agree with his opinions.

24.4.47 No bread. A lot of bakeries are closed, and there are endless line-ups in front of the ones that are still producing bread.

Finally, a new Russian newspaper that is not Communist is being published in Paris, called *New Thought*.

Aunt Sania from America described the Easter Parade in New York, where women were walking along Fifth Avenue all dressed up, wearing awful hats, and men in suits and top hats. Countess Keller also wrote to me from New York; she is disappointed by the manners of her American son-in-law and finds the city dirty and "lacking in resources for the soul."

The bodies of the prisoners condemned to death at Nuremberg have been incinerated and the ashes thrown into the Yser River.

20.5.47 I have received my American visa, after so many complications. To start with, despite the fact that my name was first on the list, the Consulate put someone else ahead of me, to "accommodate" him, leaving my visa delayed to wait for a month or perhaps more. My case was no exception. You often hear that applicants for departure make "arrangements" with employees who change the order of the names on the list. Princess W. works at the Consulate and telephoned me to inform me of the matter, asking me not to say that she was the one who told me. The employee who had made "arrangements" with the applicant started out denying it, then asked me how I got the information. I coolly lied and told her it was the gentleman in question who had told me, the Russian applicant. She seemed embarrassed then and asked me to come back tomorrow, saying that she was going to "check." The next day all she said to me was, "Will you please go and see Miss C. I think she might have a number for you." Miss C. said to me at once, "I see no reason why you should not have your visa right now."

Now that I have my visa for America in my possession, an official document with a big red seal, am I really happy to have a visa? My feeling is more something like, "Now, it's done. No use looking back." In essence, I am leaving with a very heavy heart. Nothing draws me to America and Americans. My decision was dictated by fatigue, by the hope of no longer having to struggle to eat or keep moving... Perhaps I am creating illusions for myself. Can America really be a "safe harbour" for us Europeans?

3.6.47 I have begun sorting my things. God, what useless objects! Some of them have been in my trunks for ten years without ever being taken out, waiting for better times that never came. I am torn between the desire to take a lot of little nothings with me, dear for the memories and the atmosphere they evoke, and the promise I made myself not to be attached to the past anymore or to material things. I gave Barbos the albums of Petrovskoye I had reverently preserved in the turmoil, because he is the one who represents the continuity of the family now...[152]

Aunt Sania came through Paris. Extraordinary for her age, she flew by airplane for the first time in her life at seventy-seven years old and did not shut her eyes all night "because it was so fascinating to see the moon two steps away" and because she could not stop thinking about her youngest son Alexander, an aviator who died in 1935 during a night flight. He had always described the beauty of a night flight to her with so much enthusiasm, the pilot's sense of communion with the stars and the dome of the heavens.

She was surprised to see men in cafés during working hours. In America, one only sees women during the day. American women told her that they go out with friends and have lunch with them but have never met their husbands.

---

152 Petrovskoye is the name of the village for which the Zweguintzoff family estate, the country childhood home of Countess Hendrikoff, was named. The village, near Borisoglebsk on the Russian Steppes, is very run down today. The family home was torn down just after the Revolution and the materials and foundation from the house were used to build a clubhouse for the village. It was certainly not an improvement. The outbuildings were used for a children's summer camp. As of September 2011, all that remains is the derelict clubhouse, the crumbling foundation and steps, the vines that covered the original house and some outbuildings.

18.7.47   I am swimming in paperwork. I had to complete a "change of address" and submit it to the Town Hall. The employee asked me with a charming smile if I had brought a stamped paper with me and a certificate of residence. I had forgotten that one must always have a stamped paper in one's pocket! To be allowed to take my personal effects with me, I have to fill out an application and have my signature witnessed at the *Commissariat*; that signature has to be certified by the Mayor, his signature authenticated by the Prefect, and that signature finally certified by the Ministry of Foreign Affairs. All the offices are open the same hours and are located in different parts of the city.

21.7.47   Spent my whole afternoon at the Prefecture. I had to extend my French exit visa. Fortunately, I had armed myself with every imaginable legal document – stamped paper, residence certificate – including photos. Just to renew my visa, I was asked for all those supporting documents! I took my place in line at one o'clock in the courtyard of the Prefecture. We were kept in order by two big officers on one side and fences on the other. Despite the large signs stating that the Prefecture's departments are open without interruption from nine o'clock in the morning to four-thirty in the afternoon, we were only allowed to enter in single file starting at two o'clock. The weather was stormy and rain had started falling in torrents. I was the only one who had an umbrella and, as soon as I opened it, four people hurried under its shelter, saying to me, "We follow you faithfully." The other people in the line tried to shelter themselves from the rain any way they could by pressing against the walls or hastily opening newspapers to hold over their heads. One of the women near me told me that she is Swiss and has her Swiss passport in her possession, which allows her to enter her country without any problem; yet, in spite of that, she has to have a French exit visa. She said, "Why not allow district *Commissariats* to issue exit visas, as they do for French citizens? Surely the district *Commissaires* know us better than they know French citizens, because they are always dealing with foreigners."

Finally, at 2:10, one of the officers shouted in a loud voice, "Go ahead!" and it was the rush of the strong crushing the weak. Inside the room, we had to line up again. Then it was the calvary of authentications. At the police station, that was done automatically; an orderly in the hallway stamped my document, took it and brought it back almost immediately with the certified signature of the *Commissaire*. Things do not work that way at the Seine Prefecture. Although the offices are supposed to stay open until four-thirty, it had been such a beautiful day that the employees had simply taken a holiday. This was announced to me by the sole official remaining on site, who came out of his office at the sound of my footsteps echoing in the deserted hallway. Moreover, the gentleman was very kind, because he suggested, as a favour to me, that I leave him my certificates, which he would have authenticated in my absence. He told me to come and get them Monday evening after work. I trusted him and agreed.

27.7.47 Eight-hour line-up at the Prefecture to start with, ending up at the Exchange Control Office. I was in the courtyard at the Prefecture starting at eight-thirty in the morning. Around ten o'clock, the sun started to roast us and, around eleven o'clock, we were red and sweating, pressed between two fences like sardines and moving forward like turtles. When my turn finally came to go into the room, the counters had no more stamps, and we had to wait for an hour for someone to go get them. I had to line up again at the Exchange Control Office to get a permit to buy dollars in cash and a $250 cheque. I was so dazed in the end that I could no longer remember the right name of the bank where I had recently opened an account to purchase the cheque in dollars. The employee was getting impatient, quite rightly in any case, and kept on saying, "Look here, Madame, you can always remember the name of your bank."

I answered, "Not after lining up for eight hours."

12.8.47 I have now been sailing on the *Mauretania* since seven o'clock in the evening. The last days in Paris remain obscured in fog in my memory, errands, packing, farewells... I had the impression I was being buried, and the letters of farewell I received reminded me of obituaries. It is a certainty that I will never see older friends again, like Mary Eristoff's mother. And others? I have been gripped by a dreadful feeling of fear the last few days. What am I going to find on the other side of the ocean? Did I fail in courage by abandoning a struggle that seemed beyond my strength over the long haul? All those questions remain unanswered for the time being. I have now severed my ties with Europe and turned another page in the book of my life.

I left the house around ten o'clock in the morning. Fortunately, Nicholas Zweguintzoff[153] came to pick me up in a taxi; it is still quite an issue to find one. Many people were to accompany me to the station… It would have been a relief to be able to burst into tears, but I could not even cry…

The train stopped once at Caen. That city and Lisieux were badly hit in the bombings. In Lisieux, the cathedral stands oddly intact in the midst of a heap of ruins. Along the way, we had a visit from the ticket, passport, and currency checkers. An American couple were questioned at length about how they had exchanged their dollars in France. Since they did not have proof recorded on their passports that they had exchanged their money legally at a bank teller, they had to pay a fine of $250.

The *Mauretania* was waiting for its passengers at anchor in the harbour at Cherbourg because the port is still half demolished, and a tender took us out to board. A cord on the tender separated first and second class passengers from tourist class, which I was. French customs never opened my luggage on the whole trip. It was really worth the trouble to run from one administration to the next to get permits that apparently were of no interest to anyone!

My heart tightened when I saw the *Mauretania's* two red smoke-stacks through the fog… Then everything happened as if we were on rollerskates. We boarded by a small gangway directly on the tourist side and were immediately snapped up by stewards who took us to our staterooms. Our luggage was brought to us in a wink. It was nearly seven o'clock and, before long, the dinner bell rang. The passengers exclaimed with surprise when they saw butter, milk, and white buns on the tables for everyone to help themselves. There are still shortages of all those products in France and I, who usually eat very little bread and rarely eat white bread, ate five buns one after another.

153 A relative of Countess Hendrikoff's (not her brother or her father, who were both also named Nicholas Zweguintzoff)

En route, I got to know a Russian woman who is married to an American. She is an experienced passenger who has already made the crossing several times, and helped me a great deal by giving me valuable advice, such as how to register immediately for the second service in the restaurant, get a table for two, rent a deck chair as soon as possible, and so on. My stateroom is located on the lower deck, somewhat of a disadvantage in the event of heavy seas and very hot weather. However, the stateroom is for two, whereas most are for four, and has a porthole, which staterooms in the middle do not. Fortunately, my companion is charming – a fine Italian woman, very nice, with whom I speak Italian.

17.8.47 The weather is splendid. We have only had two days of heavy seas, which made most of the passengers sick, but apparently I have my sea legs because I did not get sick; I have never been seasick in my life.

The days are spent lying stretched out on a deck chair on the deck. The library on board is fairly well stocked; I even found the book by Malaparte that I had heard so much about, *Kaputt*. Malaparte is said to be the illegitimate son of Prince Paolo Troubetzkoy. In the book is a story about a basket that Malaparte thinks is a basket of oysters which, in fact, contains the eyes of Yugoslavian partisans sent to Pavelitch by his Ustachis.

At eleven o'clock, the deck steward comes by with cups of consommé and crackers and, at four o'clock, with high tea – that is, tea, cakes, toast, and so on. The people are pretty awful, a band of Czechoslovakians who emigrated to America and are coming back from a visit to their relatives. They barely speak English; we had a conversation half in Russian, half in Slovenian. The women never take off the white kerchiefs tied under their chins, even for dinner. Many Israelites. Everyone complains about Europe, especially France, which is criticized for lack of effort to work and lack of friendliness to strangers. The Jews are very much against Great Britain, which they consider "kaput" and add, "We will force England to recognize our rights to Palestine. We will finally have a country."

The purser called me and asked me to help him because an old Russian lady, Madame Katchninsky, seventy-five years old, filled out her documents partly in her maiden name, as is the custom in France and Belgium, and partly in her married name. Since she does not speak a word of English, the purser could not explain it to her. I found a solution by joining the two names with a hyphen; since then, Madame Katchninsky never leaves my side and follows me everywhere, keeping a tight grip on a panel of my skirt. She is going to join her son, whom she has not seen for twenty-five years, and is absolutely appalled by the trip, forms, and so on. It is strange to see the number of modest emigrants who leave for an unknown country. People who have material possessions think twice about it, because you always become somewhat of a slave to your possessions. The ones who have nothing to lose are the ones who take the chance, often helped by relatives who have made a bit of money in America.

The purser sent me his compliments and advised me that my luggage, along with the luggage of nearly two hundred passengers, was shipped by mistake by the French railway company on the passenger liner *De Grasse* departing from Le Havre, when we departed from Cherbourg! It arrives in New York three days after our arrival in that city. The purser consoled me by saying that we were lucky our luggage was sent on a ship destined for New York, not Brazil.

We arrive tomorrow morning in New York. The humid heat of the city is starting to make itself felt, despite the ventilator fans in the staterooms and public areas.

18.8.47 In the morning, going down for breakfast, I read on the blackboard that the *Mauretania* arrives in New York at eleven-thirty. However, because of formalities, most of the passengers will only be able to disembark around four o'clock in the afternoon. The ship already looks like an anthill. Stewards are piling hand luggage near the entrance doors, and passengers are running from one deck to another to be sure not to miss the Statue of Liberty, which we ended up seeing as a grey shadow through the fog surrounding New York. The heat is oppressive, a humid, tropical heat; sweat does not dry but sticks to your clothing and your body. A passenger explained to me that is because the air holds more moisture than the human body.

The *Mauretania* slowly followed the course of the Hudson and finally ended up stopping at the Cunard dock. We had lunch around one-thirty. The waiter who served us and amused us during the voyage by his distractedness and professional inexperience, accompanied by a charming and disarming smile, thanked us when he received our tip and politely asked our nationality. "American," my companion answered, to cut short any explanations. I, however, replied "Russian."

Then our young "poet," as we had nicknamed him, became heated and asked if I am "one of those Russian princesses." He proudly declared that he belongs to the "Party." I innocently asked him, "What party?"

He answered, "The Communist Party, of course. Any worker has to belong." Then he added that his comrades in England converted him to their doctrine. Probably, being a "White Russian," I could not give him any information about life in Soviet Russia today.

I admitted that I am, in fact, an émigrée, but added that, after the war, many Russians came to France after they left their country, voluntarily or involuntarily, during the war years, and we émigrés often had the opportunity to meet them and hear their stories. There must be a serious reason for them to prefer France or some other country to their homeland. Then I said to him very seriously, "Why don't you take a trip to Russia to see the living conditions in that country personally?"

He looked at me, a bit confused, seeming to doubt my sincerity, then said to me, still with the same charming smile, "In any case, I really hope to see you again."

Countess Olga Hendrikoff, Philadelphia, 1960

PART III

For nearly twenty years after Lala left France for the United States, she lived in Philadelphia with her cousin Alexander (Sasha) Zweguintzoff, his wife Nancy, and their children Sandy and Nata. Lala taught languages at the Berlitz school in Philadelphia. When Sandy and Nata had grown up, Nancy and Sasha went back to live in Paris. Lala would have loved to do the same, but the idea was not financially practical.

In 1966 at the age of seventy-five, Lala moved yet again to a new country to start all over again. Ella and Kyril had emigrated to Canada after World War II to be with their daughter Helen, who had married a Canadian R.C.A.F. officer, Alan Carscallen, in Italy at the end of WWII. After Kyril's death, Lala moved to Canada to live with her sister. The move to Calgary was difficult: Lala felt isolated from her lifelong friends and missed her family in France, the family who sustained her during the difficult days of the war. But in Canada she had, at least, the security of her Canadian family and a comfortable life.

Lala loved horses, dogs, and children. She was compassionate and kind to children, especially those orphaned or hungry during the war. Having no children of her own, she lavished love and attention on two generations of children: Helen Shirkoff Carscallen and her sister Irina and brother Lerick; Vladimir and Michel Zweguintzoff; the next generation Sandy Zweguintzoff, Nata Zweguintzoff, and Hélène Zweguintzoff-Charveriat; and Suzanne, Stanley, Anne, and John Carscallen.

Lala was an excellent listener and thoughtful problem-solver. With her superior intellect and inquiring mind, she contributed to stimulating discussions on a wide range of topics from politics and religion to art, music and literature. She had practical skills such as hair cutting, sewing, typing and generally being able to make something out of nothing. Her knitting produced made-to-measure sweaters, hats, and mittens from scraps of wool for her great nieces and nephews. She was also an accomplished photographer.

In times of upheaval, Lala found comfort in her Russian Orthodox religion, art, literature, classical music, theatre, and opera. In happier times, a relaxing evening at home would be a glass of sherry, classical music playing on the phonograph, and knitting or reading *The Manchester Guardian*.

Countess Hendrikoff, Lala, died in 1987 at the age of 95. Her ashes are buried on the Carscallen family farm at Priddis, Alberta, overlooking Fish Creek with a view of the mountains, tall aspens and Gooseberry Hill where she loved to pick berries: a scene which never failed to remind her of her home in Russia.

AFTERWORD

Rummaging through the old Russian trunk in 2008, underneath a pile of sweaters, I rediscovered manuscripts written by my great aunt Lala in Russian and French. My mother had told me that the manuscripts were interesting. We had planned to translate the works ourselves, but my mother, who said she had "no intention of dying," suddenly did just that in 2005.

With my dubious high school French, I began to read through the World War II French manuscript. It seemed interesting, as my mother had said, but also posed many questions, the answers to which would be difficult to find. The generation before, who could have easily helped answer them, were now all dead. It was clearly up to me, the only person in the family who had the knowledge and time to pursue such an increasingly complex undertaking.

Fortunately I was able to find an expert French-to-English translator, Maureen Ranson. I asked her to read the manuscript over quickly to see if it was worth the time and expense to translate. A call from Maureen indicating that she not only found it interesting but genuinely loved it was all the encouragement needed to begin what turned out to be a four-year effort.

We had several challenges. The first one was identifying the many people mentioned in the manuscript only by initials. Solving this problem required the Russian-to-English translation of the Russian Revolution and World War I memoir, a trip to the Russian Orthodox cemetery in Sainte-Geneviève-des-Bois near Paris, extensive research, and help from my Russian cousins.

The next bump on the road appeared when I discovered a rough earlier copy of the manuscript, which was necessary to reconcile with the finished copy. Other minor problems were the multiple spellings of Russian family names, for example Zweguintzoff, Zweguintzow, Zvegintzov, Hendrikoff, Hendrikov, Gendrikov, Yendrikov, and place names that have changed in the last hundred years.

In the spring of 2009, Maureen and I travelled to France to photograph and visit some of the significant locations mentioned in the French memoir. Visits to Boulevard Suchet, Courances and the Abbey at Royaumont helped us to understand the context in which aunt Lala lived and worked.

It has been an honour to bring this historical document and Countess Hendrikoff's words to life. A work of this scope is not brought to fruition without the diligent effort, help and support of many.

Gratitude and thanks to my friend Maureen Ranson, whose attention to detail has brought Countess Hendrikoff's words to life. You have made this journey joyful. Thanks to Russian-to-English translator Evgeny Zilberov, who had the difficult task of translating a handwritten, Old Russian–style memoir into modern English.

A most wonderful aspect of this project has been discovering and reconnecting with relatives, some of whom I knew existed and some of whom turned up entirely unexpectedly. An unexpected joy was Nicholas Zvegintzov, a distant cousin with a Russian heart who provided immediate research and Russian translations, answered questions and supplied a detailed family tree – thank you for your tremendous support. Nicholas helped me track down his cousin A.A. (Sandy) Zvegintzov, the baby who aunt Lala put on the ship that carried him to safety in the United States in 1940. Many thanks to Sandy for supplying the charming picture of aunt Lala and his sister Nata on a donkey. Thank you also to Lady Natasha Gourlay for providing background information on the Russian Imperial Court from her mother's book, *A Princess Remembers* by Elizabeth Zinovieff.

I am grateful to Nina Fersen, my flower girl, for unfailing encouragement, Russian/English translations and help with Russian cultural questions.

Cousin Hélène Charvériat (née Zweguintzow), your Chateau Charvériat welcome has always been warm, the conversation stimulating, the food superb and the chauffeur services reliable – merci beaucoup.

Heartfelt thanks to Sandy Frum and Paul Klein for information about their grandmother Countess Alexandra Ruggeri-Laderchi and Léon de Rosen. Miguel Cardon de Lichtbuer Gargarine researched the Hendrikoff family – merci.

This book has brought many adventures. In the fall of 2011, my ever-patient and supportive husband, Walter, and I travelled to Russia to visit our old family homes. Without our friends inside Russia, Alix Aigunyan and Andrey Polunin, we would not have realized our dream of actually making it into rural Russia to see the old estate or got past a Soviet-era guard at the cadet school in St. Petersburg.

I would like to recognize my Canadian group: my sister Anne Carscallen, researcher extraordinaire; her husband Rowland Lorimer, Director of the Master of Publishing Program at Simon Fraser University; and my niece Julia Lorimer, the computer whiz. Their combined expertise has helped me push this book forward. I admire Kate Hanson for her perseverance and loyalty in spite of many setbacks; she was able to provide guidance, computer support and research. Thanks also to my cousin Maryetta Harper who suggested that I begin working on this project and who did the first read-through of the Russian translation.

Kelsey Attard, the major editor of both manuscripts, has been a gift. I appreciate your attention to detail, your diligence and your interest in a work that is so far away in time and place from our modern-day experience.

I cannot finish without mentioning my patient husband, who has not complained about the commitment of time and expense that has been devoted to this book in the past four years. He listened to family stories about people he never knew; he travelled with me to rural Russia with all the difficulties that entailed, using his Polish-Russian language skills and all the while keeping us safe in less-than-ideal conditions.

It is my wish in having this book published that you, the reader, will take with you a part of my great aunt Lala's philosophy and perspective. I also hope that you will be encouraged to learn more about this group of Russians – an intelligent, educated, and talented generation, but a generation lost through war.

– *Sue Carscallen*

ink/light

Inkflight Publishing
Mailing address
PO BOX 4608
Main Station Terminal
349 West Georgia Street
Vancouver, BC
Canada, V6B 4A1

For other Inkflight titles visit:
www.inkflight.com

For more on Olga Hendrikoff visit:
www.acountessinlimbo.com

The main text of this book is set in
SABON, a typeface family designed by
Jan Tschichold in 1967. The chapter
headings, and Russian characters are set
in MINION CYRILLIC, a typeface family
designed by Robert Slimbach in 1992.
The years in the chapter headings are set
in MINION PRO, a typeface family designed by Robert Slimbach in 2000. The
title of this book is set in *Chopin Script*,
a typeface designed by Claude Pelletier
in 1999. Chopin Script was originally
released under the name Diogene, and
is based on the typeface Polonaise,
designed by Phil Martin in 1977.

CPSIA information can be obtained at www.ICGtesting.com
Printed in the USA
LVOW061843220513

335071LV00008B/243/P